G000296744

STREET ATLAS
North
Hampshire

First published in 1991 by

Philip's, a division of
Octopus Publishing Group Ltd
2–4 Heron Quays, London E14 4JP

Second colour edition 2002
Second impression 2003

ISBN 0-540-08102-7 (hardback)
ISBN 0-540-08103-5 (spiral)

© Philip's 2002

Ordnance Survey®

This product includes mapping data licensed
from Ordnance Survey® with the permission of
the Controller of Her Majesty's Stationery Office.
© Crown copyright 2002. All rights reserved.
Licence number 100011710

Printed and bound in Spain
by Cayfosa-Quebecor

Contents

Digital Data

The exceptionally high-quality mapping found in this atlas is available as digital data in TIFF format, which is easily convertible to other bitmapped (raster) image formats.

The index is also available in digital form as a standard database table. It contains all the details found in the printed index together with the National Grid reference for the map square in which each entry is named.

For further information and to discuss your requirements, please contact Philip's on 020 7531 8439 or ruth.king@philips-maps.co.uk

Motorway with junction number	
Primary route – dual/single carriageway	
A road – dual/single carriageway	
B road – dual/single carriageway	
Minor road – dual/single carriageway	
Other minor road – dual/single carriageway	
Road under construction	
Pedestrianised area	
Postcode boundaries	DY7
County and unitary authority boundaries	
Railway	
Railway under construction	
Tramway, miniature railway	
Rural track, private road or narrow road in urban area	
Gate or obstruction to traffic (restrictions may not apply at all times or to all vehicles)	
Path, bridleway, byway open to all traffic, road used as a public path	

The representation in this atlas of a road, track or path is no evidence of the existence of a right of way

174
94
Adjoining page indicators

Walsall	**Railway station**
	Private railway station
	Bus, coach station
	Ambulance station
	Coastguard station
	Fire station
	Police station
	Accident and Emergency entrance to hospital
H	**Hospital**
+	**Place of worship**
i	**Information Centre** (open all year)
P	**Parking**
P&R	**Park and Ride**
PO	**Post Office**
	Camping site
	Caravan site
	Golf course
	Picnic site
Prim Sch	**Important buildings, schools, colleges, universities and hospitals**
River Medway	**Water name**
	River, stream
	Lock, weir
	Water
	Tidal water
	Woods
	Houses
Church	**Non-Roman antiquity**
ROMAN FORT	**Roman antiquity**

Acad	**Academy**	Mkt	**Market**	
Allot Gdns	**Allotments**	Meml	**Memorial**	
Cemy	**Cemetery**	Mon	**Monument**	
C Ctr	**Civic Centre**	Mus	**Museum**	
CH	**Club House**	Obsy	**Observatory**	
Coll	**College**	Pal	**Royal Palace**	
Crem	**Crematorium**	PH	**Public House**	
Ent	**Enterprise**	Recn Gd	**Recreation Ground**	
Ex H	**Exhibition Hall**	Resr	**Reservoir**	
Ind Est	**Industrial Estate**	Ret Pk	**Retail Park**	
IRB Sta	**Inshore Rescue Boat Station**	Sch	**School**	
		Sh Ctr	**Shopping Centre**	
Inst	**Institute**	TH	**Town Hall/House**	
Ct	**Law Court**	Trad Est	**Trading Estate**	
L Ctr	**Leisure Centre**	Univ	**University**	
LC	**Level Crossing**	Wks	**Works**	
Liby	**Library**	YH	**Youth Hostel**	

■ The dark grey border on the inside edge of some pages indicates that the mapping does not continue onto the adjacent page

■ The small numbers around the edges of the maps identify the 1 kilometre National Grid lines

The scale of the maps on the pages numbered in blue is 5.52 cm to 1 km • 3½ inches to 1 mile • 1: 18103

0	¼	½	¾	1 mile
0	250 m	500 m	750 m	1 kilometre

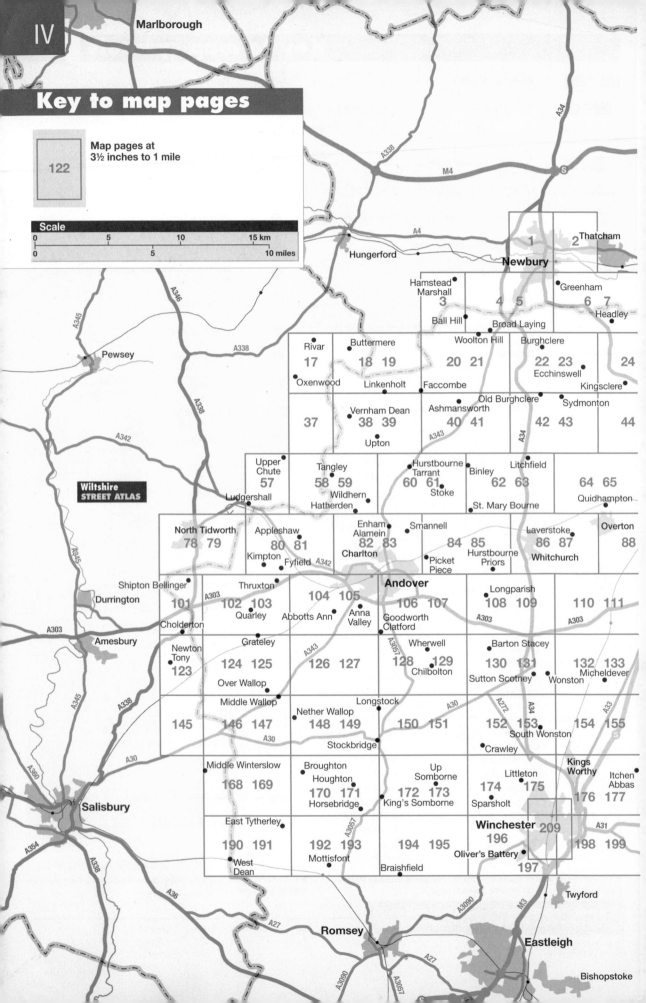

IV

Key to map pages

Map pages at
3½ inches to 1 mile

122

Scale

0 ————— 5 ————— 10 ————— 15 km

0 ————— 5 ————— 10 miles

Wiltshire
STREET ATLAS

Marlborough

Hungerford

Newbury

1 **2** Thatcham

Hamstead
Marshall
3 **4** **5** Greenham **6** **7**
Ball Hill Broad Laying Headley
Woolton Hill Burghclere

Pewsey

Rivar Buttermere **20** **21** **22** **23** **24**
17 **18** **19** Echinswell
Oxenwood Linkenholt Faccombe Kingsclere

Old Burghclere Sydmonton
Vernham Dean Ashmansworth
37 **38** **39** **40** **41** **42** **43** **44**
Upton

Upper Hurstbourne Litchfield
Chute Tangley Tarrant Binley
57 **58** **59** **60** **61** **62** **63** **64** **65**
Ludgershall Wildhern Stoke Quidhampton
Hatherden St. Mary Bourne

Enham Smannell Laverstoke Overton
North Tidworth Appleshaw Alamein **84** **85** **86** **87** **88**
78 **79** **80** **81** **82** **83** Hurstbourne Whitchurch
Kimpton Charlton Priors
Shipton Bellinger Fyfield Picket
Durrington Thruxton **104** **105** Andover Piece Longparish
101 **102** **103** **106** **107** **108** **109** **110** **111**
Cholderton Quarley Abbotts Ann Anna Goodworth
Amesbury Valley Clatford

Newton Grateley Wherwell Barton Stacey **132** **133**
Tony **124** **125** **126** **127** **128** **129** **130** **131** Micheldever
123 Chilbolton **154** **155**
Over Wallop Sutton Scotney Wonston

Middle Wallop Longstock South Wonston
Nether Wallop **150** **151** **152** **153** **154** **155**
145 **146** **147** **148** **149** Crawley
Stockbridge Kings
Worthy
Middle Winterslow Broughton Up Littleton Itchen
Houghton Somborne **174** **175** Abbas
168 **169** **170** **171** **172** **173** **176** **177**
Salisbury Horsebridge King's Somborne Sparsholt

East Tytherley Winchester **209**
190 **191** **192** **193** **194** **195** **196** **198** **199**
West Mottisfont Braishfield Oliver's Battery
Dean **197**

Twyford

Romsey

Eastleigh

Bishopstoke

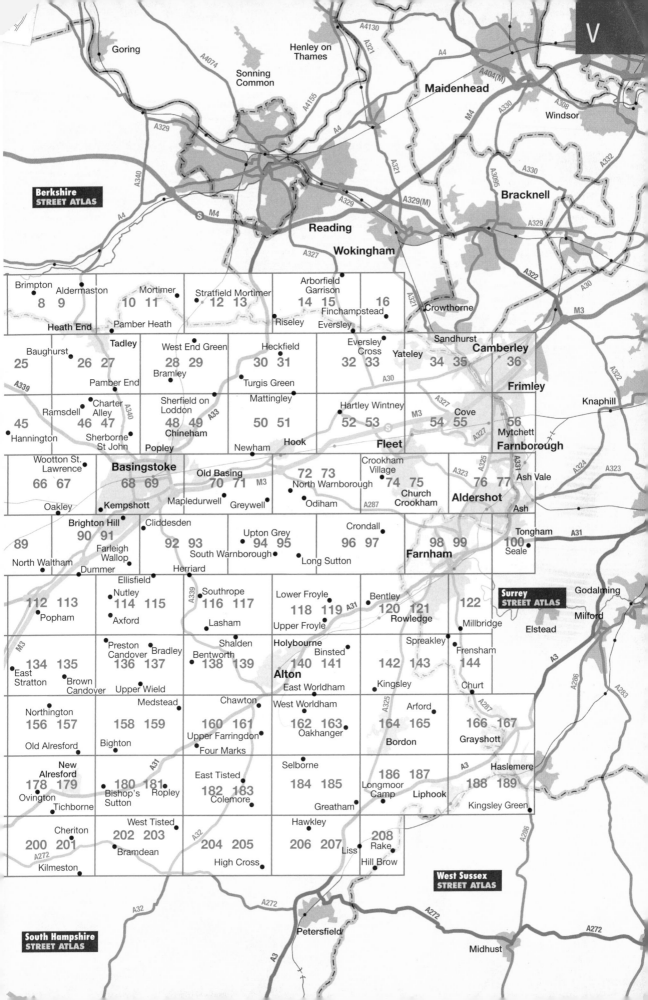

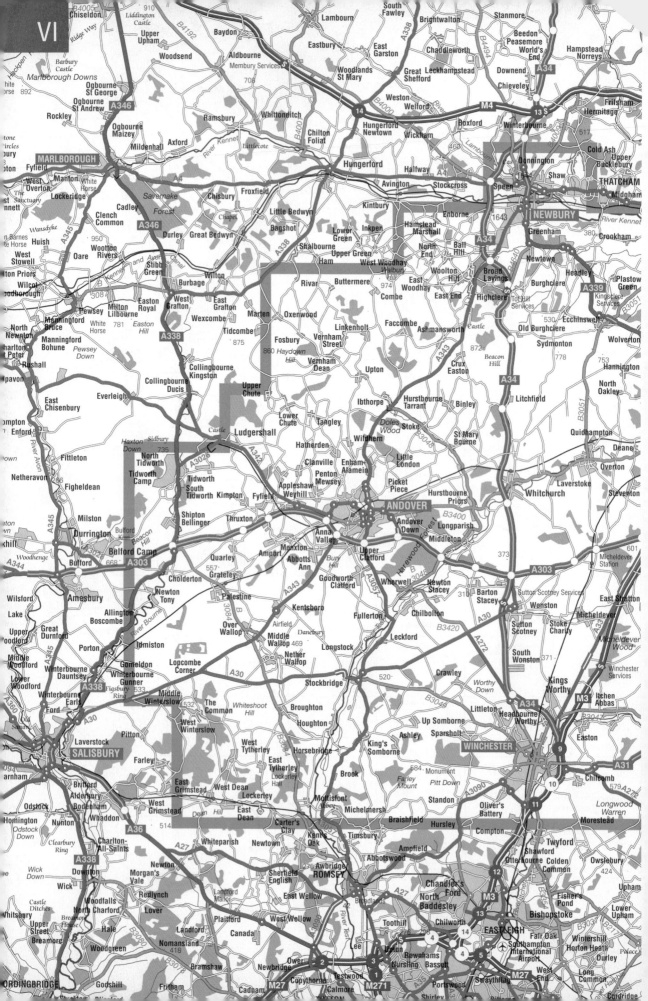

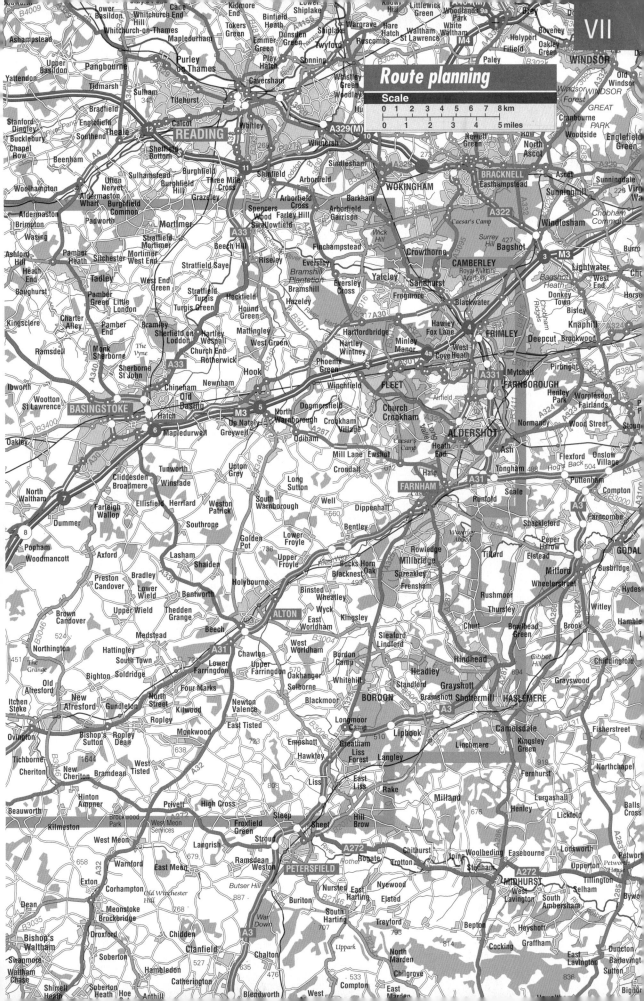

Major administrative and Postcode boundaries

Scale

| County and unitary authority boundaries |
| District boundaries |
| Postcode boundaries |
| Area covered by this atlas |

0   5   10   15 km
0   5   10 miles

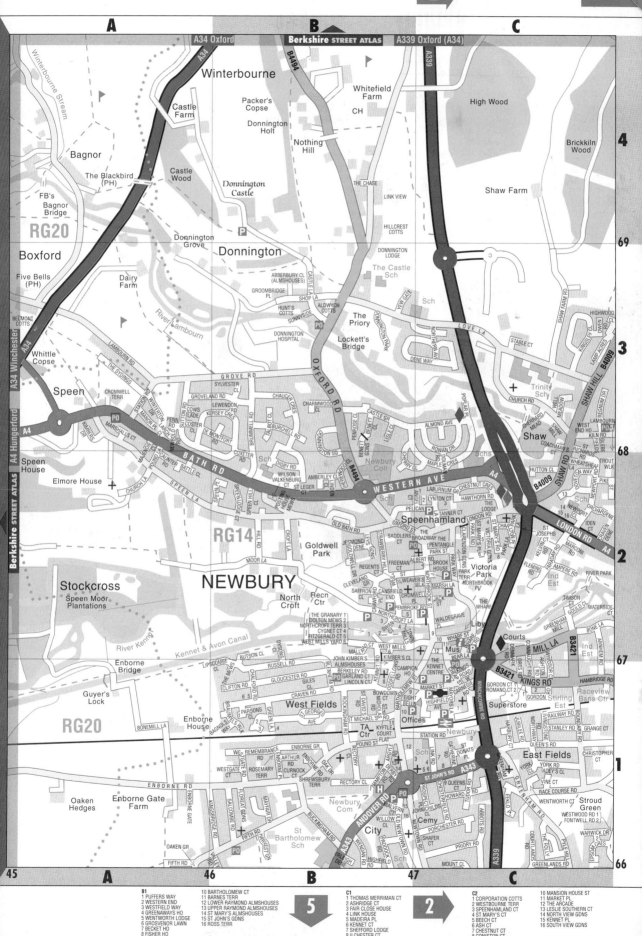

A34 Oxford
Berkshire STREET ATLAS
A339 Oxford (A34)

A   B   C

Winterbourne

Packer's Copse

Whitefield Farm

CH

High Wood

Castle Farm

Donnington Holt

Nothing Hill

Brickkiln Wood

4

Bagnor

The Blackbird (PH)

Castle Wood

Donnington Castle

THE CHASE

LINK VIEW

Shaw Farm

FB's Bagnor Bridge

Castle Wood

HILLCREST COTTS

69

RG20

Boxford

Donnington Grove

Donnington

DONNINGTON LODGE

The Castle Sch

Five Bells (PH)

Dairy Farm

ABBERBURY CL (ALMSHOUSES)

GROOMBRIDGE PL

SHOP LA

HUNT'S COTTS

SUNNYSIDE

DONNINGTON HOSPITAL

ALDWYCH COTTS

The Priory

Lockett's Bridge

YEW GATE

Sch

LOVE LA

HIGHWOOD

STABLE CT

KINGSLEY CL

LAMP ACRES

REGNUM DR

B4009

3

River Lambourn

Whittle Copse

Speen

LAMBOURN RD

THE SYDINGS

CROMWELL TERR

GROVE RD

SYLVESTER CL

GROVELAND RD

LEWENDON RD

KERSEY CRES

CHARMWOOD CL

CHAUCER CRES

COWS LADE

OXFORD RD

Trinity Sch

CHURCH RD

SHERRARD MEAD

WELL MEADOW

SHAW HILL

WEST END HO

RICHARDS

SHAW RD

Shaw

68

A4 Hungerford

A4

MARSHALLS CT

STATION RD

WINTERTON RD

MANOR PL

PENN RD

SUTTON RD

DE MONTFORT

COSTER CL

BRUMMELL RD

BURCHELL RD

TALBOT CL

PENROSE CL

BENNETT RD

LISLE CL

CASTLE GR

ALMOND AVE

ROWAN DR

POPLAR PL

Coachman's Ct

St Richards

KILN FIELDS

GLEBE

NEWPORT

ORCHARDENE

13

Speen House

Elmore House

CHURCH LA

SPEEN LA

BATTLE CL

SPEEN PL

CALCUTER RD

HILL RD

COXETER RD

DIGBY CL

WILSON

VALKENBURG

ST LEGER CT

AMBERLEY CL

BENNETT RD

Newbury Coll

WESTERN AVE

Sch

ANGEL

PELICAN

LYNTON CT

HAWTHORN RD

The Lodge

HUTTON CL

WHEATSHEAF

WAY

PIKE

NEWPORT

IDEN CL

CRAVEN

A4

B4009

2

RG14

Goldwell Park

MOOR LA

CROFT LA

OLD BATH RD

Sch

OXFORD ST

STRAWBERRY HILL

THE PENTANGLE

PARK ST

SADDLERS

CLAREN DON

ST MARY'S RD

Victoria Park

ST JOSEPHS

KELVIN

MARCONI

FLEMING RD

AMPERE RD

RIVER PARK

Ind Est

LONDON RD

NEWBURY

Stockcross

Speen Moor Plantations

North Croft

Recn Ctr

JESMOND DENE

REGENTS PL

CLEVELAND

SAFFRON

FREEMAN RD

ALBERT RD

BROOK HOUSE

PARK WAY

Victoria Park

NORTHBROOK PV

TIMSON LA

WATERSIDE

River Kennet

Kennet & Avon Canal

THE GRANARY 1
DOLTON MEWS 2
NORTHCROFT TERR 3
CYGNET CT 4
FITZGERALD CT 5
WEST MILLS YARD 6

CRAWFORD

SWAN

NORTHCROFT LA

WEAVER'S

CANSFIELD END

CROMWELL RD

PEMBROKE RD

WEST MILLS

WALDEGRAVE

JACK ST

WHARF ST

The Wharf

Liby

GREENHAM MILL

BONE LA

B3421

Ind Est

67

Enborne Bridge

Guyer's Lock

LIPSCOMBE CL

THE MEWS

CHALCROFT RD

CLIFTON RD

BUTSON CL

DYSONS CL

RUSSELL RD

GLOUCESTER RD

GILES RD

CRAVEN RD

BERKELEY RD

JOHN KIMBER'S ALMSHOUSES

GARLAND CT

LINCOLN CT

BOWDOWN

KIMBER'S CL

CAMPION HO

MALLARD

BARTHOLOMEW ST

MARKET ST

BELLS

HIGHFIELD AVE

The Kennet Centre

BEAR LA

DENMARK

WINDSOR CT

MILL LA

HAMBRIDGE RD

Courts

Mus

B3421

KINGS RD

Raceview Bsns Ctr

RG20

Enborne House

BONEMILL LA

BRAUNES WLK

BAGNOLS WAY

PARSONS ST

GREEN LA

St GEORGE'S AVE

ROCKINGHAM RD

St DAVID'S RD

St MICHAEL RD

POUND ST

KYFTLE COURT FLAT

West Fields

Offices

TA Ctr

STATION RD

Newbury

WINCHCOMBE RD

Superstore

GORDON CT 1
ROMANO CT 2

Stirling Est

HARBURY RD

NORTHWAY

LIVINGSTONE RD

STANLEY RD

JUBILEE RD

GRANGE CT

East Fields

CHRISTOPHER CT

1

Oaken Hedges

Enborne Gate Farm

ENBORNE RD

REMEMBRANCE RD

WESTGATE RD

WESTGATE CT

ARTHUR RD

ROSEMARY TERR

ENBORNE GR

ENBORNE GATE

OLD DR

RECTORY RD

SHREWSBURY TERR

RECTORY CL

Newbury Com

HAMPTON RD

ANDOVER RD

St JOHN'S RD

MALVERN

WILLOW RD

City

St Bartholomew Sch

KINGSBRIDGE RD

SALCOMBE RD

MAYFAIR DR

BUCKINGHAM RD

FLOREAT GDNS

St DONATS CT

ARGYLE RD

CATHERINE RD

QUEEN'S RD

PROSPECT RD

CHESTERFIELD RD

JOHN CHILD'S RD

OLD NEWTOWN RD

NEWTOWN RD

PORCHESTER RD

SHAFER RD

Cemy

PRIORY RD

A343

GREENHAM RD

KENDRICK RD

York RD

JADEY'S CL

VINE CT

RACE COURSE RD

WENTWORTH CT

Stroud Green

WESTWOOD RD 1
FONTWELL RD 2

WARWICK DR

THE FOLLY

EPSOM CL

A339

Oaken Gr

OAKEN GR

FIFTH RD

HARVEST GN

VALLEY RD

St John's RD

HIGHFIELD RD

WENDAN RD

PADDOCK RD

MOUNT CL

COURTLANDS RD

GREENLANDS RD

PYLE HILL

PIKE

66

45   A   46   B   47   C

2
5
2

B1
1 PUFFERS WAY
2 WESTERN END
3 WESTFIELD WAY
4 GREENAWAYS HO
5 WENTWORTH LODGE
6 GROSVENOR LAWN
7 BECKET HO
8 FISHER HO
9 IMPERIAL CT
10 BARTHOLOMEW CT
11 BARNES TERR
12 LOWER RAYMOND ALMSHOUSES
13 UPPER RAYMOND ALMSHOUSES
14 ST MARY'S ALMSHOUSES
15 ST JOHN'S GDNS
16 ROSS TERR

C1
1 THOMAS MERRIMAN CT
2 ASHRIDGE CT
3 FAIR CLOSE HOUSE
4 LINK HOUSE
5 MADEIRA PL
6 KENNET CT
7 SHEFFORD LODGE
8 ILCHESTER CT
9 HILARY HOUSE

C2
1 CORPORATION COTTS
2 WESTBOURNE TERR
3 SPEENHAMLAND CT
4 ST MARY'S CT
5 BEECH CT
6 ASH CT
7 CHESTNUT CT
8 CONISTON CT
9 BRIDGE ST
10 MANSION HOUSE ST
11 MARKET PL
12 THE ARCADE
13 LESLIE SOUTHERN CT
14 NORTH VIEW GDNS
15 KENNET PL
16 SOUTH VIEW GDNS

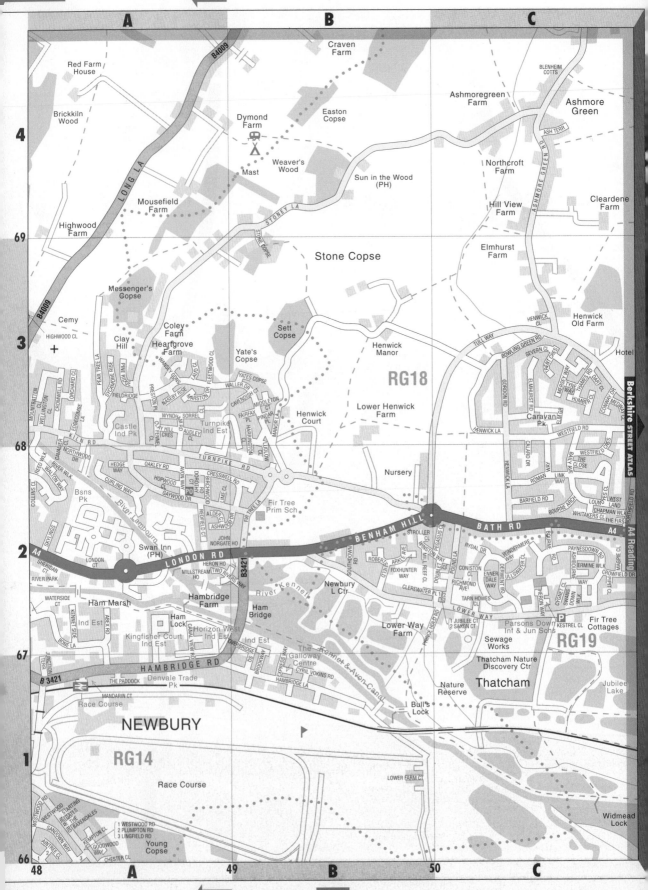

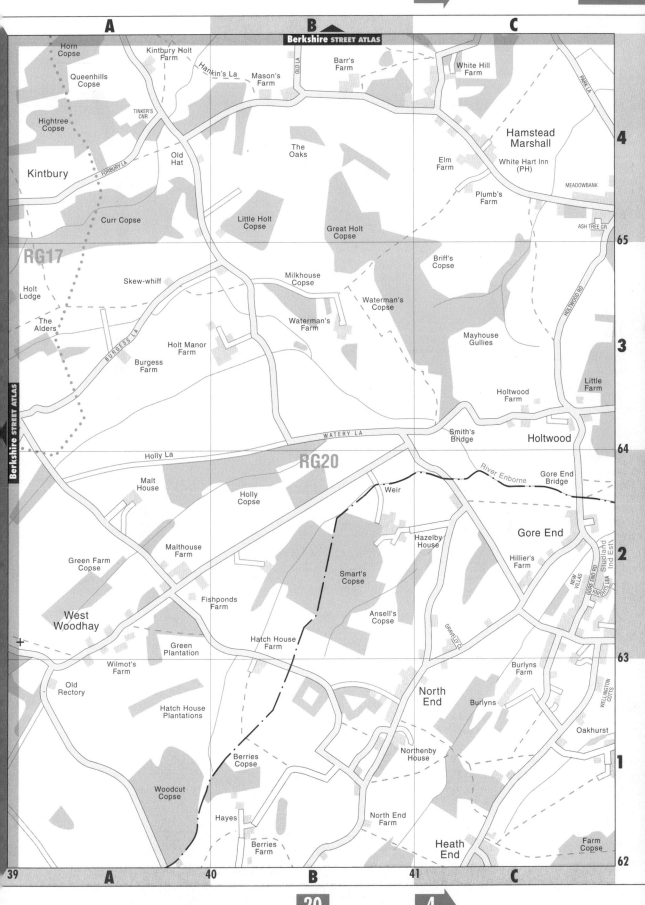

Berkshire STREET ATLAS

Berkshire STREET ATLAS

A — **B** — **C**

4
65
3
64
2
63
1
62

39   **A**   40   **B**   41   **C**

Horn Copse
Kintbury Holt Farm
Hankin's La
Mason's Farm
Old La
Barr's Farm
White Hill Farm
PARK LA
Queenhills Copse
TINKER'S CNR
The Oaks
Hamstead Marshall
Hightree Copse
Elm Farm
White Hart Inn (PH)
MEADOWBANK
Old Hat
Kintbury
FORBURY LA
Plumb's Farm
ASH TREE GR
Curr Copse
Little Holt Copse
Great Holt Copse
Briff's Copse
HOLTWOOD RD
RG17
Holt Lodge
Skew-whiff
Milkhouse Copse
Waterman's Copse
Little Farm
The Alders
BURGESS LA
Waterman's Farm
Mayhouse Gullies
Holt Manor Farm
Holtwood Farm
Burgess Farm
Smith's Bridge
Holtwood
WATERY LA
Holly La
RG20
River Enborne
Gore End Bridge
Malt House
Holly Copse
Weir
Gore End
Malthouse Farm
Hazelby House
Hillier's Farm
Studland Ind Est
Green Farm Copse
Smart's Copse
NEW VILLAS
GORE END RD
KNIGHTS LEA
Fishponds Farm
Ansell's Copse
GRAVEL LA CL
West Woodhay
Green Plantation
Hatch House Farm
North End
Burlyns Farm
WELLINGTON COTTS
Wilmot's Farm
63
Old Rectory
Burlyns
Oakhurst
Hatch House Plantations
Berries Copse
Northenby House
Woodcut Copse
Hayes
North End Farm
Heath End
Farm Copse
Berries Farm

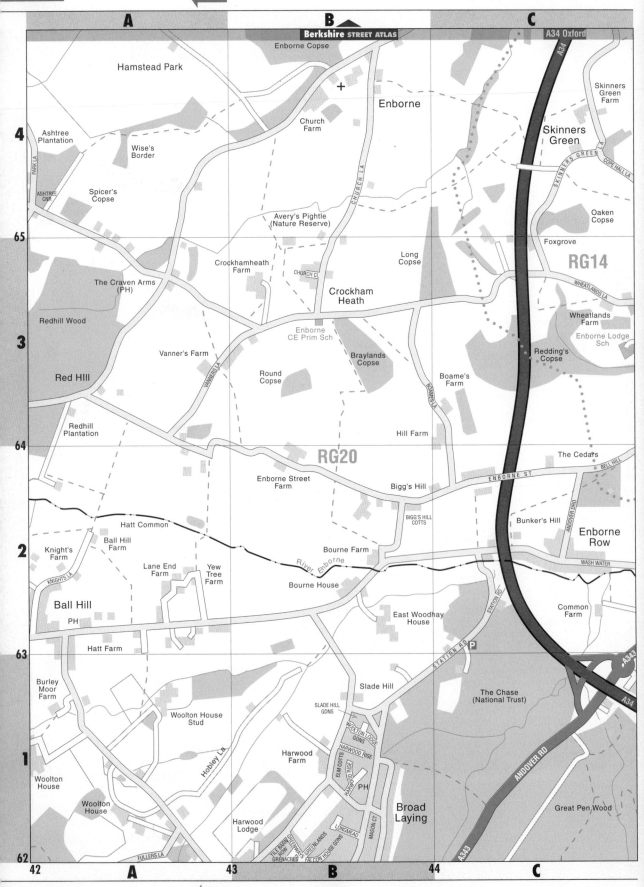

Berkshire STREET ATLAS

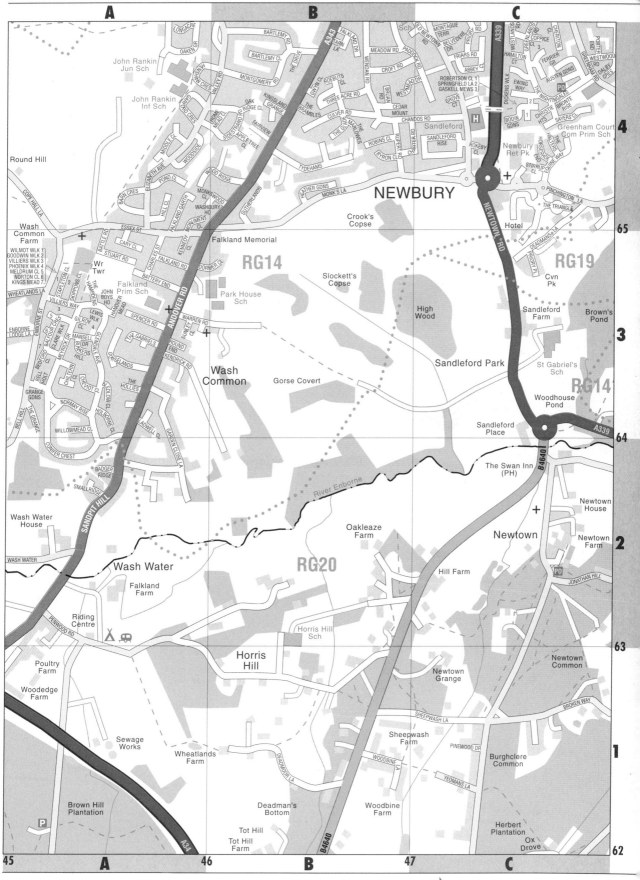

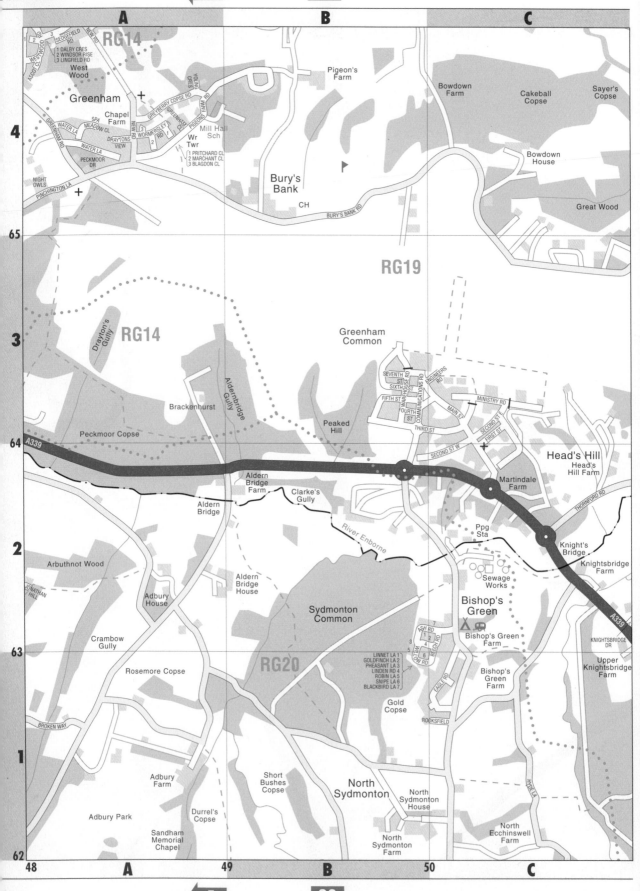
A   B   C

RG14

1 DALBY CRES
2 WINDSOR RISE
3 LINGFIELD RD

SEDGEFIELD RD

West Wood

Greenham

Pigeon's Farm

Bowdown Farm

Cakeball Copse

Sayer's Copse

Chapel Farm

SPA MEADOW CL

GREYBERRY COPSE RD

GREENHAM RD

PIGEONS RD

YOUNG CRES

NEW RD

Mill Hall Sch

Bowdown House

4

WORMERSLEY RD

DRAYTONS VIEW

Wr Twr

1 PRITCHARD CL
2 MARCHANT CL
3 BLAGDON CL

Bury's Bank

Great Wood

WATER LA

PECKMOOR DR

GREENHAM LA

NIGHT OWLS

PINCHINGTON LA

CH

BURY'S BANK RD

65

RG19

Drayton's Gully

RG14

Greenham Common

3

Brackenhurst

Aldernbridge Gully

Peaked Hill

SEVENTH ST

SIXTH ST

FIFTH ST

FOURTH ST

THIRD ST

WAREHOUSE RD

COMMUNICATIONS RD

ENGINEERS RD

MAIN ST

MINISTRY RD

SECOND ST

FIRST ST

Head's Hill

Peckmoor Copse

SECOND ST W

Head's Hill Farm

64

A339

Aldern Bridge Farm

Clarke's Gully

Martindale Farm

THORNFORD RD

Aldern Bridge

Ppg Sta

Knight's Bridge

2

Arbuthnot Wood

Aldern Bridge House

River Enborne

Sewage Works

Knightsbridge Farm

JONATHAN HILL

Adbury House

Sydmonton Common

Bishop's Green

Bishop's Green Farm

KNIGHTSBRIDGE DR

Crambow Gully

CH RD

BEECH RD

Bishop's Green Farm

Upper Knightsbridge Farm

63

Rosemore Copse

RG20

WILLOW RD

LINNET LA 1
GOLDFINCH LA 2
PHEASANT LA 3
LINDEN RD 4
ROBIN LA 5
SNIPE LA 6
BLACKBIRD LA 7

EAGLE RD

BROKEN WAY

Gold Copse

ROOKSFIELD

1

Adbury Farm

Short Bushes Copse

North Sydmonton

North Sydmonton House

MORELA

Adbury Park

Durrel's Copse

Sandham Memorial Chapel

North Sydmonton Farm

North Ecchinswell Farm

62

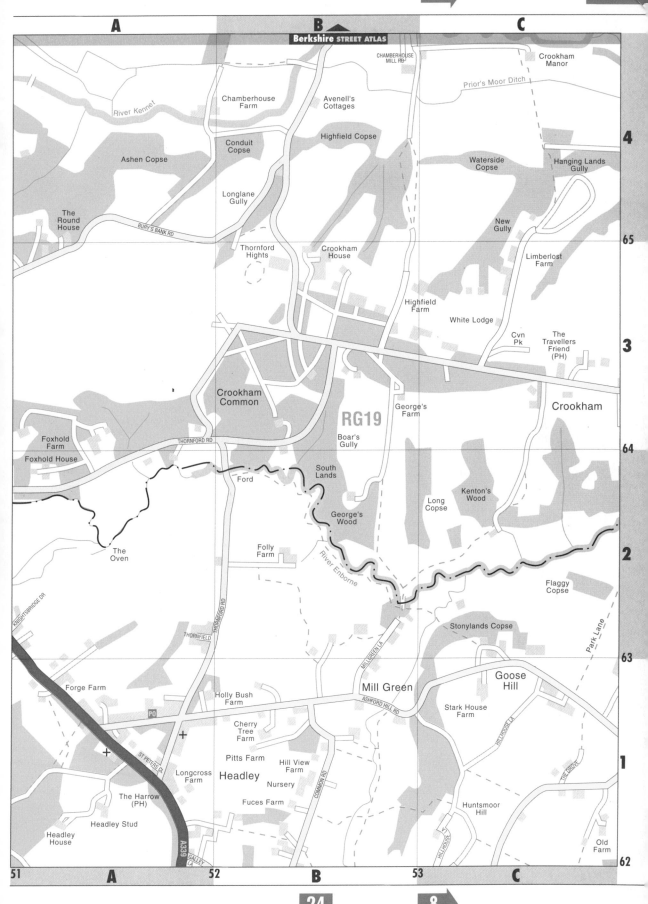

Berkshire STREET ATLAS

A
B
C

CHAMBERHOUSE MILL RD

Crookham Manor

Prior's Moor Ditch

River Kennet

Chamberhouse Farm

Avenell's Cottages

Highfield Copse

4

Conduit Copse

Ashen Copse

Waterside Copse

Hanging Lands Gully

Longlane Gully

The Round House

BURY'S BANK RD

New Gully

65

Thornford Hights

Crookham House

Limberlost Farm

Highfield Farm

White Lodge

Cvn Pk

The Travellers Friend (PH)

3

Crookham Common

George's Farm

RG19

Crookham

Boar's Gully

64

Foxhold Farm

THORNFORD RD

Foxhold House

Ford

South Lands

Kenton's Wood

George's Wood

Long Copse

The Oven

Folly Farm

River Enborne

Flaggy Copse

2

Stonylands Copse

Park Lane

63

Forge Farm

Mill Green

Goose Hill

Holly Bush Farm

ASHFORD HILL RD

Stark House Farm

PO

MILLGREEN LA

HILLCROSS LA

Cherry Tree Farm

+

Pitts Farm

Hill View Farm

THE DRIVE

1

Longcross Farm

Headley

Nursery

COMMON RD

+

ST PETERS CL

KNIGHTSBRIDGE DR

THORNFIELD

THORNFORD RD

Fuces Farm

Huntsmoor Hill

The Harrow (PH)

Headley Stud

HILLHOUSE LA

Old Farm

Headley House

A339

GALLEY LA

62

A

B

Berkshire STREET ATLAS

C

Woolhampton

Brimpton Mill

King's Bridge

River Kennet

BRIMPTON RD

4

The Lynch

Bonds Gully

Gravel Pit

East Field Copse

Manor Farm

MANOR VIEW

65

Stone House

Burnell's Farm

PO

Weir

Shalford Farm

BACK LA

Manor Farm

Holdaway's Farm

CHURCH LA

PH

Brimpton

ENBORNE WAY

BANNISTER PL

3

Brimpton CE Prim Sch

Bannister's Wood

MANOR LA

RG7

Chaplin's Wood

Upper Hyde End Farm

HYDE END LA

Arundell's Copse

Able Bridge

64

Little Park House

Little Park Farm

Oak Cottage

Hyde End

Stockwell Farmhouse

Park Copse

Hyde End Wood

Boot Farm

Hyde End Farm

2

Park Gully Bridge

River Enborne

Inwood Copse

BACK LA

Brimpton Common

Oxford Bridge

Blacknest Farm

RG19

HOCKFORD LA

BRIMPTON LA

63

Riddings Farm

Ashford Hill Farm

The Pineapple Inn (PH)

B3051

RIDDINGS LA

WOODHOUSE LA

Woodhouse Farm

Broom Close Row

ASHFORD HILL RD

1

Woodlands Farm

Brook Farm

LITTLE ALDERSHOT LA
THE COUNCIL HOUSES 2

The Ship Inn (PH)

RG26

Kingsclere Woodlands

Ashford Hill

OLD LA

Chippings Gully

FARM ALLEY

Whitehall Farm

Ashford Hill Prim Sch

CHAPEL LA

B3051

Redlands Copse

62

54

A

55

B

56

C

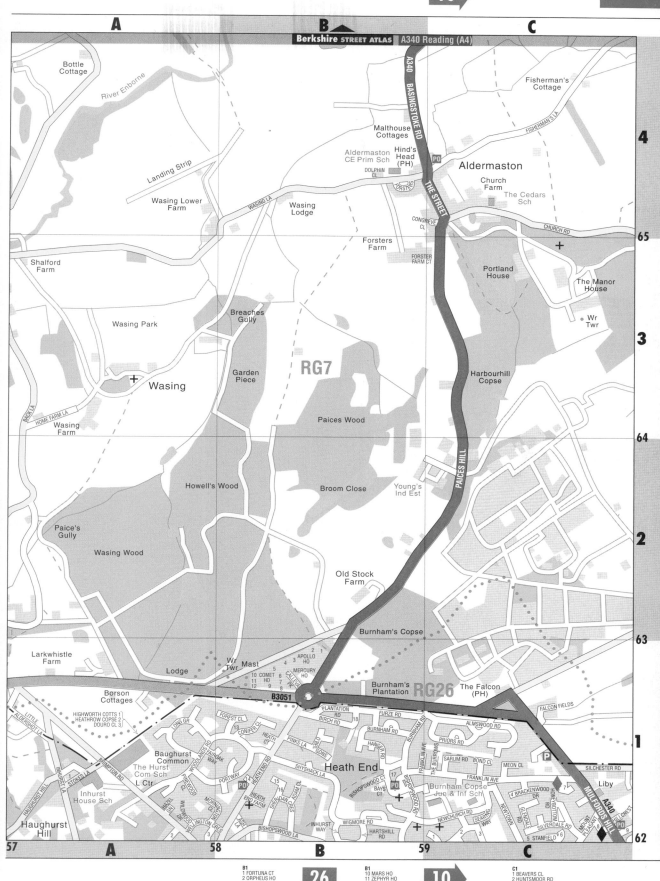

A340

BASINGSTOKE RD

THE STREET

Bottle Cottage

River Enborne

Fisherman's Cottage

FISHERMAN'S LA

Malthouse Cottages

Aldermaston CE Prim Sch

Hind's Head (PH)

PO

Aldermaston

Landing Strip

Wasing Lower Farm

WASING LA

Wasing Lodge

DOLPHIN CL

FORSTERS

Church Farm

The Cedars Sch

CHURCH RD

4

CONGREVE CL

Forsters Farm

65

Shalford Farm

FORSTER FARM CT

Portland House

The Manor House

Wr Twr

Breaches Gully

RG7

Wasing Park

Garden Piece

Harbourhill Copse

3

Wasing

BACK LA

HOME FARM LA

Wasing Farm

Paices Wood

PAICES HILL

64

Howell's Wood

Broom Close

Young's Ind Est

Paice's Gully

Wasing Wood

2

Old Stock Farm

Burnham's Copse

63

Larkwhistle Farm

Lodge

Wr Twr

Mast

APOLLO HO

MERCURY HO

COMET HO

CALLUM

Burnham's Plantation

RG26

The Falcon (PH)

FALCON FIELDS

Borson Cottages

HIGHWORTH COTTS 1
HEATHROW COPSE 2
DOURO CL 3

B3051

PLANTATION RD

BIRCH RD

FURZE RD

BURNHAM RD

ALMSWOOD RD

PRIORS RD

SILCHESTER RD

1

LITTLE ALDERSHOT LA

BRIMPTON RD

LONG GR

FOREST CL

CONIFER CL

HEATH CT

PINKS LA

3RD GDNS

HANGER RD

BURNHAM AVE

FRANKLIN AVE

THE BURROWS

SARUM RD

BOND CL

MEON CL

P

Liby

Baughurst Common

The Hurst Com Sch L Ctr

WOODLANDS RD

FAIROAK WAY

PORTWAY

PIREWOOD CL

HEATH END RD

SHYSHACK LA

Heath End

FRANKLIN AVE

Burnham Copse Jun & Inf Sch

BRACKENWOOD DR

HONEYBOTTOM RD

A340

MULFORDS HILL

Inhurst House Sch

HAZEL GN

WILDMOOR DR

MORNINGTON CL

WELLINGTON CRES

ASH CL

HEATH END RD

SHERIDAN CRES

BAYS CT

BISHOPSWOOD RD

NEWCHURCH RD

NEWTOWN

SEARING WAY

GLENDALE RD

SILVERDALE RD

LIMEMINT

PLEASANT

HILLCREST

PO

Haughurst Hill

HAUGHURST HILL

STOKES LA

INHURST LA

INHURST WAY

WIGMORE RD

BISHOPSWOOD LA

HARTSHILL RD

STANFIELD

62

Berkshire STREET ATLAS

Aqua Vitae Copse

Ufton Park

Brent's Gully

Padworth

Upper Church Farm

Upper Lodge Farm

The Old Rectory

SILVER LA

Padworth Gully

Springhill Farm

Wrays Farm

RECTORY RD

The Croft

MAY'S LA

Hatch Farm House

The Round Oak (PH)

65

CHURCH RD

SPRING LA

RAMPTONS LA

The Birches

REDLANE HILL

Court Farm

RAGHILL

P

Padworth Common

BLOCK COTTS

3

Raghill Farm

Old Warren

Burnt Common

Budd's Firs

Black Pightle

REDLA

Aldermaston Park

RG7

CHAPEL LA

+

WELSHMAN'S RD

64

Little Heath

Valentine Wood Ind Est

Fox Hill

2

Decoy Pond

Alders Slade

Benyon's Inclosure

Aldermaston Soke

SOKE RD

Hungry Hill

Pond Farm

63

Upper Moor's Gully

WINKWORTH LA

SECOND AVE

FIRST AVE

Catthaw Lands Copse

Soke Pig Farm

White House Farm

Catthawlands Farm

PELICAN RD

WAKEFORD CT

SILCHESTER RD

KINGS RD

1

+

Silchester CE Prim Sch

SCHOOL LA

+ Mus

RG26

P

SPENCER CL

JUNE CL

CHURCH RD

STROUD CL

SPRINGFIELD RD

CLAPPS GATE

WAKEFORD CL

KNOLLYS RD

ERSKINE RD

IMPSTONE RD

PAMBER RD

Silchester

P

Calleva Arms (PH)

P

TADLEY COMMON RD

Tadley Court

PAMBER HEATH RD

ILEX CL

Pamber Heath

Silchester Common

Tadley Common

CHURCH RD

VALLEY WAY

ROMANS GATE

THE GLEN

Roman Fields 1

Little London Rd 2

DUKES RIDE

SYMPSON RD

ARNEWOOD AVE

WESTLYN RD

EASTLYN RD

HEATH RD

BURNEY BIT

WHISTLERS LA

GORSELANDS

62

60

A

61

B

62

C

12

Berkshire STREET ATLAS

Oval Pond
Cowpond Piece
Roundoak Piece
Gibbet Piece
CAMP RD
PADWORTH RD
FOUR HOUSES CNR
FOUR HOUSES CNR CVN SITE
ISLAND FARM RD
Mast
Water Tower
READING RD
P
Five Oaken
Warennes Wood
Starvale Woods
Mowbray's Piece
Holden's Firs
LONGMOOR LA
Bridge's Farm
Lukin's Wood
BREWERY COMM
NIGHTINGALE LA
4
Fifty Acre Piece
Hundred Acre Piece
College Piece
Pickling Yard Plantation
Chaplin's Copse
GROVES LA
THE CRESCENT
SPRING RD
WOODSIDE CL
WINDMILL CT
WINDMILL RD
65
Stockwell's Piece
STEPHENS FIRS
SWEEZER'S PIECE
BIRCHLAND CL
RAVENSWORTH RD
LAMBWOOD
ST CATHERINE'S HILL
STEPHENS FIRS
FIRS END
BIRCH LA
STEPHEN'S CL
STEPHEN'S RD
LEIGH FIELD
PINE DR
BRIARLEA RD
WINDMILL CNR
THE BEVERS
HEATHLEA
KING ST
BADGERS CROFT
Liby
Mortimer Hill Farm
WINDMILL CNR
FAIRFIELD PK
WEST END RD
CROFT RD
VICTORIA RD
GLENAPP GRANGE
P
PO
GARTH RD
Mortimer St John's CE Sch
PH
THE STREET
ORCHARD RD
CAMPBELL'S GREEN
THE AVENUE
HAMMOND HEATH
3
WELSHMAN'S RD
CHAPEL RD
ROWLAND'S CL
THE BRIDGES
Turner's Arms (PH)
Mortimer West End
STANMORE GDNS
LOVES WOOD
ST MARY'S RD
ST JOHN'S RD
Mortimer
Summerlug
RG7
CHURCH RD
BACK LA
West End Farm
Lovegrove's Farm
Simms's Copse
SIMMS FARM LA
DRURY LA
64
Red Lion (PH)
Mortimer West End
West End Brook
Simms Stud Farm
TURK'S LA
Windabout Copse
Tanhouse Bridge
2
Stone Hill
Nine Acre Copse
Simms's Plantation
Brocas Land Farm
PITFIELD LA
63
P
WALL LA
Kiln Yard Copse
Sheepgrove Farm
Silchester Brook
AMPHITHEATRE
The Drove
CALLEVA ROMAN TOWN (remains of)
Manor Farm
CHURCH LA
PARK LA
1
P
CLAPPERS FARM RD
Silchester Hall
62

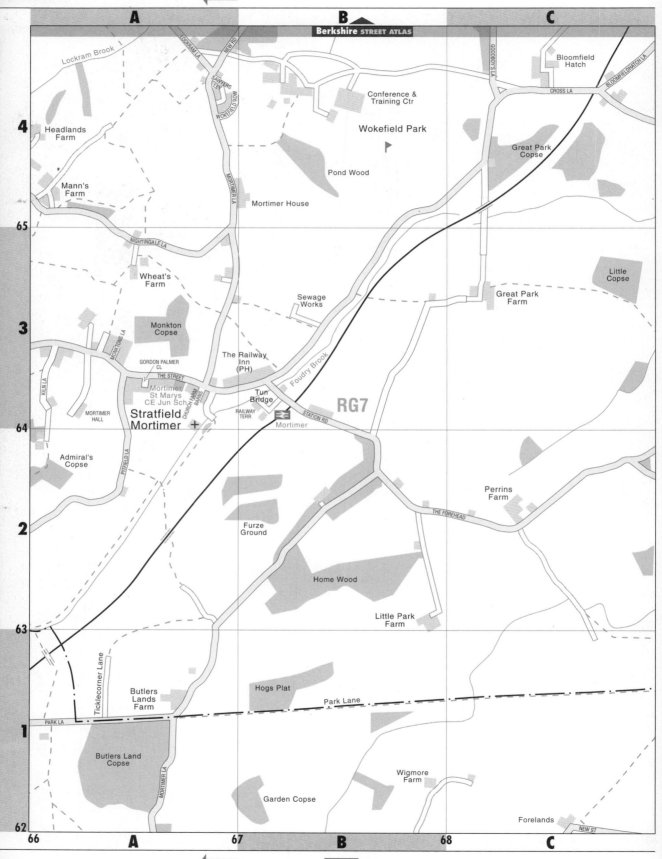

Berkshire STREET ATLAS

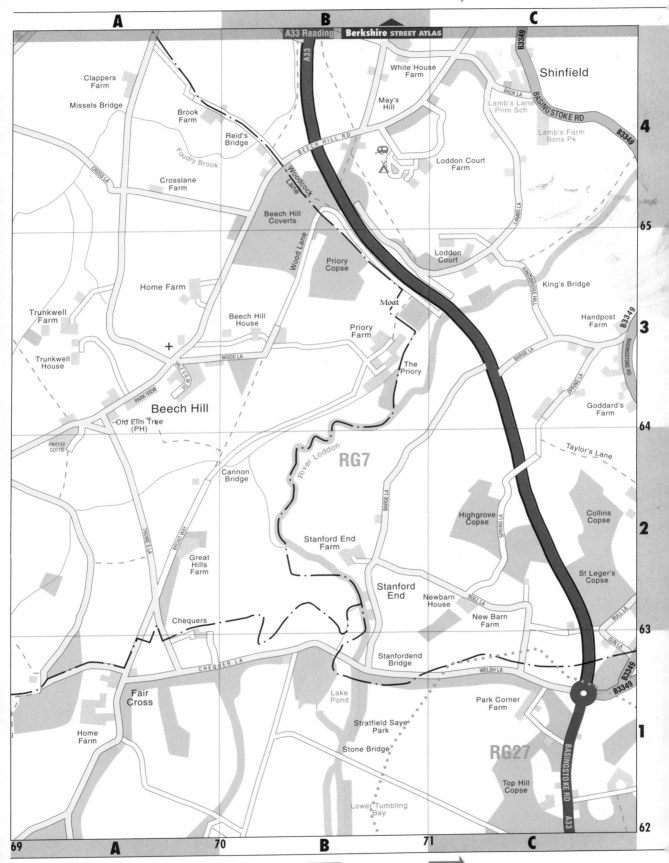

A   B   C

A33 Reading   **Berkshire** STREET ATLAS

Shinfield

B3349

Clappers Farm

Missels Bridge

Brook Farm

Reid's Bridge

White House Farm

May's Hill

BACK LA

Lamb's Lane Prim Sch

Lamb's Farm Bsns Pk

BASINGSTOKE RD

B3349   **4**

CROSS LA

Foudry Brook

Crosslane Farm

BEECH HILL RD

Woodcock Lane

Beech Hill Coverts

Wood Lane

Priory Copse

Loddon Court Farm

LAMBS LA

65

Home Farm

Trunkwell Farm

Beech Hill House

Moat

Priory Farm

The Priory

Loddon Court

KINGSBRIDGE HILL

King's Bridge

Handpost Farm

B3349

3

Trunkwell House

WOOD LA

VALE VIEW RD

BARGE LA

BASINGSTOKE RD

SPRING LA

PARK VIEW

Beech Hill

Old Elm Tree (PH)

Goddard's Farm

64

PRIORY COTTS

Cannon Bridge

River Loddon

RG7

Taylor's Lane

THORPE'S LA

BROAD WAY

Great Hills Farm

Stanford End Farm

BARGE LA

SPRING LA

Highgrove Copse

Collins Copse

2

St Leger's Copse

Stanford End

Newbarn House

BULL LA

New Barn Farm

BULL LA

SUN LA

Chequers

Stanfordend Bridge

WELSH LA

Park Corner Farm

B3349

B3349

63

CHEQUER LA

Fair Cross

Lake Pond

Stratfield Saye Park

Stone Bridge

RG27

BASINGSTOKE RD

1

Home Farm

Top Hill Copse

A33

Lower Tumbling Bay

62

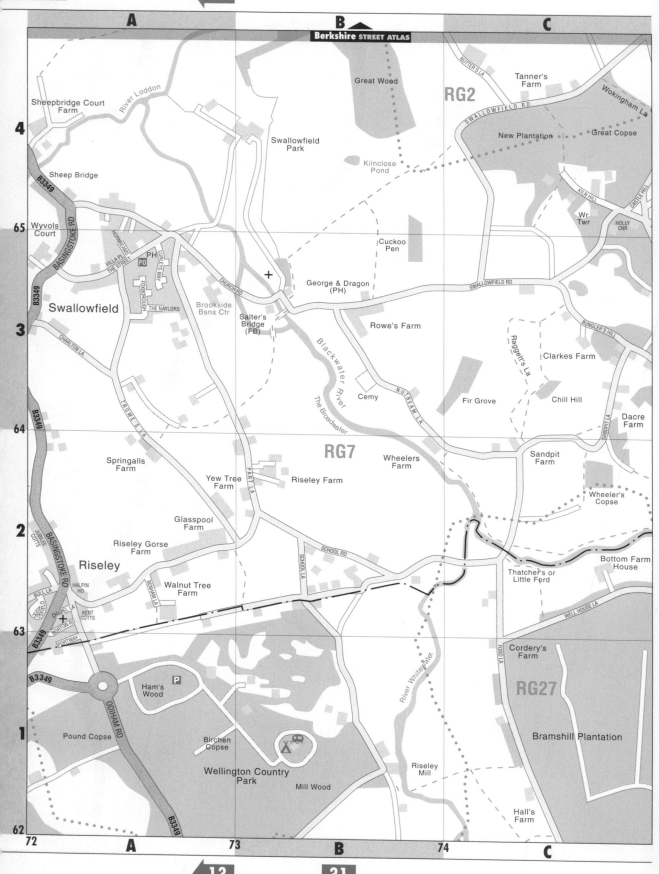

Berkshire STREET ATLAS

A   B   C

Great Wood

RG2

Nutter's La

Tanner's Farm

Wokingham La

Sheepbridge Court Farm

River Loddon

Swallowfield Park

Swallowfield Rd

New Plantation

Great Copse

4

Kilnclose Pond

Kiln Hill

Castle Hill

Sheep Bridge

Wr Twr

Holly Cnr

B3349

65

Wyvols Court

Horsecroft

The Street

Villa Pl

PO

Curley's Way

Church Rd

Cuckoo Pen

Swallowfield Rd

PH

Foxborough

The Naylors

George & Dragon (PH)

3

Swallowfield

Charlton La

Brookside Bsns Ctr

Salter's Bridge (FB)

Rowe's Farm

Raggett's La

Bungler's Hill

Clarkes Farm

B3349

Blackwater River

Cemy

Nutbean La

Fir Grove

Chill Hill

Dacre Farm

64

Trowe's La

The Broadwater

RG7

Wheelers Farm

Sandpit La

Sandpit Farm

Springalls Farm

Part La

Yew Tree Farm

Riseley Farm

2

Glasspool Farm

Wheeler's Copse

Jubilee Cotts

Riseley Gorse Farm

School La

School Rd

Bottom Farm House

Riseley

Basingstoke Rd

Halpin Ho

Benham La

Walnut Tree Farm

Thatcher's or Little Ford

Well House La

Bull La

Kent Cotts

63

Chapel La

Norton Rd

Portway

B3349

Cordery's Farm

Ford La

RG27

B3349

Ham's Wood

P

River Whitewater

1

Odiham Rd

Pound Copse

Birchen Copse

Bramshill Plantation

Wellington Country Park

Mill Wood

Riseley Mill

Hall's Farm

B3349

62

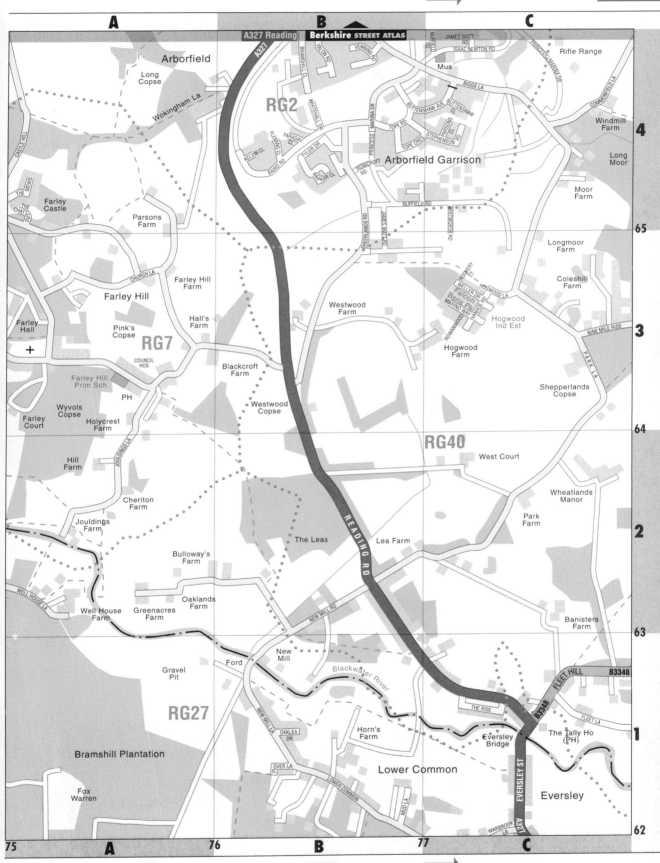

A327 Reading **Berkshire** STREET ATLAS

Arborfield

Long Copse

RG2

Wokingham La

JAMES WATT RD
ISAAC NEWTON RD

Mus

Rifle Range

PRINCESS MARINA DR

COMMONFIELD LA

Windmill Farm

BIGGS LA

BRAMSHILL CL

VALON RD

VENNING RD

WHITEHALL DR

FARADAY CL

FLEMING CL

BAIRD RD

KELVIN CL

TYLER DR

BAKER CL

BOWCROFT RD

BUTTENSHAW AVE

TOPE RD

TOPE CRES

PARSONS CL

STEPHENSON

BUTTENSHAW CL

Arborfield Garrison

4

Long Moor

Moor Farm

THE MEWS

THE CHASE

Farley Castle

Parsons Farm

NUFFIELD RD

65

CASTLE HILL

ASHERLANDS RD

JAMES SUTTON DR

WHITWORTH RD

Longmoor Farm

Coleshill Farm

CHURCH LA

Farley Hill Farm

Farley Hill

Hall's Farm

Westwood Farm

BROADLEY CL

WELLER DR

HOGWOOD LA

MARINO WAY

Falcon
Bsns Pk

Hogwood
Ind Est

NINE MILE RIDE

3

Farley Hall

+

Pink's Copse

RG7

COUNCIL HOS

Blackcroft Farm

ROWANWOOD

Hogwood Farm

PARK LA

Shepperlands Copse

Farley Hill Prim Sch

PH

Westwood Copse

64

Wyvols Copse

Holycrest Farm

RG40

West Court

Wheatlands Manor

Farley Court

Hill Farm

JOULDINGS LA

Cheriton Farm

Park Farm

2

Jouldings Farm

Bulloway's Farm

The Leas

Lea Farm

Banisters Farm

Oaklands Farm

REA DING RD

Well House Farm

Greenacres Farm

WELL HOUSE LA

NEW MILL RD

63

Gravel Pit

Ford

New Mill

Blackwater River

FLEET HILL

B3348

THE RISE

B3348

RG27

NEW MILL LA

OAKLEA DR

Horn's Farm

Eversley Bridge

FLEET LA

The Tally Ho (PH)

1

Bramshill Plantation

OVER LA

LOWER COMMON

Lower Common

EVERSLEY ST

Eversley

Fox Warren

MUD LA

A327

WARBROOK LA

62

A

76

B

77

C

15

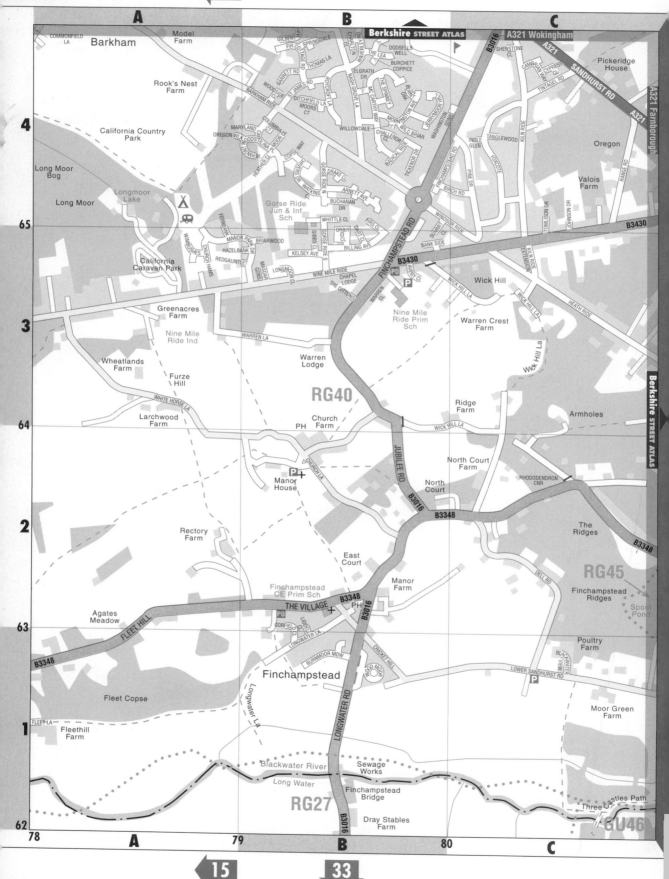

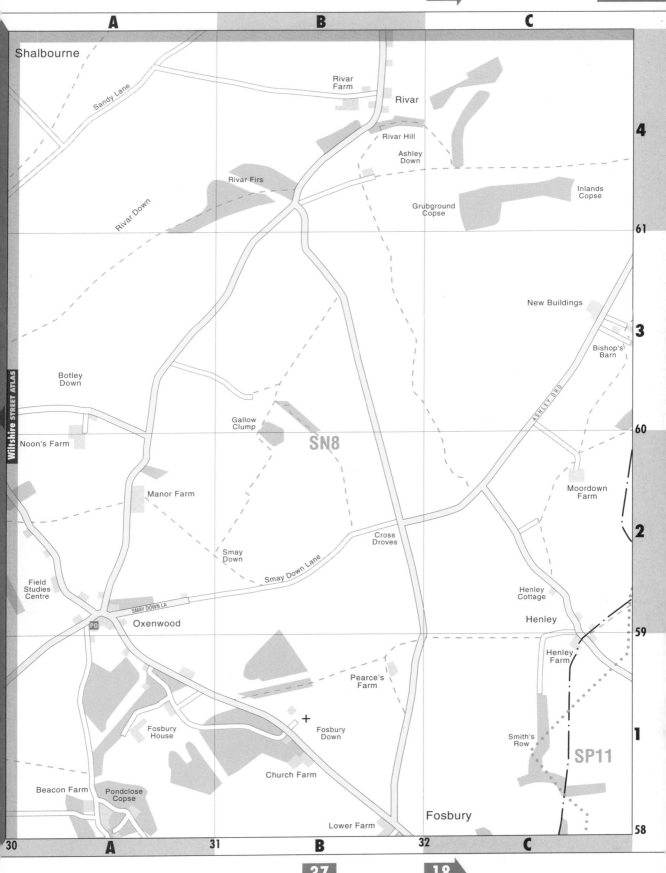

Shalbourne

Sandy Lane

Rivar
Farm

Rivar

Rivar Hill

Ashley
Down

Rivar Firs

Rivar Down

Grubground
Copse

Inlands
Copse

New Buildings

Bishop's
Barn

Botley
Down

Gallow
Clump

SN8

ASHLEY DRO

Noon's Farm

Manor Farm

Moordown
Farm

Cross
Droves

Smay
Down

Smay Down Lane

Henley
Cottage

Field
Studies
Centre

SMAY DOWN LA

PO

Oxenwood

Henley

Henley
Farm

Pearce's
Farm

Smith's
Row

Fosbury
House

+

Fosbury
Down

SP11

Beacon Farm

Pondclose
Copse

Church Farm

Fosbury

Lower Farm

Wiltshire STREET ATLAS

4

61

3

60

2

59

1

58

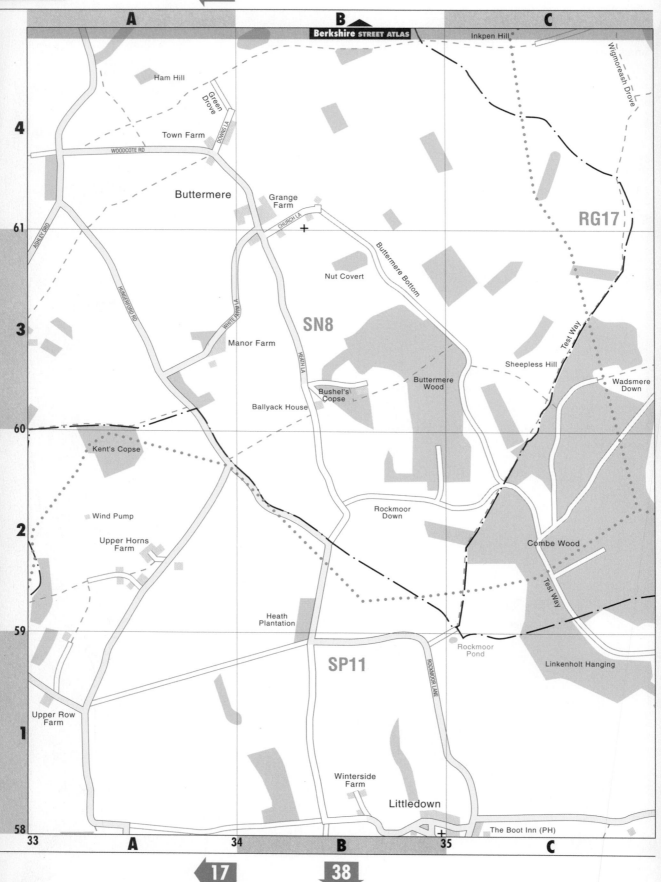

Berkshire STREET ATLAS

Ham Hill

Green Drove

Town Farm

DOWNS LA

WOODCOTE RD

Buttermere

Grange Farm

CHURCH LA

Nut Covert

Buttermere Bottom

RG17

Inkpen Hill

Wigmoreash Drove

ASHLEY DRO

HUNGERFORD RD

WHITE FARM LA

SN8

HEATH LA

Manor Farm

Bushel's Copse

Ballyack House

Buttermere Wood

Sheepless Hill

Test Way

Wadsmere Down

Kent's Copse

Wind Pump

Upper Horns Farm

Rockmoor Down

Combe Wood

Test Way

Heath Plantation

SP11

ROCKMOOR LANE

Rockmoor Pond

Linkenholt Hanging

Upper Row Farm

Winterside Farm

Littledown

The Boot Inn (PH)

Berkshire STREET ATLAS

A   B   C

Wright's Lane

Walbury Hill

West Woodhay Down

RG20

4

Wright's Farm

Summer Hill

P

Sandpits Down

Waylarer's Walk

61

Combe

Lower Farm

Park Wood

Manor Farm

CHURCH LA

Sugglestone Down

Combe Hill

3

RG17

Mast

Eastwick

Summerton's Down

60

Hogs Hole

Ruffian's Copse

Combe Bottom

Combe Wood

2

Limber Copse

Birch Copse

Highdown

59

Ken's Wood

Test Way

Down Copse

SP11

Hart Hill Down

1

Cleve Hill Down

Iron's Hill

Manor House

Pump House

Faccombe

Linkenholt

PO

58

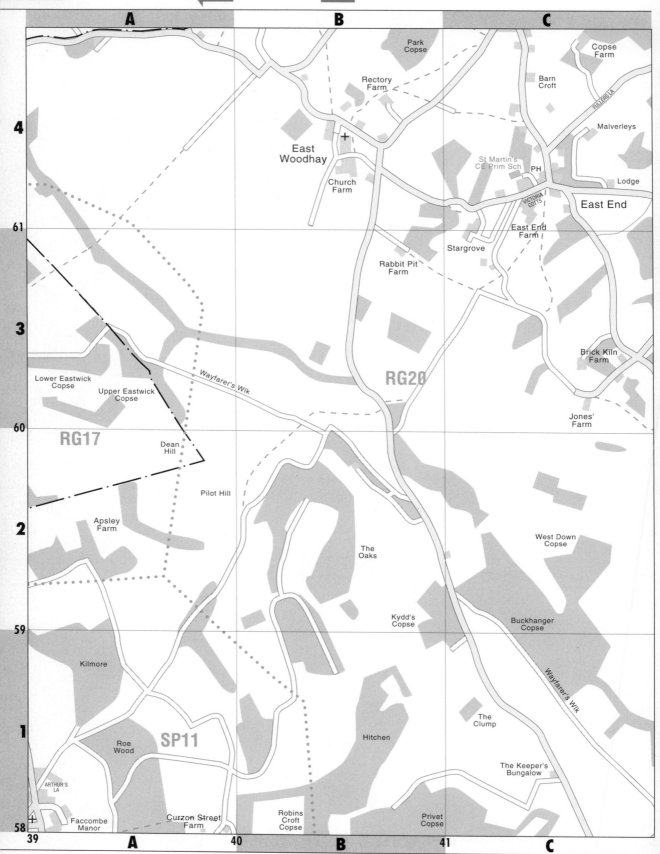

A B C

Park
Copse

Rectory
Farm

Copse
Farm

Barn
Croft

FULLERS LA

4

East
Woodhay

Malverleys

St Martin's
CE Prim Sch

PH

Church
Farm

VICTORIA COTTS

Lodge

East End

61

East End
Farm

Stargrove

Rabbit Pit
Farm

RG20

Brick Kiln
Farm

3

Lower Eastwick
Copse

Wayfarer's Wlk

Upper Eastwick
Copse

Jones'
Farm

60

RG17

Dean
Hill

Pilot Hill

West Down
Copse

2

Apsley
Farm

The
Oaks

Kydd's
Copse

Buckhanger
Copse

59

Wayfarer's Wlk

Kilmore

1

SP11

The
Clump

Roe
Wood

Hitchen

The Keeper's
Bungalow

ARTHUR'S
LA

Faccombe
Manor

Curzon Street
Farm

Robins
Croft
Copse

Privet
Copse

58

39 A 40 B 41 C

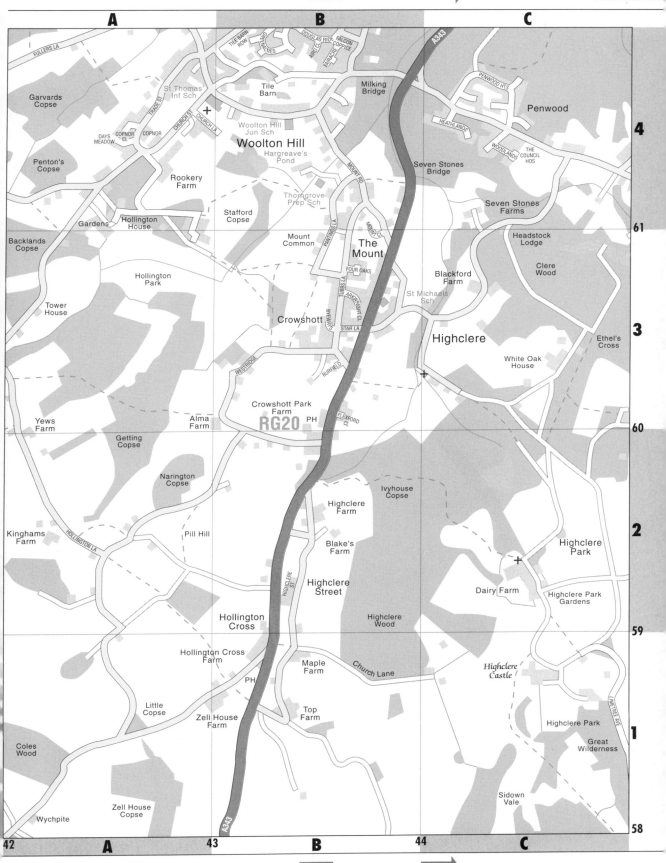

A   B   C

FULLERS LA

Garvards
Copse

Tile Barn
Row

GREENACRES

Douglas Ride

FALCON
COPPICE

AIRD CL

FAIRACRE

Tile Barn

Milking
Bridge

A343

PENWOOD HTS

Penwood

St Thomas'
Inf Sch

TRADE ST

CHURCH ST

COPNOR
CL

DAYS
MEADOW

COPNOR

CHURCH LA

Woolton Hill
Jun Sch

Woolton Hill

HEATHLANDS

WOODLANDS

THE
COUNCIL
HOS

Penton's
Copse

Hargreave's
Pond

Seven Stones
Bridge

Rookery
Farm

MOUNT RD

4

Gardens

Hollington
House

Stafford
Copse

Thorngrove
Prep Sch

PANTINGS LA

Mount
Common

The
Mount

Seven Stones
Farms

61

Backlands
Copse

Hollington
Park

FOUR OAKS

TUBBS LA

St Michaels
Sch

Blackford
Farm

Headstock
Lodge

Clere
Wood

Tower
House

Crowshott

ARKWRIGHT CL

BAKERY CL

STAR LA

Highclere

White Oak
House

Ethel's
Cross

3

Yews
Farm

WESTRIDGE

Alma
Farm

BURFIELD

Crowshott Park
Farm

RG20

PH

FLEXFORD
CL

60

Getting
Copse

Narington
Copse

Ivyhouse
Copse

2

Kinghams
Farm

HOLLINGTON LA

Pill Hill

Highclere
Farm

Blake's
Farm

Highclere
Park

HIGHCLERE ST

Highclere
Street

Dairy Farm

Highclere Park
Gardens

Hollington
Cross

Highclere
Wood

59

Hollington Cross
Farm

PH

Maple
Farm

Church Lane

Highclere
Castle

Little
Copse

Zell House
Farm

Top
Farm

Highclere Park

LIMETREE AVE

Great
Wilderness

1

Coles
Wood

Sidown
Vale

Wychpite

Zell House
Copse

58

42   A   43   B   44   C

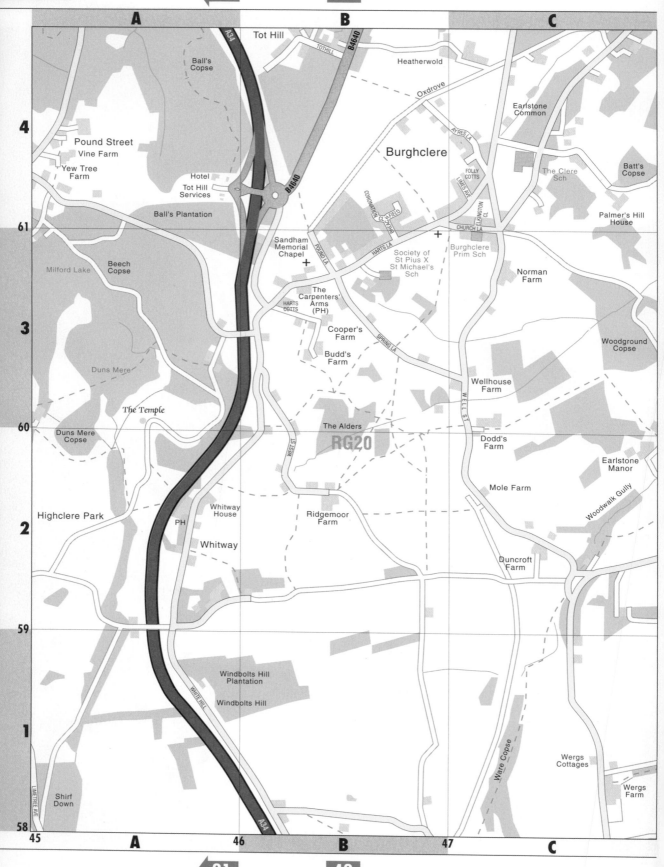

A

B

C

Tot Hill

Ball's Copse

Heatherwold

Oxdrove

Earlstone Common

4

Pound Street

Vine Farm

Burghclere

AYRES LA

The Clere Sch

Batt's Copse

Yew Tree Farm

Hotel

Tot Hill Services

FOLLY COTTS

LIMES AVE

Palmer's Hill House

Ball's Plantation

ELLINGTON CL

CHURCH LA

Burghclere Prim Sch

61

Milford Lake

Beech Copse

Sandham Memorial Chapel

CORONATION CL

FIELD

Society of St Pius X St Michael's Sch

Norman Farm

HARTS LA

POUND LA

3

Duns Mere

HARTS COTTS

The Carpenters' Arms (PH)

Cooper's Farm

SPRING LA

Woodground Copse

Budd's Farm

Wellhouse Farm

The Temple

The Alders

WELL ST

Dodd's Farm

Earlstone Manor

60

Duns Mere Copse

RG20

Woodwalk Gully

Mole Farm

Highclere Park

Whitway House

Ridgemoor Farm

Duncroft Farm

2

PH

WEST ST

Whitway

59

Windbolts Hill Plantation

WHITE HILL

Windbolts Hill

Ware Copse

1

Wergs Cottages

Wergs Farm

LIMETREE AVE

Shirf Down

A34

58

45

A

46

B

47

C

A
B
C

High Wood

Dovey's
Copse

Frith Copse

North Ecchinswell
Farm

4

Pentico

Brock's
Copse

Brock's
Green

Stud
Farm

HYDE LA

Hyde
Farm

The
Laurels

Badmore Copse

Whitehouse
Farm

61

Waterleas
Copse

Birch
Copse

Swait's
Farm

Kisby's
Farm

3

Woodside Farm

Longmeadow
Row

Long Copse

Malthouse
Farm

Earlstone
Farm

RG20

Lower Berry Wood

60

P

+

Cowhouse
Farm

Crowmarsh
Copse

Ecchinswell
& Sydmonton
CE Prim Sch

Southwood
Copse

Hobb's
Copse

Upper Berry
Wood

Ecchinswell

WOODLEYS
OAKFIELDS CL

MILL LA

Mill
Bridge

Frobury Park
Copse

2

Caveley
Copse

WHITE HILL

PH

Clere House
Farm

ECCHINSWELL RD

59

Watership
Farm

Laundry
Cottages

Glasshanger
Copse

Nuthanger
Farm

Nuthanger
Copse

1

Fishpond
Copse

Isle Copse

Isle Hill

Quarry
Copse

Fossicks

Hill Field
Farm

58

48
A
49
B
50
C

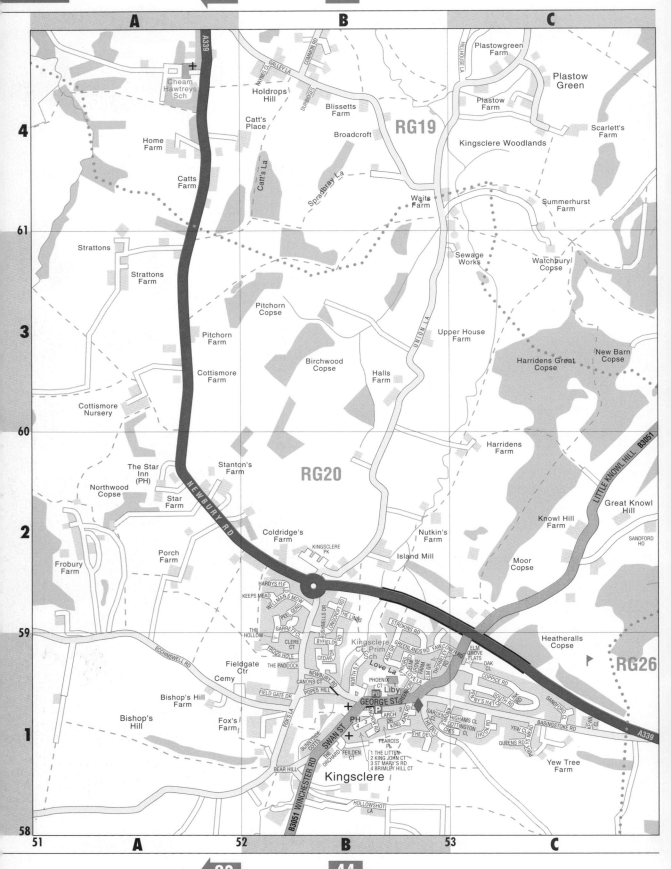

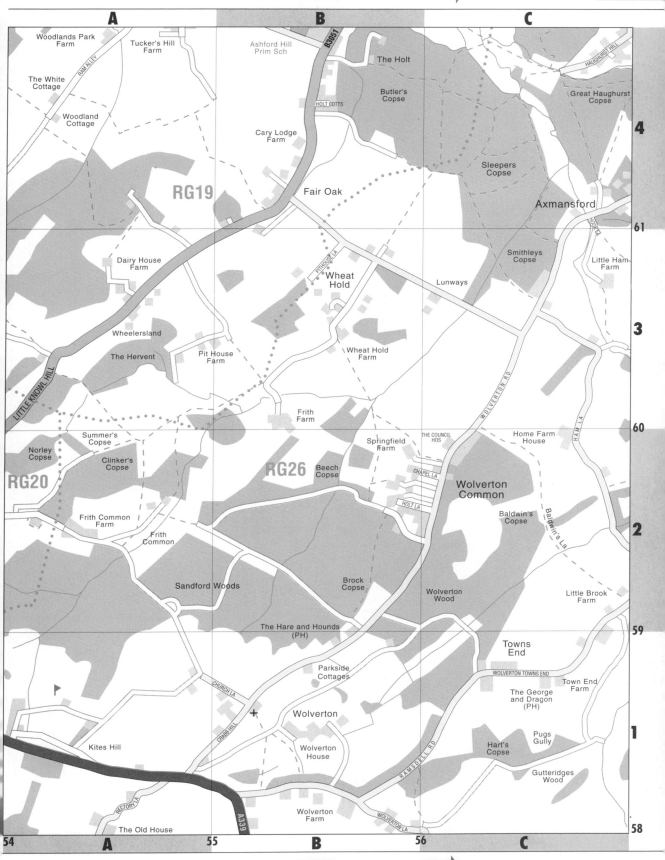

A
B
C

Woodlands Park Farm
Tucker's Hill Farm
RAM ALLEY
The White Cottage
Woodland Cottage

Ashford Hill Prim Sch
B3051
The Holt
HOLT COTTS
Butler's Copse
Cary Lodge Farm

HAUGHURST HILL
Great Haughurst Copse

4

RG19
Fair Oak

Sleepers Copse

Axmansford

Dairy House Farm
PITHOUSE LA
Wheat Hold
Lunways
Smithleys Copse
Little Ham Farm

HOCK LA

61

3

Wheelersland
The Hervent
Pit House Farm
Frith Farm
Wheat Hold Farm
WOLVERTON RD
HAM LA

LITTLE KNOWL HILL

Summer's Copse
Springfield Farm
THE COUNCIL HOS
Home Farm House

60

Norley Copse
Clinker's Copse
RG26
Beech Copse
CHAPEL LA
Wolverton Common
Baldwin's Copse
BALDWIN'S LA

RG20
Frith Common Farm
Frith Common
HOLT LA

2

Sandford Woods
Brock Copse
Wolverton Wood
Little Brook Farm

The Hare and Hounds (PH)

59

Towns End

Parkside Cottages
WOLVERTON TOWNS END
Town End Farm

CHURCH LA
The George and Dragon (PH)

CRABB HILL
Wolverton
1

Kites Hill
Wolverton House
RAMSDELL RD
Hart's Copse
Pugs Gully

Gutteridges Wood

RECTORY LA
A339
Wolverton Farm
WOLVERTON LA

The Old House

54
A
55
B
56
C

58

C4
7 BORDON CL | 14 CANDOVER CL
1 WOODCOTT HO | 8 SWANWICK WLK | 15 HARTLEY GDNS
2 LITCHFIELD HO | 9 OSIER HO | 16 ROTHERWICK RD
3 MULFORDS HILL | 10 CHERITON CL
4 GORSELANDS | 11 BRAMDEAN CL
5 ROSEBANK CL | 12 APPLESHAW CL
6 SAUNDERS GDN | 13 TOMLINS CL

A **B** **C**

Haughurst
Hill

Inhurst

PH

1 LAKELANDS
2 HEATH END RD
3 BISHOPSWOOD LA

INHURST WAY 4
HARTSHILL RD 5

HUNTSMOOR RD

WHITEDOWN RD

Gulley Copse

CH

Bishopswood
Jun & Inf
Schs

Great
Copse

Bullers Farm

Baughurst

4

Inhurst
Farm

Grantham
Farm

Curtis
Farm

Upper
Farm

Copse
Close

Hawley
Farm

61

Westfield
Copse

West View
Farm

RIMES'S LA

CHURCH BROOK

Hook Lane

Manor Farm

Oak House

The Well
House

Well Farm

The
Wellington Arms
(PH)

Church Brook
Farm

3

Causeway
Farm

Church Green
Farm

Pudding
Hill

Browning Hill

Moor
Copse

Witches'
Gully

Church Farm

RG26

Washer's
Copse

60

HILL SIDE

Browninghill
Farm

Browninghill
Copse

Baughurst
House

Hillside
Farm

Monts
Farm

Browninghill Green

Tadley
Place

Sunny Side

2

Pound Green

Browns
Farm

Baughurst
Copse

Coombe House
Farm

The
King's Peace

Malthouse
Farm

Stratton
Manor

59

Belmont

Great
Copse

Combe House
Farm

Wyeford
Farm

Stoneylands
Copse

GAULDY LANE

Moyglare
Farm

HOLLYBUSH LA

Witch Lane
Farm

Hog Park
Copse

1

Batt's
Copse

Pollards House

Stony Heath

Colliers
Copse

OLD VYNE LA

West Heath

The
Bothy

HOLLY
BUSH COTTS

Firs Court
Farm

THE COMMON

58

57 **A** **58** **B** **59** **C**

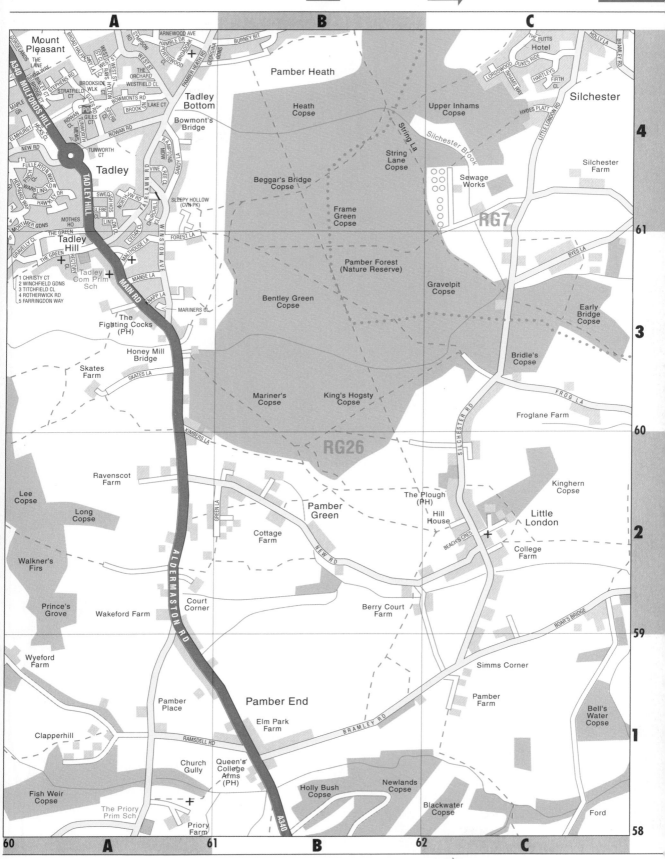

A **B** **C**

Mount Pleasant

Pamber Heath

The Butts Hotel

Silchester

Heath Copse

Upper Inhams Copse

Tadley Bottom

Bowmont's Bridge

String La

Silchester Brook

Silchester Farm

4

Tadley

String Lane Copse

Sewage Works

Beggar's Bridge Copse

RG7

Tadley Hill

Sleepy Hollow (CVN PK)

Frame Green Copse

61

Forest La

1 CHRISTY CT
2 WINCHFIELD GDNS
3 TITCHFIELD CL
4 ROTHERWICK RD
5 FARRINGDON WAY

Tadley Com Prim Sch

Pamber Forest (Nature Reserve)

Gravelpit Copse

Byes La

Early Bridge Copse

The Fighting Cocks (PH)

Bentley Green Copse

Bridle's Copse

3

Honey Mill Bridge

Skates Farm

Mariner's Copse

King's Hogsty Copse

FROG LA

Froglane Farm

60

RG26

Ravenscot Farm

Lee Copse

Kinghern Copse

Long Copse

Pamber Green

The Plough (PH)

Little London

Hill House

Cottage Farm

Green La

New Rd

Silchester Rd

Beach's Cres

College Farm

2

Walkner's Firs

Prince's Grove

Wakeford Farm

Court Corner

Berry Court Farm

Boar's Bridge

59

Wyeford Farm

Simms Corner

Pamber Place

Pamber End

Elm Park Farm

Pamber Farm

Bell's Water Copse

Clapperhill

Aldermaston Rd

Ramsdell Rd

Bramley Rd

1

Church Gully

Queen's College Arms (PH)

Holly Bush Copse

Newlands Copse

Blackwater Copse

Ford

Fish Weir Copse

The Priory Prim Sch

Priory Farm

A3⁴⁰

58

60 **A** 61 **B** 62 **C**

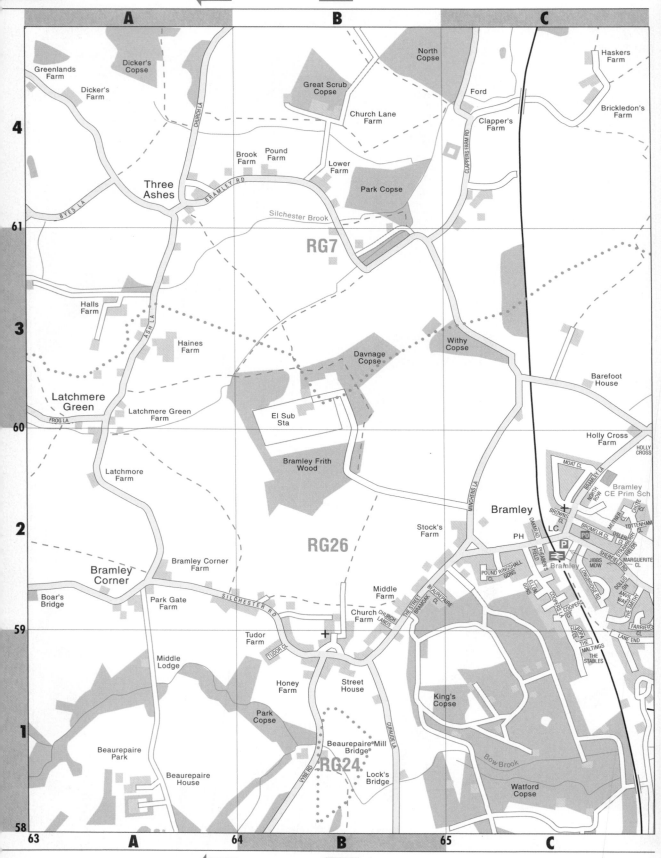

A   B   C

4

61

RG7

3

Latchmere
Green

60

2

RG26

Bramley

1

RG24

58

63   A   64   B   65   C

Greenlands
Farm

Dicker's
Copse

Dicker's
Farm

North
Copse

Haskers
Farm

Great Scrub
Copse

Ford

Brickledon's
Farm

Church Lane
Farm

Clapper's
Farm

Brook
Farm

Pound
Farm

Lower
Farm

Three
Ashes

BRAMLEY RD

Park Copse

CHURCH LA

CLAPPERS FARM RD

Silchester Brook

BYES LA

Halls
Farm

ASH LA

Haines
Farm

Davnage
Copse

Withy
Copse

Barefoot
House

Latchmere Green
Farm

FROG LA

El Sub
Sta

Bramley Frith
Wood

Holly Cross
Farm

HOLLY
CROSS

Latchmore
Farm

MINCHENS LA

Bramley
CE Prim Sch

MOAT CL

BROMLEY LA

NORTH
ROW

CHUTE CL

METHUEN CL

TOTTENHAM
CL

BROWNS
CL

OAKMEAD
CL

BROMELIA CL

OSLER CT

STRAWBERRY
FIELDS

PO

Stock's
Farm

Bramley
Corner

Bramley Corner
Farm

SILCHESTER RD

Middle
Farm

PH

LC

SHERFIELD RD

PHEABEN'S

MARGUERITE
CL

JIBBS
MDW

DOLLIS

Boar's
Bridge

Park Gate
Farm

THE STREET

BRAMOAK
CL

BEAUREPAIRE
CL

Church
Farm

CHURCH
LANDS

Bramley

POUND RINGSHALL
GDNS

ELM
GDNS

COOPERS
CT

COOPERS LA

ANVIL
WAY

FARRIERS
CL

THE
SMITHY

Middle
Lodge

Tudor
Farm

TUDOR CL

Honey
Farm

Street
House

VYNE RD

CUFAUDE LA

King's
Copse

LONGBRIDGE RD

ELVETHAM
CL

LANE END

THE
MALTINGS

THE
STABLES

59

Park
Copse

Beaurepaire Mill
Bridge

Lock's
Bridge

Bow Brook

Watford
Copse

Beaurepaire
Park

Beaurepaire
House

4

61

3

60

2

59

1

58

Lavell's Farm

Dollery's Farm

The Four Horse Shoes (PH)

LAVELL'S LA

THE SPRINGS

West End Green

Parson's Farm

GREEN LA

New Inn (PH)

NEW ST

Stratfield Saye

Herriot's Farm

FAIR OAK LA

King's Farm

MORTIMER LA

Purdue's Farm

RG7

Ives Farm

Fair Oak Green

STRATFIELD SAYE RD

Southend Farm

Heywood's Farm

Pizzie Green

OLIVER'S LA

Ladyland Copse

Tubbs Copse

The Fishery

Oliver's Farm

FOLLY LA

Folly Farm

RG26

MILL LA

River Loddon

RG27

POTTERS LA

A33

Lillymill Farm

Newhouse Farm

Bramley Green

Green Farm

59

LANE END

SHERFIELD RD

St Barbara's

WOODLAND DR

THE MEWS

Sewage Works

Flood's Farm

HARTLEY LA

GERMAN RD

OFFICERS ROW

TA Ctr

1 HERRIDGE CL
2 THORNTON CL
3 BARTLETT CL
4 ILLINGWORTH CL
5 THE LIMES
6 DEERFIELD CL
7 ST MARY S CT

Bew Bridge

THE MEADOWS

MORTIMER RD

BRAMLEY RD

Long Bridge

LONGBRIDGE RD

READING RD

Longbridge Mill

Hartley Wood Common

LC LC

Sherfield Green

WILLOW WAY

BOW GN

POPLAR CL

GREENWAY

BULLSDOWN CL

BOW DR

CARPENTERS CL

WESTON HOUSE CL

MILL LA

A33

P

Sherfield on Loddon

Sherfield Farm

Bull's Down Copse

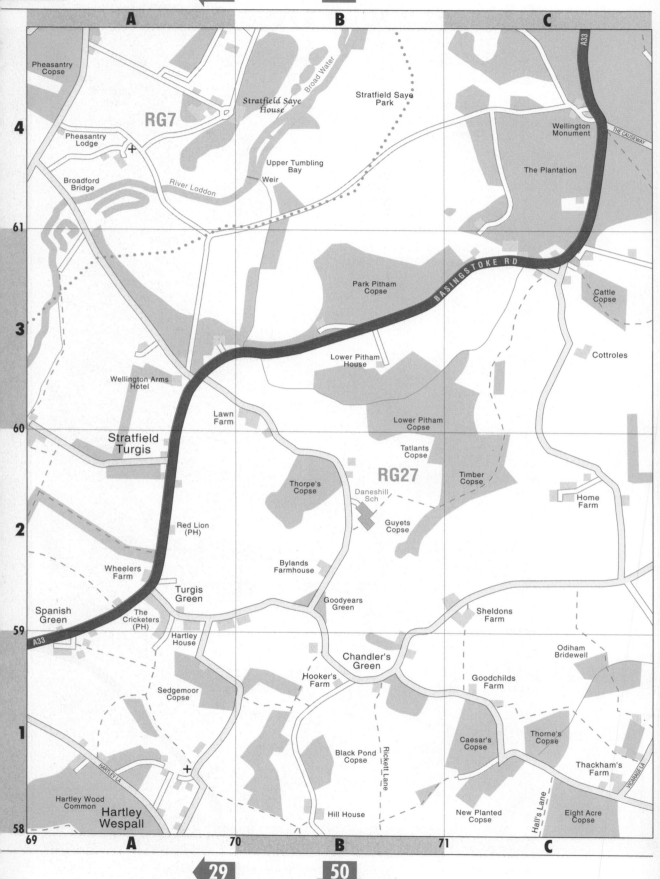

A B C

4

61

3

60

2

59

1

58

Pheasantry
Copse

RG7

Pheasantry
Lodge

Broadford
Bridge

River Loddon

Weir

Broad Water

Stratfield Saye
House

Upper Tumbling
Bay

Stratfield Saye
Park

Wellington
Monument

A33

THE CAUSEWAY

The Plantation

Park Pitham
Copse

BASINGSTOKE RD

Cattle
Copse

Cottroles

Lower Pitham
House

Lower Pitham
Copse

Wellington Arms
Hotel

Lawn
Farm

Stratfield
Turgis

Tatlants
Copse

RG27

Timber
Copse

Home
Farm

Thorpe's
Copse

Daneshill
Sch

Red Lion
(PH)

Guyets
Copse

Wheelers
Farm

Bylands
Farmhouse

Turgis
Green

Goodyears
Green

Sheldons
Farm

Odiham
Bridewell

Spanish
Green

The Cricketers
(PH)

A33

Hartley
House

Chandler's
Green

Goodchilds
Farm

Hooker's
Farm

Sedgemoor
Copse

Caesar's
Copse

Thorne's
Copse

HARTLEY LA

Black Pond
Copse

Rickett Lane

Thackham's
Farm

VICARAGE LA

Hartley Wood
Common

Hartley
Wespall

Hill House

New Planted
Copse

Hall's Lane

Eight Acre
Copse

69 70 71

A B C

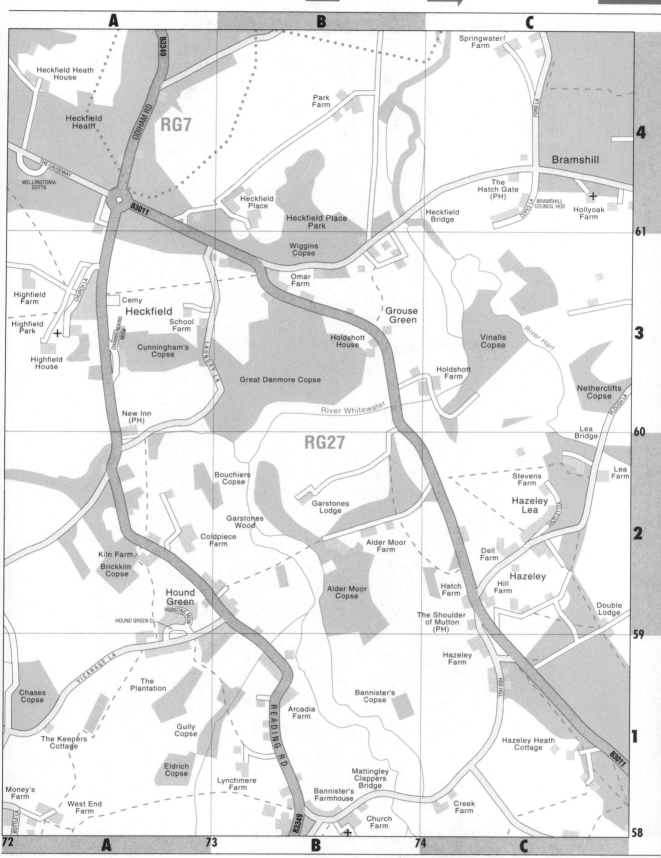

31
15

A | B | C

WARBROOK LA

St Neot's Sch

Bramshill Plantation

ST NEOT'S RD

Warbrook (Con Ctr)

A327

B3272 READING RD

Warren Farm

4

Yalden's Farm

A327

Church Farm

61

Refuse Tip

PLOUGH LA

Heath Warren

Moor Place Farm

Cudbury Clump

3

RG27

Peatmoor Copse

THE QUADRANGLE

LAKESIDE DR

READING DR N

READING DR S

GREENRIDGE CL

LOWER POOL RD

MANSION DR

PHEASANTRY DR

60

The Welsh Drive

Three Castles Path

Warren Heath

Sir Richard's Drive

2

Bramshill Park

Bramshill House (Police Coll)

Deer Park

Long Water

High Bridge

Birch Bottom

Sand & Gravel Pit

59

River Hart

Chalwin's Copse

Hulford's Copse

Hazeley Heath

Crabtree Copse

Crabtree Lodge

1

Purdies Farm

Warren Hill Farm

Warren Hill Plantation

B3011

B3011

Hatts Cottage

Hazeley Heath

SPRINGWELL LA

HULFORDS LA

A30

STAR HILL

A30

Star Hill

58

31
52

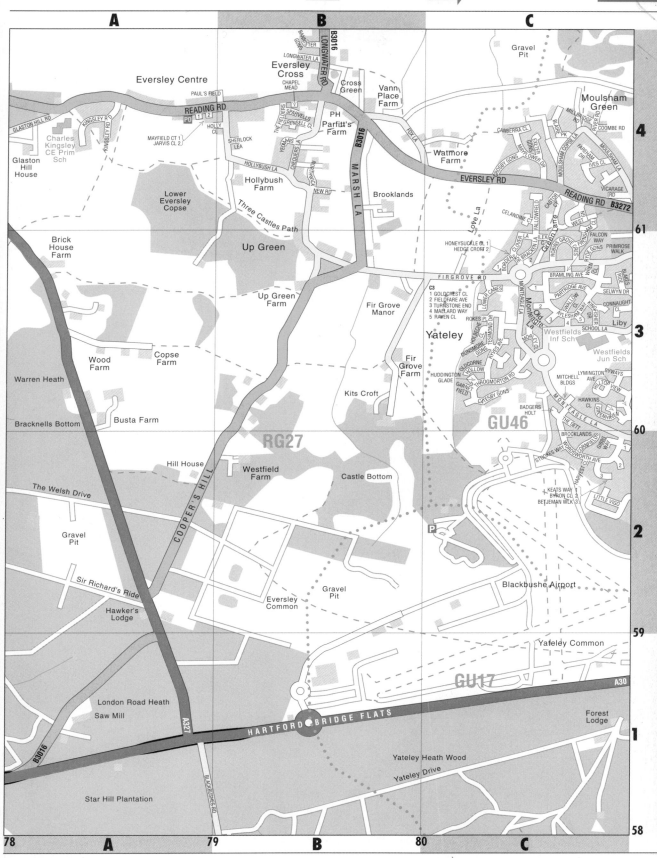

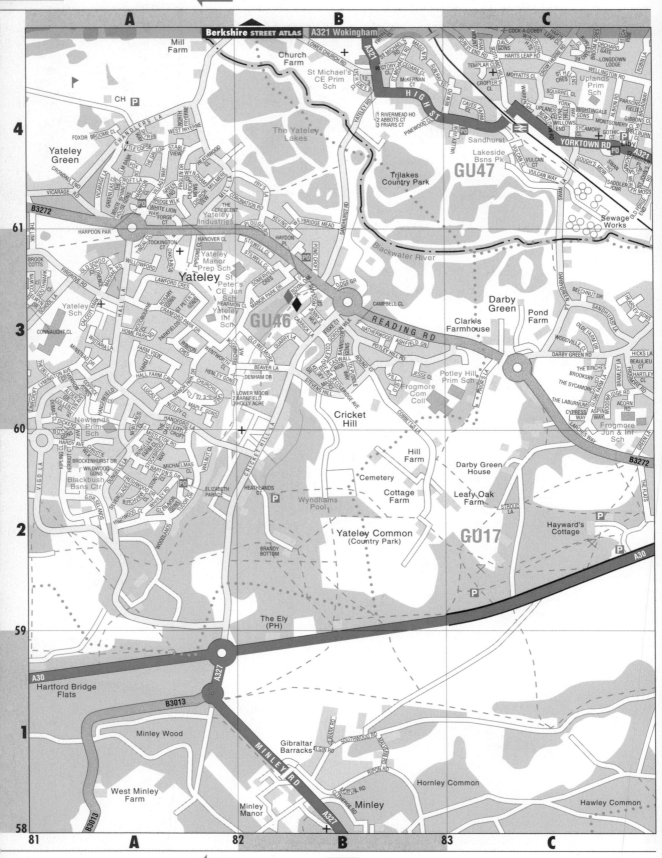

Berkshire STREET ATLAS   A321 Wokingham

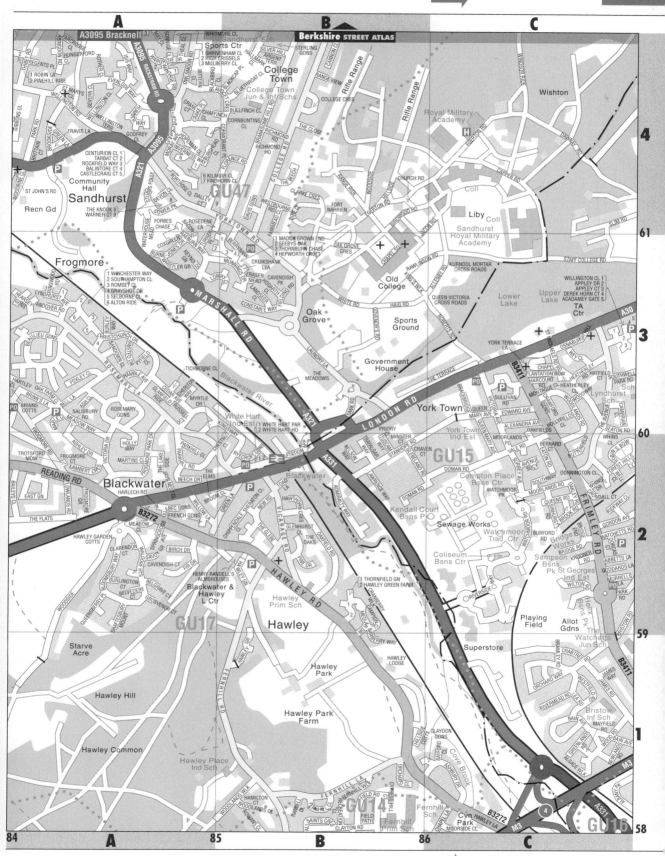

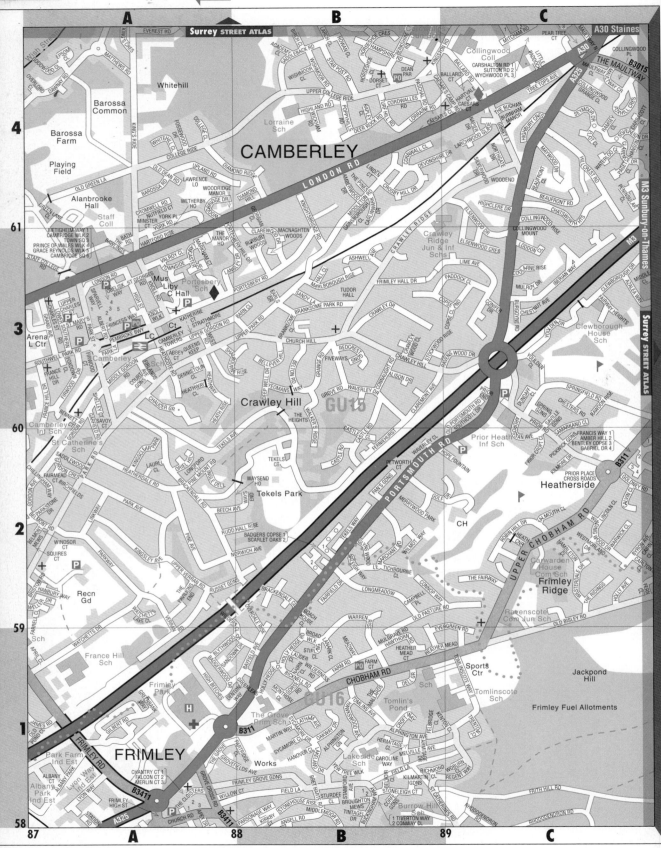

35

Surrey STREET ATLAS

A30 Staines

THE MAULTWAY

B3015

M3 Sunbury-on-Thames

Surrey STREET ATLAS

CAMBERLEY

LONDON RD

Whitehill

Barossa
Common

Barossa
Farm

Playing
Field

Alanbrooke
Hall

Staff
Coll

Arena
L Ctr

Camberley
Inf Sch

St Catherine's
Sch

Crawley Hill

GU15

Collingwood
Coll

Lorraine
Sch

Crawley
Ridge
Jun & Inf
Schs

Clewborough
House
Sch

Heatherside

Collingwood
Mount

Prior Heath
Inf Sch

Prior Place
Cross Roads

UPPER CHOBHAM RD

Carwarden
House
Com Sch

Frimley
Ridge

Ravenscote
Com Jun Sch

Tekels Park

PORTSMOUTH RD

Golf

CH

France Hill
Sch

Recn
Gd

Frimley
Park

The Grove
Prim Sch

FRIMLEY

B311

GU16

CHOBHAM RD

Tomlin's
Pond

Sports
Ctr

Tomlinscote
Sch

Jackpond
Hill

Frimley Fuel Allotments

Park Farm
Ind Est

Albany
Park
Ind Est

FRIMLEY RD

A325

B3411

B3411

Lakeside
Sch

Works

A30

A325

M3

35   56

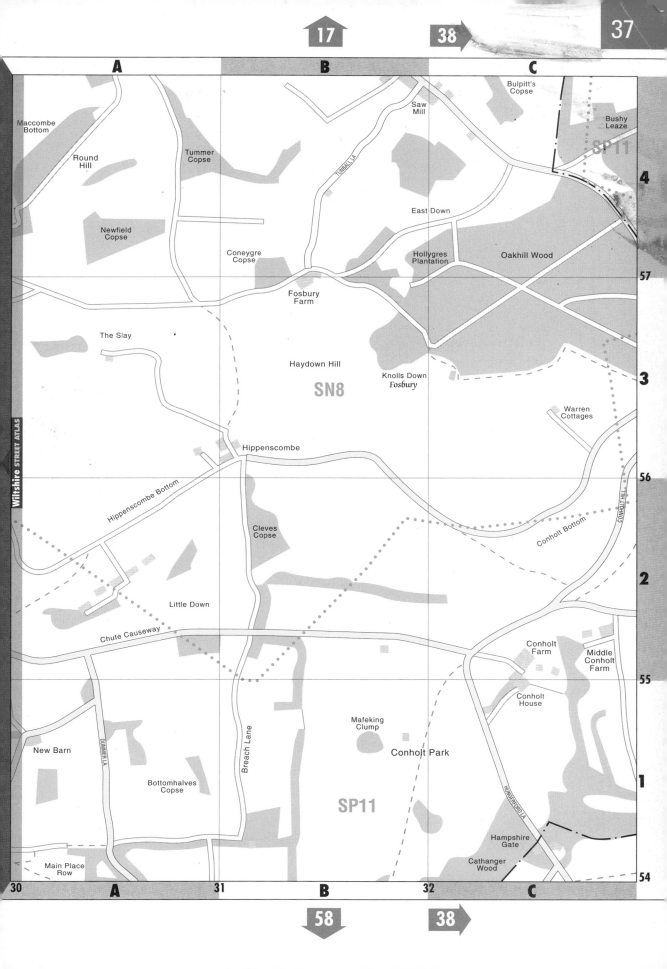

A

B

C

Littledown

Flowers
Farm

Stoney
Drove

Gambles
Cottage

Vernham
Row

Vernham Street

4

CHURCH LA

Box Farm

Church Lane

Hatch Lane

SN8

BOWERS LA

Bank Farm

57

Vernham
Bank

HATCHBURY LA

HAYDOWN LEAS

+

Sargent's
Farm

THE DELL

Vernham Manor

BULPITS HILL

The
George
Inn
(PH)

SHEPHERDS RISE

Vernham Dean
Gillum's CE
Prim Sch

BACK LA

DEAN TERR

3

Vernham Dean

SCHOOL CL

Woodside

BUTTS DENE CL

CONHOLT HILL

Poplars
Farm

Boats
Copse

SP11

56

Thornycombe
Wood

Assam
Wood

Upton
Manor

Ankers Farm

Kiblet Down

CONHOLT LA

2

Knyghten
Mere

Whitegate Firs

Crown
Inn
(PH)

HILLSIDE

55

Lower Conholt
Farm

Little Bourne
Farm

Forty Acres Wood

Oakdown
Copse

Mascombe
Copse

Rushmore
Cottages

Rushmoor
Cottage

Conholt
Down

Rushmore
Farm

1

Well Bottom

Rushmore Down

Bleekfield
Firs

Cow
Down

54

33

A

34

B

35

C

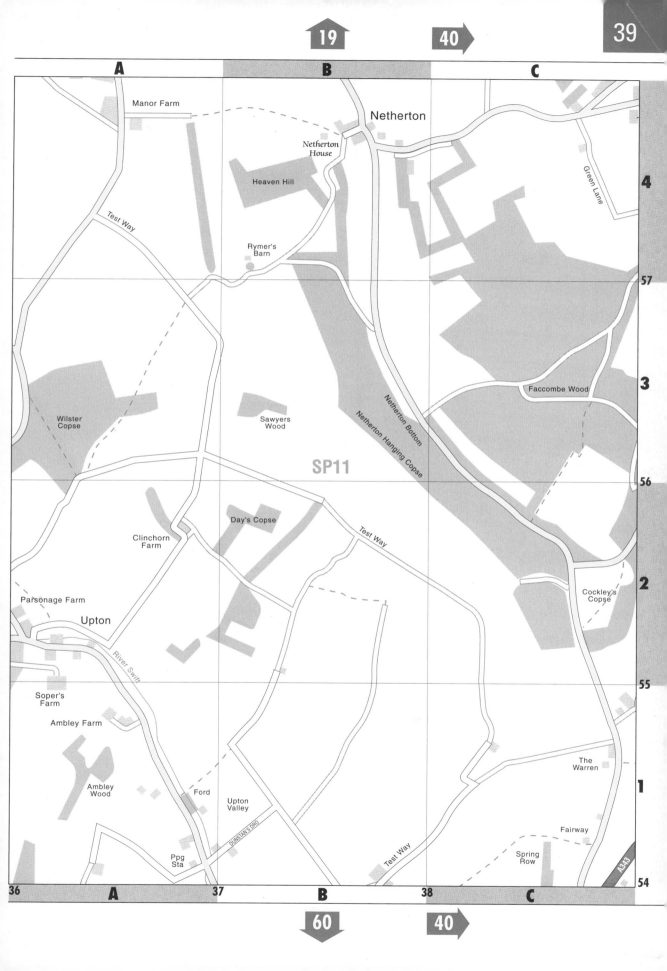

Manor Farm

Netherton

Netherton House

Green Lane

Heaven Hill

4

Test Way

Rymer's Barn

57

Wilster Copse

3

Faccombe Wood

Sawyers Wood

Netherton Bottom

Netherton Hanging Copse

SP11

56

Day's Copse

Clinchorn Farm

Test Way

Cockley's Copse

2

Parsonage Farm

Upton

River Swift

55

Soper's Farm

Ambley Farm

The Warren

1

Ambley Wood

Ford

Upton Valley

DUNSTAN'S DRO

Test Way

Fairway

Ppg Sta

Spring Row

A343

54

39
20

A   **B**   **C**

PH

Robins
Croft
Copse

Privet Copse

The Isle

Manor
Farm

Woodhay
Poor

The Plough
(PH)

Ashmansworth

4

Bartlett's
Down

HIGHFIELD

London Lane

Steeles
Farm

PO

Spencefield
Copse

Codley
Copse

Alexander
Farm

Hipple La

57

Hall Lane

RG20

Kimmer Farm

Church
Farm

+

3

The
Bushes

Lower
Manor
Farm

A343

Faccombe Wood

56

Sidley
Wood

Ten
Acre
Brow

2

Sidley
Bottom

Doyley
Manor

SP11

Lye
Copses

Doyley Manor
Farm

DOILEY HILL

P

Lye
Farm

55

Esseborne
Manor
(Hotel)

Doiley
Wood

Splatts
Copse

Long
Copse

1

Doiley Hill
Farm

DOILEY BOTTOM

Sladen
Green
Farm

A343

Sladen
Green

54

Lower
Doiley
Farm

39   **A**   40   **B**   41   **C**

39
61

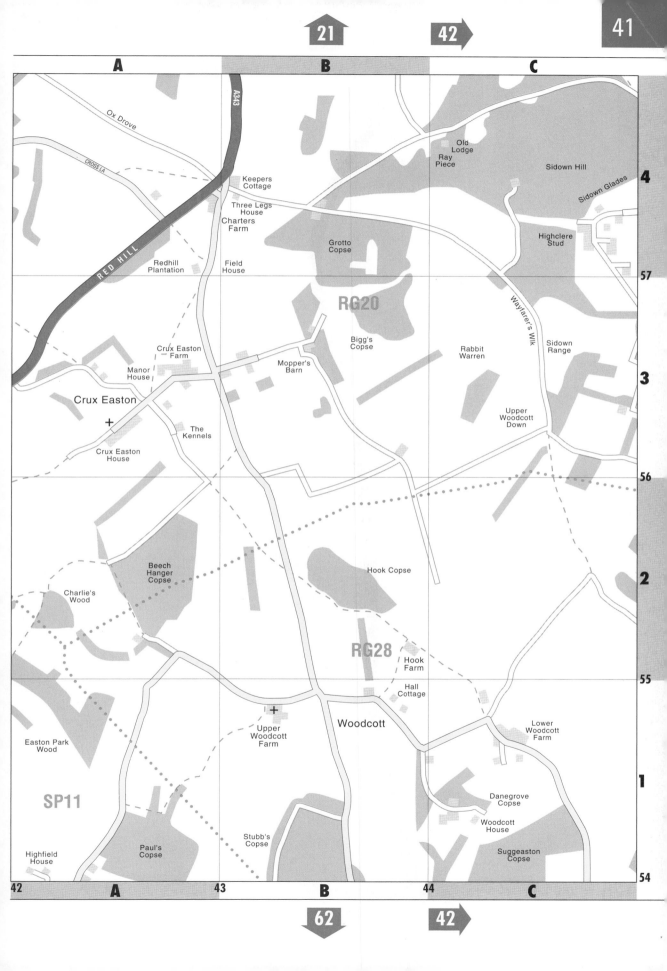

A34

Lanecombe
Copse

Ivory
Farm

BEACON PASS

Manor
Farm

WEIR
COTTS

Old
Burghclere

Hall

P

THE LIME KILN
COTTS

4

Grave

57

Beacon Hill

RG20

Black
Valley

3

Wayfarer's Walk

Down Farm

56

Hare Warren
Down

Chapman's Dell

Great Litchfield
Down

Lower Woodcott
Down

Thorndown
Plantation

2

55

Shell's
Copse

RG28

1

Bixley
Copse

Little Down

Old Orchard
Copse

A34

JUBILEE CL

Down Farm

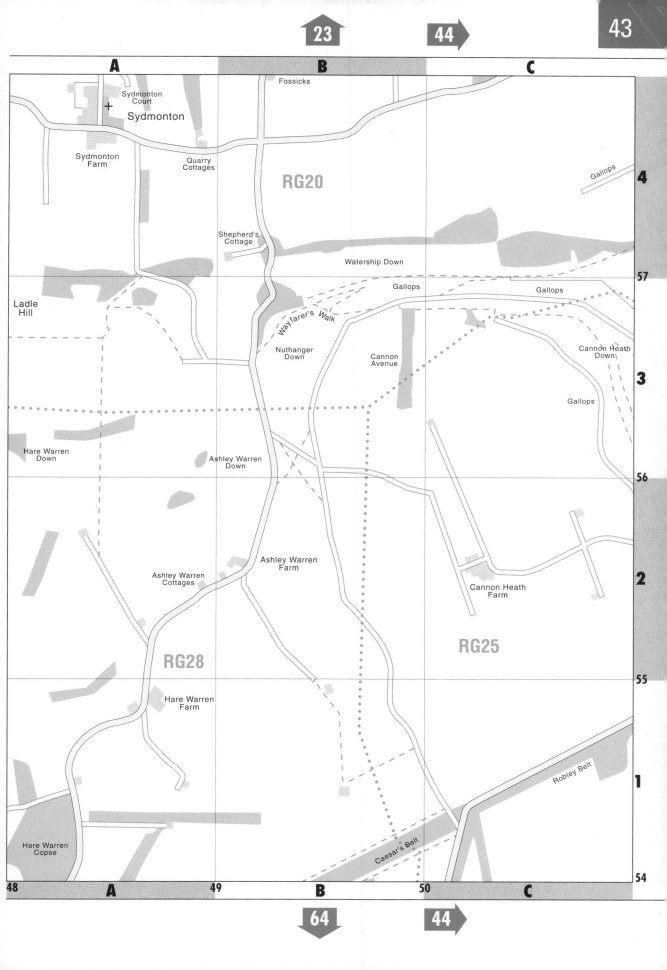

A | B | C

Fossicks

Sydmonton
Court
✛
Sydmonton

Sydmonton
Farm

Quarry
Cottages

RG20

Gallops

4

Shepherd's
Cottage

Watership Down

57

Ladle
Hill

Gallops

Gallops

Wayfarer's Walk

Nuthanger
Down

Cannon Heath
Down

Cannon
Avenue

3

Gallops

Hare Warren
Down

Ashley Warren
Down

56

Ashley Warren
Farm

Ashley Warren
Cottages

Cannon Heath
Farm

2

RG25

RG28

55

Hare Warren
Farm

Robley Belt

1

Hare Warren
Copse

Caesar's Belt

54

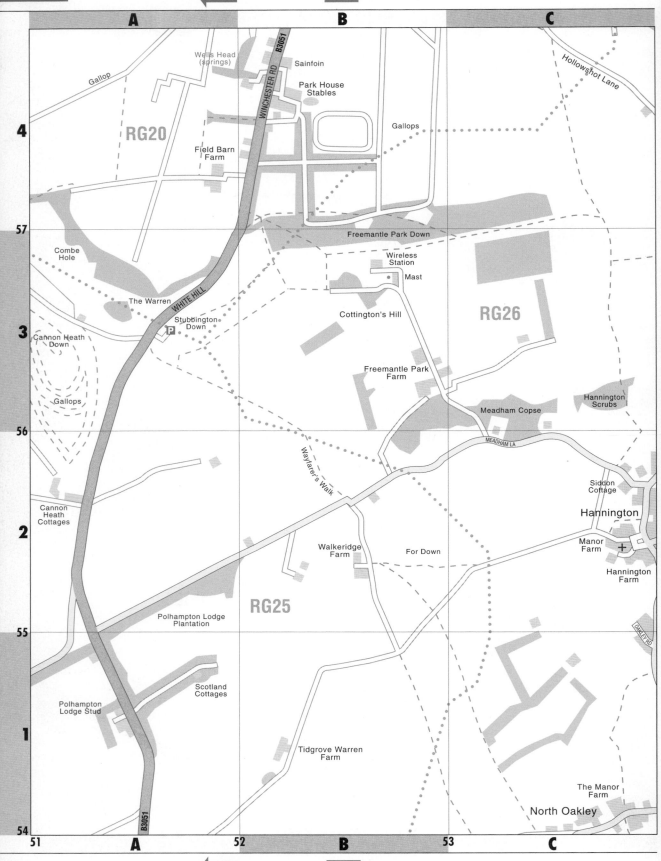

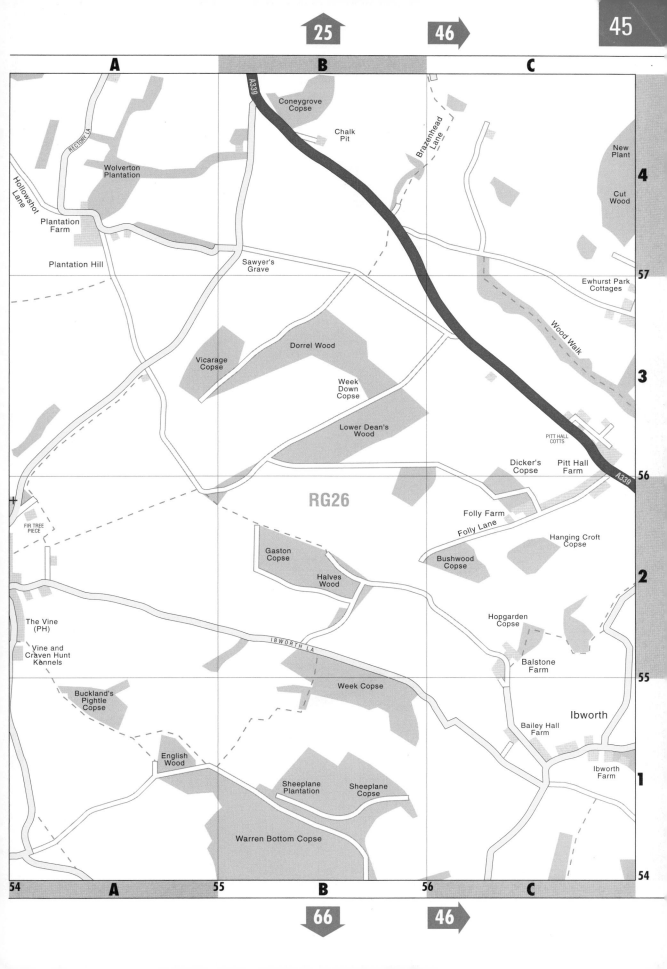

A
B
C

A339
Coneygrove
Copse
Chalk
Pit

Brazenhead Lane

New
Plant

RECTORY LA

Wolverton
Plantation

Cut
Wood

4

Hollowshot Lane

Plantation
Farm

Plantation Hill

Sawyer's
Grave

57

Ewhurst Park
Cottages

Dorrel Wood

Wood Walk

Vicarage
Copse

Week
Down
Copse

3

Lower Dean's
Wood

PITT HALL
COTTS

Dicker's
Copse

Pitt Hall
Farm

56

A339

RG26

+

FIR TREE
PIECE

Folly Farm

Folly Lane

Hanging Croft
Copse

Gaston
Copse

Halves
Wood

Bushwood
Copse

2

The Vine
(PH)

Hopgarden
Copse

Vine and
Craven Hunt
Kennels

IBWORTH LA

Balstone
Farm

55

Buckland's
Pightle
Copse

Week Copse

Ibworth

Bailey Hall
Farm

English
Wood

Ibworth
Farm

1

Sheeplane
Plantation

Sheeplane
Copse

Warren Bottom Copse

54

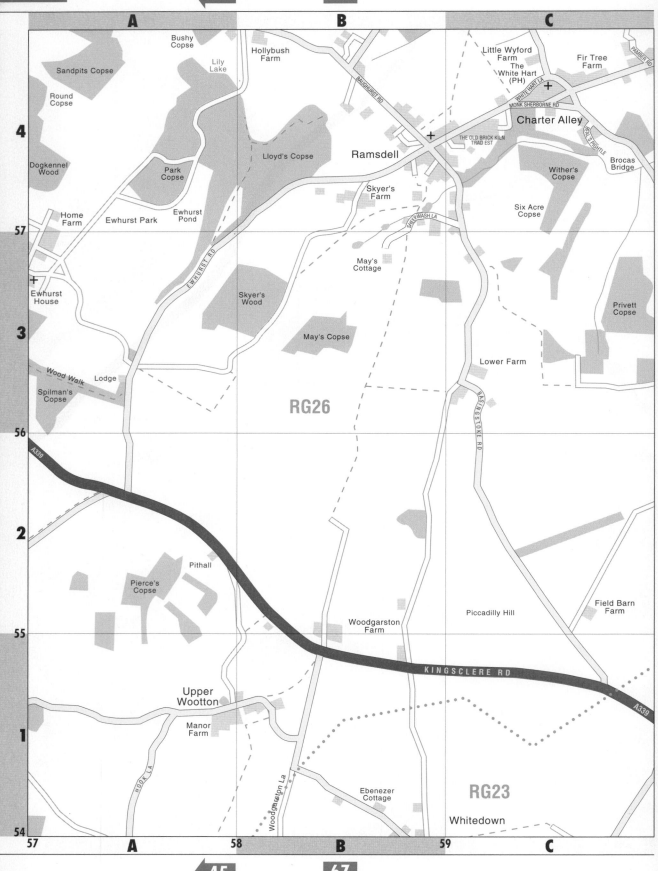

A **B** **C**

Bushy Copse

Sandpits Copse

Lily Lake

Hollybush Farm

Little Wyford Farm
The White Hart (PH)

Fir Tree Farm

PAMBER RD

Round Copse

BAUGHURST RD

WHITE HART LA

MONK SHERBORNE RD

Charter Alley

4

Dogkennel Wood

Park Copse

Lloyd's Copse

Ramsdell

THE OLD BRICK KILN TRAD EST

Wither's Copse

Brocas Bridge

BEAL'S PIGHTLE

Home Farm

Ewhurst Park

Ewhurst Pond

Skyer's Farm

Six Acre Copse

57

EWHURST RD

SHERWASH LA

Ewhurst House

Skyer's Wood

May's Cottage

Privett Copse

3

May's Copse

Lower Farm

Wood Walk

Lodge

BASINGSTOKE RD

Spilman's Copse

RG26

56

A339

Field Barn Farm

2

Pithall

Pierce's Copse

Woodgarston Farm

Piccadilly Hill

A339

55

KINGSCLERE RD

Upper Wootton

1

Manor Farm

HOOK LA

Woodgarston La

Ebenezer Cottage

RG23

Whitedown

54

57 **A** **58** **B** **59** **C**

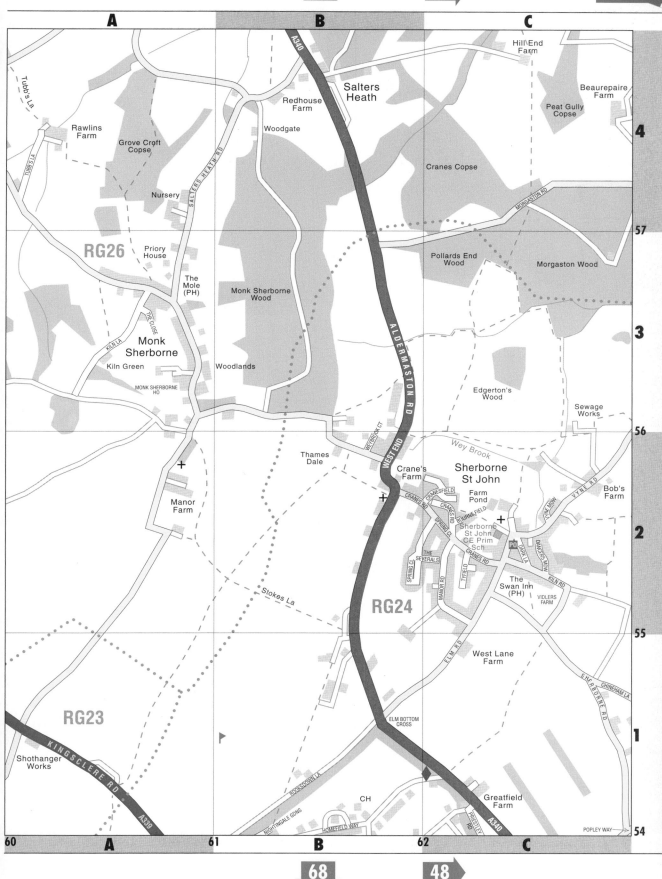

A   **B**   **C**

Tubb's La

Rawlins Farm

Grove Croft Copse

Nursery

RG26

Priory House

The Mole (PH)

KILN LA

THE CLOSE

Monk Sherborne

Kiln Green

MONK SHERBORNE HO

Woodlands

Redhouse Farm

Woodgate

SALTERS HEATH RD

A340

Salters Heath

Hill\End Farm

Peat Gully Copse

Beaurepaire Farm

Cranes Copse

MORGASTON RD

Pollards End Wood

Morgaston Wood

Monk Sherborne Wood

ALDERMASTON RD

Edgerton's Wood

Sewage Works

Manor Farm

Thames Dale

WETBROOK CT

WEST END

Crane's Farm

CRANES RD

CRANESFIELD

BOURNEFIELD

Wey Brook

Sherborne St John

Farm Pond

BARK LA

VYNE RD

DANCERS MDW

Bob's Farm

SPRING CL

Sherborne St John CE Prim Sch

PO

THE SEVERALS

MANOR RD

CRANES RD

TYFIELD

The Swan Inn (PH)

KILN RD

Vidlers Farm

RG24

Stokes La

West Lane Farm

ELM RD

S HERBORNE RD

CHINEHAM LA

RG23

KINGSCLERE RD

Shothanger Works

A339

ELM BOTTOM CROSS

ROOKSDOWN LA

NIGHTINGALE GDNS

HOMEFIELD WAY

CH

Greatfield Farm

PRIESTLEY RD

A340

POPLEY WAY →

57

4

3

56

2

55

1

54

60   **A**   61   **B**   62   **C**

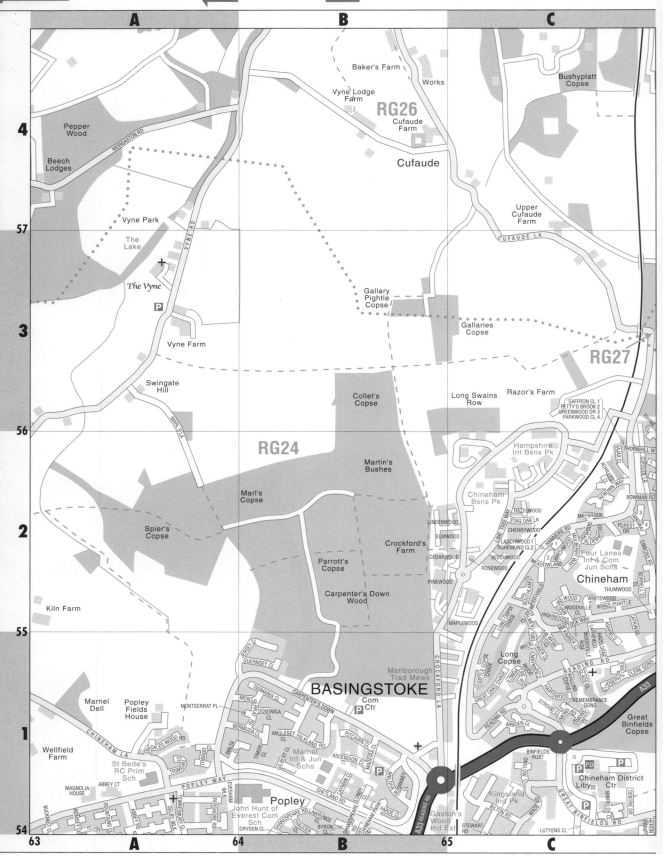

A   B   C

4

Pepper Wood

Beech Lodges

Baker's Farm

Works

Vyne Lodge Farm

RG26

Cufaude Farm

Cufaude

Bushyplatt Copse

57

Vyne Park

The Lake

The Vyne

P

Upper Cufaude Farm

CUFAUDE LA

3

Vyne Farm

Gallary Pightle Copse

Gallaries Copse

RG27

Swingate Hill

Collet's Copse

Long Swains Row

Razor's Farm

SAFFRON CL 1
PETTY'S BROOK 2
GREENWOOD DR 3
PARKWOOD CL 4

56

MARL'S LA

RG24

Martin's Bushes

Hampshire Int Bsns Pk

THORNHILL W

AJAX CL

Chineham Bsns Pk

HAZELWOOD

STAG OAK LA

RENOWN WAY

ACHILLES CL

BOWMAN RD

TANGWAY

2

Marl's Copse

Spier's Copse

Parrott's Copse

Crockford's Farm

LIME TREE WAY
LINDENWOOD
CHERRYWOOD
ELMWOOD
CEDARWOOD
BEECHWOOD
PINEWOOD

HAMMORE RD
LARCHWOOD 1
AGHEMUND CL 2

BIRCHWOOD

MULBERRY WAY

MEADOWLAND
ROSEWOOD

FOREST DR

Four Lanes Int & Com Jun Schs

MAYBROOK

Chineham

THUMWOOD

Carpenter's Down Wood

MAPLEWOOD

WOODVILLE CL
WHITEWOOD
KINGS PIGHTLE

SOUTHDOWN
MERRYFIELD

HIGHMOORS

MATTOCK WAY

GIBBONS RD
SCHNELL'S

CATKIN CL

55

Kiln Farm

JERSEY CL

GUERNSEY CL

Marlborough Trad Mews

Long Copse

READING RD

+

JOSEPH'S CL

CLERE GDNS

A33

1

Marnel Dell

Popley Fields House

MONTSERRAT PL

TASMANIA CL

CARPENTER'S DOWN

BASINGSTOKE

Com Ctr

P

BINFIELDS RDBT

Great Binfields Copse

Wellfield Farm

CHINEHAM LA

STRICKLEY WOOD RD
TOBAGO CL
IMANIA

BERMUDA CL

GILBERT CL

TIMOR CL
DOMINICA CL
MONTSERRAT CL

ANGLESEY
FALKLAND RD

PITCAIRN CL

ASCENSION CL
MADEIRA CL

Marl Infant & Jun Schs

P

P

BINFIELDS CL

P PO

Chineham District Liby

Kingsland Ind Pk

P

Chineham District Ctr

P

HERON PARK

MAGNOLIA HOUSE

St Bede's RC Prim Sch

ABBEY CT

POPLEY WAY

Popley

John Hunt of Everest Com Sch

DRYDEN CL

SHAKESPEARE RD
LAWRENCE

CHAUCER

BYRON CL

READING RD

Gaston's Wood Ind Est

STEWART RD

BILTON RD

WADE RD

GREAT BINFIELDS RD

LUTYENS CL

CENTRE DR

54

BUCKFAST CL
ROMSEY RD
FOUNTAINS RD

Sch

TEWKESBURY CT

SELBY WALK

ABBE RD

PERSHORE RD

EVESHAM WLK

SHETLAND RD
CAYMAN CL
CHINEHAM PARK

FAROE CL

A33 READING RD

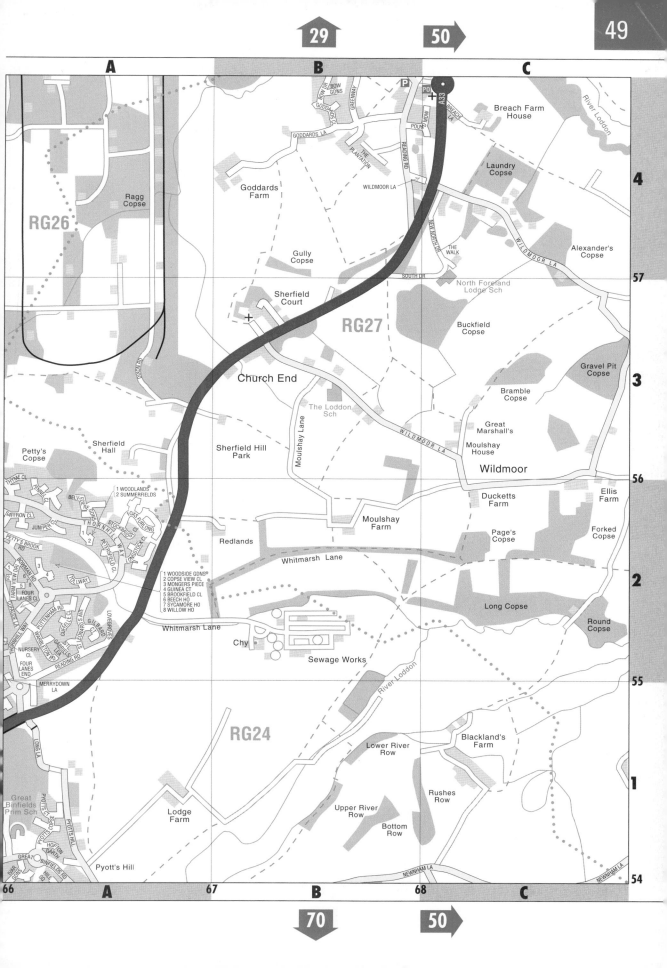

A

B

C

P

PO

Breach La

A33

Breach Farm House

River Loddon

Bow Dr

Bow Gdns

Greenway

Goddards Cl

Goddards La

The Plantation

Reading Rd

Pound

Mdw

Laundry Copse

4

Goddards Farm

Wildmoor La

New North Dr

The Walk

Wildmoor La

Alexander's Copse

RG26

Ragg Copse

Gully Copse

South Dr

North Foreland Lodge Sch

57

Sherfield Court

RG27

Buckfield Copse

Gravel Pit Copse

Church End

The Loddon Sch

Bramble Copse

3

Dixon Rd

Petty's Copse

Sherfield Hall

Sherfield Hill Park

Moulshay Lane

Wildmoor La

Great Marshall's

Moulshay House

Thyme Cl

Finne Cl

Belvedere Gdns

Saffron Cl

Juniper Cl

1 WOODLANDS
2 SUMMERFIELDS

Ios Furlong

Wildmoor

56

Thornhill Way

Stockbps

Longstock Cl

Petersfield Cl

Ducketts Farm

Ellis Farm

Petty's Brook Rd

Bowman Rd

Moulshay Farm

Page's Copse

Forked Copse

Redlands

2

Farm View Dr

Four Lanes Cl

Loddley

1 WOODSIDE GDNS
2 COPSE VIEW CL
3 MONGERS PIECE
4 GUINEA CT
5 BROOKFIELD CL
6 BEECH HO
7 SYCAMORE HO
8 WILLOW HO

Whitmarsh Lane

Long Copse

Round Copse

Thornhill Way

Puttenham Rd

Duffel Cl

Gabriels

St Leonards Ave

Gilbard Cl

Lovegroves

Whitmarsh Lane

Chy

Sewage Works

River Loddon

55

Nursery Cl

Wagbeton Cl

Reading Rd

Four Lanes End

Merrydown La

RG24

Lower River Row

Blackland's Farm

Long La

1

Great Binfields Prim Sch

Pyotts Copse

Hopton

Pyotts Hill

Lodge Farm

Upper River Row

Bottom Row

Rushes Row

Great Binfields Rd

Binfields Sq

Pyott's Hill

Newnham La

Newnham La

54

66

A

67

B

68

C

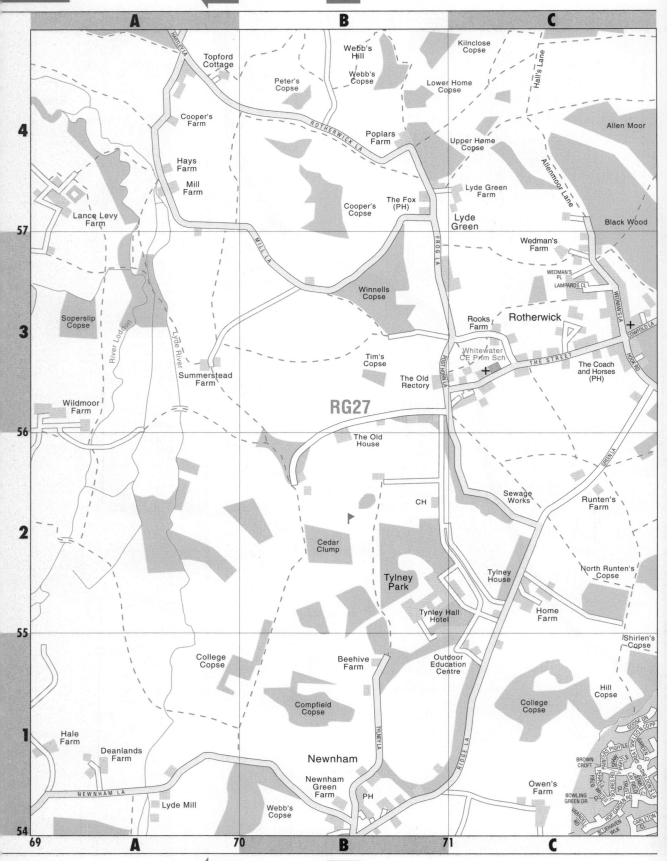

A
B
C

4

57

3

56

2

55

1

54

69
A
70
B
71
C

HAMLEY LA

Topford
Cottage

Cooper's
Farm

Hays
Farm

Mill
Farm

Lance Levy
Farm

Soperslip
Copse

River Loddon

Lyde River

MILL LA

Summerstead
Farm

Wildmoor
Farm

Webb's
Hill

Peter's
Copse

Webb's
Copse

ROTHERWICK LA

Poplars
Farm

Cooper's
Copse

The Fox
(PH)

Winnells
Copse

Tim's
Copse

The Old
Rectory

RG27

The Old
House

Cedar
Clump

CH

Kilnclose
Copse

Lower Home
Copse

Upper Home
Copse

Hall's Lane

Allen Moor

Allenmoor Lane

Lyde Green
Farm

Lyde
Green

Black Wood

Wedman's
Farm

WEDMAN'S
PL

LAMPARDS CL

Rooks
Farm

Rotherwick

FROG LA

POST HORN LA

Whitewater
CE Prim Sch

THE STREET

WEDMAN'S LA

COWFOLD LA

HOOK RD

The Coach
and Horses
(PH)

GREEN LA

Sewage
Works

Runten's
Farm

North Runten's
Copse

Tylney
House

Home
Farm

Shirlen's
Copse

Hill
Copse

Tylney
Park

Tynley Hall
Hotel

College
Copse

Beehive
Farm

Compfield
Copse

Outdoor
Education
Centre

RIDGE LA

TYLNEY LA

Hale
Farm

Deanlands
Farm

NEWNHAM LA

Lyde Mill

Newnham

Newnham
Green
Farm

Webb's
Copse

PH

Owen's
Farm

College
Copse

GOSSE GN

SHELDON COPP

PAINTERS PIGHTLE

GAMDEL

PIGHTLE

FERREL

FIELD

SCURES RD

TRUST CL

STABLE CT

LAY FIELD

OSMELS CL

BROWN
CROFT

BOWLING
GREEN DR

HOP GARDEN RD

VARNDEL
RD

BLUEHAVEN WLK

CARLETON
CL

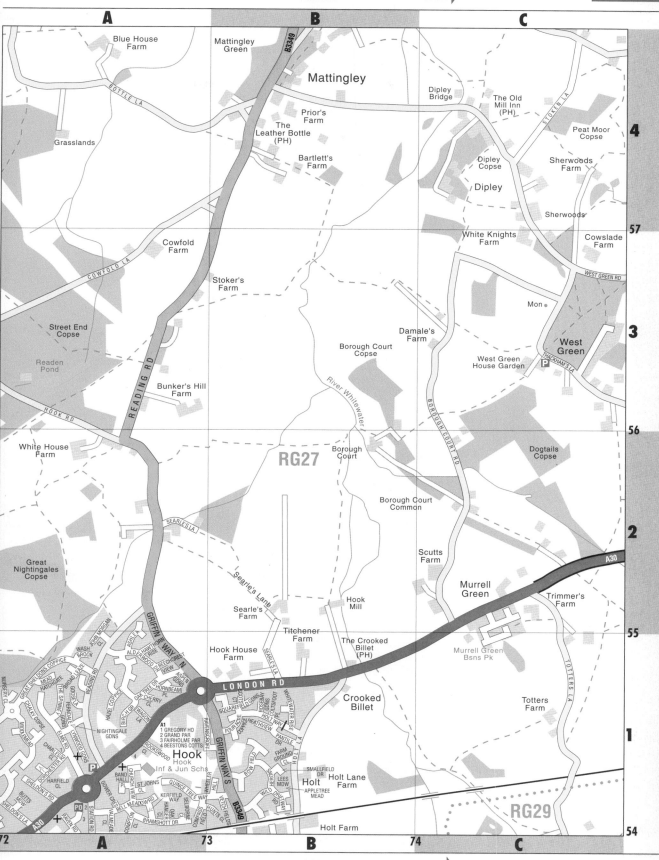

B2
1 ANDOVER DR
2 BENTLEY DR
3 DUNLEY DR
4 EVERSLEY DR
5 EMERY DOWN DR
6 HAZELEY DR
7 HECKFIELD DR
8 KIMPTON DR
9 LISS DR
10 LONGMOOR CT
11 LONG SUTTON DR
12 MATTINGLEY DR
13 MICHELDEVER DR
14 MEDSTEAD DR
15 OVINGTON DR
16 NUTLEY DR
17 PAMBER DR
18 UPPER MOUNT ST
19 LOWER MOUNT ST

C1
1 BLUEBELL WLK
2 SNOWDROP WLK
3 PRIMROSE WLK
4 PEAR TREE AVE
5 CLARENDON HO
6 HARTFIELD HO
7 CHURCH CT
8 FIRCROFTS
9 VICTORIA GDNS
10 MEADOW CT
11 SOVEREIGN CT
12 HART CTR
13 NORTH MALL
14 CARNIVAL SQ
15 OAKLEY PL
16 SOUTH MALL
17 CALTHORPE SQ
18 VICTORIA CT
19 COTSWOLD CT

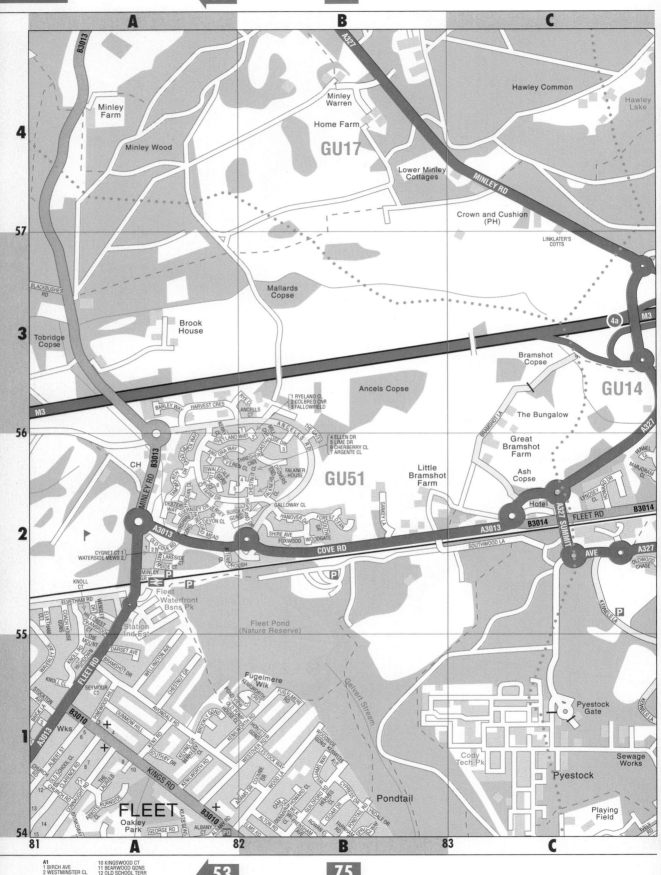

A   B   C

4

57

3

56

2

55

1

54

81   82   83

Minley Farm
Minley Wood

Minley Warren
Home Farm

GU17

Hawley Common

Hawley Lake

Lower Minley Cottages

MINLEY RD

Crown and Cushion (PH)

LINKLATER'S COTTS

BLACKBUSHES RD

Mallards Copse

4a

M3

Tobridge Copse

Brook House

Bramshot Copse

GU14

M3

Ancels Copse

A327

BARLEY WAY   HARVEST CRES

RYE CL

1 RYELAND CL
2 COLBRED CNR
3 FALLOWFIELD

ANCELLS CT

ANCELLS RD   THE GATE

BRAMSHOT LA

The Bungalow

Great Bramshot Farm

4 ELLEN DR
5 LIME DR
6 CHERBERRY CL
7 ARGENTE CL

CH

B3013

MINLEY RD

Little Bramshot Farm

Ash Copse

GU51

FENNEL CL

MARJORAM CL

LYNDSEY DR

HOWARD DR

Hotel

A327   FLEET RD   B3014

GALLOWAY CL

SANKEY LA

B3014

SUMMIT

A3013

OLD COVE RD

CYGNET CT 1
WATERSIDE MEWS 2

LAKESIDE CT

MINLEY GR

COVE RD

SOUTHWOOD LA

A3013

AVE   A327   OLDWOOD CHASE

KNOLL CT

P

Fleet Waterfront Bsns Pk

Station Ind Est

P   P

P

KENNEL LA

P

Pyestock Gate

ELVETHAM RD

COACH HOUSE

HILLCREST DR

CRANBROOK CT

THE MOUNT

DARSET AVE

Fleet Pond (Nature Reserve)

Gelvert Stream

KNOLL RD

HIGHDOWN

SEYMOUR CT

BRAMSHOT DR

WELLINGTON AVE

CHESTNUT AVE

Fugelmere Wlk

KENILWORTH CRES

FUGELMERE RD

B3010

FLEET RD

KNOLL CL

A3013

Wks

STOCKTON AVE

BRICK LA

DUNMOW HILL

PINEWOOD HILL

AVONDALE RD

KENT RD

SOUTHBY DR

POND VIEW

OLD PUMP HO

HOUSE DR

WOOD LA

KENILWORTH RD

GDNS

WOODSIDE GDNS

KENWITH AVE

Cody Tech Pk

Sewage Works

ALBERT ST

OLD SCHOOL CL

CLARENCE RD

THE LAURELS

BURNSIDE

ABBOTS

KENILWORTH RD

KINGS RD

KEATS GDNS

ADAMS CT

COOMBE DR

WOOD LA

ALTON RD

ELMS RD

ALBANY RD

GEORGE RD

FLEET

Oakley Park

B3010

PO

LIAMS WAY

CYPRESS DR

CEDAR DR

FARNHAM RD

PONDTAIL RD

SPRUCE RD

ROWAN CL

GUILDFORD RD

Pondtail

Pyestock

Playing Field

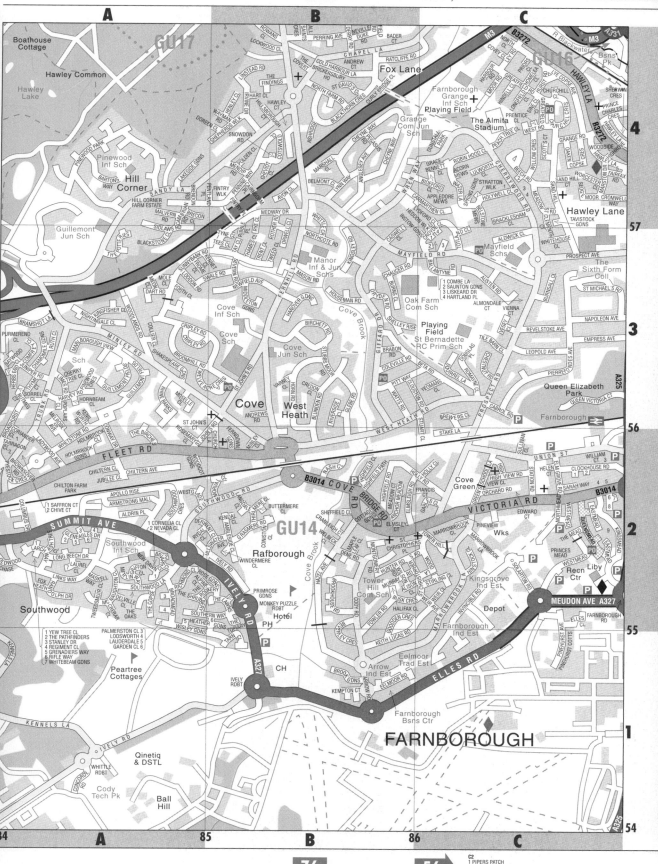

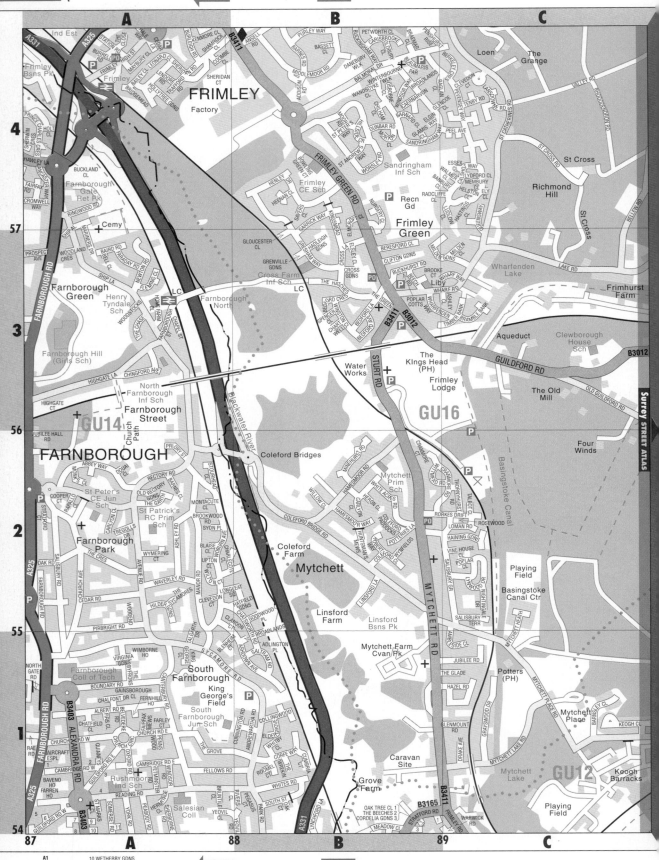

A1
1 CAMBRIDGE CT
2 BARTON CT
3 DENBY CT
4 REDE CT
5 NEELEM CT
6 KASHMIR CT
7 BULLER CT
8 WYKEHAM HO
9 ALEXANDRA CT

10 WETHERBY GDNS
11 SOMERSET CT

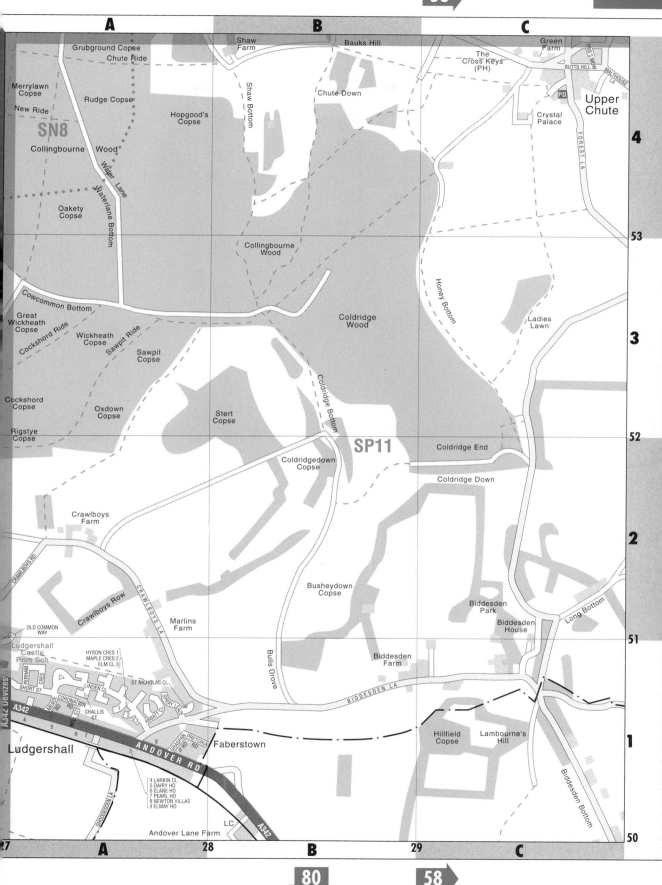

A
B
C

Grubground Copse
Chute Ride

Shaw
Farm
Bauks Hill

The
Cross Keys
(PH)

Green
Farm

TRIB'S MDW

BUTTS HILL

MALTHOUSE LA

Merrylawn
Copse

Chute Down

PO

New Ride

SN8

Shaw Bottom

**Upper
Chute**

Rudge Copse

Hopgood's
Copse

Crystal
Palace

FOREST LA

4

Collingbourne Wood

Water Lane

Waterlane Bottom

53

Oakety
Copse

Collingbourne
Wood

Honey Bottom

Ladies
Lawn

Cowcommon Bottom

Great
Wickheath
Copse

Coldridge
Wood

3

Cockshord Ride

Wickheath
Copse

Sawpit Ride

Sawpit
Copse

Cockshord
Copse

Oxdown
Copse

Stert
Copse

Coldridge Bottom

Rigstye
Copse

Coldridge End

52

Coldridgedown
Copse

SP11

Coldridge Down

Crawlboys
Farm

2

CRAWLBOYS RD

Busheydown
Copse

Biddesden
Park

Long Bottom

Biddesden
House

CRAWLBOYS LA

Marlins
Farm

OLD COMMON
WAY

Crawlboys Row

Ludgershall
Castle
Prim Sch

HYSON CRES 1
MAPLE CRES 2
ELM CL 3

Bulls Drove

Biddesden
Farm

51

PERHAM CRES

SHORT ST

St Nicholas Cl.

LINDEN CL

SPRAY LEAZE

BIDDESDEN LA

MEADE
CORONATION
RD

BELL ST

CHALLIS
CT

ABBATT CL

Faberstown

Hillfield
Copse

Lambourne's
Hill

1

A342 DEVIZES

A342

4
5
6
7
8

Ludgershall

GRASPAN RD

PRETORIA RD

ANDOVER RD

8

Biddesden Bottom

SHODDESDEN LA

4 LARKIN CL
5 DAIRY HO
6 ELANE HO
7 PEARL HO
8 NEWTON VILLAS
9 ELMAY HO

LC

A342

Andover Lane Farm

50

27
A
28
B
29
C

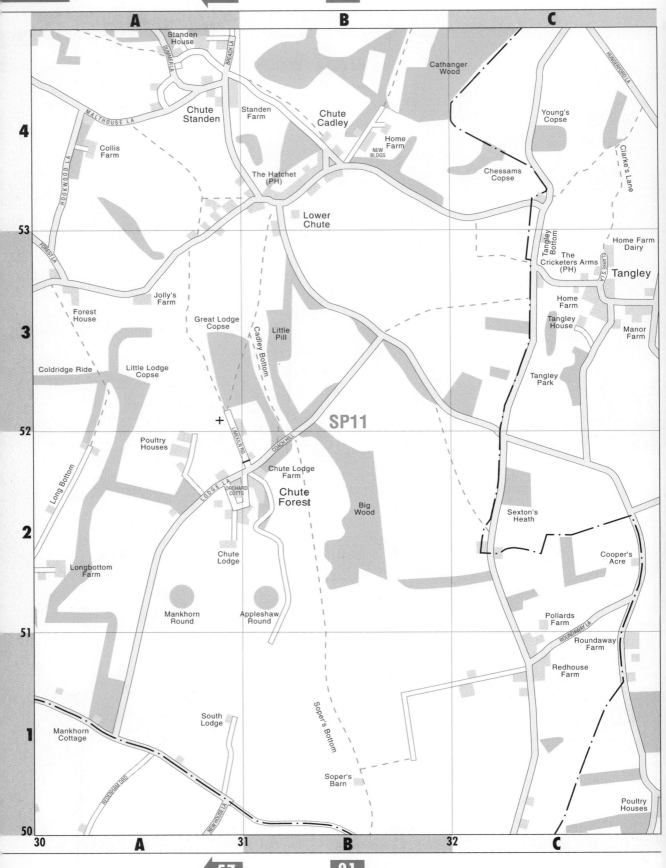

A

Standen House

Chute Standen

Standen Farm

Chute Cadley

Cathanger Wood

Young's Copse

DUNMER LA

BREACH LA

Home Farm

NEW BLDGS

Clarke's Lane

HUNGERFORD LA

MALTHOUSE LA

Collis Farm

The Hatchet (PH)

Chessams Copse

HOOKWOOD LA

Lower Chute

4

Tangley Bottom

Home Farm Dairy

53

FOREST LA

Jolly's Farm

The Cricketers Arms (PH)

Tangley

Forest House

Great Lodge Copse

Little Pill

Home Farm

Manor Farm

3

CADLEY BOTTOM

Tangley House

Coldridge Ride

Little Lodge Copse

CLARKE'S LA

Tangley Park

SP11

Poultry Houses

LIMEKILN RD

COACH HILL

Sexton's Heath

2

Chute Lodge Farm

Big Wood

LODGE LA

ORCHARD COTTS

Cooper's Acre

Longbottom Farm

Chute Forest

Long Bottom

Chute Lodge

Pollards Farm

ROUNDAWAY LA

Mankhorn Round

Appleshaw Round

51

Roundaway Farm

Redhouse Farm

South Lodge

Soper's Bottom

1

Mankhorn Cottage

REDENHAM DRO

Soper's Barn

Poultry Houses

NEWHOUSE LA

50

30   A   31   B   32   C

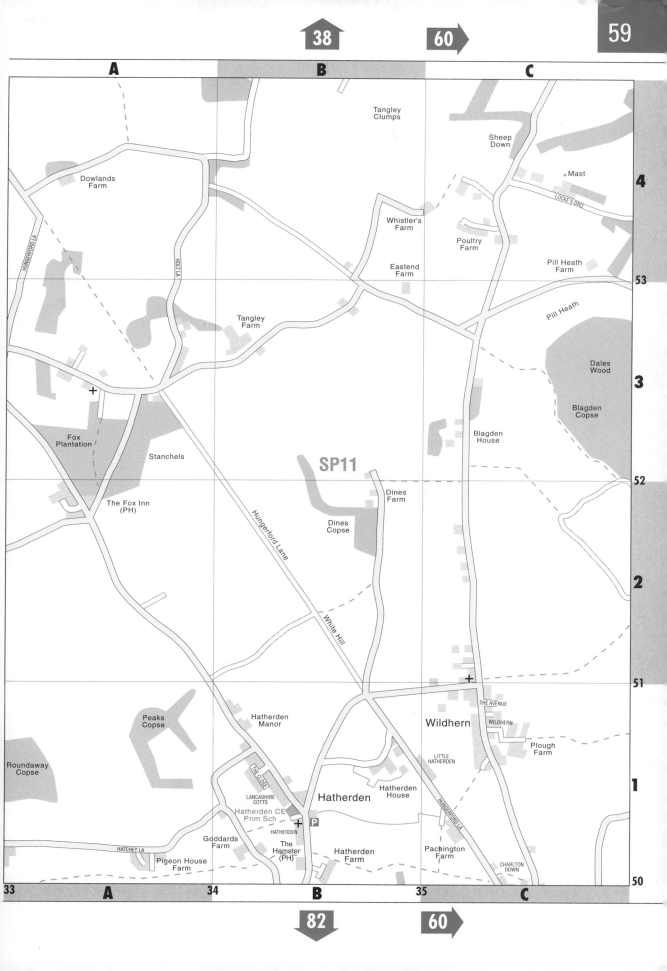

59
39

A   B   C

4

Locke's Barn

Locke's Dro

Ibthorpe

Upper Ibthorpe Farm

Ibthorpe Manor Farm

HORSESHOE LA

Prosperous Farm

A343

Yewtree Farm

Adams Farm

Test Way

Hurstbourne Tarrant

DOLOMANS LA

DINES CL

The Rank

The Dene

Windmill Hill Down

WINDMILL LA

Dolomans La

KNIGHTS YD

PO

THE CRESCENT

DEAN RISE

53

Windmills Farm

Windmills

Windmill Hill

DOCTORS DRO

The George and Dragon (PH)

B3048 CHURCH ST

VICTORIA PL

River Swift

Parsonage Farm

STOKE RD

B3048

Hurstbourne Tarrant CE Prim Sch

Lower Farm

3

Blagden Copse

Hurstbourne Hill

Hurstbourne Common

Bourne Rivulet

SP11

Doles Copse

Test Way

52

Doles Wood

2

Doles Farm

Doles House

Bourne Park

Frenches Farm

Rag Wood

51

Lee's Wood

Rag Copse

Frenche's Lodge

1

Green Dro

Great Stubbage

Long Copse

Straits Copse

A343 NEWBURY RD

MACCULLUM RD

Ridges Copse

50

36   A   37   B   38   C

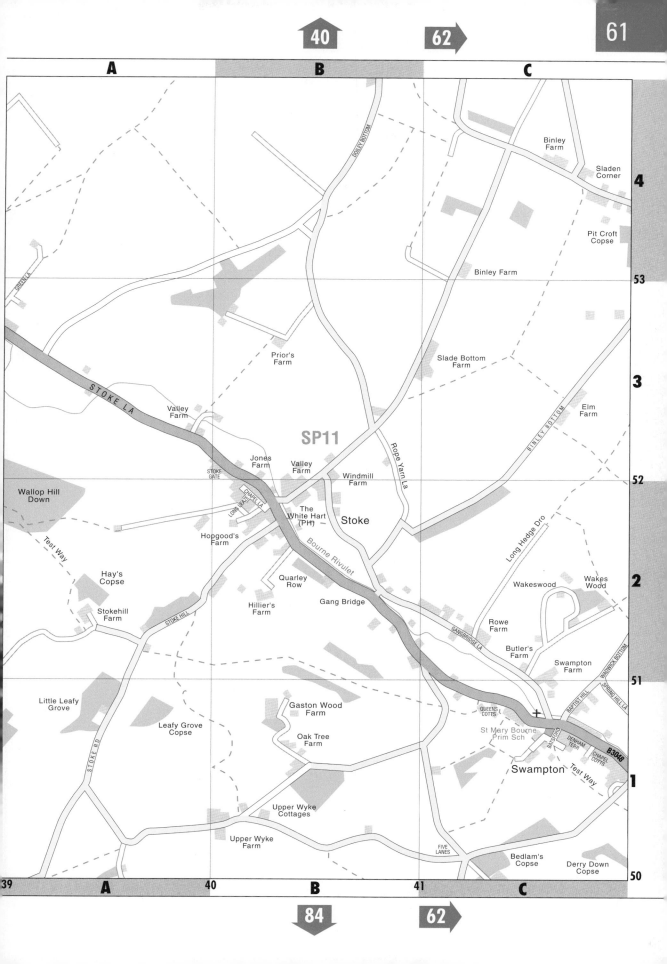

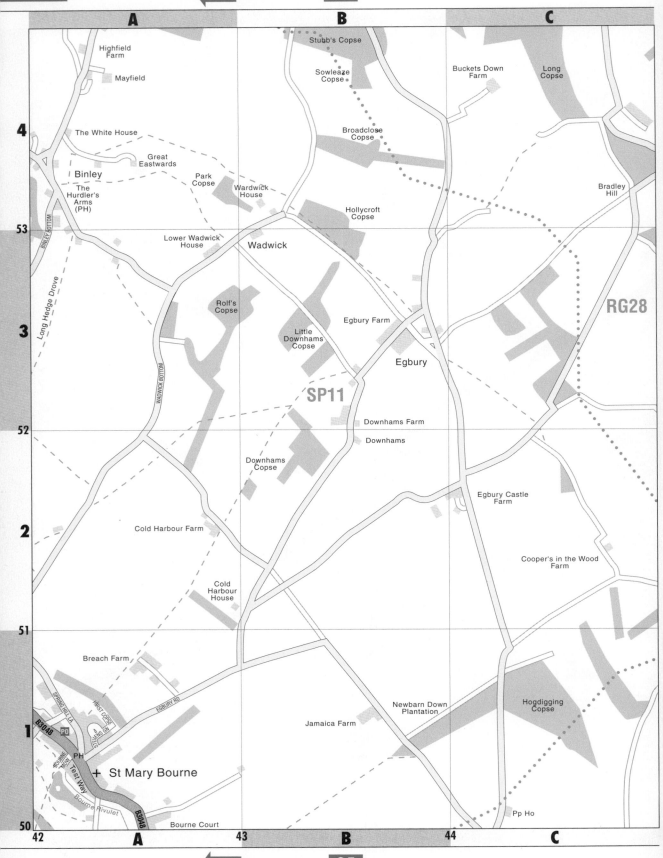

A   B   C

4

Highfield Farm

Mayfield

The White House

Great Eastwards

Binley

The Hurdler's Arms (PH)

Park Copse

Wardwick House

Stubb's Copse

Sowleaze Copse

Broadclose Copse

Hollycroft Copse

Buckets Down Farm

Long Copse

Bradley Hill

53

Lower Wadwick House

Wadwick

Long Hedge Drove

3

Rolf's Copse

Little Downhams Copse

Egbury Farm

Egbury

SP11

RG28

Wadwick Bottom

52

Downhams Farm

Downhams

Downhams Copse

Cold Harbour Farm

2

Egbury Castle Farm

Cooper's in the Wood Farm

Cold Harbour House

51

Breach Farm

Springhill La

Hirst Copse

Egbury Rd

Stevens Gn

Newbarn Down Plantation

Hogdigging Copse

B3048

PO

1

PH

Bourne Mdw

Test Way

+ St Mary Bourne

Jamaica Farm

Bourne Rivulet

B3048

Pp Ho

50

Bourne Court

42   43   44

A   B   C

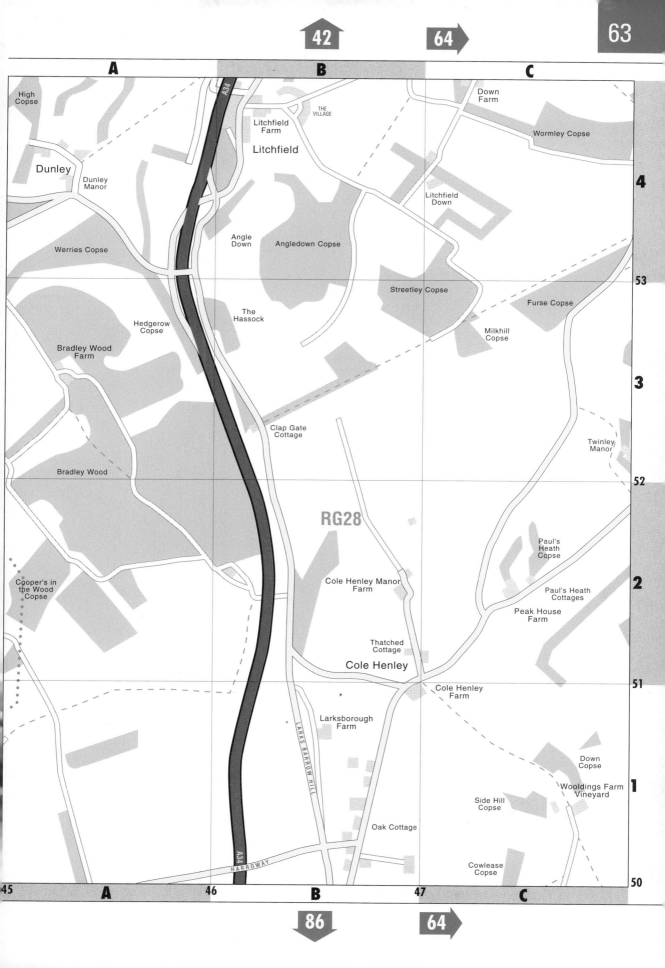

63
43

A **B** **C**

Palmer's
Bushes

Owls
Lodge

Caesar's Belt

4

Robley Belt

Ridgeway
Copse

53

Keeper's Cottage

Old Farmhouse

Ridgeway
Farm

Willesley Warren
Cottages

Dunn's
Wood

Willesley Warren
Farm

3

Paul's
Wood.

RG25

Twinley
Manor

52

Little Twinley's
Copse

RG28

The
Peak

Whitnal

2

New
Barn

La
Bresse

51

TWINLEY LA

COURT DRO

1

Harroway Belt

The
Orchards

The
Cottage

Lordsfield
Plantation

Ash Bed
Plantation

Northfield
Plantation

Northington Belt

Sewage
Works

50

48 49 50

A **B** **C**

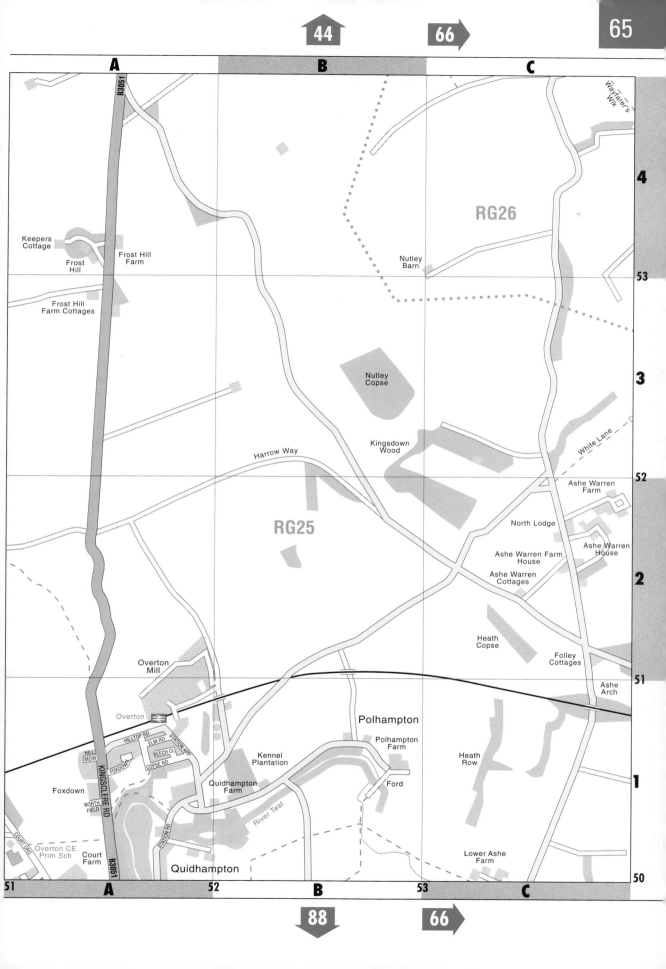

44
66

A
B
C

4

53

3

52

2

51

1

50

Wayfarer's Wlk

RG26

Keepers Cottage

Frost Hill

Frost Hill Farm

Frost Hill Farm Cottages

Nutley Barn

Nutley Copse

Kingsdown Wood

Harrow Way

White Lane

Ashe Warren Farm

RG25

North Lodge

Ashe Warren Farm House

Ashe Warren House

Ashe Warren Cottages

Heath Copse

Folley Cottages

Ashe Arch

Overton Mill

B3051

Overton

Polhampton

HILLTOP RD
ELM RD
BEECH CL
COPSE RD
STATION APP
HILL MDW
FOXDOWN
KINGSCLERE RD
NORTH FIELD

Foxdown

Kennel Plantation

Quidhampton Farm

Polhampton Farm

Ford

Heath Row

River Test

STATION RD

COURT DRO
Overton CE Prim Sch
Court Farm

B3051

Quidhampton

Lower Ashe Farm

51
A
52
B
53
C

88
66

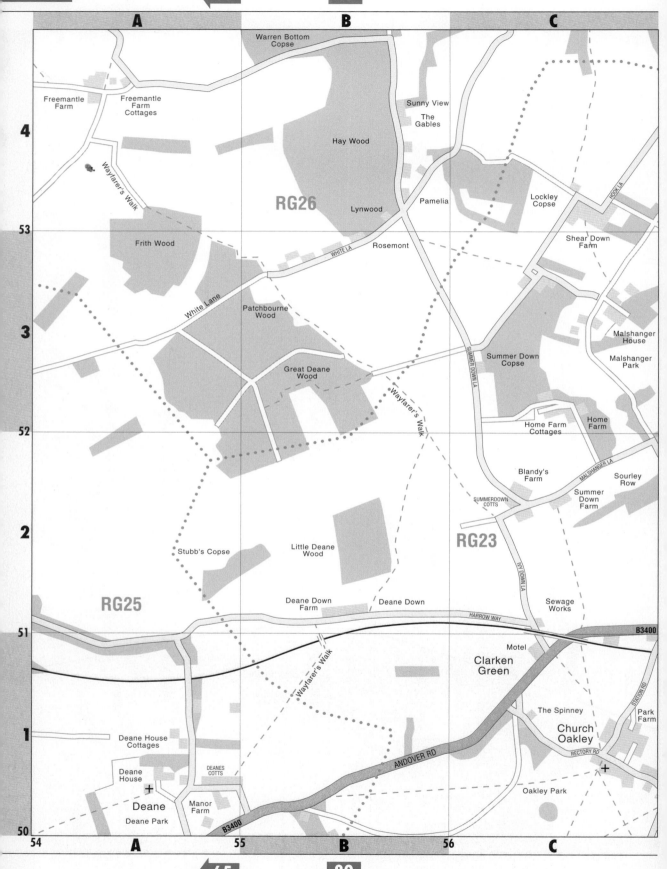

A   **B**   **C**

4

Freemantle Farm

Freemantle Farm Cottages

Warren Bottom Copse

Wayfarer's Walk

Sunny View

The Gables

Hay Wood

RG26

Lynwood

Pamelia

Lockley Copse

HOOK LA

53

Frith Wood

WHITE LA

Rosemont

Shear Down Farm

White Lane

Patchbourne Wood

3

SUMMER DOWN LA

Summer Down Copse

Malshanger House

Malshanger Park

Great Deane Wood

Wayfarer's Walk

52

Home Farm Cottages

Home Farm

MALSHANGER LA

Blandy's Farm

Sourley Row

SUMMERDOWN COTTS

Summer Down Farm

2

Stubb's Copse

Little Deane Wood

RG23

IVY DOWN LA

Sewage Works

RG25

Deane Down Farm

Deane Down

HARROW WAY

51

B3400

Motel

Clarken Green

Wayfarer's Walk

STATION RD

The Spinney

Park Farm

1

Deane House Cottages

DEANES COTTS

Church Oakley

RECTORY RD

Deane House

Manor Farm

ANDOVER RD

Oakley Park

+

Deane

Deane Park

B3400

50

54   **A**   55   **B**   56   **C**

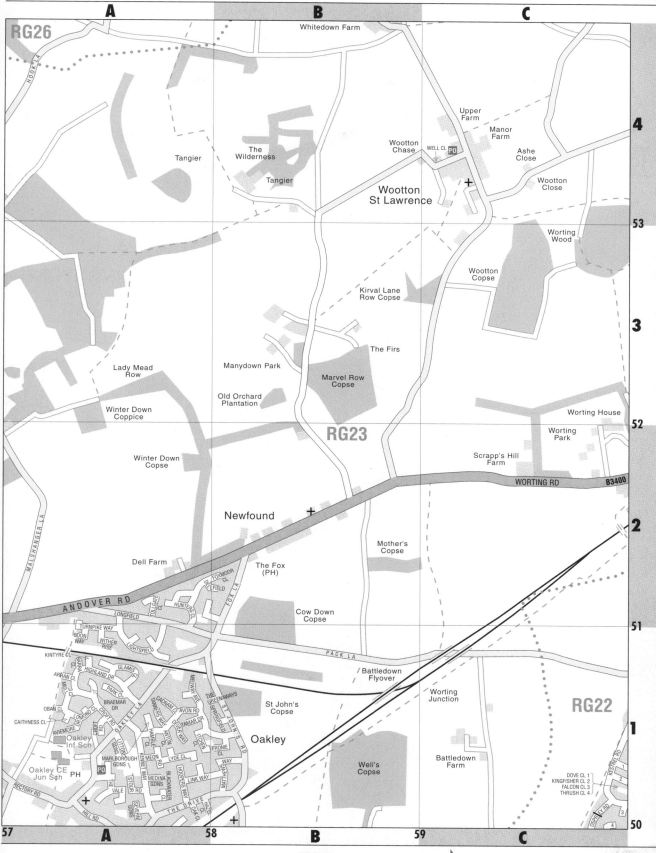

RG26

A   B   C

HOOK LA

Whitedown Farm

Tangier

The Wilderness

Tangier

Upper Farm

Manor Farm

Wootton Chase

WELL CL   PO

Ashe Close

Wootton Close

Wootton St Lawrence

Worting Wood

4

53

Kirval Lane Row Copse

Wootton Copse

Lady Mead Row

The Firs

Manydown Park

Marvel Row Copse

Old Orchard Plantation

Worting House

Winter Down Coppice

RG23

Worting Park

52

Scrapp's Hill Farm

Winter Down Copse

WORTING RD   B3400

Newfound

Mother's Copse

2

Dell Farm

FOXMOOR CL

The Fox (PH)

MALSHANGER LA

ANDOVER RD

LFIELD

TOLLGATE CL

HUNTERS CL

FOX LA

Cow Down Copse

Battledown Flyover

51

LONGFIELD

Turnpike Way

BOON WAY

WITHER RISE

LIGHTSFIELD

PACK LA

KINTYRE CL

HIGHLAND DR

BARRA CL

GLAMIS

MILL CL

PARK CL

ARRAN CL

MEDWAY AVE

CADNAM CL

TANNERS WAY

THE GREENAWAYS

ST JOHN'S RD

AVON RD

DEVER WAY

SPRINGFIELD

St John's Copse

Worting Junction

RG22

OBAN CL

BRAEMAR DR

OAKLEY LA

TAMAR DR

ANTON

ITCHEN

CAITHNESS CL

LOMOND CL

CROFT RD

LITTON GDNS

HAMBLE

Oakley

AVIEMORE

Oakley Inf Sch

KENNET WAY

MEON

FROME CL

YDE CL

1

DOVE CL 1
KINGFISHER CL 2
FALCON CL 3
THRUSH 4

Oakley CE Jun Sch

PO

PH

MARLBOROUGH GDNS

STOUR RD

MEDINA GDNS

BLACKWATER CL

HOOPERS WAY

MATTHEWS WAY

LINK WAY

KESTREL RD

RECTORY RD

THE VALE

SEVERN GDNS

THE DRIVE

HAZEL

OAK CL

Well's Copse

Battledown Farm

OSPREY RD

HILL RD

57   A   58   B   59   C   50

67
47

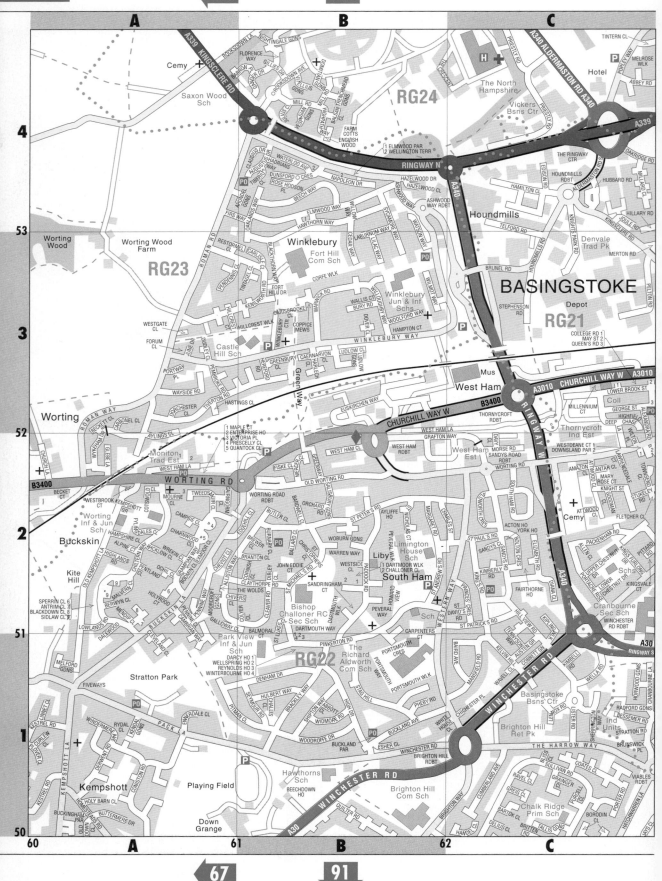

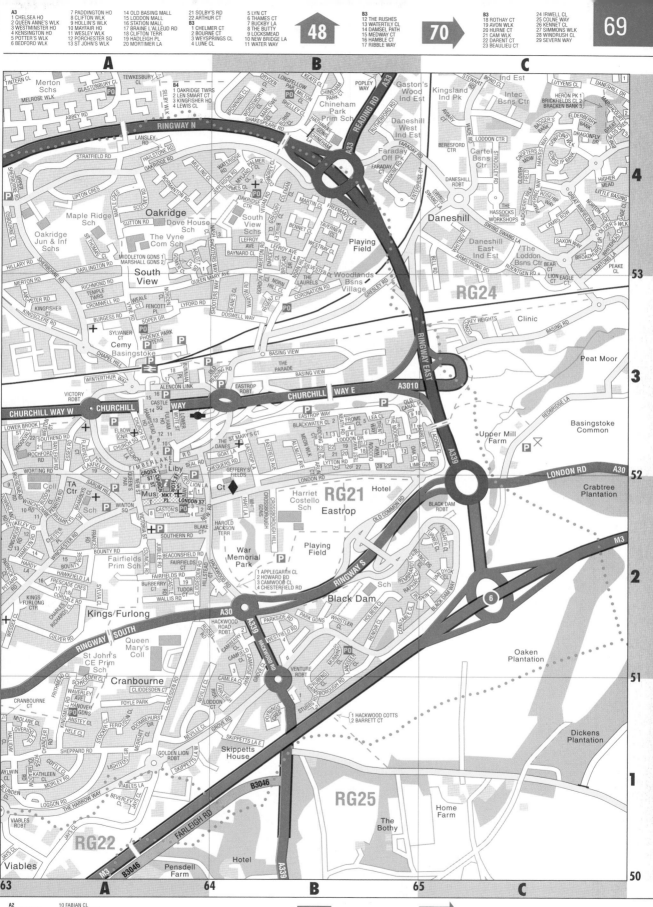

69
49

A **B** **C**

NEWNHAM LA

Bain's Wood

Lower Mill

Lower Mill Farm

Elliot's Copse

Poors Farm

POORS FARM RD

POT LA

Gold's Farm

4

Oliver's Battery
Motte & Baileys

Bartons La

1 POPPY FIELDS
2 GREAT BINFIELDS CRES
3 AMPORT CL
4 BRICKFIELDS CL
5 CHARLDON GN
6 TRELLIS DR
7 CAVELL CT
8 COPSE FIELD
9 BEDDINGTON CT

Wildwood Farm

Round Copse

WATER END LA

A30

Barton's Mill

RILEY LA

Cemy

1 CHESTNUT BANK
2 CHAPEL CL

Bushy Lease Copse

Hodd's Copse

VIrnell's Copse

ASHMOOR LA

53

Grange Farm

Brown's Farm

St Mary's CE Jun Sch

RG24
OLD BASING

Hodd's Farm

Hodd's Hill

Andwell

RG27 Priory Farm

Lyde River

The Crown (PH)

Basing House
(remains of)

Old Basing Inf Sch

East Moor

Andwell Moor

M3

3

Basingstoke Common

Hatch

LONDON RD

Swannill Nursery

Basingfield

PH

GREYWELL RD

OAK TREE COTTS

GREYWELL RD

COB TREE COTTS

52 A30

Crabtree Plantation

P

BASINGFIELD CL

KEMBERS LA

M3

2

New Park

Huish Farm

Huish House

Webb's Farm

Mapledurwell

The Gamekeepers (PH)

TUNWORTH RD

FROG LA

DOWN LA

Dicken's Lane Plantation

Moorhams Cottage

Moorhams Copse

RG25

Nunnery Hill

Manor Farm

51

Sheetlands Copse

Gray's Farm

1

Blackdown Farm

POLECAT CNR

Ragmore

66 **A** **67** **B** **68** **C**

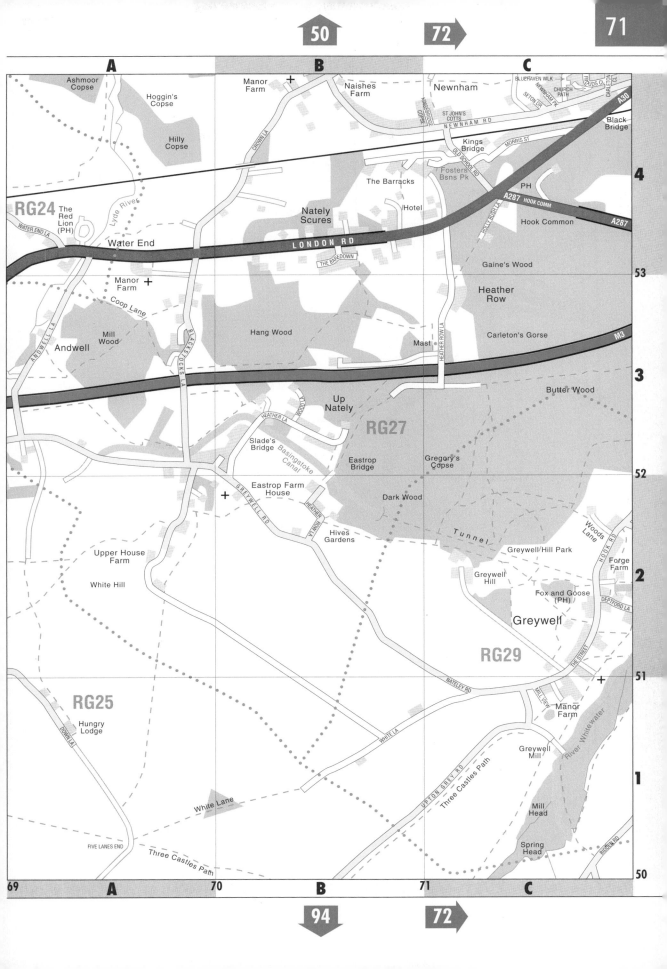

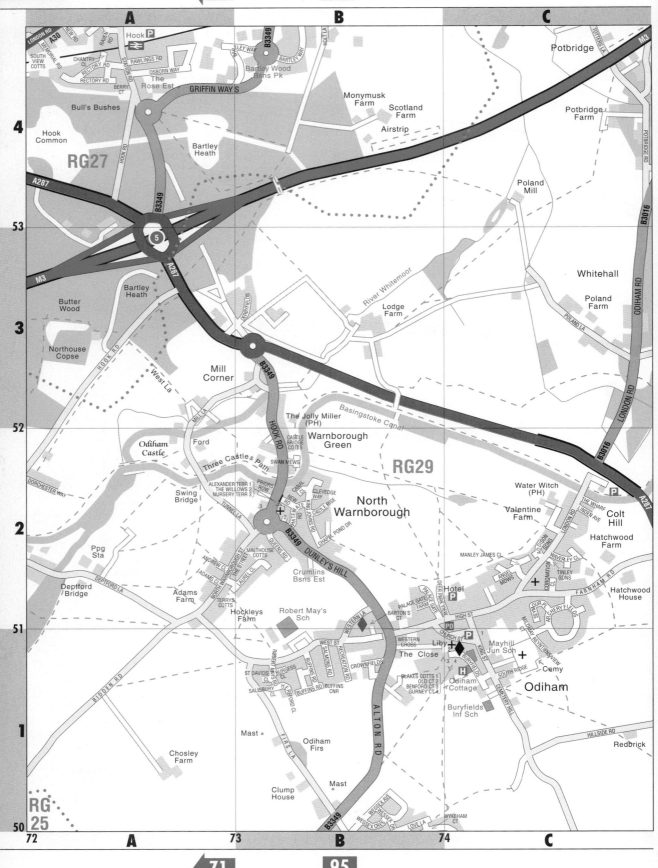

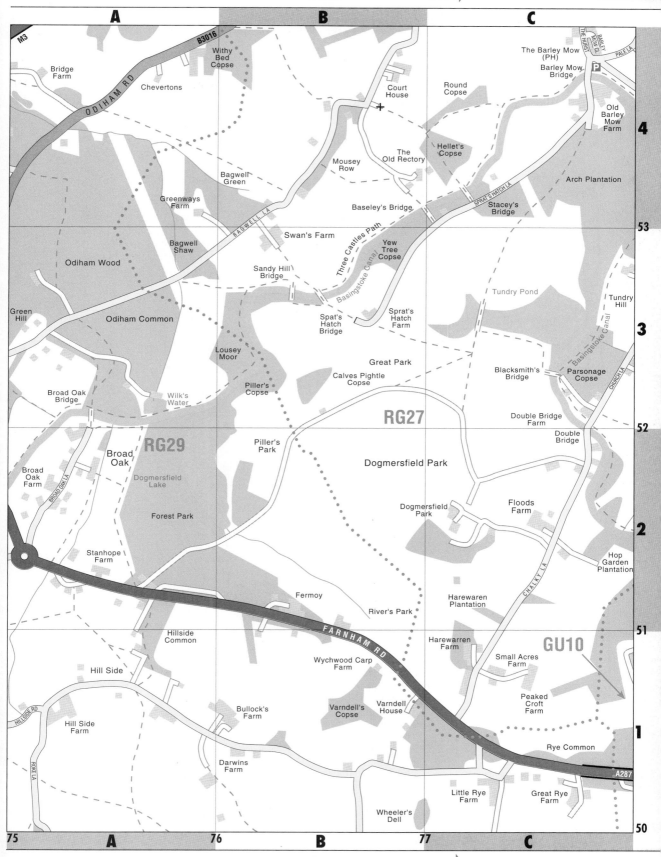

M3

ODIHAM RD
B3016

Bridge Farm

Chevertons

Withy Bed Copse

Court House

Round Copse

The Barley Mow (PH)

THE HURST
BARLEY MOW CL
PALE LA

Barley Mow Bridge

P

Old Barley Mow Farm

4

Mousey Row

The Old Rectory

Hellet's Copse

Bagwell Green

Greenways Farm

Baseley's Bridge

SPRAT'S HATCH LA

Stacey's Bridge

Arch Plantation

BAGWELL LA

Swan's Farm

Three Castles Path

Yew Tree Copse

53

Bagwell Shaw

Sandy Hill Bridge

Basingstoke Canal

Tundry Pond

Tundry Hill

Odiham Wood

Green Hill

Odiham Common

Spat's Hatch Bridge

Sprat's Hatch Farm

Basingstoke Canal

CHURCH LA

3

Lousey Moor

Great Park

Blacksmith's Bridge

Parsonage Copse

Broad Oak Bridge

Piller's Copse

Calves Pightle Copse

Wilk's Water

RG27

Double Bridge Farm

Double Bridge

52

Piller's Park

RG29

Broad Oak Farm

BROAD OAK LA

Broad Oak

Dogmersfield Lake

Forest Park

Dogmersfield Park

Dogmersfield Park

Floods Farm

Hop Garden Plantation

2

Stanhope Farm

Fermoy

River's Park

Harewaren Plantation

CHALKY LA

GU10

FARNHAM RD

Hillside Common

HILLSIDE RD

Hill Side

Wychwood Carp Farm

Harewarren Farm

Small Acres Farm

51

Peaked Croft Farm

Hill Side Farm

ROKE LA

Bullock's Farm

Varndell's Copse

Varndell House

Rye Common

1

A287

Darwins Farm

Little Rye Farm

Great Rye Farm

Wheeler's Dell

50

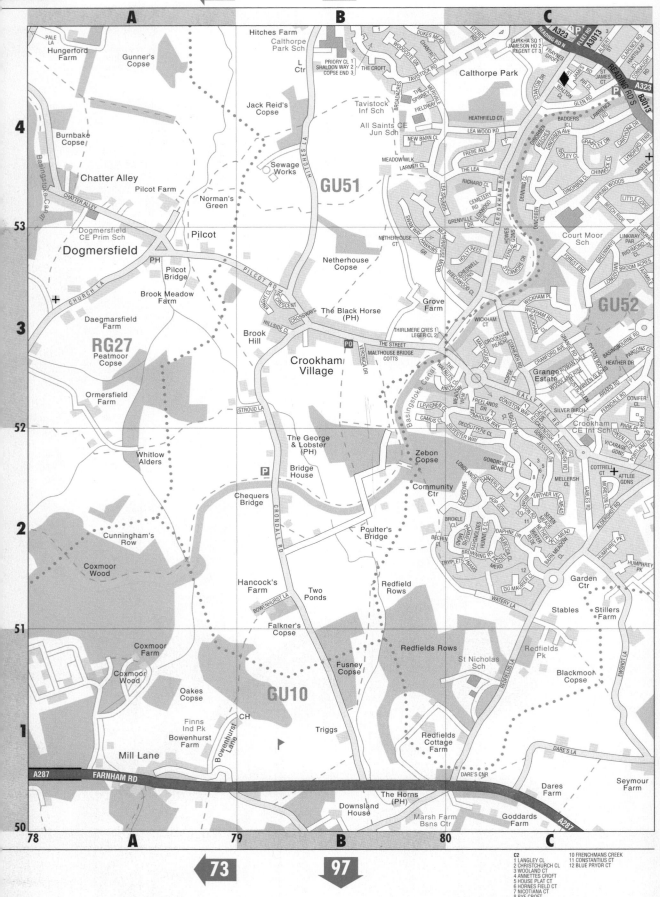

C2
1 LANGLEY CL
2 CHRISTCHURCH CL
3 WOOLAND CT
4 ANNETTES CROFT
5 HOUSE PLAT CT
6 HORNES FIELD CT
7 NICOTIANA CT
8 RYE CROFT
9 TWISELL THORNE
10 FRENCHMANS CREEK
11 CONSTANTIUS CT
12 BLUE PRYOR CT

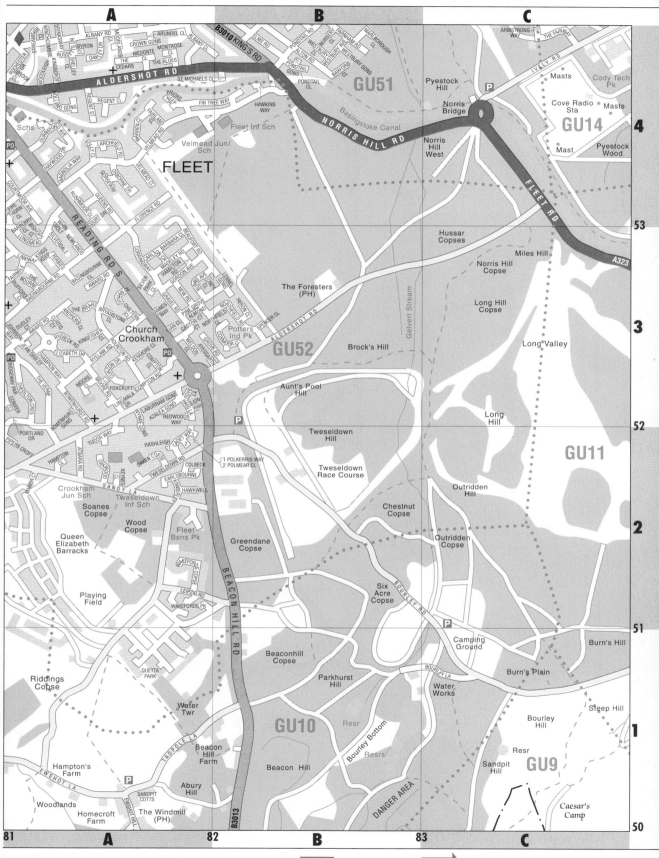

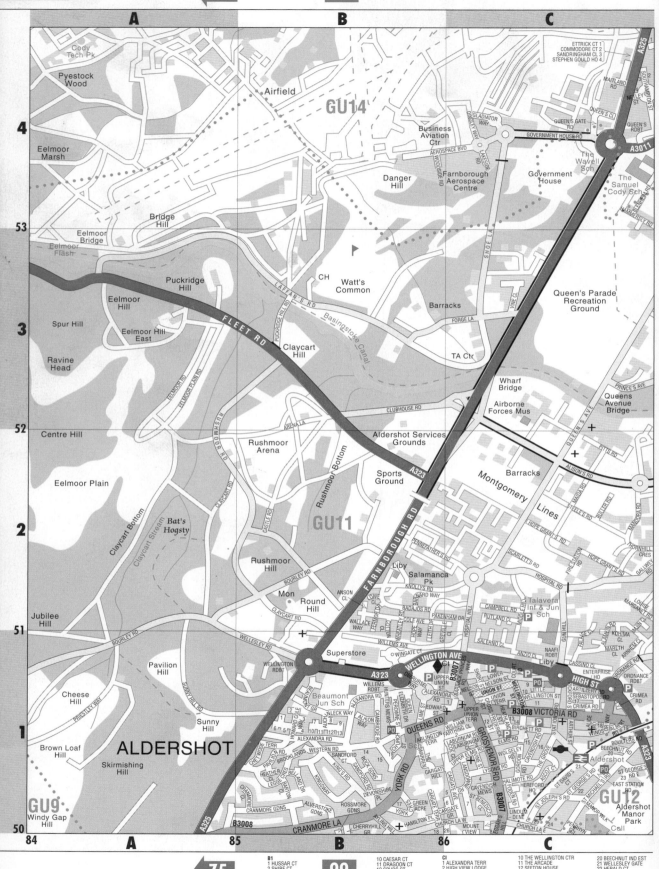

75
55

A
B
C

4

53

3

52

2

51

1

50

84
A
85
B
86
C

GU14
Airfield

ETTRICK CT 1
COMMODORE CT 2
SANDRINGHAM CL 3
STEPHEN GOULD HO 4

Cody Tech Pk
Pyestock Wood

Business Aviation Ctr

Danger Hill

Government House

The Wavell Sch

The Samuel Cody Sch

Eelmoor Marsh

Farnborough Aerospace Centre

Bridge Hill

Eelmoor Bridge

Eelmoor Flash

Puckridge Hill

Watt's Common
CH

Barracks

Queen's Parade Recreation Ground

Eelmoor Hill

FLEET RD

Spur Hill

Eelmoor Hill East

Claycart Hill

Ravine Head

Wharf Bridge

Airborne Forces Mus

Queens Avenue Bridge

TA Ctr

FORGE LA

Centre Hill

CLUBHOUSE RD

Aldershot Services Grounds

Montgomery Lines

Barracks

Eelmoor Plain

Rushmoor Arena

Rushmoor Bottom

Sports Ground

A323

GU11

Claycart Bottom

Bat's Hogsty

Claycart Stream

Rushmoor Hill

Liby

Salamanca Pk

Talavera Inf & Jun Sch

Jubilee Hill

Mon

Round Hill

Superstore

Wellington Ave

Liby

Pavilion Hill

Wellington Rdbt

Beaumont Jun Sch

Queens Rd

High St

Victoria Rd

Aldershot

Cheese Hill

Sunny Hill

Brown Loaf Hill

Skirmishing Hill

York Rd

Grosvenor Rd

Aldershot Manor Park

GU9

Windy Gap Hill

B3008

Cranmore La

GU12

75
99

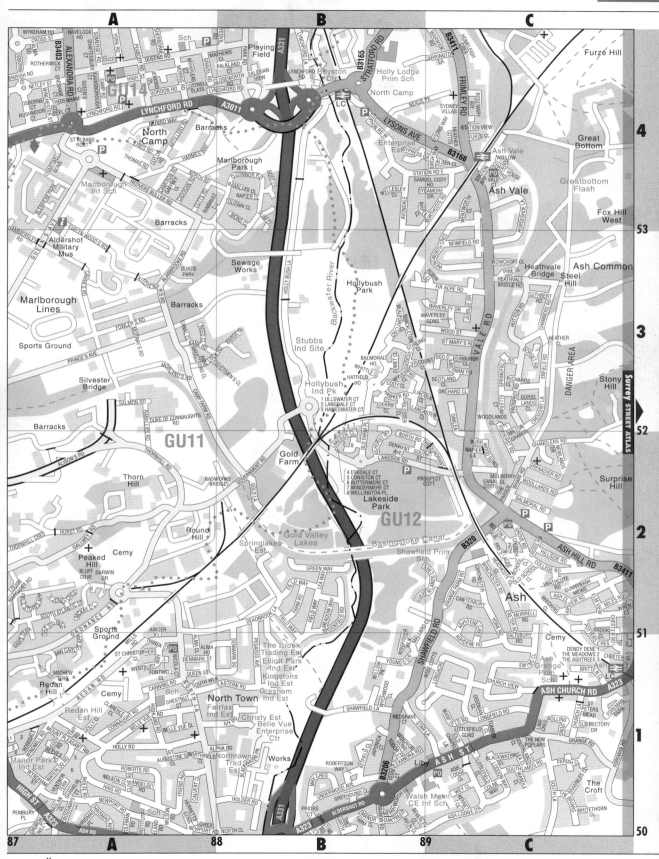

A1
1 REDAN GDNS
2 AMBER CT
3 POUND RD
4 WINDMILL CT
5 SUNNY VIEW CL
6 BEMBRIDGE CT
7 RYDE CT

C3		C4						
1 MELKSHAM HO		1 COLLINS CT		7 CHESTNUT AVE		14 WILSON HO		
2 SAVERNAKE HO		2 VOCKINS CL		8 ROWAN CT		15 PRINCES CT		
3 CALNE HO		3 AUCHINLECK HO		9 SWINDON HO				
4 PEWSEY HO		4 CUNNINGHAM HO		10 DEVIZES HO				
5 WESTBURY HO		5 MONTGOMERY HO		11 WARMINSTER HO				
		6 ALEXANDER HO		12 SALISBURY HO				
				13 TROWBRIDGE HO				

A338 Marlborough

Sidbury Hill Plantation

Gason Hill

Mill Path

Zouch Prim Sch

Chalkpit Hill

BOURNE VIEW

LUDGERSHALL RD

Clarendon Hill Plantation

Clarendon Hill

Clarendon Jun & Inf Schs

Mast

L Ctr
THE WHITE HO

Seven Barrows

Liby

Dunch Hill

St George's Cl

Hampshire Cross

Tidworth Camp

Hamilton Ct

SP9

PLANTATION RD

FURZE HILL RD

Clarendon Terr

THE MALL

BULFORD RD

DANGER AREA

CH

THE AVENUE

Tidworth House

Hare Warren

South Tidworth

Tidworth Park

Home Farm

HUMBER LA

Sports Ground

ARCOT RD

Milston Drove

The Belt

Sewage Works

Old Rectory

Ashdown Copse

South Park Lodge

The Cross Belt

TIDWORTH RD

SALISBURY RD

A338

PENNINGS RD

PARK RD

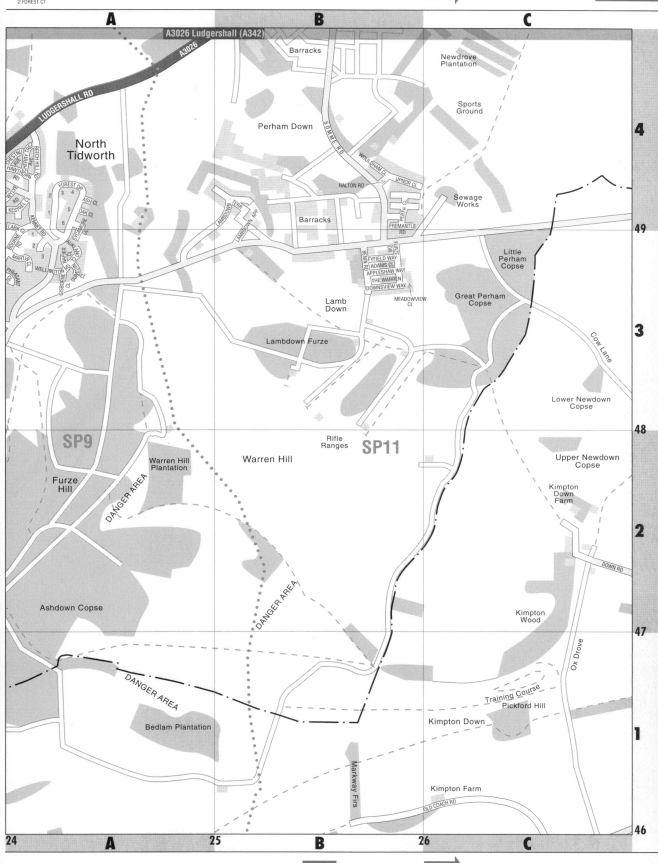

A3026 Ludgershall (A342)

LUDGERSHALL RD

A3026

North
Tidworth

Barracks

Perham Down

Newdrove
Plantation

Sports
Ground

SOMME RD

WOULDHAM CL

UPNOR CL

HALTON RD

Barracks

PERTH CL

Sewage
Works

FREMANTLE RD

LAMBDOWN TERR

LAMBDOWN APP

FURZE DR

BENIN RD

FYFIELD WAY
ADAMS CL
APPLESHAW WAY
THE WARREN
DOWNSVIEW WAY

MEADOWVIEW CL

Little
Perham
Copse

Lamb
Down

Great Perham
Copse

Lambdown Furze

Cow Lane

Lower Newdown
Copse

Rifle
Ranges

SP11

SP9

Warren Hill

Upper Newdown
Copse

Warren Hill
Plantation

Kimpton
Down
Farm

Furze
Hill

DANGER AREA

DANGER AREA

Kimpton
Wood

DOWN RD

Ashdown Copse

Ox Drove

DANGER AREA

Training Course

Pickford Hill

Bedlam Plantation

Kimpton Down

Markway Firs

Kimpton Farm

OLD COACH RD

CHESTNUT RD
BEECH HILL RD
CHERRY TREE
HAWTHORN RD
WYLYE RD
KESTREL CL
FOREST DR
ASH CL
OAK CL
KENNET RD
LARK CL
BOURNE RD
STICKLAND DR
PLUM LANE
GISBORNE RD
NAPIER CL
WELLINGTON
MARTIN
PHEASANT CL

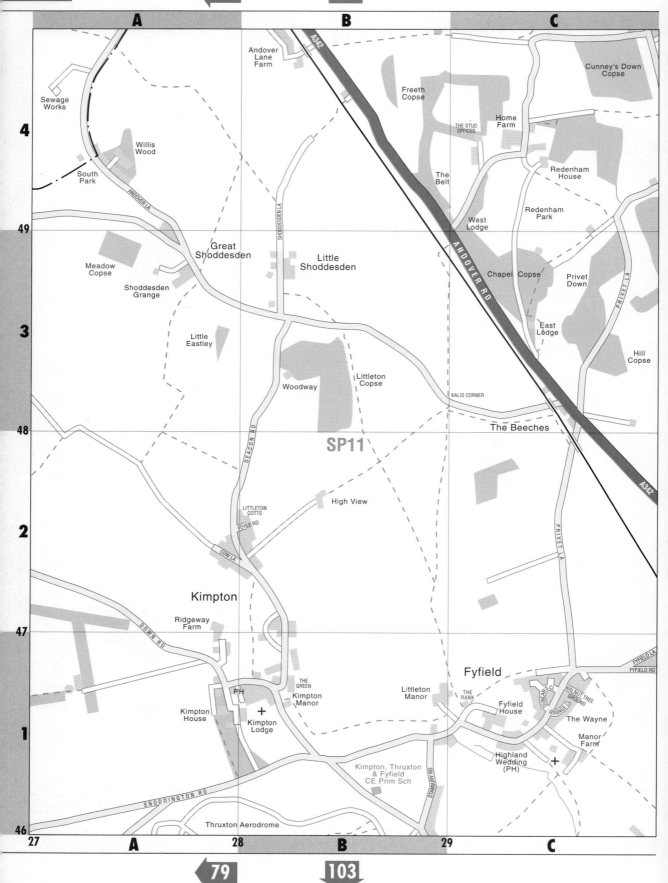

A   B   C

Sewage
Works

South
Park

ANDOVER LA

Willis
Wood

Meadow
Copse

Shoddesden
Grange

Great
Shoddesden

Little
Eastley

Andover
Lane
Farm

A342

SHODDESDEN LA

Little
Shoddesden

Woodway

Littleton
Copse

DEACON RD

SP11

LITTLETON
COTTS

FOYLE RD

High View

COW LA

Kimpton

Ridgeway
Farm

DOWN RD

Kimpton
House

PH

THE
GREEN

Kimpton
Manor

Kimpton
Lodge

Kimpton, Thruxton
& Fyfield
CE Prim Sch

STANBURY RD

SNODDINGTON RD

Thruxton Aerodrome

Freeth
Copse

THE STUD
OFFICES

The
Belt

West
Lodge

Home
Farm

Redenham
House

Redenham
Park

ANDOVER RD

Chapel Copse

East
Lodge

Privet
Down

Cunney's Down
Copse

PRIVET LA

Hill
Copse

KALIS CORNER

The Beeches

A342

PRIVET LA

Fyfield

Littleton
Manor

THE
RANK

DUNCANS CL

WALNUT TREE
GROUND

GRANGE CL

Fyfield
House

FYFIELD LA

FYFIELD RD

The Wayne

Manor
Farm

Highland
Wedding
(PH)

27   A   28   B   29   C

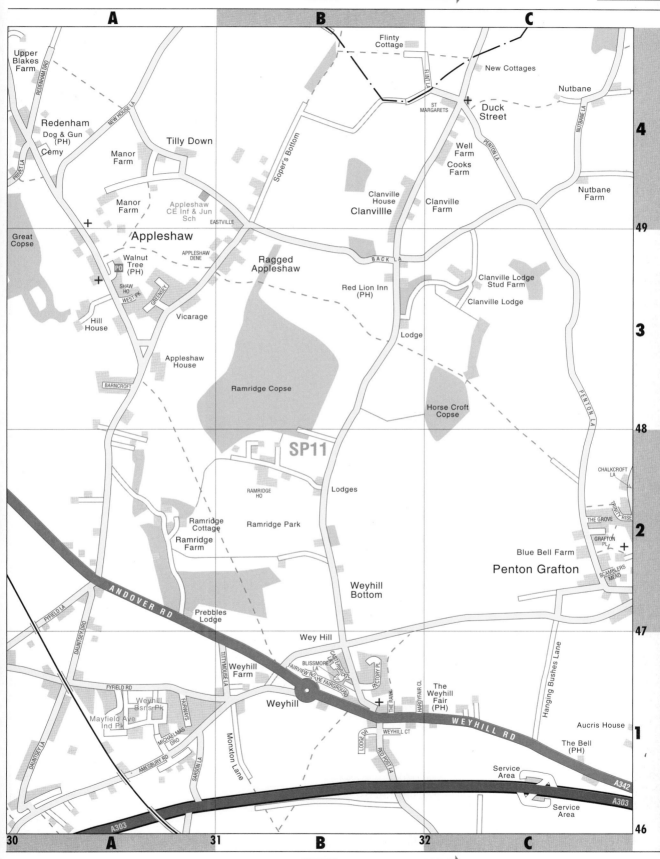

A   B   C

Upper Blakes Farm

REDENHAM DRO

NEW HOUSE LA

Redenham
Dog & Gun (PH)
Cemy

Manor Farm

Tilly Down

Flinty Cottage

FLINT LA

New Cottages

St Margarets

Nutbane

Duck Street

4

PRIORY LA

Manor Farm

Appleshaw CE Inf & Jun Sch

EASTVILLE

Soper's Bottom

Well Farm

Cooks Farm

PENTON LA

Nutbane Farm

NUTBANE LA

Great Copse

Appleshaw

APPLESHAW DENE

Clanville House

Clanville

Clanville Farm

49

Walnut Tree (PH)

PO

SHAW HO

WEST PK

GREENSLY

Ragged Appleshaw

BACK LA

Red Lion Inn (PH)

Clanville Lodge Stud Farm

Clanville Lodge

Hill House

Vicarage

Lodge

3

BARNCROFT

Appleshaw House

Ramridge Copse

Horse Croft Copse

PENTON LA

SP11

48

Ramridge HO

Lodges

CHALKCROFT LA

TRINITY RISE

THE GROVE

Ramridge Cottage

Ramridge Park

GRAFTON PL

2

Ramridge Farm

Blue Bell Farm

SCAMBLERS MEAD

Penton Grafton

ANDOVER RD

Prebbles Lodge

Weyhill Bottom

47

PYFIELD LA

DAUNTSEY DRO

TITTYMOUSE LA

Weyhill Farm

Wey Hill

FAIRVIEW RD

BLISSMORE LA

CASTOPROCK

THE FAIRGROUND

RECTORY PL

THE RANK

HARDYFAIR CL

The Weyhill Fair (PH)

HANGING BUSHES LANE

Aucris House

FYFIELD RD

FAIRWAYS

Weyhill Bsns Pk

Weyhill

Monxton Lane

WEYHILL RD

The Bell (PH)

1

Mayfield Ave Ind Pk

MICHAELMAS DRO

SARSON LA

LODGE DR

WEYHILL CT

REDPOST LA

Service Area

A342

DAUNTSEY LA

AMESBURY RD

Service Area

A303

A303

30   A   31   B   32   C

46

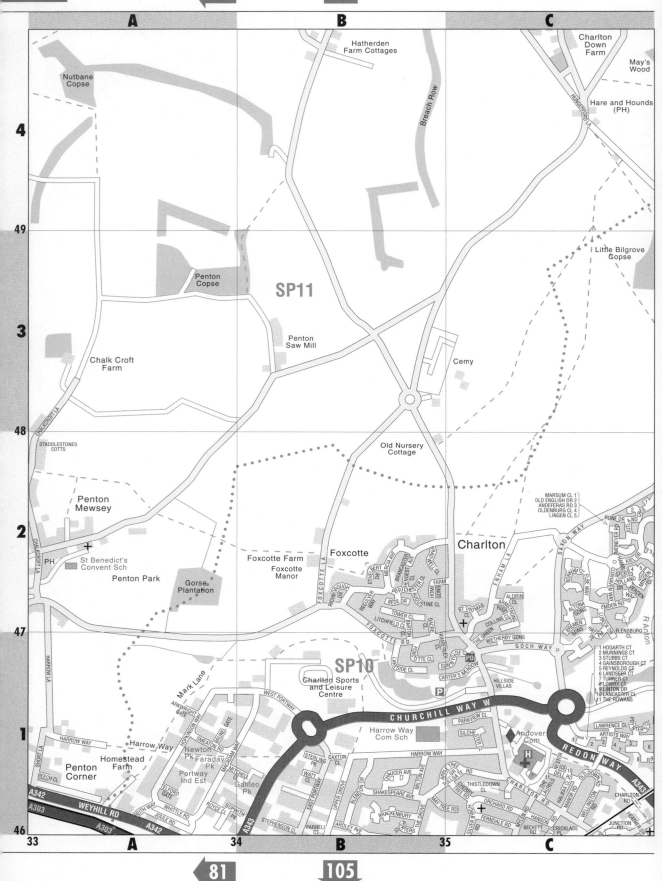

A   B   C

Nutbane
Copse

Hatherden
Farm Cottages

Charlton
Down
Farm

May's
Wood

Hare and Hounds
(PH)

4

Penton
Copse

SP11

Little Bilgrove
Copse

49

Chalk Croft
Farm

Penton
Saw Mill

Cemy

3

48

STADDLESTONES
COTTS

Old Nursery
Cottage

MARSUM CL 1
OLD ENGLISH DR 2
ANDEFERAS RD 3
OLDENBURG CL 4
LINGEN CL 5

Penton
Mewsey

Charlton

2

PH

St Benedict's
Convent Sch

Penton Park

Gorse
Plantation

Foxcotte Farm

Foxcotte Manor

Foxcotte

St Tho Mas

The Green

1 HOGARTH CT
2 MUNNINGS CT
3 STUBBS CT
4 GAINSBOROUGH CT
5 REYNOLDS CT
6 LANDSEER CT
7 TURNER CT
8 LOWRY CT
9 LINTON DR
10 LANCASTER CL
11 THE ROWANS

47

SP10

Charlton Sports
and Leisure
Centre

HILLSIDE
VILLAS

P

CHURCHILL WAY W

REDON WAY

1

Harrow Way

Harrow Way
Com Sch

Andover
Com

H

LAWRENCE CL
ARTISTS WAY

Penton
Corner

Homestead
Farm

Newton
Pk

Faraday
Pk

Portway
Ind Est

Galileo
Pk

CHARLTON RD

A342

WEYHILL RD

A303

A303   A342

A343

46

33   A   34   B   35   C

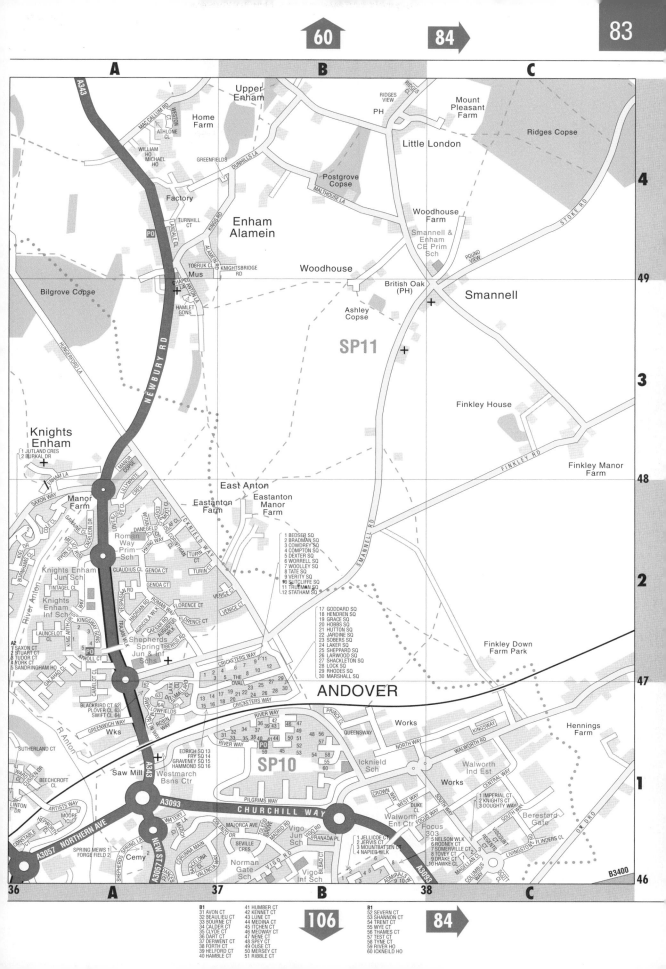

A B C

4

49

3

48

2

47

1

46

Upper Enham

Home Farm

WESTON RD
MAC CALLUM RD
ATHLONE CL
WILLIAM HO
MICHAEL HO
GREENFIELDS
DUNHILLS LA

Factory

TURNHILL CT
LANDALE CL
PO
KINGS RD
ALAMEIN RD

Enham Alamein

TOBRUK CL
Mus
KNIGHTSBRIDGE RD
CHAPEL
ASHTON LA
HAMLET GDNS
NEWBURY RD

Bilgrove Copse

HUNGERFORD LA

Postgrove Copse
MALTHOUSE LA

Little London

RIDGES VIEW
PH

Mount Pleasant Farm

Ridges Copse

STOKE RD

Woodhouse Farm

Smannell & Enham CE Prim Sch

Woodhouse

British Oak (PH)
POUND VIEW

Smannell

Ashley Copse

SP11

Finkley House

FINKLEY RD

Finkley Manor Farm

Knights Enham
1 JUTLAND CRES
2 BURKAL DR
ENHAM LA

MANOR COPSE

East Anton

Eastanton Farm

Eastanton Manor Farm

SMANNELL RD

Manor Farm
SAXON WAY
COL CL
GAVIMER CL
CHERLEON DR
LOVEDEAN CL
LILLYWHITE CRES
Roman Way Prim Sch
WITAN RD
EDGBY CL
OLAF CL
CORINTHIAN
ICKNIELD WAY
TURIN
TURIN

KIEL DR
RYON CL
MELFORT RISE
VIKING WAY
DANEGELD
KING WAY
GENOA CT
GENOA CT

BURNHAMS RD
River Anton
Knights Enham Jun Sch
TINTAGEL CL
Knights Enham Inf Sch
CLAUDIUS CL
HADRIAN RD
ROMAN WAY
VESPASIAN RD
AGRICOLA WLK
CAESAR RD
AUGUSTUS RD
FLORENCE CT
FLORENCE CT
VENICE CT
VENICE CT

1 BEDSER SQ
2 BRADMAN SQ
3 COWDREY SQ
4 COMPTON SQ
5 DEXTER SQ
6 WORRELL SQ
7 WOOLLEY SQ
8 TATE SQ
9 VERITY SQ
10 SUTCLIFFE SQ
11 TRUEMAN SQ
12 STATHAM SQ

17 GODDARD SQ
18 HENDREN SQ
19 GRACE SQ
20 HOBBS SQ
21 HUTTON SQ
22 JARDINE SQ
23 SOBERS SQ
24 LAKER SQ
25 SHEPPARD SQ
26 LARWOOD SQ
27 SHACKLETON SQ
28 LOCK SQ
29 RHODES SQ
30 MARSHALL SQ

LAUNCELOT CL
A2
1 SAXON CT
2 STUART CT
3 TUDOR CT
4 YORK CT
5 SANDRINGHAM HO
KINGSWAY GDNS
KING ARTHUR
ATHOLL CT
PO
Shepherds Spring Jun & Inf Schs
TIBERIUS RD
TRAJAN WLK

CRICKETERS WAY
6
7 9 11
8 10 12
5
3 THE OVAL
4
25
21 22 23 24
20
26
27 28 29
30
CRICKETERS WAY

ANDOVER

Finkley Down Farm Park

CAMELET CL
GALAHAD CL
BLACKBIRD CT 62
PLOVER CL 63
SWIFT CL 64
MALLARD
LARK
DOVE
SWAN
MARTIN WAY
LOWFIELDS
ROBIN WAY
62
63
64
13 14 15 16
17 18 19
GREENWICH WAY
Wks
R Anton

RIVER WAY
32 34 37 39 43
31 33 35 38 40 41 44
36 42 46 47
48 49 50 51
45 52 53
PO
59

SUTHERLAND CT
EDRICH SQ 13
FRY SQ 14
GRAVENEY SQ 15
HAMMOND SQ 16
Saw Mill
A3343
Westmarch Bsns Ctr

SP10

RIVER WAY
54 55 56 57 58 60

Works

PRINCE CL
QUEENSWAY
NORTH WAY
Icknield Sch

Works
WALWORTH RD
KINGSWAY
CENTRAL WAY
Walworth Ind Est

Hennings Farm

LINTON DR
BEECHCROFT CL
WARDLE ROW
CHICHESTER CL
ARTISTS WAY
MOORE CL
HEPWORTH CL
CONSTABLE CL
A3057 NORTHERN AVE
W41 ERY LA
A3343
A3093
Walworth Ent Ctr
CROWN WAY
WEST WAY
DUKE CL
SOUTH WAY
Focus 303
1 IMPERIAL CT
2 KNIGHTS CT
3 DOUGHTY WAY
VISCOUNT
SOUTH WAY
REGENTS
Beresford Gate
LIVINGSTONE CT
OX DRO
MAGELLAN CT
COLUMBUS WAY

PILGRIMS WAY
CHURCHILL WAY
MAJORCA AVE
COLENZO DR
TOLEDO CL
MARCH CL
VIGO RD
BILBAO CT
GRANADA PL
1 JELLICOE CT
2 JERVIS CT
3 MOUNTBATTEN CT
4 NAPIER WLK
ADMIRALS WAY
A3093
5 NELSON WLK
6 RODNEY CT
7 SOMERVILLE CT
8 TOVEY CT
9 DRAKE CT
10 HAWKE CL
FLINDERS CL

SPRING MEWS 1
FORGE FIELD 2
NEW STREET
A3057
Cemy
SHEPHERDS SPRING LA
CORUNNA MAIN
BARCELONA CL
VALENCIA CL
SEVILLE CRES
Norman Gate Sch
Vigo Jun Sch
Vigo Inf Sch
VIGO RD

B3400

B1		
31 AVON CT	41 HUMBER CT	52 SEVERN CT
32 BEAULIEU CT	42 KENNET CT	53 SHANNON CT
33 BOURNE CT	43 LUNE CT	54 TRENT CT
34 CALDER CT	44 MEDINA CT	55 WYE CT
35 CLYDE CT	45 ITCHEN CT	56 THAMES CT
36 DART CT	46 MEDWAY CT	57 TEST CT
37 DERWENT CT	47 NENE CT	58 TYNE CT
38 FORTH CT	48 SPEY CT	59 RIVER HO
39 HELFORD CT	49 OUSE CT	60 ICKNIELD HO
40 HAMBLE CT	50 MERSEY CT	
	51 RIBBLE CT	

B1
52 SEVERN CT
53 SHANNON CT
54 TRENT CT
55 WYE CT
56 THAMES CT
57 TEST CT
58 TYNE CT
59 RIVER HO
60 ICKNIELD HO

83
61

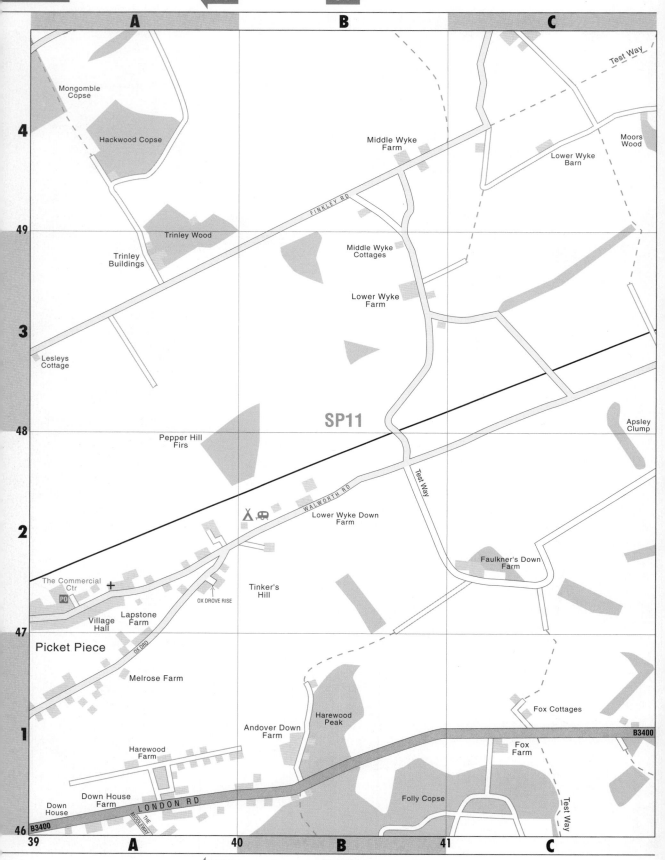

83
107

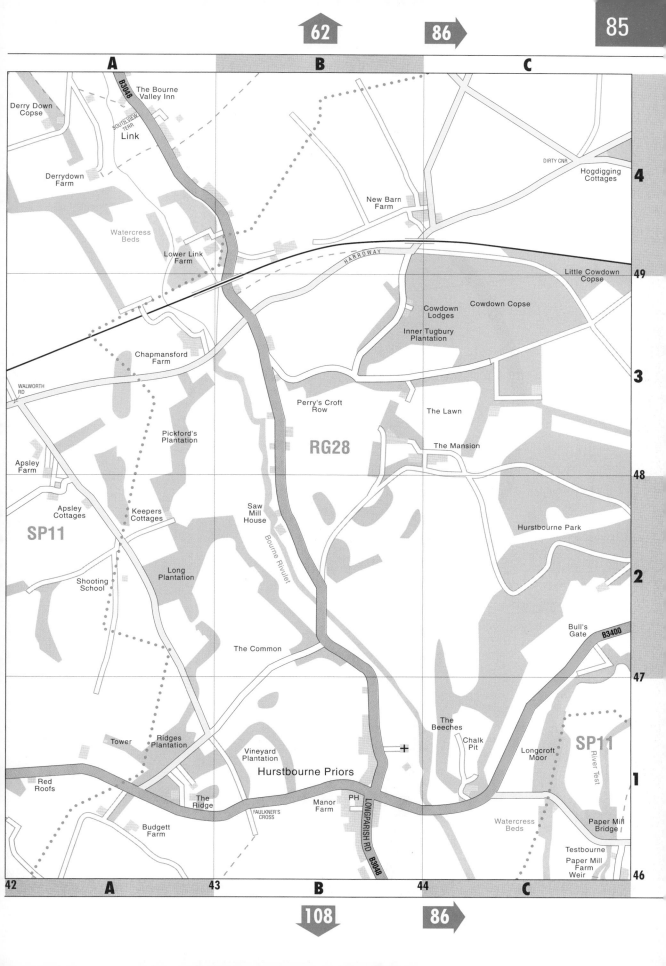

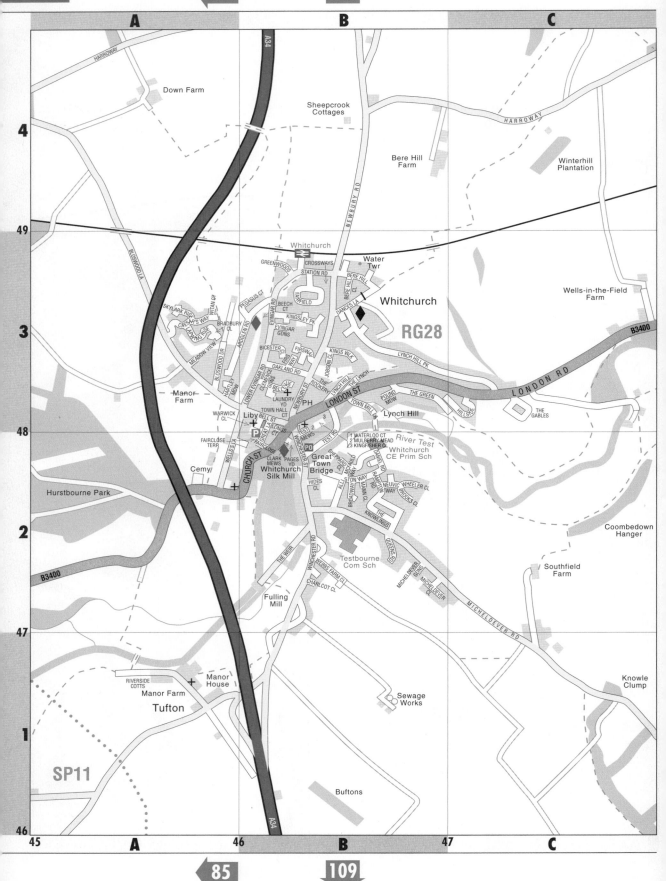

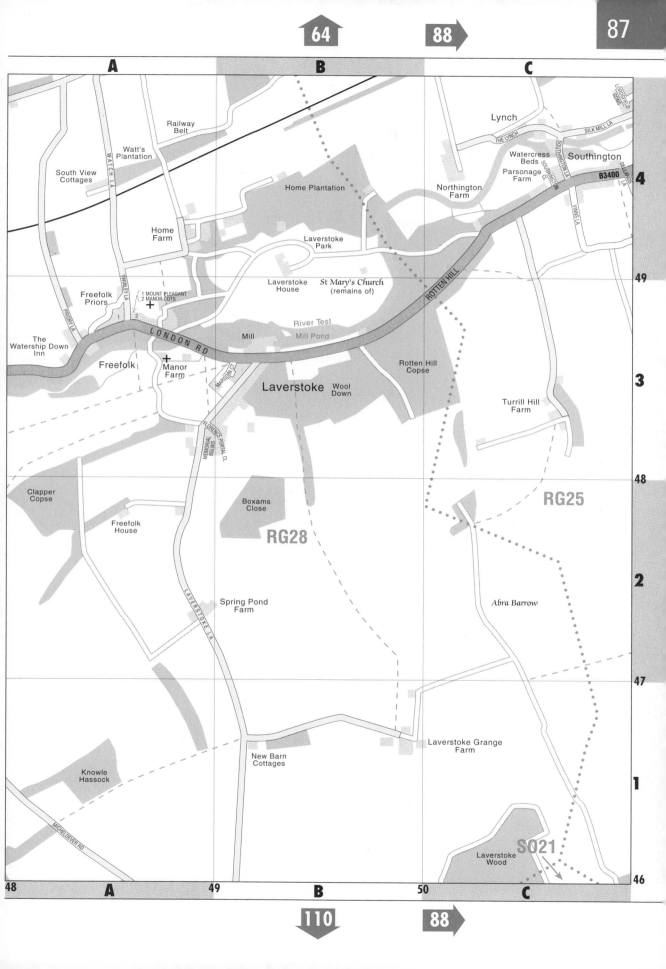

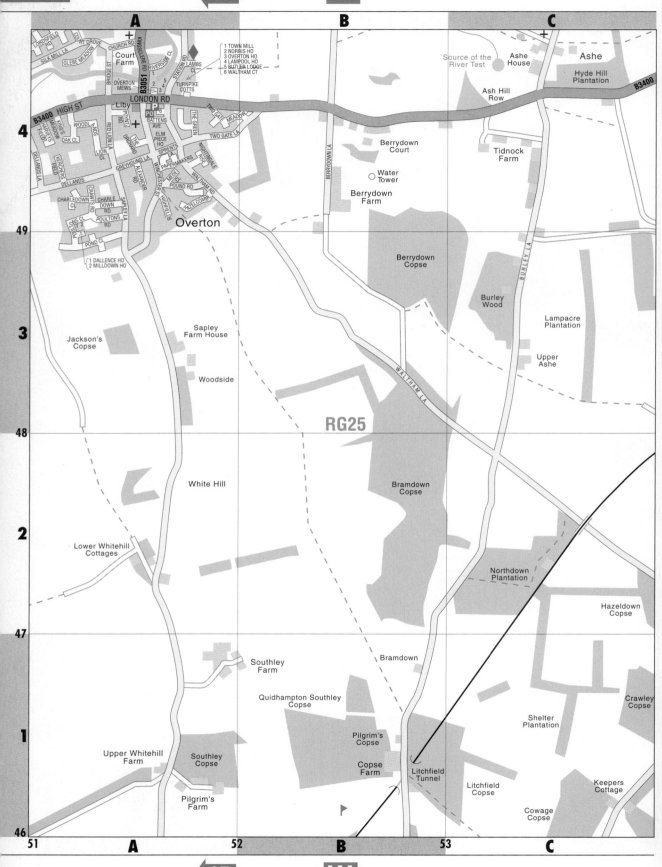

1 TOWN MILL
2 NORRIS HO
3 OVERTON HO
4 LAMPOOL HO
5 BUTLER LODGE
6 WALTHAM CT

Source of the
River Test

Ashe House

Ashe

Hyde Hill
Plantation

B3400

Ash Hill
Row

Tidnock
Farm

Berrydown
Court

Water
Tower

Berrydown
Farm

Burley
Wood

Burley La

Lampacre
Plantation

Upper
Ashe

Berrydown La

Court Farm

Overton
Mews

B3051

Liby

London Rd

Two Gate Meadow

Two Gate La

The Green

Turnpike
Cotts

Station Rd

Lambs
Cl

B3400 High St

Kingsclere Rd

Church Rd

Silk Mill La

Glebe Meadow

Lordsfield
Cott

Bridge St

Riverside Cl

Battens
Ave

Elm
Piece
Ho

Sprents

Nightingale
Rise

Paperhamkers

Woodl

King's
Meadow

Harry's
Field

Oak Cl

Red Lion La

Lion
Cl

The Orchard

Pywitz
Rd

Alexander

Greyhound La

Winchester Highfields

Waltham Rd

Pound Rd

Hatelcomb

Delllands La

Kerchers
Field

Charledown
Cl

Crawls
Rd

Charle
Down
Rd

Poultons
Rd

Sapley
La

SMS Cl

Pond Cl

Delllands

Overton

1 DALLENCE HO
2 MILLDOWN HO

Berrydown
Copse

49

Jackson's
Copse

Sapley
Farm House

Woodside

3

RG25

Waltham La

48

White Hill

Bramdown
Copse

Lower Whitehill
Cottages

2

Northdown
Plantation

Hazeldown
Copse

47

Southley
Farm

Bramdown

Quidhampton Southley
Copse

Crawley
Copse

Pilgrim's
Copse

Shelter
Plantation

1

Copse
Farm

Litchfield
Tunnel

Litchfield
Copse

Keepers
Cottage

Upper Whitehill
Farm

Southley
Copse

Pilgrim's
Farm

Cowage
Copse

46

51

A

52

B

53

C

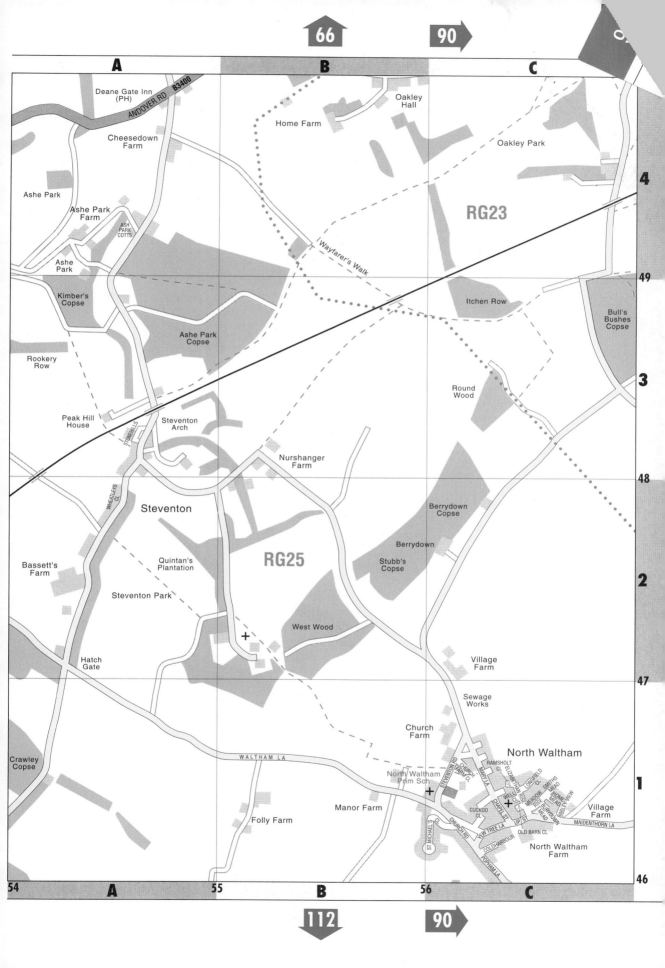

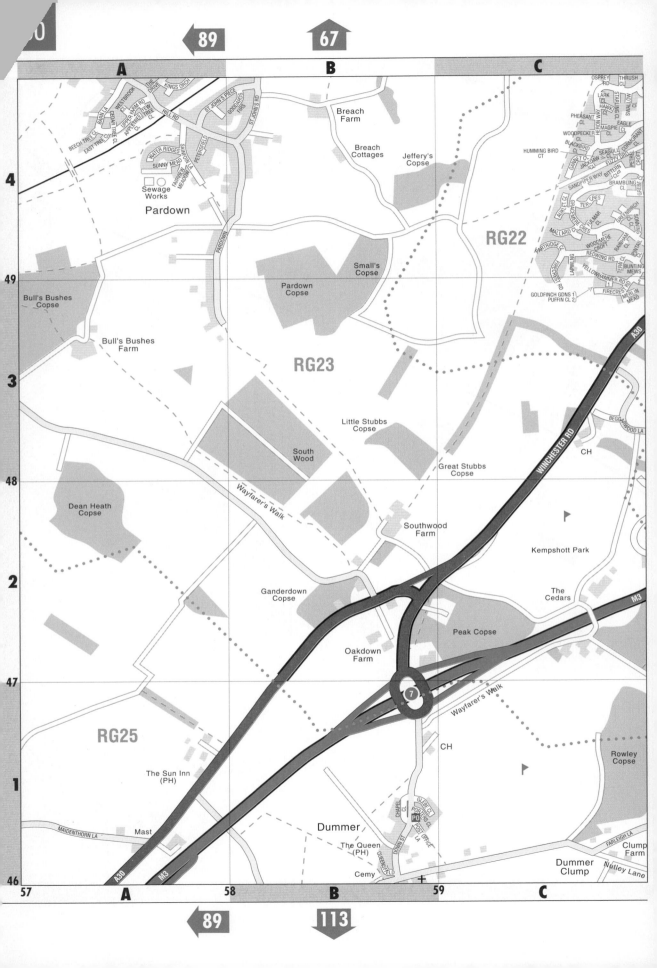

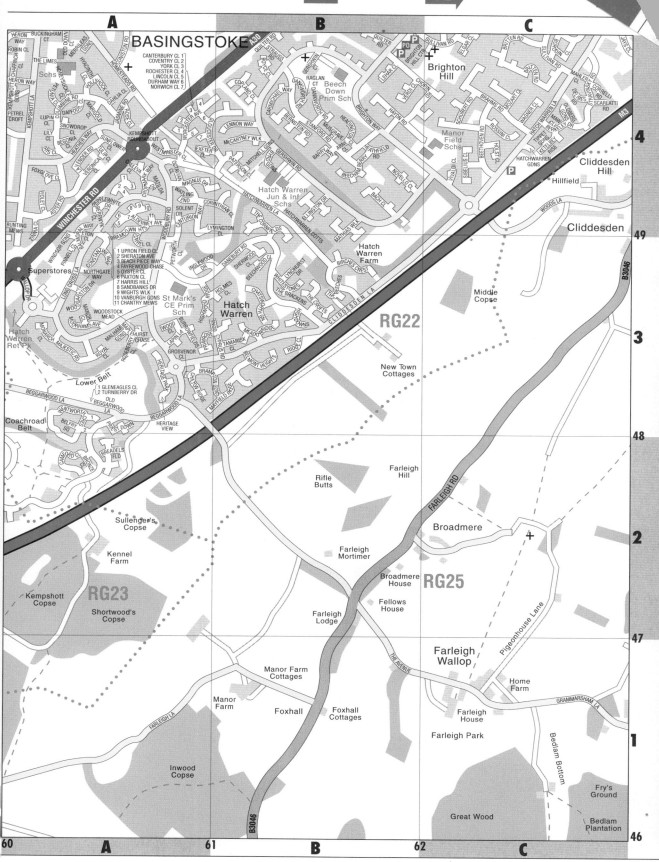

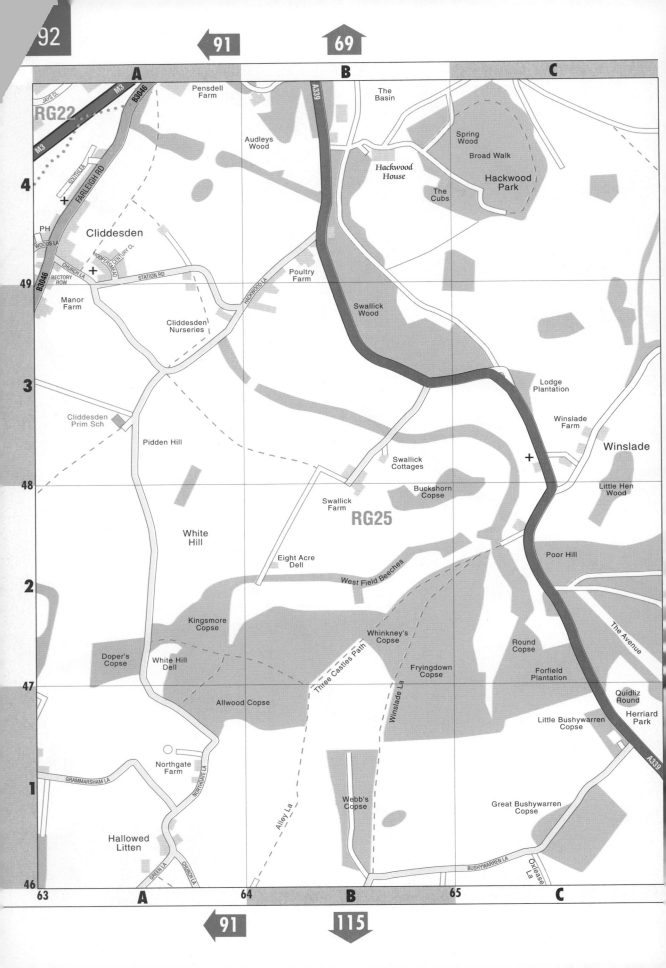

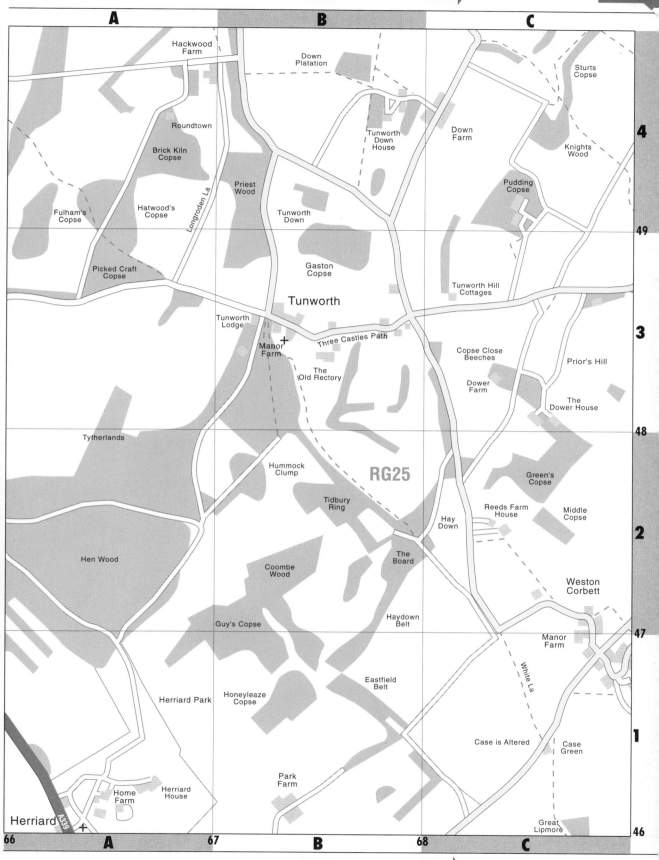

A   **B**   **C**

Three Castles Path

Three Castles
Path

Upton Grey Rd

Four Lanes
End

Bidden
Water

Ford
Farm

FORD LA

Bidden Grange
Farm

BIDDEN RD

Lower Bidden
Farm

Dean
Plantation

4

Bidden

GASTON LA

RG25

Gaston
Copse

49

Cleves
Farm

CLEVES LA

Upton Grey
House

THE ARBORETUM

Manor
Farm

WOODMANFIELD

Little Dean
Farm

LITTLE DEAN LA

3

CEMETERY LA

Upton
Grey

+

LITTLE HODDINGTON

Little
Hoddington

The Hoddington
Arms
(PH)

PO

SOUTH HILL

WESTON CL

The Village
Farm

UMBREY HILL

Tile Barn
Farm

48

WESTON RD

Weston
Mark

Hoddington Park

HODDINGTON
COTTS

*Hoddington
House*

THE OLD ORCHARD 1
NASH MEADOWS 2

Lee's
Farm

1
2

Hoddington
Farm

Dean Farm
House

LEES HILL

2

Weston Patrick
House

RG29

CHURCH VIEW

47

Manor
Farm

+

Weston Patrick

Dean
Copse

ALTON ROAD
COTTS

B3349

Hoddington

Privett
Copse

Westers Lane

1

Wood Lane
End

Little Park
Copse

Long La

B3349

PACKSE LA

46

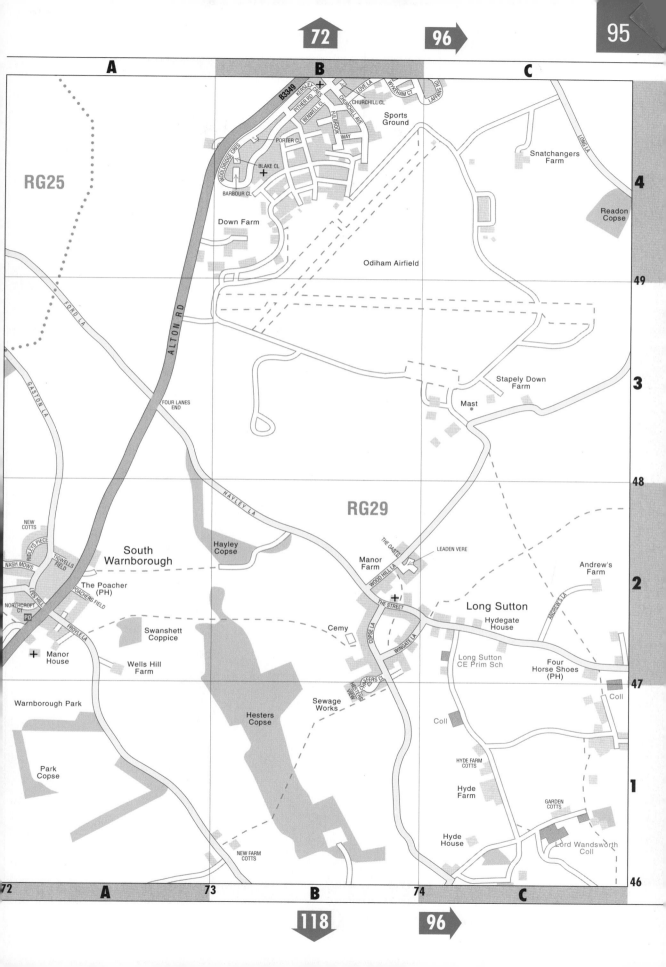

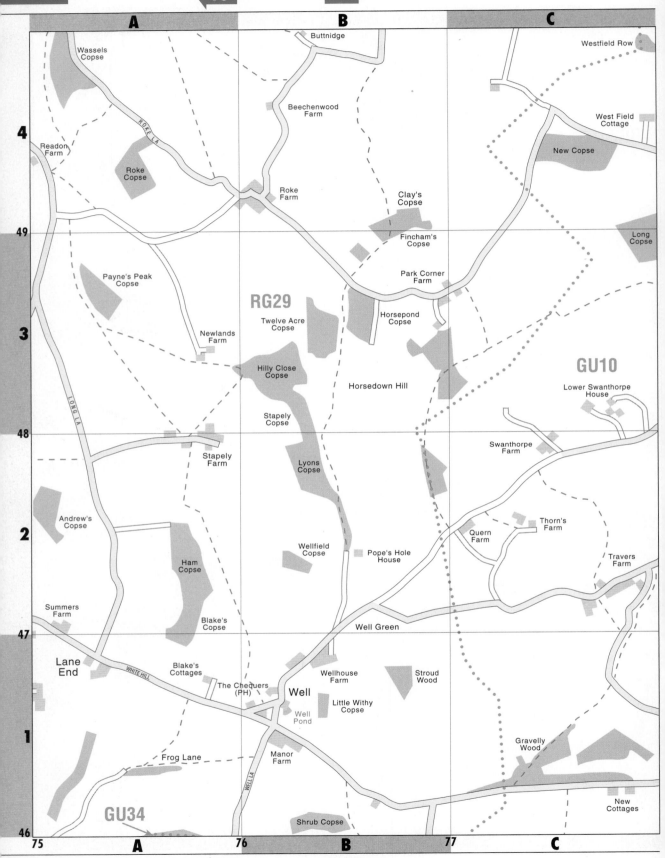

A B C

Buttnidge

Wassels
Copse

Beechenwood
Farm

Westfield Row

West Field
Cottage

4

ROKE LA

Readon
Farm

Roke
Copse

Roke
Farm

Clay's
Copse

New Copse

Fincham's
Copse

Long
Copse

49

Payne's Peak
Copse

Park Corner
Farm

RG29

Twelve Acre
Copse

Horsepond
Copse

GU10

Newlands
Farm

Lower Swanthorpe
House

3

LONG LA

Hilly Close
Copse

Horsedown Hill

Stapely
Copse

Swanthorpe
Farm

48

Stapely
Farm

Lyons
Copse

Andrew's
Copse

Thorn's
Farm

Quern
Farm

Travers
Farm

2

Ham
Copse

Wellfield
Copse

Pope's Hole
House

Summers
Farm

Blake's
Copse

Well Green

47

Lane
End

WHITE HILL

Blake's
Cottages

The Chequers
(PH)

Well

Wellhouse
Farm

Stroud
Wood

Gravelly
Wood

1

Little Withy
Copse

Well
Pond

WELL LA

Frog Lane

Manor
Farm

GU34

New
Cottages

46

Shrub Copse

75 A 76 B 77 C

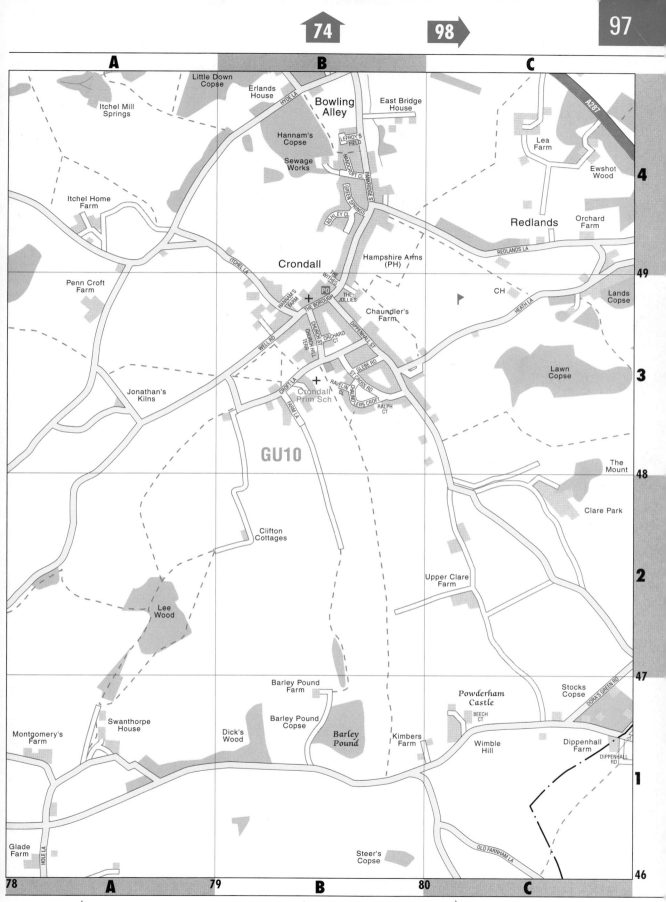

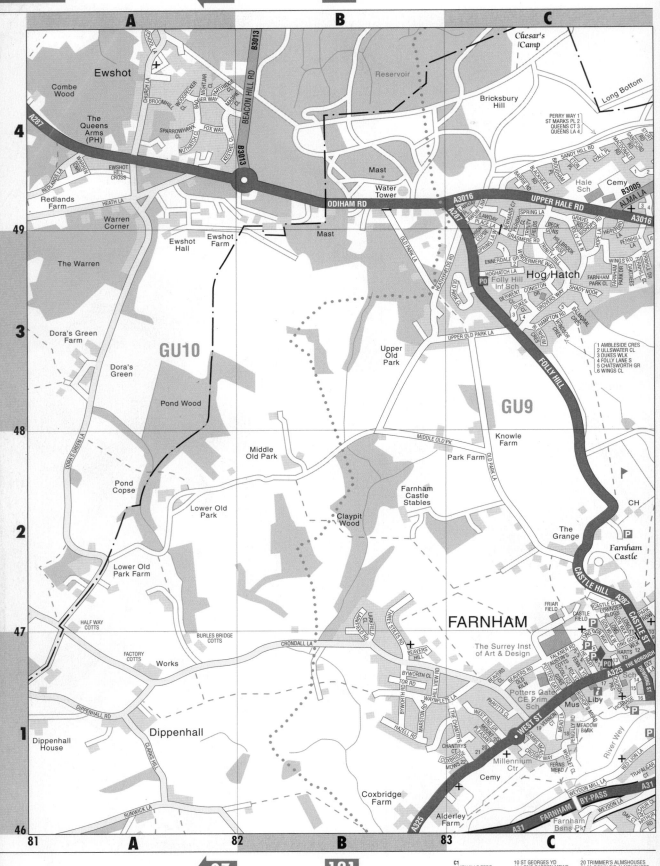

C1
1 MELVILLE TERR
2 LOVETT HO
3 WESTMEAD
4 COBBETTS MEWS
5 LION AND LAMB WAY
6 TIMBER CL
7 CRAVEN HO
8 ARUNDELL PL
9 THE MEWS
10 ST GEORGES YD
11 LONG GARDEN MEWS
12 OLD KILN COURTYARD
13 LION AND LAMB YD
14 UPPER CHURCH LA
15 MIDDLE CHURCH LA
16 LOWER CHURCH LA
17 WEAVERS YD
18 BROOKMEAD CT
19 OLD TOWN MEWS
20 TRIMMER'S ALMSHOUSES
21 McDONALD'S ALMSHOUSES
22 SAMPSON'S ALMSHOUSES

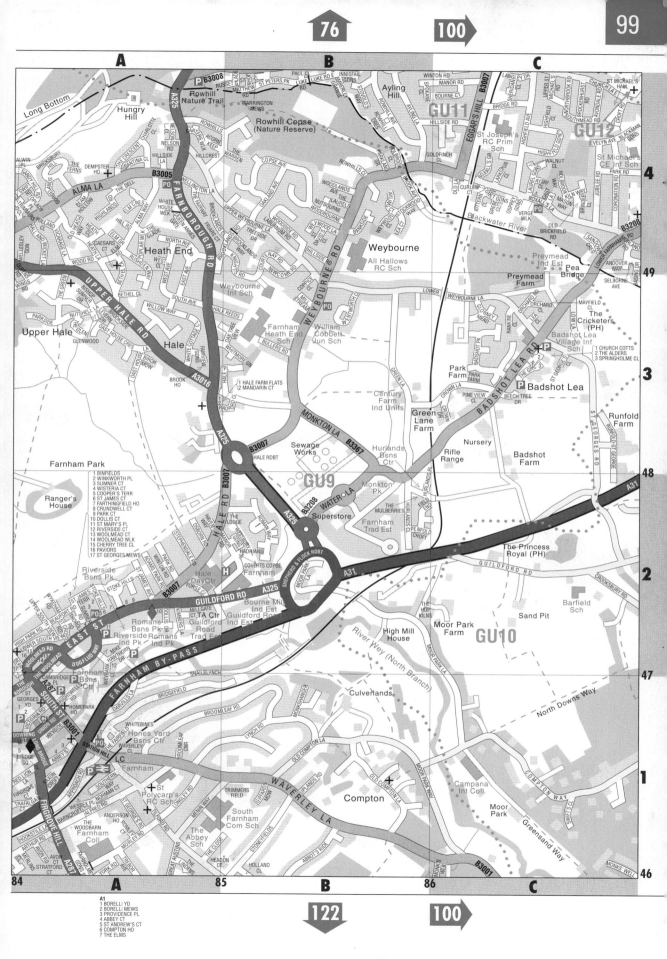

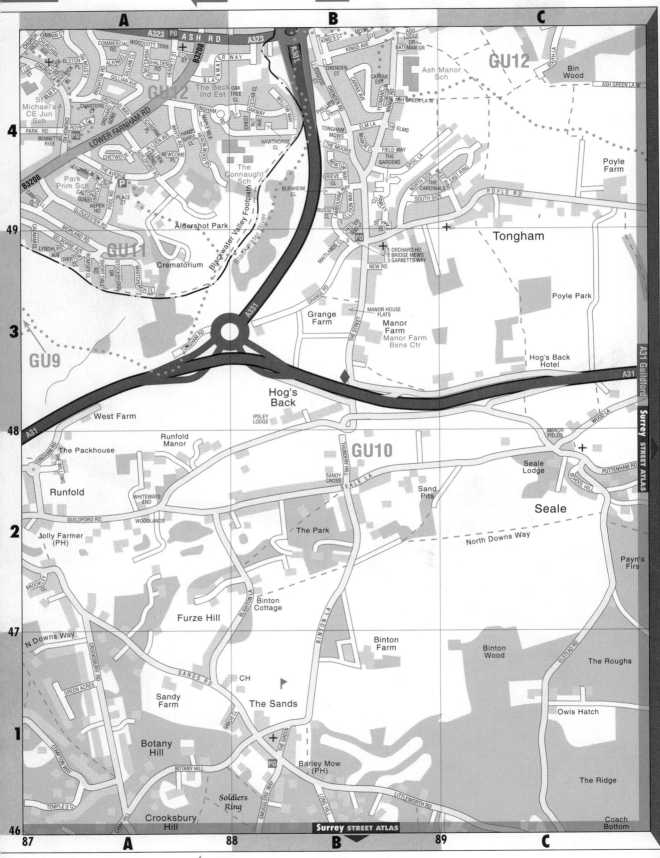

A B C

CHURCH
HILL
IMRAN CT
LEE
CHURCH CL
ELSTON
CHURCHILL AVE
COMMERCIAL RD
WOODCOTT TERR
PO
A323
ASH RD
A323
B3208
A331
KING'S CT
MOOR
ASH LODGE DR
BATEMAN GR

GU12

Bin Wood

4

St Michael's CE Jun Sch
Park RD
PO
GU12
LOWER FARNHAM RD
The Beck Ind Est
OAK TREE CL
CEDAR CL
WILLOW WAY
Tongham RD
HAWTHORNE CL
The Connaught Sch
OXENDEN CT
CARFAX AVE
CARFAX EST
MANOR RD
ASH GREEN LA W
Ash Manor Sch
ASH GREEN LA W
Poyle Farm

Park Prim Sch
P
The Avenue
GEORGE GDNS
CHETWODE
GUILDFORD RD
BLENHEIM CL
NEWTON WAY
GRIEVE CL
LAMBOURNE WAY
TONGHAM MDWS
ELM LA
THE ELMS
FIELD WAY
THE GARDENS
SPOIL LA
NORTH SIDE
WEST RING
EAST RING
THE CARDINALS
SOUTH SIDE
POYLE RD

49

Aldershot Park
Blackwater Valley Footpath
Blackwater River
RUSSET CL
CHESTER WAY
ST PAUL'S
PINKLEY
1 ORCHARD HO
2 BRIDGE MEWS
3 GARBETTS WAY
PO
NEW RD
Tongham
Poyle Park

GU11
Crematorium
MAITLANDS CL
GRANGE RD
Grange Farm
MANOR HOUSE FLATS
THE STREET
Manor Farm
Manor Farm Bsns Ctr
Hog's Back Hotel

3

GU9
TONGHAM RD
A331

West Farm
IPSLEY LODGE
Hog's Back
A31
A31 Guildford
Surrey STREET ATLAS

48

A31
TONGHAM RD
The Packhouse
The Willows
Runfold Manor
CEDAR LA
THUNDERY HILL
GU10
SANDY CROSS
SEALE LA
Sand Pits
MANOR FIELDS
WOOD LA
Seale Lodge
PUTTENHAM RD
SCHOOL HILL

2

Jolly Farmer (PH)
Runfold
GUILDFORD RD
WHITEWAYS END
WOODLANDS
The Park
North Downs Way
Seale
Payn's Firs

BROOKLEY CL
BLIGHTON LA
Binton Cottage
BINTON LA
Binton Farm
Binton Wood
ELSTEAD RD
The Roughs

47

N Downs Way
CROOKSBURY RD
SANDS RD
CH
Furze Hill
GREEN ACRES
Sandy Farm
SANDS DR
The Sands
THE GREEN
Owls Hatch

1

COMPTON WAY
Botany Hill
BOTANY HILL
PO
Barley Mow (PH)
LITTLEWORTH RD
The Ridge

TEMPLE'S CL
CAMP HILL
Crooksbury Hill
Soldiers Ring
SMUGGLERS WAY
LONG HILL
Coach Bottom

46

87 A 88 B 89 C

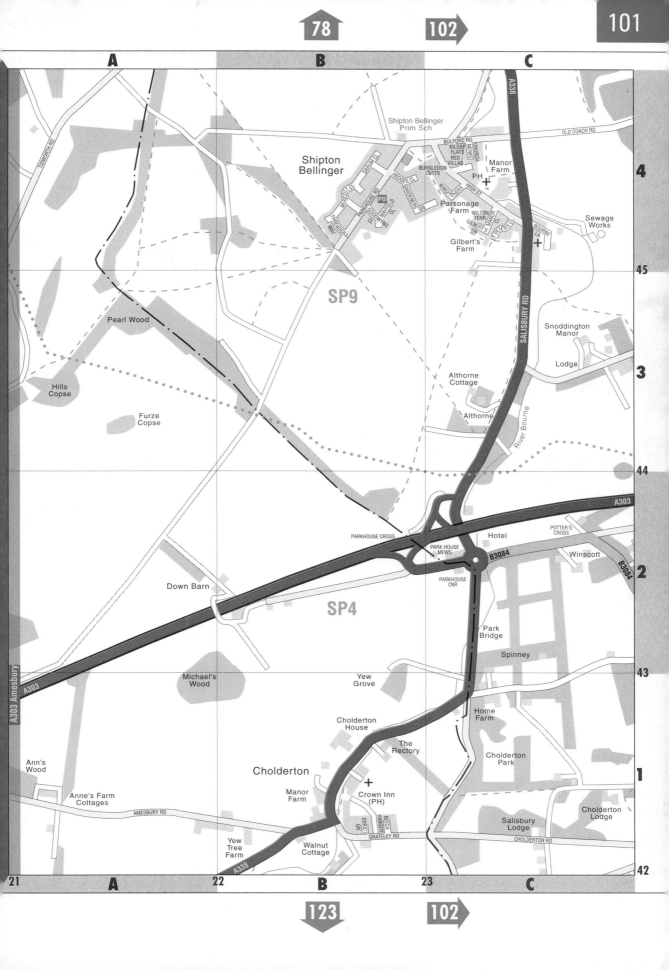

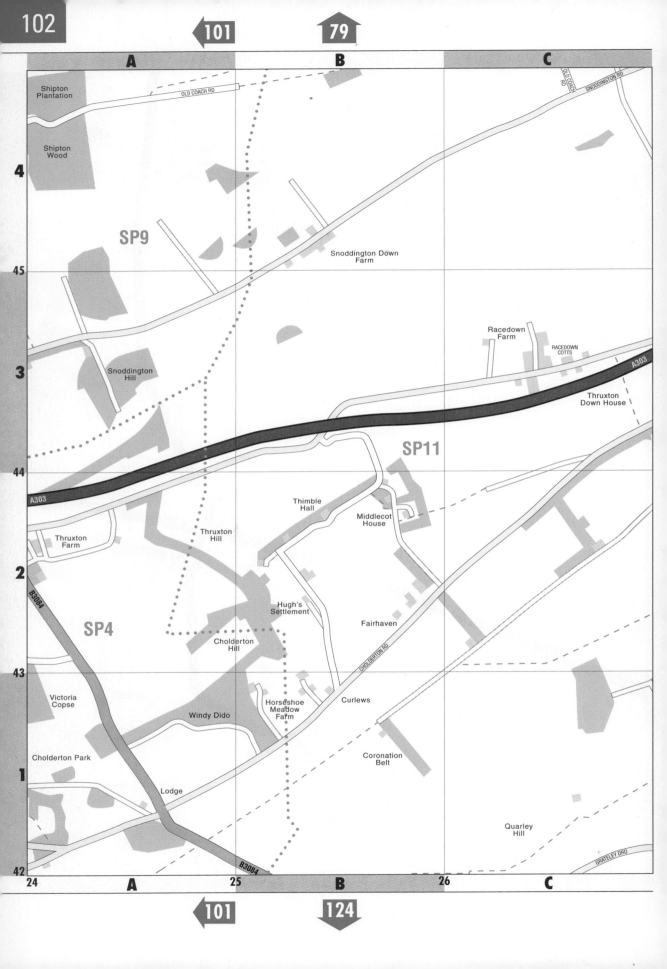

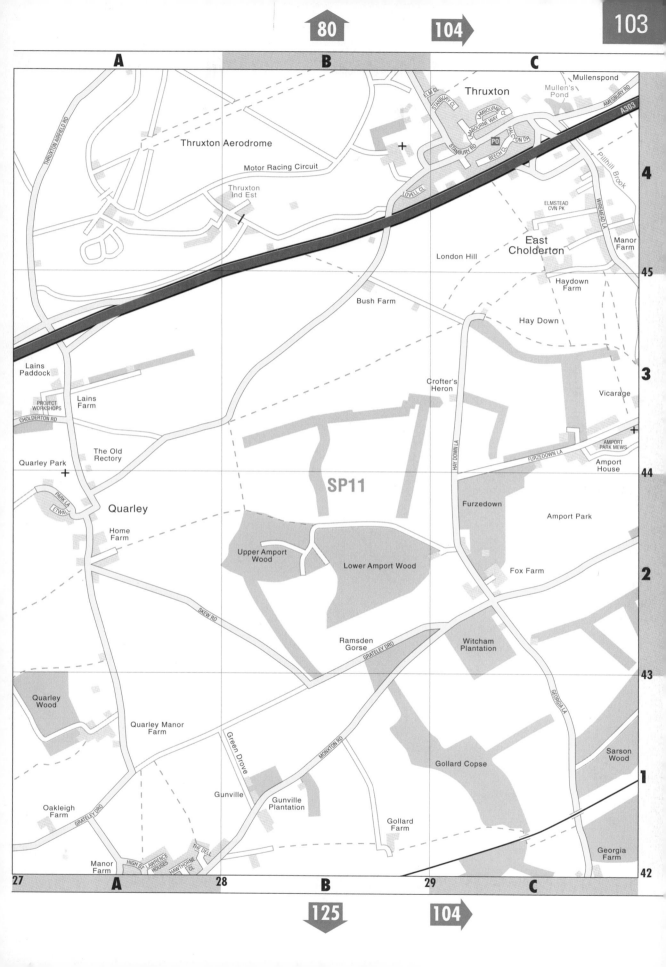

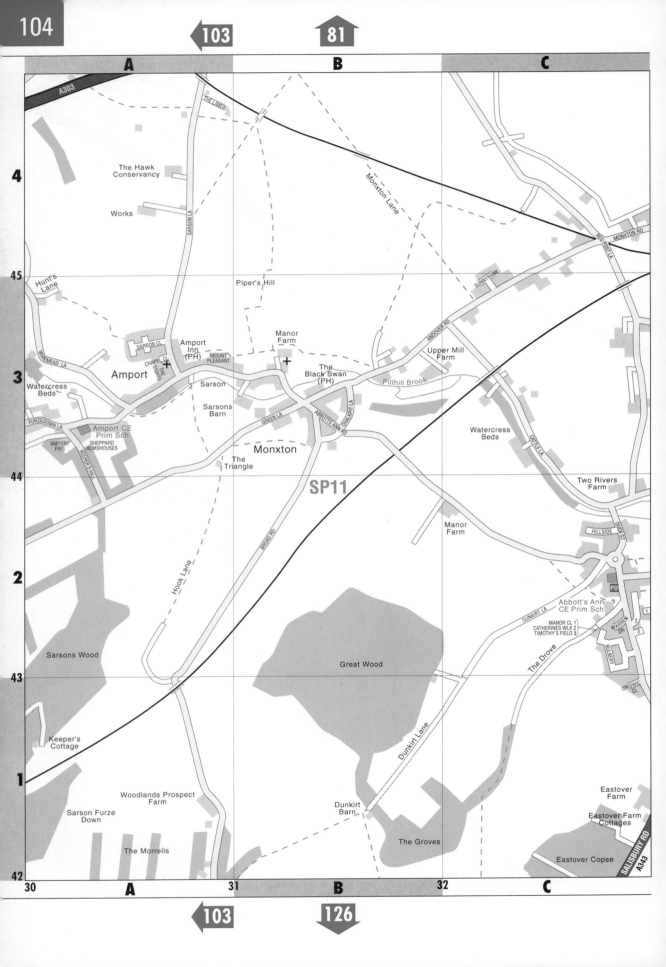

A   **B**   **C**

A303

THE LIMES

4

The Hawk
Conservancy

Monxton Lane

Works

MONXTON RD

RED POST LA

45

Hunt's
Lane

SARSON LA

Piper's Hill

SUNNYBANK

WREMEAD LA

SARSON CL

CHAPEL CL

Amport
Inn
(PH)

MOUNT
PLEASANT

Manor
Farm

ANDOVER RD

Upper Mill
Farm

3

Amport

THE EIGHTS

Sarson

The Black
Swan
(PH)

Pillhill Brook

Watercress
Beds

FURZEDOWN LA

Sarsons
Barn

GREEN LA

ABBOTTS ANN RD

CHALKPIT LA

Watercress
Beds

CATTLE LA

AMPORT
FIRS

KEEPER'S HIL

Amport CE
Prim Sch

SHEPPARD
ALMSHOUSES

Monxton

The
Triangle

Two Rivers
Farm

44

SP11

HILLSIDE

DUCK ST

Manor
Farm

Hook Lane

BROAD RD

2

PO

Abbott's Ann
CE Prim Sch

DUNKIRT LA

WARREN DR

MANOR CL 1
CATHERINES WLK 2
TIMOTHY'S FIELD 3

BILBERY

Sarsons Wood

Great Wood

The Drove

CRISWIC
CL

43

Dunkirt Lane

Keeper's
Cottage

1

Woodlands Prospect
Farm

Dunkirt Barn

Eastover
Farm

Sarson Furze
Down

Eastover Farm
Cottages

SALISBURY RD

The Morrells

The Groves

Eastover Copse

A343

42

30   **A**   **31**   **B**   **32**   **C**

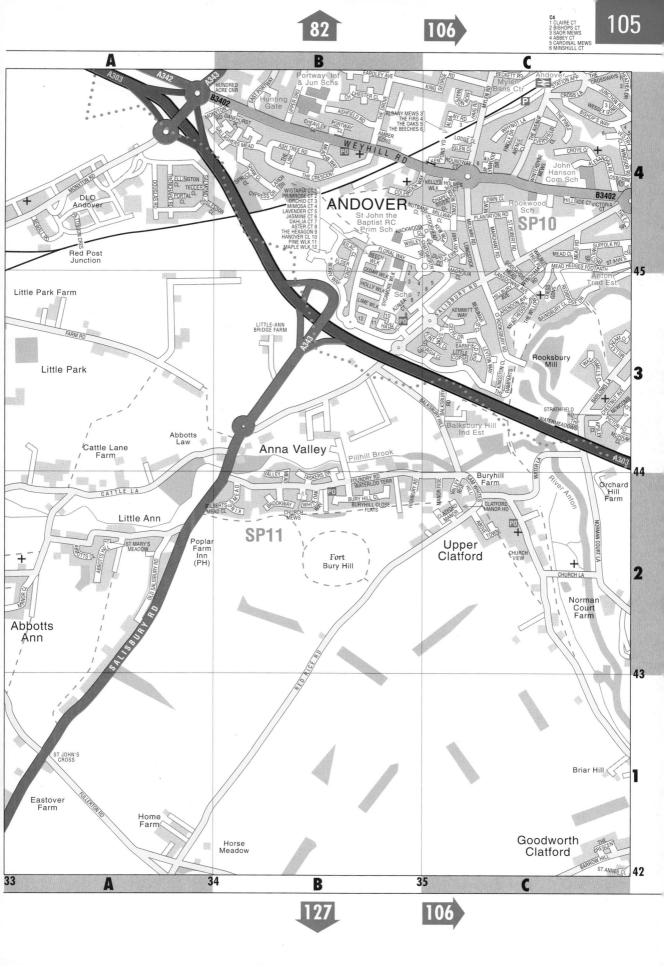

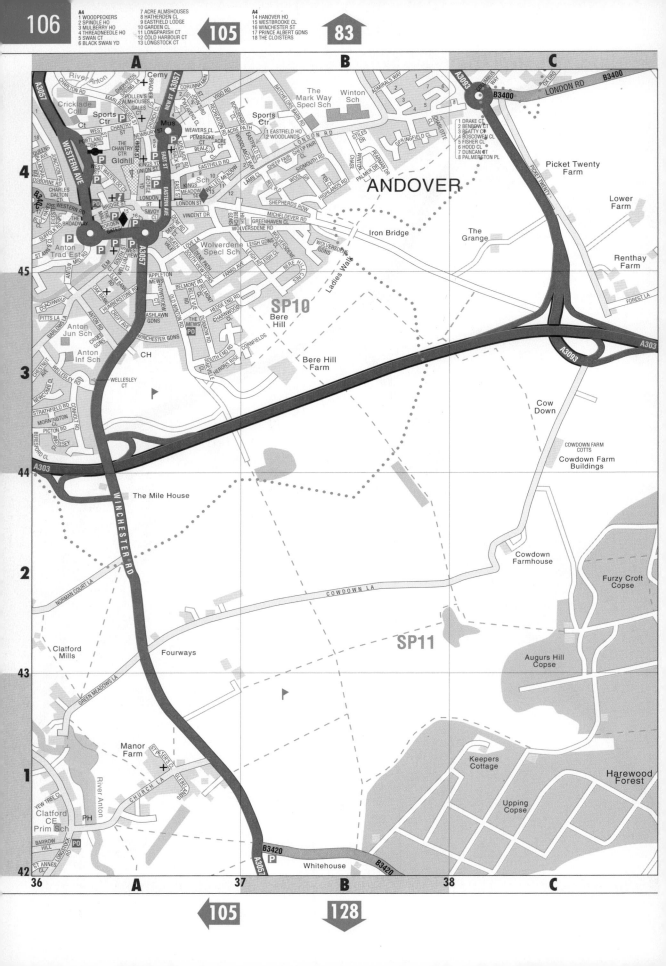

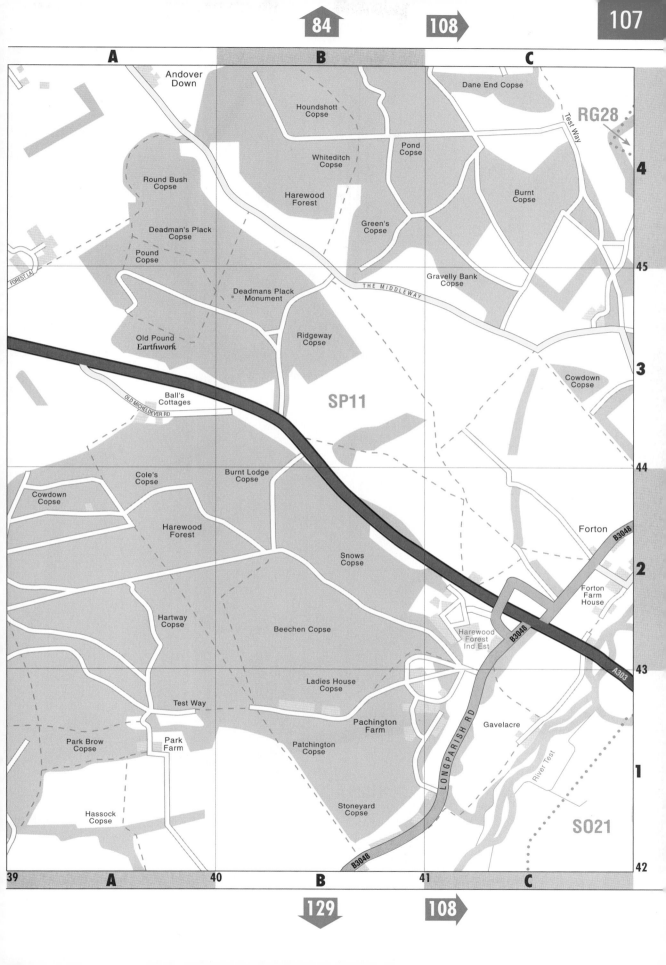

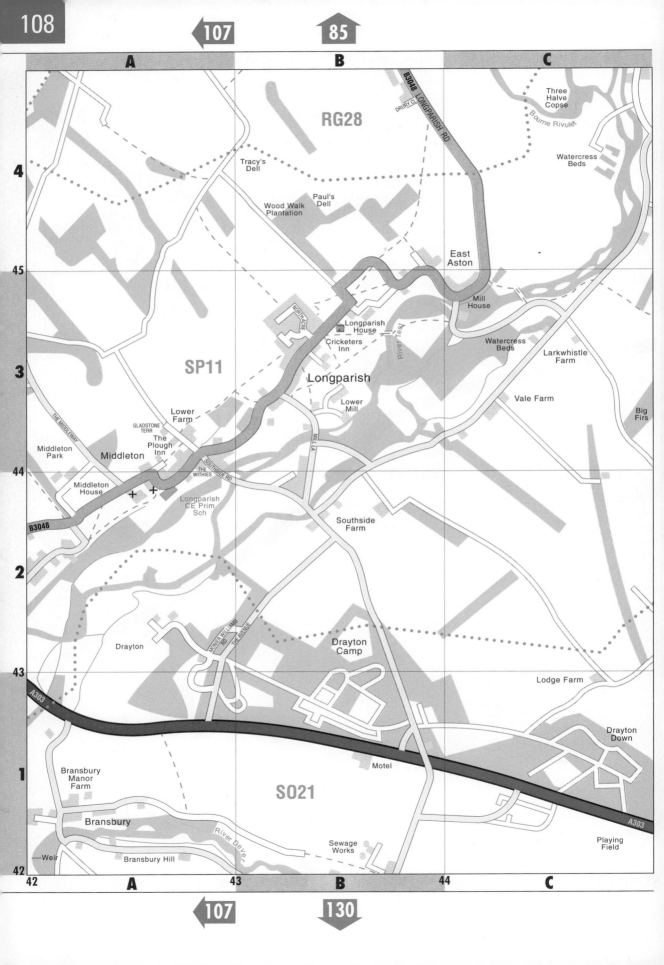

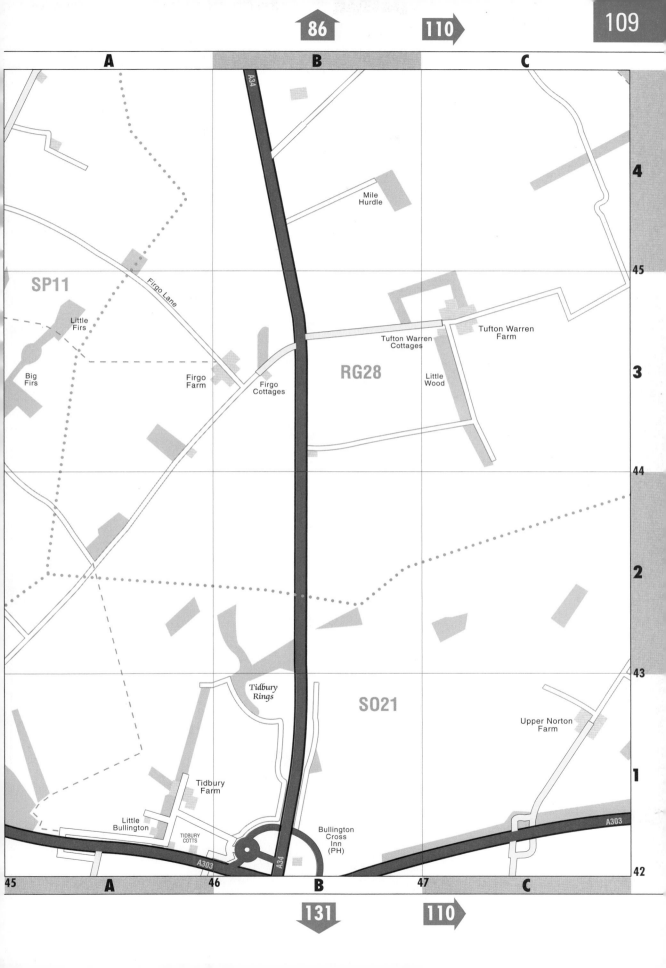

A
B
C

4

45

SP11

Little
Firs

Big
Firs

Firgo Lane

Firgo
Farm

Firgo
Cottages

A34

Mile
Hurdle

Tufton Warren
Cottages

Tufton Warren
Farm

RG28

Little
Wood

3

44

SO21

2

43

Tidbury
Rings

Upper Norton
Farm

1

Tidbury
Farm

Little
Bullington

TIDBURY
COTTS

Bullington
Cross
Inn
(PH)

A303

A303

A34

42

45
A
46
B
47
C

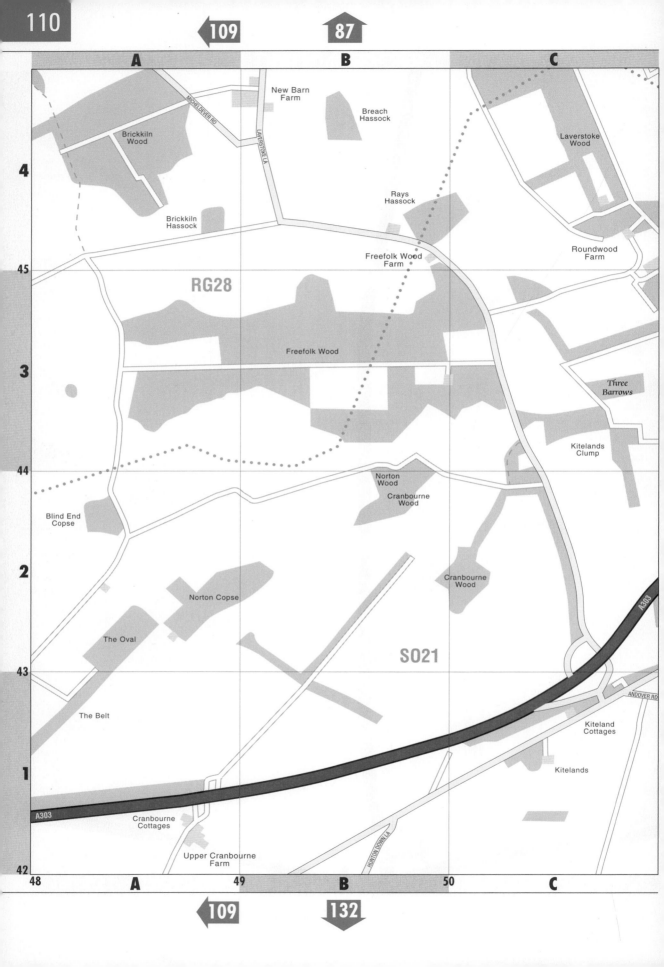

109
87

A B C

New Barn
Farm

Breach
Hassock

Laverstoke
Wood

MICHELDEVER RD

Brickkiln
Wood

LAVERSTOKE LA

4

Rays
Hassock

Roundwood
Farm

Brickkiln
Hassock

Freefolk Wood
Farm

45

RG28

Freefolk Wood

Three
Barrows

3

Kitelands
Clump

44

Norton
Wood

Cranbourne
Wood

Blind End
Copse

2

Cranbourne
Wood

Norton Copse

The Oval

SO21

43

A303

ANDOVER RD

The Belt

Kiteland
Cottages

1

Kitelands

A303

Cranbourne
Cottages

HUNTON TOWN LA

Upper Cranbourne
Farm

42

48 A 49 B 50 C

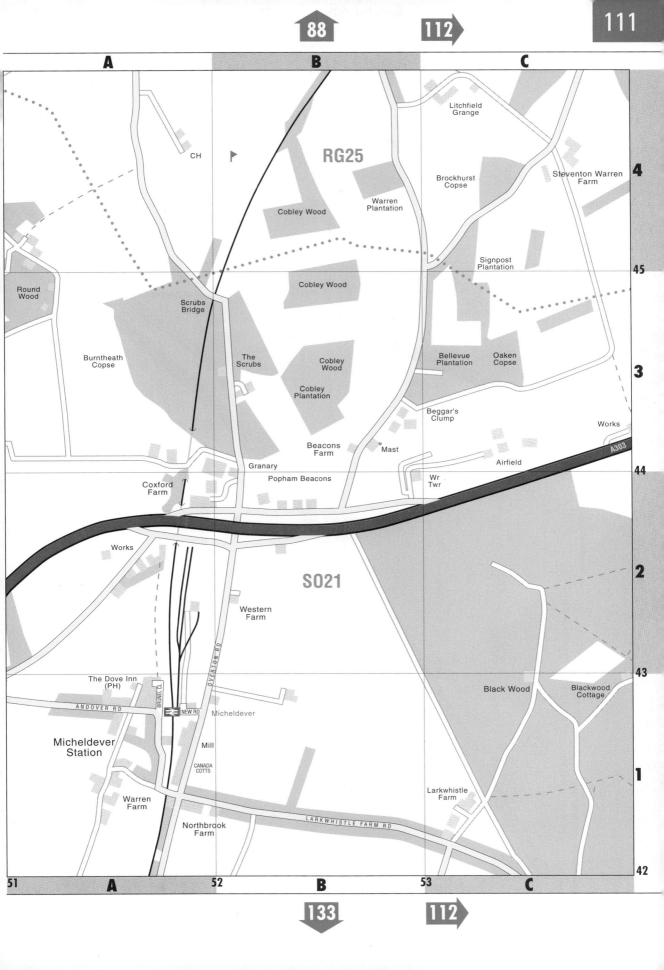

111
89

A   B   C

RG25

Ashen Grove
Copse

The Fox
(PH)

Wheatsheaf
Hotel

POPHAM LA

A30

A303

M3

4

45

Crem

Misholt
Copse

Waltham Trinleys

Hellier's
Copse

Bramley
Wood

Cocksford Firs
East

3

Cocksford
Down

A303

West Farm

44

Popham Court
Farm

Popham

Popham Court
Farm

Black Wood

2

SO21

Bittley
Copse

The Old
Vicarage

43

Vicarage
Farm

College Wood

BRADLEY
COTTS

Bradley
Farm

Manor Farm

1

Woodmancott

London
Lodge

Rownest
Wood

THE CALVERT CTR

Innersdown
Farm

42

A33   M3

54   55   56

A   B   C

111
134

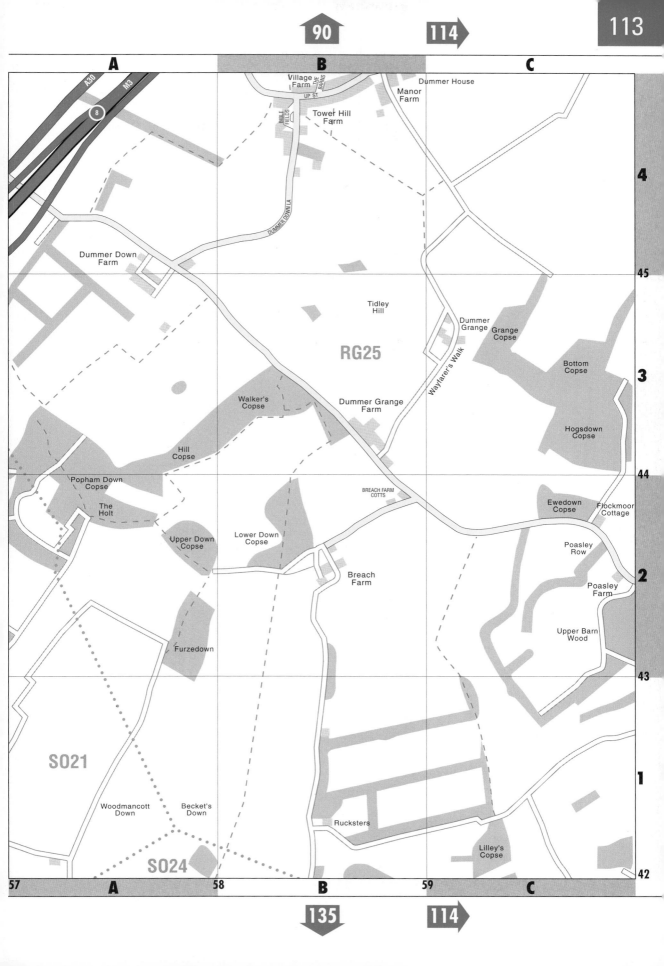

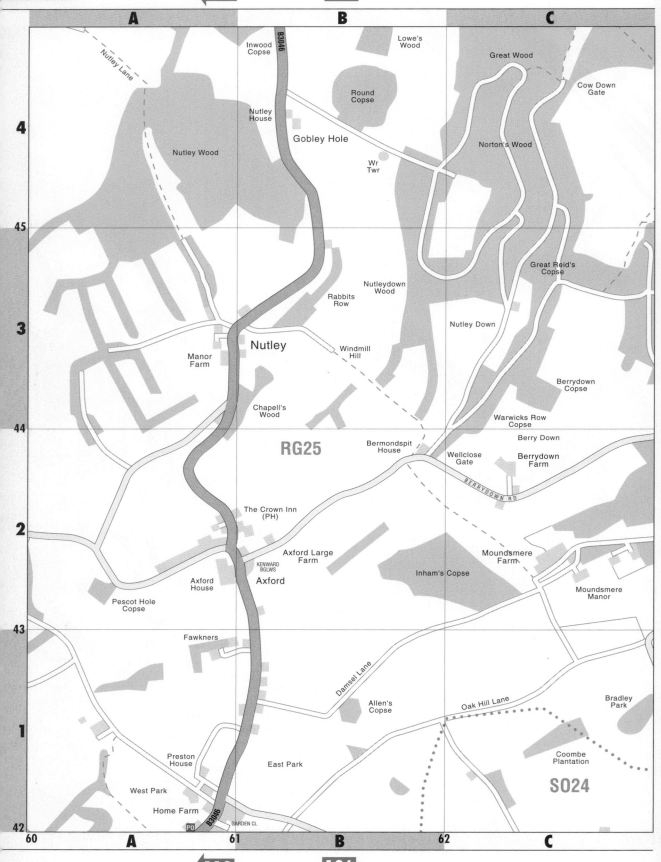

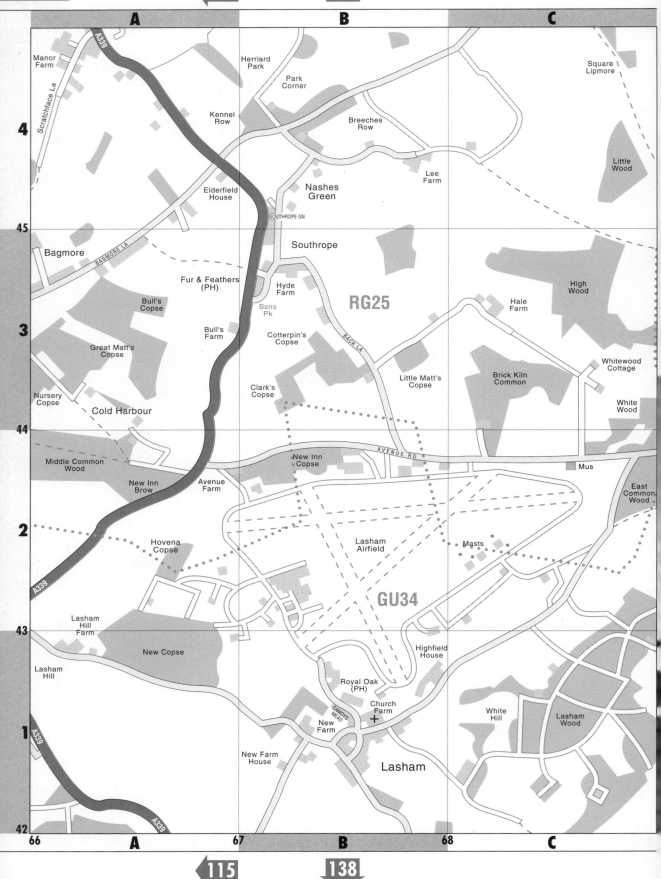

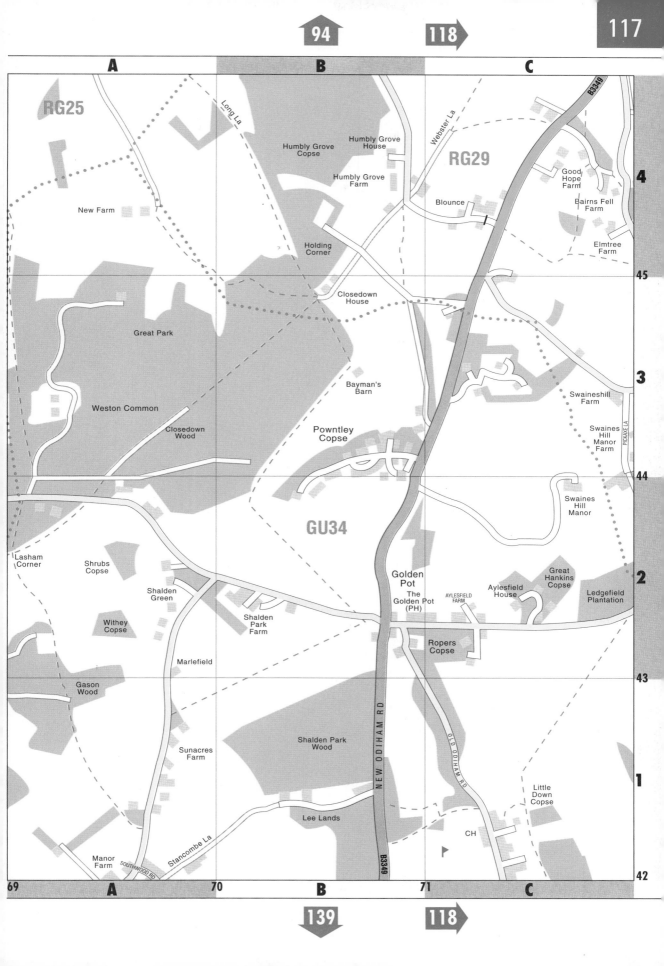

117
95

A   **B**   **C**

New Farm

Vinney
Copse

Sheephouse
Copse

White House
Farm

Highnam
Copse

4

Pickaxe
Copse

Sutton
Common

45

RG29

West
View

Great
Wood

Gaston
Copse

3

Little
Wood

Broadlands
Copse

PICKAXE LA

SUNCROFT LA

Yarnhams
Farm

Hawkins
Wood

44

Beech Hangers Lane

Mast

Liddenfield
Copse

Stowell
Copse

Dicket's
Plantation

Yarnhams
Cottages

Stowell
Cottage

2

Fielders
Copse

Shrub Croft
Copse

Ham Wood

GU34

Masts

43

Brockham Hill
Farm Cottages

BROCKHAM HILL LA

Peakham
Copse

Holybourne
Down

Spollycombe
Copse

Brockham Hill
Barn

New Lane

1

Round
Wood

Howard's
Lane

42

72   **A**   **73**   **B**   **74**   **C**

A
B
C

RG29

Sheephouse Copse

RG29

The Beeches

The Drove

Hangers Hyle Copse

High Wood

Isnage Farm

4

Stenes Copse

Husseys Lane

Crest Hill Farm

WELL LA

Silvester's Copse

45

Copse Hill Farm

Chalk Pit

GU10

3

Rock House Farm

Eastholes Copse

Hodges Farm

Lower Froyle

Blackacre Copse

Pax Hill

Shortlands Copse

The Prince of Wales (PH)

HUSSEYS LA

Husseys Farm

The Hanger

Saintburyhill Farm

Saintbury Hill

Silvesters Farm

Brocas Farm

Crocks Farm

44

BARNFIELD CL

PARK LA

The White House

HOLMWOOD COTTS

WESTBURN FIELDS

The Anchor Inn (PH)

Coldrey Farm

PAX HILL

BAMBER LA

Meml

COLDREY COTTS

A31

GU34

Highway House

2

Rye Bridge

Blundens Farm

Cemy

GID LA

43

Upper Froyle

ISINGTON LA

Isington Mill

THE SQUARE

Treloar Sch

River Wey

Isington

West End Farm

College Farm

Froyle Mill

The Miller's House Farm

1

Colthouse Lane

Quarry Bottom

Isington Farm

ISINGTON RD

West End

Shrubbery House

Hen and Chicken (PH)

Chestnut Copse

Gaston Copse

Greatfield Cottage

A31

42

A   B   C

4

Locks Grove

Gasson's Coppice

Highcombes Farm

Cheek's Farm

OLD FARNHAM LA

RUNWICK LA

Grover's Farm

Willey Copse

BURY COURT COTTS

Bury Court

Hill Farm

45

Perryland

Wallfield Copse

IDLEFIELD COTTS

CRONDALL RD

Northbrook Farm

Northbrook

East Green

MARSH LA

A31

Irelands

3

Jenkyn Place

CHURCH LA

HOLE LA

Hole La

Broadhatch House

Welche's House

Marsh House

The Bull Inn (PH)

GU10

Bentley

Bentley CE Prim Sch

SCHOOL LA

Turk's Mill

LONGCROFT

BABS FIELDS

EGGARS FIELD

BONNERS FIELD

PO

Bentley Bsns Pk

44

OAKWAY

SOUTH VIEW COTTS

THE POLLARDS

The Star (PH)

RECTORY LA

Bentley Ind Ctr

White Bridge

Cotton's Copse

South Green Farm

A31

Marelands

Holt Pound Inclosure

Sewage Works

River Wey

GRAVEL HILL RD

2

Bentley Green Farm

Alice Holt Forest

STATION RD

Forest Wlks

P

Anstey Bridge

WEY BANK

43

P   Bentley

Alice Holt Farm

ISINGTON RD

Isington Close

PARK CL

ALICE HOLT COTTS

A325

THROAKMEAD

GU34

Aldix Copse Farm

BLACKNEST RD

Westminster House

Lodge Inclosure

Alice Holt Lodge

1

Plain Piece

Catham Copse

Redcap Copse

Broadview Farm

THE GLADE

BACK LA

A325

42

Blacknest Ind Pk

78   A   79   B   80   C

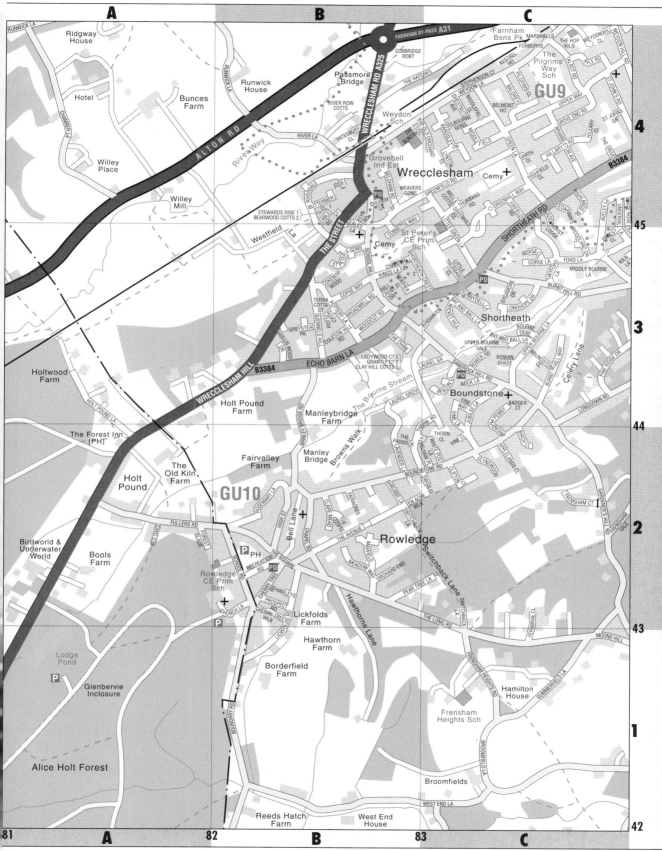

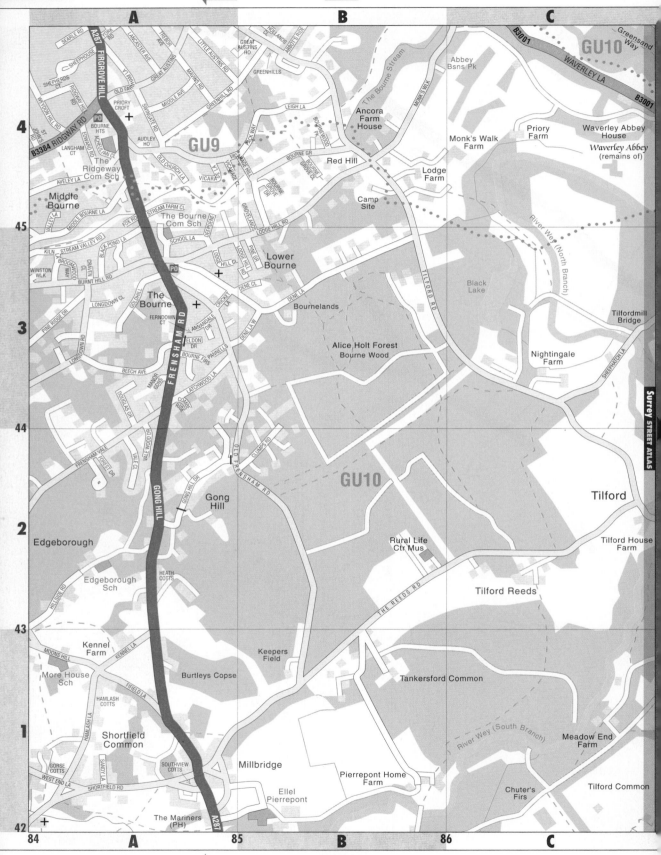

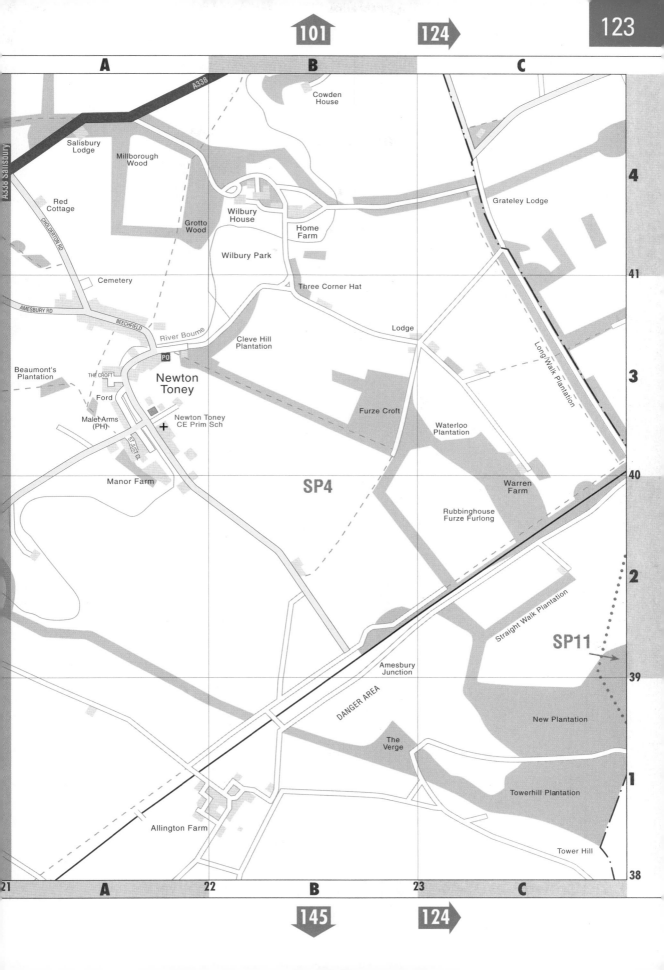

A   B   C

A338 Salisbury

Cowden House

Salisbury Lodge

Millborough Wood

4

Red Cottage

CHOLDERTON RD

Grotto Wood

Wilbury House

Home Farm

Grateley Lodge

Wilbury Park

Cemetery

41

AMESBURY RD

BEECHFIELD

River Bourne

Three Corner Hat

Cleve Hill Plantation

Lodge

Long Walk Plantation

Beaumont's Plantation

PO

THE CROFT

Newton Toney

3

Ford

Furze Croft

Waterloo Plantation

Malet Arms (PH)

Newton Toney CE Prim Sch

ST JUST CL

Manor Farm

SP4

Warren Farm

40

Rubbinghouse Furze Furlong

Straight Walk Plantation

2

SP11

Amesbury Junction

New Plantation

39

DANGER AREA

The Verge

Towerhill Plantation

1

Allington Farm

Tower Hill

38

21   A   22   B   23   C

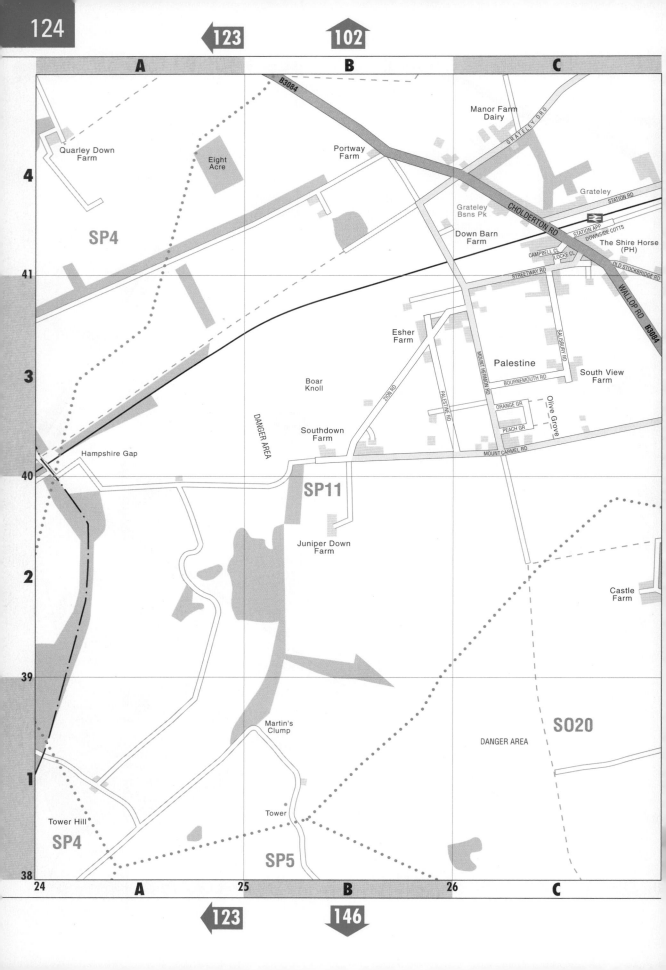

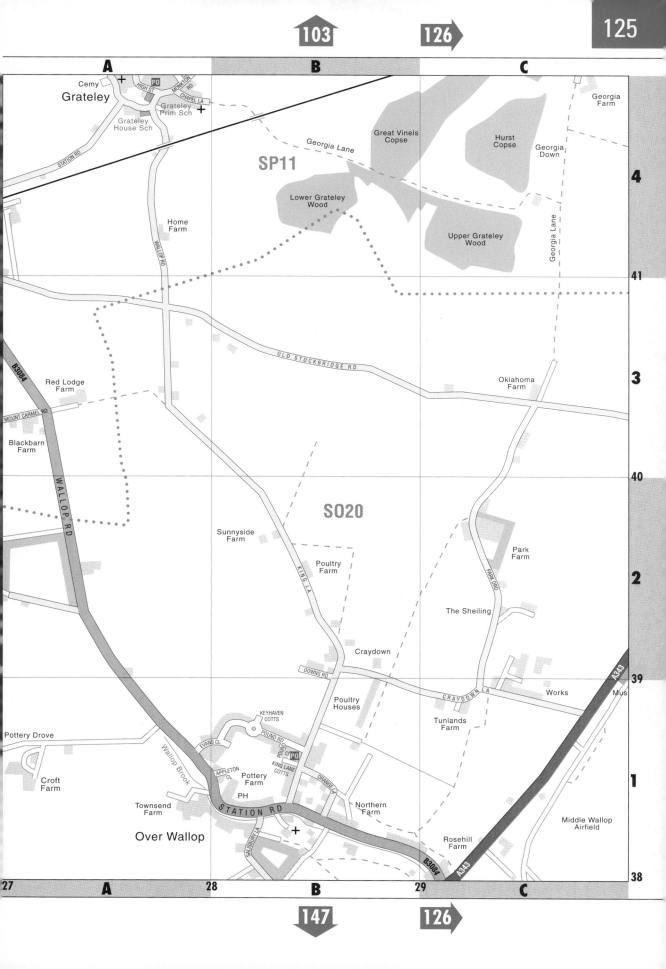

125
104

A **B** **C**

4

Old Prospect
Farm

Prospect
Farm

Eastover
Copse

Cossical
Copse

Stonehanger
Copse

Abbotts Ann Down

41

Down Farm

SALISBURY RD

SP11

Chestnut
Cottage

Dunkirt
House

Monxton
Oakcuts

3

OLD STOCKBRIDGE RD

Saxley Farm

Married
Quarters

Kentsboro

40

Towers

MAPLE
CL

SYCAMORE
CRES

1 CL

Kentsboro
Farm

SERGEANT CL
TAPPING CL
BENTA CL
WILSON CL
SEK KONG CL
FALAISE RD
BE AGLE
CL

BIRCH
AVE

2 3 4
PINE CL

5
BEECH
CL

6

LARCH CL

ELM CL

WILLOW WAY

CHESTNUT CRES

Married
Quarters

1 HAWTHORN HILL
2 POPLAR PATH
3 CHERRY WLK
4 ASH PATH
5 DANEBURY VIEW
6 LAUREL PL
7 HOLLY WLK

7

OAK
CL

Upper Oakcuts
Copse

Mast

2

SO20

Mus Of Army Flying
Explorers World

39

Knock Wood

Down
Farm

1

Middle Wallop
Airfield

Sewage
Works

38

30 **A** **31** **B** **32** **C**

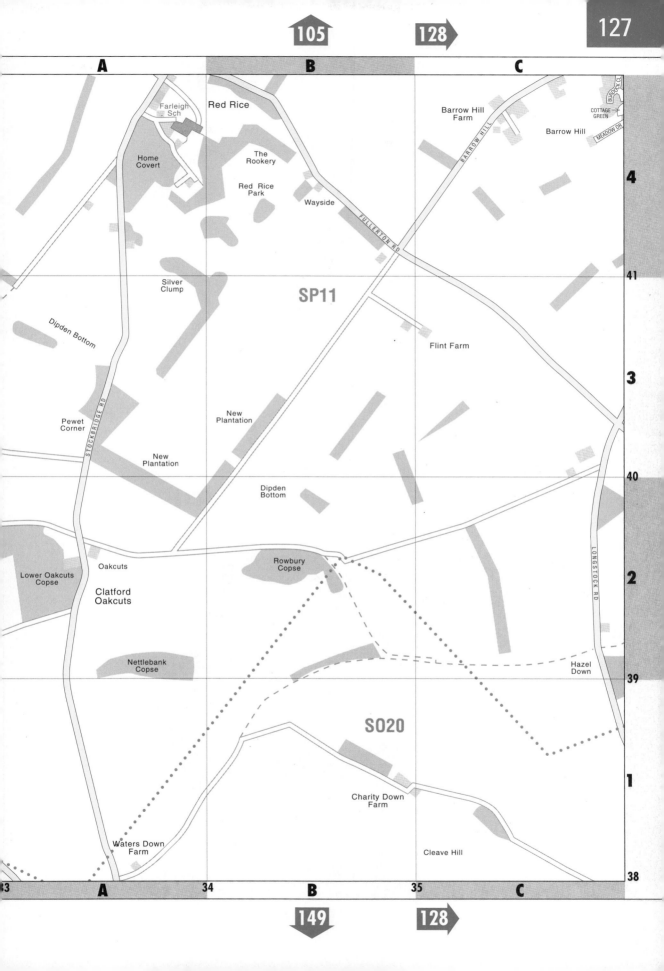

A
B
C

Farleigh Sch
Red Rice
Home Covert
The Rookery
Red Rice Park
Wayside
Barrow Hill Farm
Barrow Hill
BURDOCK CL
COTTAGE GREEN
MEADOW DR

BARROW HILL

4

FULLERTON RD

Silver Clump

SP11

41

Dipden Bottom

Flint Farm

STOCKBRIDGE RD

New Plantation

3

Pewet Corner

New Plantation

Dipden Bottom

40

Oakcuts

Rowbury Copse

LONGSTOCK RD

2

Lower Oakcuts Copse

Clatford Oakcuts

Hazel Down

Nettlebank Copse

39

SO20

Charity Down Farm

1

Waters Down Farm

Cleave Hill

38

33

A
34
B
35
C

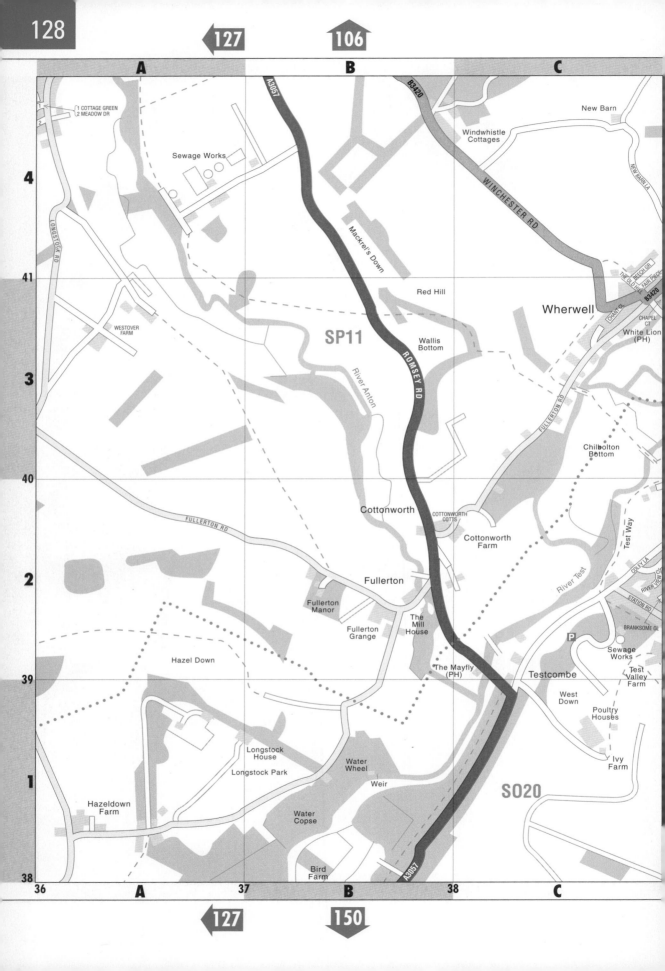

1 COTTAGE GREEN
2 MEADOW DR

Sewage Works

LONGSTOCK RD

A3067

B3420

New Barn

Windwhistle
Cottages

WINCHESTER RD

NEW BARN LA

4

41

WESTOVER
FARM

Mackrel's Down

Red Hill

SP11

River Anton

Wallis
Bottom

ROMSEY RD

Wherwell

THE OLD THE
CHAPEL
FAIR CROSS
BEECH GR
CHANT CL

B3420

CHAPEL
CT

White Lion
(PH)

3

FULLERTON RD

Chilbolton
Bottom

FULLERTON RD

40

Cottonworth

COTTONWORTH
COTTS

Cottonworth
Farm

Test Way

COLEY LA

River Test

RIVER VIEW

STATION RD

2

Fullerton

Fullerton
Manor

Fullerton
Grange

The
Mill
House

BRANSOME CL

P

Sewage
Works

Test
Valley
Farm

Hazel Down

The Mayfly
(PH)

Testcombe

West
Down

Poultry
Houses

39

Longstock
House

Longstock Park

Water
Wheel

Weir

SO20

Ivy
Farm

1

Hazeldown
Farm

Water
Copse

Bird
Farm

A3067

38

36
A
37
B
38
C

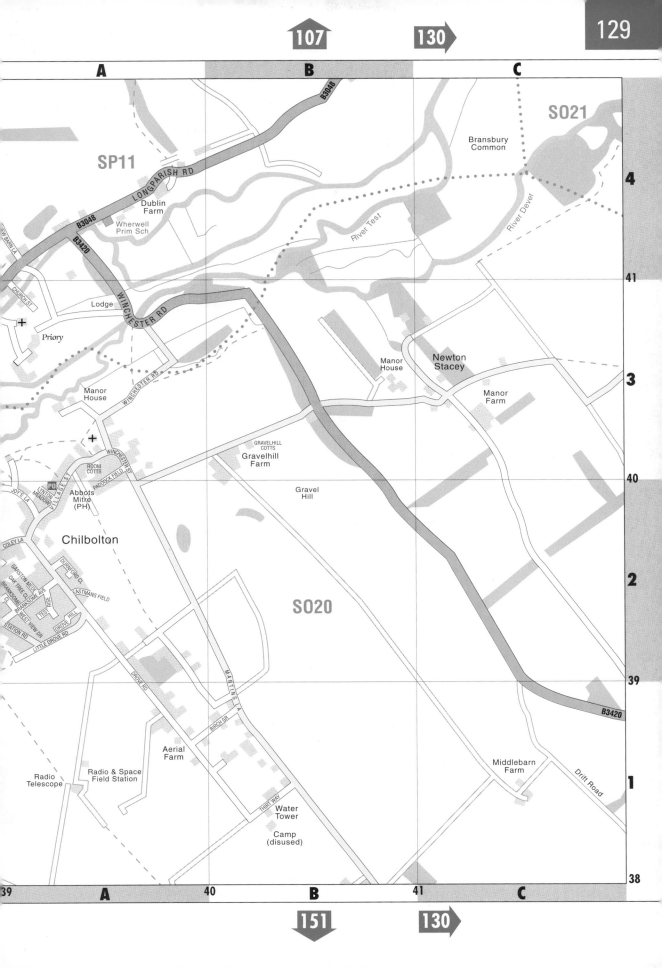

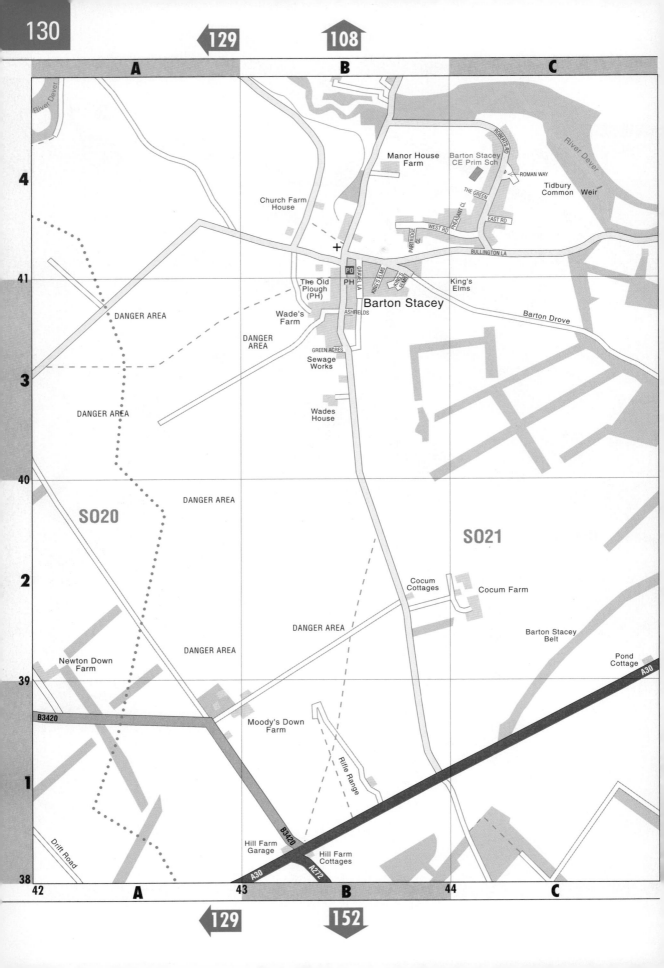

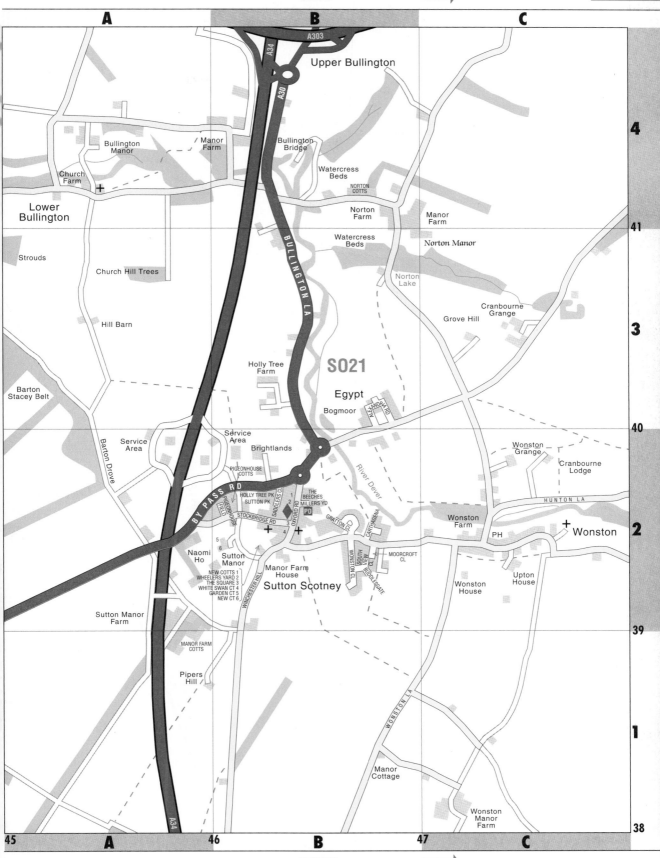

A   B   C

Upper Bullington

A303

A34

A30

Manor Farm

Bullington Manor

Bullington Bridge

Church Farm

Watercress Beds

NORTON COTTS

4

Lower Bullington

Norton Farm

Manor Farm

41

Strouds

Watercress Beds

Norton Manor

Church Hill Trees

Norton Lake

BULLINGTON LA

Grove Hill

Cranbourne Grange

Hill Barn

3

Barton Stacey Belt

Holly Tree Farm

SO21

Egypt

Bogmoor

ALEXANDRA RD

Barton Drove

Service Area

Service Area

Brightlands

Wonston Grange

Cranbourne Lodge

40

PIGEONHOUSE COTTS

River Dever

HUNTON LA

BY PASS RD

PIGEONHOUSE FIELD

HOLLY TREE PK
SUTTON PK

THE BEECHES
MILLERS YD

PO

Wonston Farm

Wonston

STOCKBRIDGE RD

SADDLERS CL

OXFORD RD

GRATTON CL

CARTHAGENA

PH

2

5

6

Naomi Ho

Sutton Manor

WINCHESTER HILL

Manor Farm House

NEW COTTS 1
WHEELERS YARD 2
THE SQUARE 3
WHITE SWAN CT 4
GARDEN CT 5
NEW CT 6

Sutton Scotney

WONSTON CL

HUDSON VIEW CL

BIDDLEGATE

MOORCROFT CL

Wonston House

Upton House

Sutton Manor Farm

MANOR FARM COTTS

39

Pipers Hill

WONSTON LA

1

Manor Cottage

Wonston Manor Farm

38

45   A   46   B   47   C

131
110

A

B

C

4

Hunton Down
Farm

Victoria Cottages

Counsellor's
Walk

41

HUNTON DOWN LA

Hunton Grange
Farm

New
Cottages

Weston Down
Cottages

Chestnut Villas

3

Norsebury
Ring

Northbrook
House

WESTON DOWN RD

40

SO21

Hunton Manor
Farm

Hunton

Norsebury
Farm

Hunton
Manor

Lower
Norsebury

Northbrook

NORTHBROOK

HUNTON LA

Norsebury
House

Weston
Colley

2

Norsebury
Cottages

WESTON
COLLEY

Weston
Farm

River Dever

Michaels

Stoke
Charity

PO

OLD STOKE RD

39

Borough
Farm

1

38

A

49

B

50

C

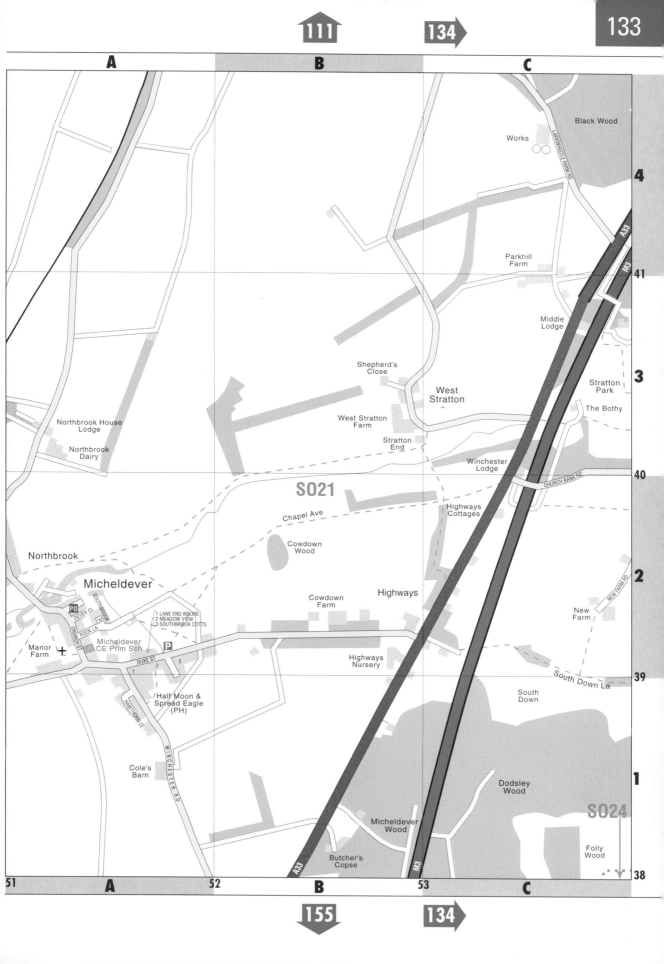

4

41

3

40

2

39

1

38

Black Wood

Works

LARKWHISTLE FARM RD

Parkhill
Farm

Middle
Lodge

A33

M3

Stratton
Park

The Bothy

Shepherd's
Close

West
Stratton

West Stratton
Farm

Stratton
End

Winchester
Lodge

CHURCH BANK RD

SO21

Chapel Ave

Highways
Cottages

Cowdown
Wood

Northbrook House
Lodge

Northbrook
Dairy

Northbrook

Micheldever

Highways

Cowdown
Farm

New Farm RD

New
Farm

PO

SOUTHBROOK

DEVER CL

ROOK LA

1 LANE END BGLWS
2 MEADOW VIEW
3 SOUTHBROOK COTTS

P

Manor
Farm

Micheldever
CE Prim Sch

CHURCH ST

DUKE ST

1 2 3

Highways
Nursery

South Down La

South
Down

Half Moon &
Spread Eagle
(PH)

HAWTHORN CL

WINCHESTER RD

Cole's
Barn

Dodsley
Wood

SO24

Micheldever
Wood

A33

M3

Butcher's
Copse

Folly
Wood

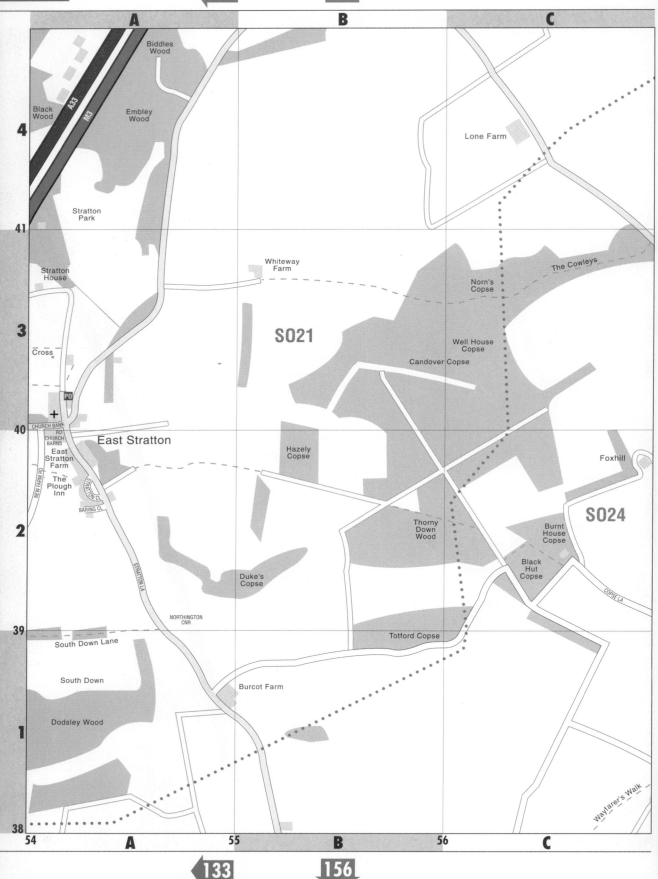

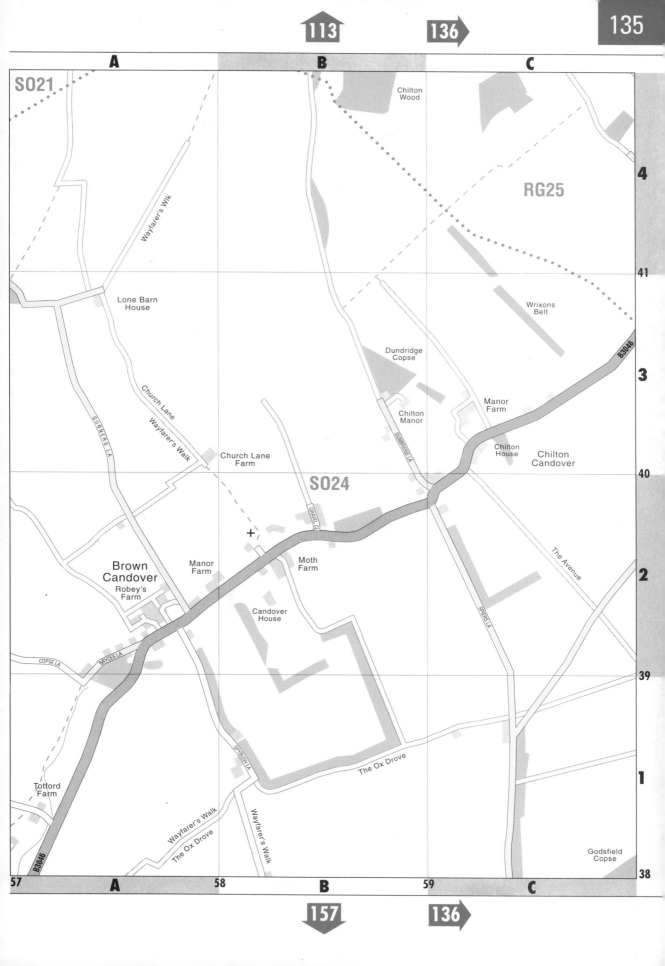

SO21

Chilton
Wood

RG25

4

41

Lone Barn
House

Wrixons
Belt

B3046

Dundridge
Copse

Church Lane

3

Wayfarer's Wlk

Wayfarer's Walk

GUNNERS LA

Manor
Farm

DUNBRIDGE LA

Chilton
Manor

Chilton
House

Chilton
Candover

Church Lane
Farm

40

SO24

+

GRAVEL CL

Brown
Candover

Manor
Farm

Moth
Farm

The Avenue

Robey's
Farm

SPEERS LA

2

Candover
House

COPSE LA

BRYCES LA

39

SPYBUSH LA

The Ox Drove

Tottford
Farm

1

Wayfarer's Walk

Wayfarer's Walk

The Ox Drove

Godsfield
Copse

B3046

38

135
114

A **B** **C**

B3046

Preston Candover CE Prim Sch

North Hall

The Purefoy Arms (PH)

STENBURY
DR

Manor Farm

South Hall

Preston Candover

Fairview Farm

Lower Farm

RG25

Bradley Corner

Down La

Three Castles Path

Preston Down

Park Copse

4

B3046

Preston Grange

Down Farm

41

Buds Hill

Windmill Hill

3

The Ox Drove

Down Farm Dairy

40

Chilton Down

Bangor Copse

Wield Wood Lodge

SO24

Caigers Farm

2

Dandelys Copse

Wield Wood Farm

Wield Wood

Wield Manor Farm

39

Juniper Hill

Wield Wood

Upper Wield

PO

Wield House Farm

WIELD GRANGE

1

Godsfield Copse

Armsworth Hill Farm

Three Castles Path

Barton Copse

38

60 **A** 61 **B** 62 **C**

135
158

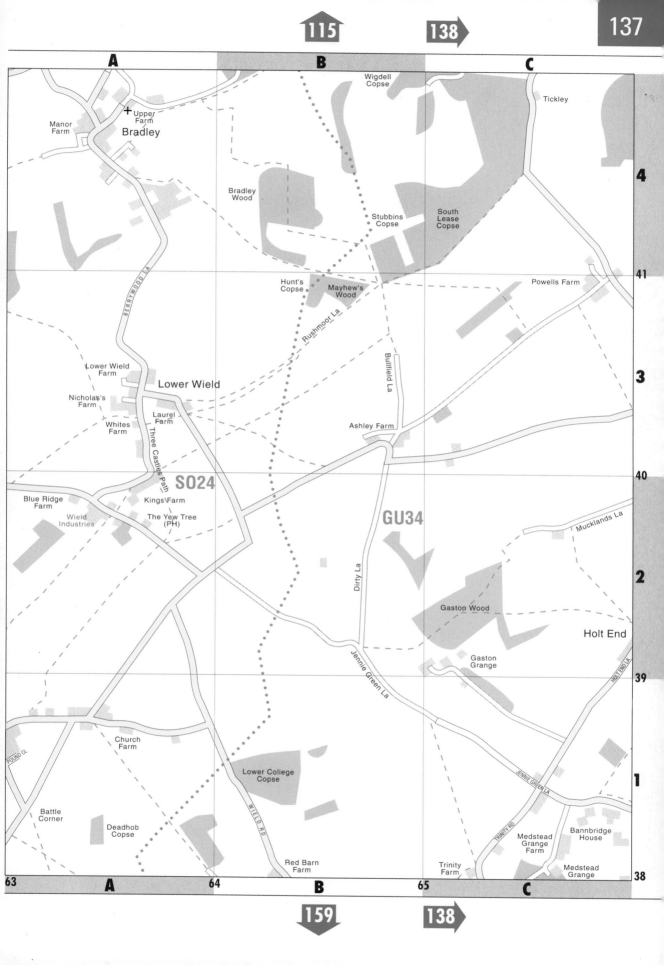

A B C

Wigdell Copse

Tickley

Manor Farm

+ Upper Farm

Bradley

4

Bradley Wood

Stubbins Copse

South Lease Copse

BERRYWOOD LA

41

Powells Farm

Hunt's Copse

Mayhew's Wood

Rushmoor La

Lower Wield Farm

Lower Wield

Bullfield La

3

Nicholas's Farm

Laurel Farm

Whites Farm

Three Castles Path

Ashley Farm

SO24

40

Blue Ridge Farm

Kings Farm

GU34

Mucklands La

Wield Industries

The Yew Tree (PH)

2

Gaston Wood

Dirty La

Holt End

Gaston Grange

39

HOLT END LA

Church Farm

Jennie Green La

Lower College Copse

POUND CL

1

JENNIE GREEN LA

Battle Corner

Deadhob Copse

WIELD RD

TRINITY RD

Medstead Grange Farm

Bannbridge House

Red Barn Farm

Trinity Farm

Medstead Grange

38

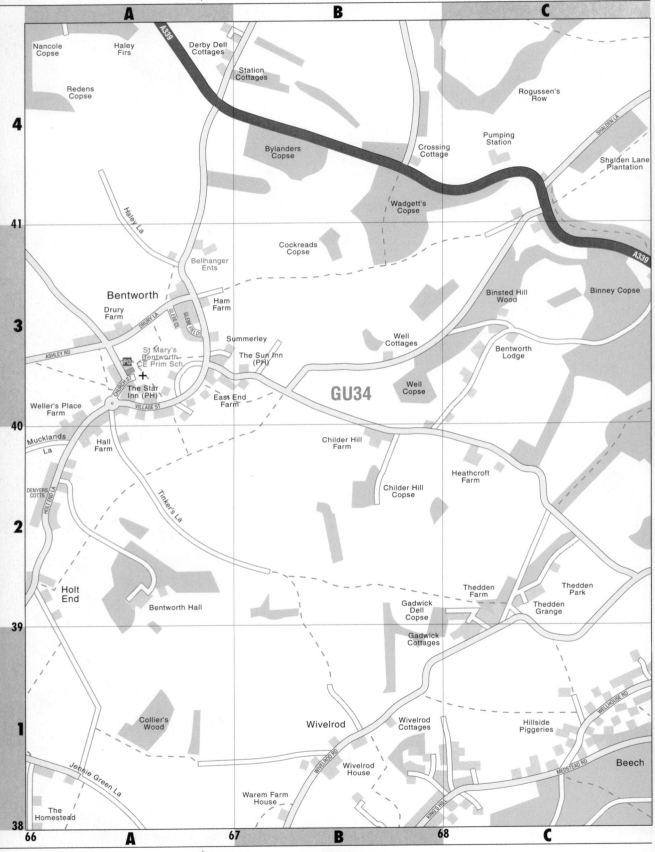

137
116

A

B

C

4

41

3

40

2

39

1

38

Nancole
Copse

Haley
Firs

Derby Dell
Cottages

A339

Station
Cottages

Rogussen's
Row

Redens
Copse

SHALDEN LA

Bylanders
Copse

Crossing
Cottage

Pumping
Station

Shalden Lane
Plantation

Haley La

Wadgett's
Copse

A339

Cockreads
Copse

Bellhanger
Ents

Bentworth

Ham
Farm

Binsted Hill
Wood

Binney Copse

Drury
Farm

DRURY LA

GLEBE CL

GLEBE FIELDS

Summerley

Well
Cottages

Bentworth
Lodge

ASHLEY RD

St Mary's
Bentworth
CE Prim Sch

The Sun Inn
(PH)

PO

CHURCH ST

The Star
Inn (PH)

East End
Farm

GU34

Well
Copse

VILLAGE ST

Weller's Place
Farm

Mucklands
La

Hall
Farm

Childer Hill
Farm

Heathcroft
Farm

DENYERS
COTTS

HOLT END LA

Tinker's La

Childer Hill
Copse

Holt
End

Bentworth Hall

Thedden
Farm

Thedden
Park

Gadwick
Dell Copse

Thedden
Grange

Gadwick
Cottages

Collier's
Wood

Wivelrod

Wivelrod
Cottages

Hillside
Piggeries

WELLHOUSE RD

Beech

Jennie Green La

WIVELROD RD

Wivelrod
House

MEDSTEAD RD

The
Homestead

Warem Farm
House

KING'S HILL

66

A

67

B

68

C

137
160

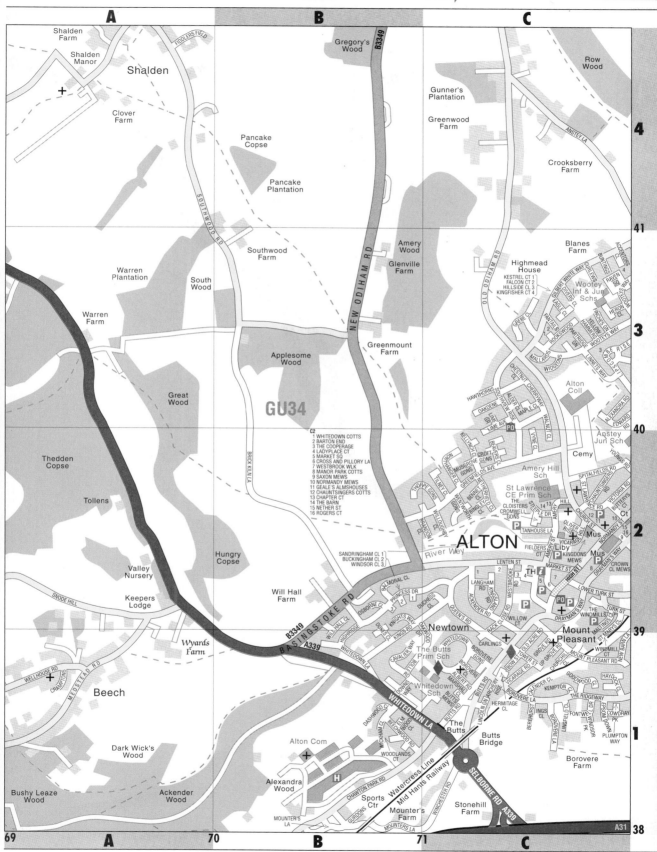

A   B   C

Shalden Farm
Shalden Manor
FIDDLERS FIELD
Shalden
Clover Farm

Gregory's Wood
B3349

Row Wood

Gunner's Plantation
Greenwood Farm

ANSTEY LA

Crooksberry Farm

4

Pancake Copse
Pancake Plantation

SOUTHWOOD RD

NEW ODIHAM RD

Amery Wood
Glenville Farm

41

Blanes Farm

Highmead House
KESTREL CT 1
FALCON CT 2
HILLSIDE CL 3
KINGFISHER CT 4

GILBERT WHITE WAY
CURLEWS
BUNTINGS
RAVEN SQ

ACKENDERS

OLD ODIHAM RD

Wootey Inf & Jun Schs

Warren Plantation
Southwood Farm

South Wood

Warren Farm

Great Wood

Southwood Farm

Applesome Wood

GU34

Greenmount Farm

GREBE RD
RANZALS
PINTAILS
EAGLE CL
PARTRIDGE GN
FINCHES CR
WOOTEY'S WAY
HERON RD
AXMINSTERS

Alton Coll

GILBERT
CHESTNUT
CHERRYWAY
WALNUT CL
SOUTHVIEW RISE
MAPLE CL

THE RISE

Anstey Jun Sch

3

Thedden Copse

Tollens

BRICK KILN LA

C2
1 WHITEDOWN COTTS
2 BARTON END
3 THE COOPERAGE
4 LADYPLACE CT
5 MARKET SQ
6 CROSS AND PILLORY LA
7 WESTBROOK WLK
8 MANOR PARK COTTS
9 SAXON MEWS
10 NORMANDY MEWS
11 GEALE'S ALMSHOUSES
12 CHAUNTSINGERS COTTS
13 CHAPTER CT
14 THE BARN
15 NETHER ST
16 ROGERS CT

HAWTHORNS
OAKDENE
LIME AVE
KELLYNCH CL
BEAVERS CL
MUSGROVE GDNS
CROFT GDNS
GREENFIELDS AVE

Amery Hill Sch

St Lawrence CE Prim Sch
THE CLOISTERS
CROMWELL GDNS

SPITALFIELDS RD

Cemy

VICTORIA RD
BUTTER'S CT

40

Valley Nursery

Hungry Copse

THORPE GDNS

WILLOUGHBY

WENTWORTH GDNS
BRANDON CL

River Wey

SANDRINGHAM CL 1
BUCKINGHAM CL 2
WINDSOR CL 3

BALMORAL CL

STEEPLE DR

OLIVER RISE

CHURCH ST
NORMANDY CT

Mus
Liby
Mus
Kingdons Mews
CROWN CL MEWS

2

Keepers Lodge

SNODE HILL

Wyards Farm

WILL HALL CL
HIGHRIDGE

Will Hall Farm

BASINGSTOKE RD

B3349
A339

OSBORNE CL
PRINCESS DR
DUCHESS CL

WHITEDOWN LA

KNIGHTS WAY
KINGS RD

LENTEN ST

Newtown

LANGHAM RD
WESTBROOKE
ACKENDER RD
QUEEN'S RD

MARKET ST
HIGH ST
LOWER TURK ST

THE WINDMILLS
TURK ST
MALTINGS CL

Mount Pleasant

WINDMILL CT
NEW BARN LA

39

Beech

WELLHOUSE RD
MEDSTEAD RD
CRAMPTONS

Dark Wick's Wood

Bushy Leaze Wood

Ackender Wood

DASHWOOD CL
WICKHAM CL
BEECHWOOD RD
WHITEDOWN LA

Alton Com

Alexandra Wood

MOUNTER'S LA

H

Sports Ctr

Watercress Line
Mid Hants Railway

CAVALIER WAY

The Butts Prim Sch

Whitedown Sch

WINCHESTER RD

The Butts

Butts Bridge

SELBORNE RD
A339

Mounter's Farm

Stonehill Farm

CHAWTON PARK RD

WOODLANDS CT

CHURCHILL CL
VICARAGE RD
MOUNT PLEASANT RD
GOODWOOD CL
THE RIDGEWAY
HAYOCK CL
COWDRAY
EPSOM CL
WINDSOR PK
FONTWELL
PLUMPTON WAY

Borovere Farm

1

69   A   70   B   71   C   A31   38

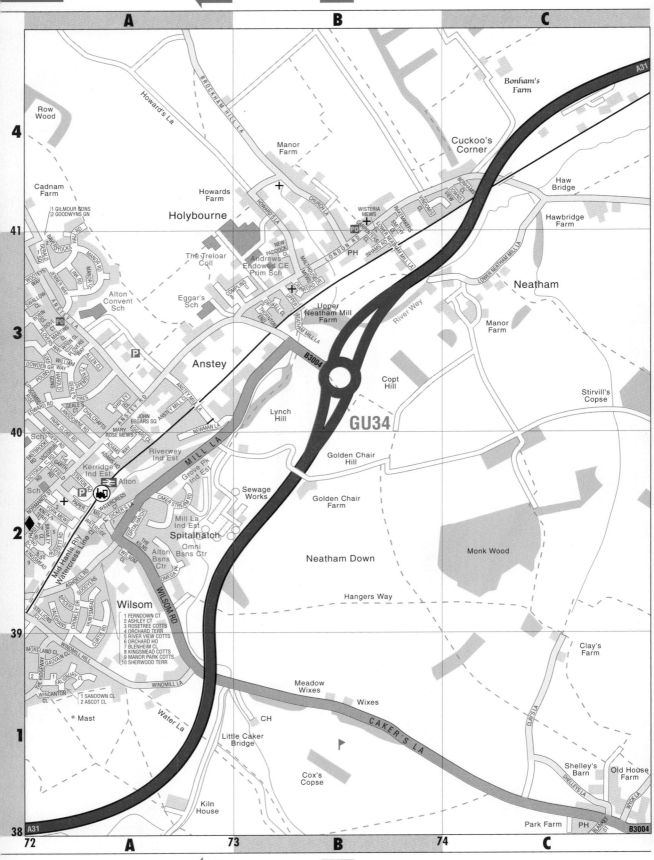

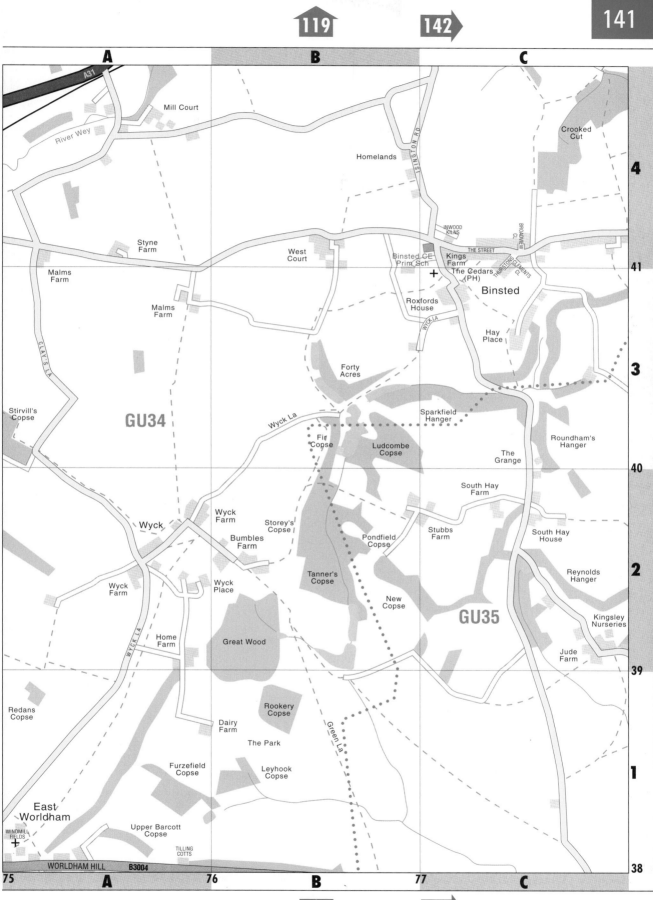

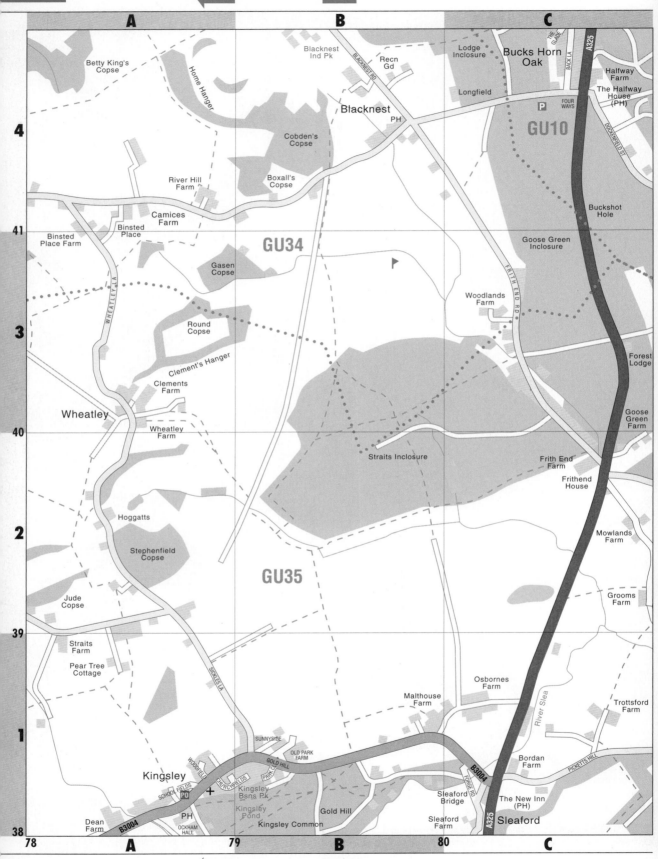

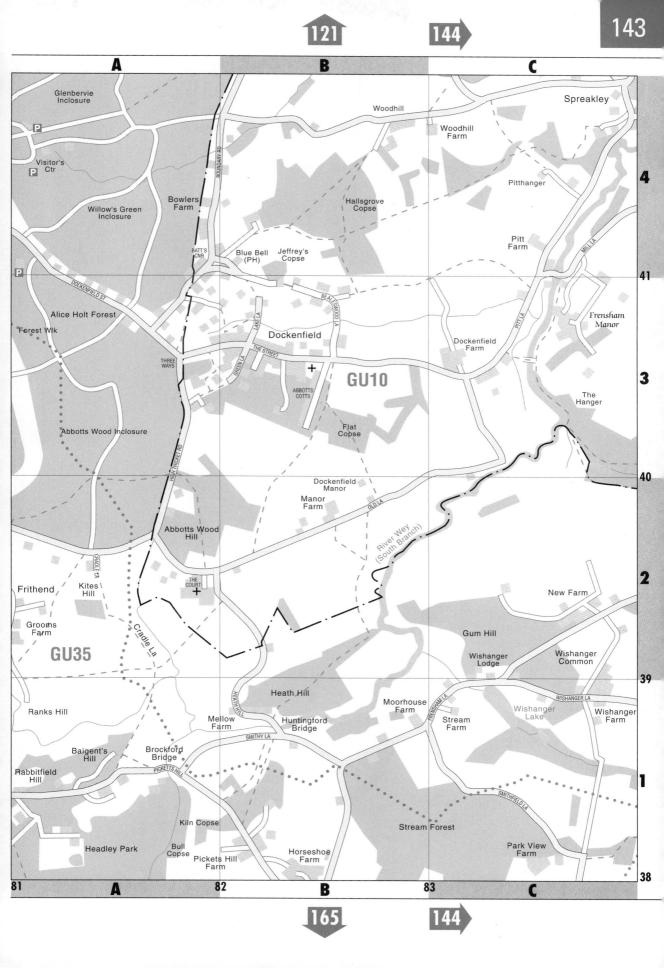

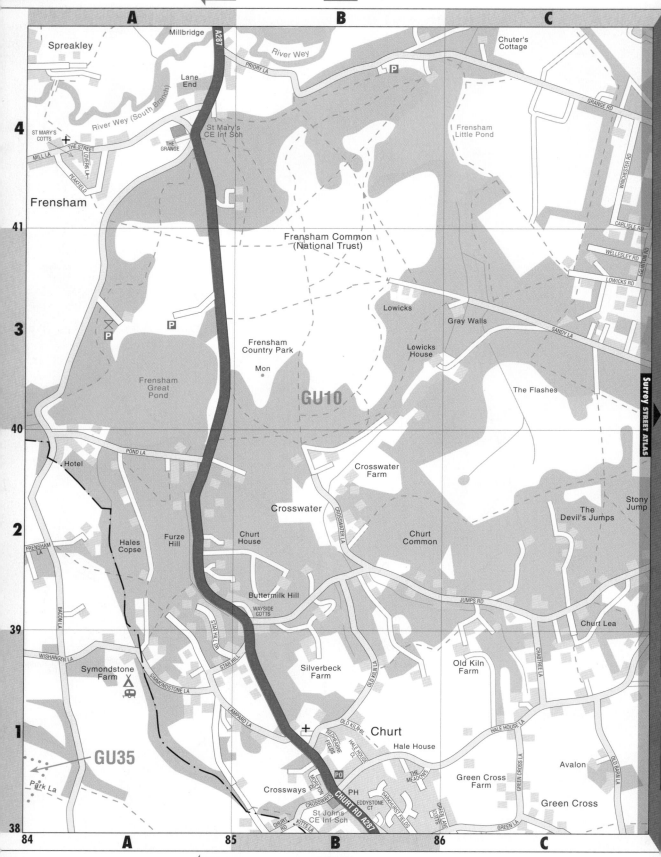

Surrey STREET ATLAS

Spreakley

Millbridge

Lane End

Frensham

River Wey (South Branch)

St Mary's COTTS

MILL LA

PEAKFIELD

THE STREET

LOVERS LA

THE GRANGE

St Mary's CE Inf Sch

A287

PRIORY LA

River Wey

P

Chuter's Cottage

GRANGE RD

WINCHESTER RD

NORTH RD

CARLISLE RD

WELLESLEY RD

LOWICKS RD

Frensham Little Pond

Frensham Common (National Trust)

P

Frensham Country Park

P

Frensham Great Pond

Mon

GU10

Lowicks

Lowicks House

Gray Walls

SANDY LA

The Flashes

POND LA

Hotel

FRENSHAM LA

Crosswater Farm

Crosswater

The Devil's Jumps

Stony Jump

Hales Copse

Furze Hill

Church House

CROSSWATER LA

Churt Common

The

BACON LA

Buttermilk Hill

WAYSIDE COTTS

JUMPS RD

Churt Lea

STAR HILL DR

STAR HILL

Silverbeck Farm

OLD KILN LA

Old Kiln Farm

CRABTREE LA

WISHANGER LA

Symondstone Farm

SIMONDSTONE LA

LAMPARD LA

OLD KILN RD

Churt

Hale House

HALE HOUSE LA

GREEN CROSS LA

OLD BARN LA

GU35

Park La

REDINGENE FIELDS

HALE HOUSE CL

Crossways

CROSSWAYS

MONKTON LA

PO

CHURT RD A287

PH

EDDYSTONE CT

THE MEADOWS

PARCHURST FIELDS

GREEN LANE COTTS

Green Cross Farm

Avalon

Green Cross

St Johns CE Inf Sch

CHURT RD

KITTS LA

GREEN LA

84   A   85   B   86   C

4

41

3

40

2

39

1

38

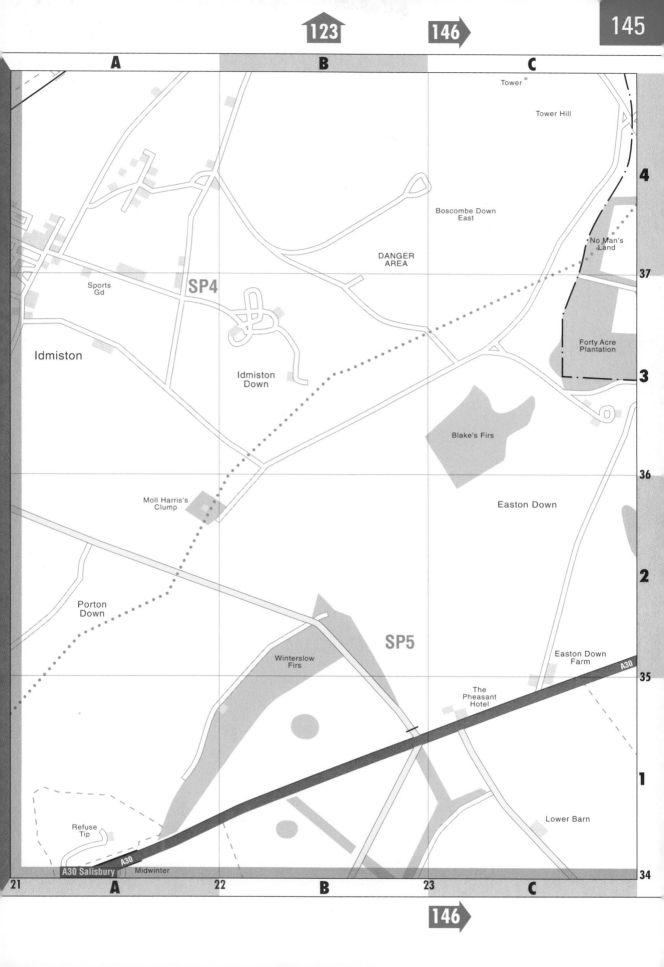

Tower

Tower Hill

A
B
C

4

Boscombe Down
East

No Man's
Land

DANGER
AREA

37

Forty Acre
Plantation

Sports
Gd

SP4

Idmiston
Down

3

Blake's Firs

Idmiston

36

Moll Harris's
Clump

Easton Down

2

Porton
Down

SP5

Winterslow
Firs

Easton Down
Farm

A30

35

The
Pheasant
Hotel

1

Refuse
Tip

Lower Barn

A30 Salisbury   Midwinter

A30

21   22   23   34

A
B
C

A   B   C

SP4

SO20

Suddern
Hill

4

Isle of Wight
Hill

DANGER AREA

Jack's Bush
Farm

Bush
Farm

A343

37

3

Roche Court
Down

Little Firs
Farm

36

Little
Firs

Easton
Down

SP5

Hollom Down
Farm

Firs
Farm

The
Anchorage

2

LOPCOMBE
CORNER

A343

MOUNT
HEIGHTS

Lopcombe Corner
Farm

Cherry View
Farm

A30

Popple Light
Copse

A30

35

1

Gutteridge
Farm

Ashley's
Copse

Ramshill Drove

Bussle
Wood

Burretts
Grove

Warren
Court
Farm

Roche Court
Farm

Roche
Court

34

24   A   25   B   26   C

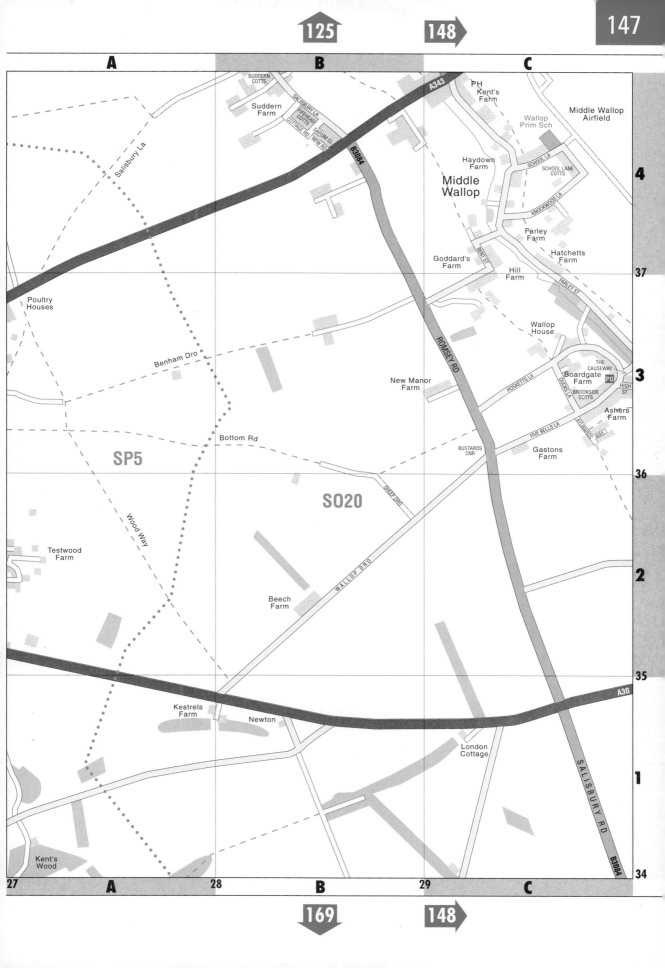

125
148
169
148

A

B

C

4

37

3

36

2

35

1

34

27

28

29

SUDDERN COTTS

Suddern Farm

SALISBURY LA

FREHEAD COTTS

COTTAGE RD

SARUM CL

NEW RD

B3084

A343

PH Kent's Farm

Wallop Prim Sch

Middle Wallop Airfield

Haydown Farm

SCHOOL LA

SCHOOL LANE COTTS

Middle Wallop

KNOCKWOOD LA

Salisbury La

Parley Farm

Hatchetts Farm

Goddard's Farm

BENT ST

Hill Farm

FARLEY ST

Poultry Houses

Wallop House

ROMSEY RD

Benham Dro

New Manor Farm

HOSKETTS LA

THE CAUSEWAY

Boardgate Farm

PO

BROOKSIDE COTTS

BUCKS LA

HIGH ST

Ashers Farm

Bottom Rd

BUSTARDS CNR

FIVE BELLS LA

AYLWARDS WAY

Gastons Farm

SP5

36

SO20

SHEEP DRO

WALLOP DRO

Wood Way

Testwood Farm

Beech Farm

Kestrels Farm

Newton

London Cottage

SALISBURY RD

A30

Kent's Wood

B3084

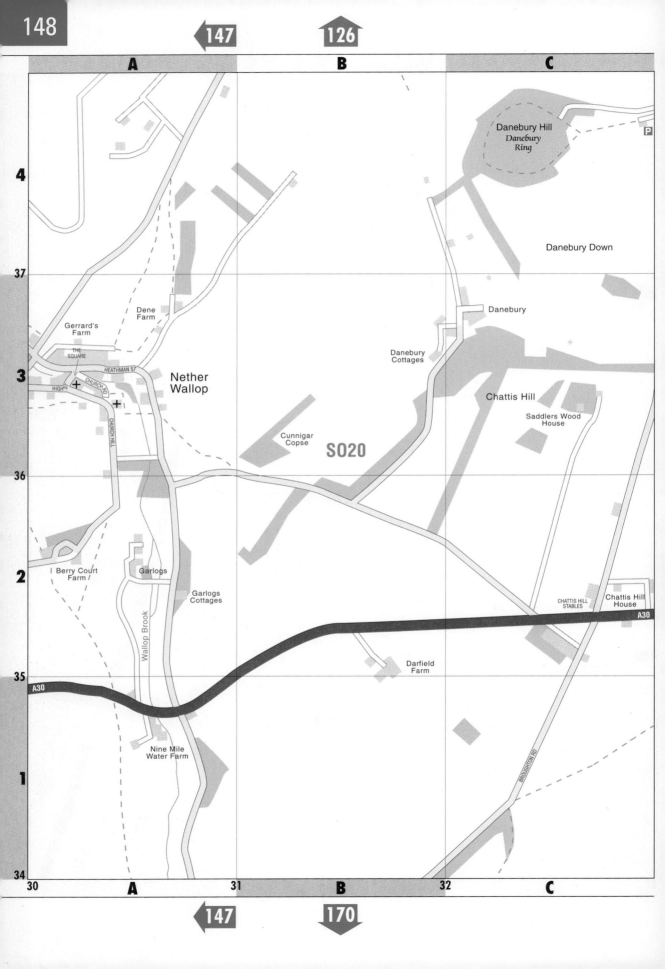

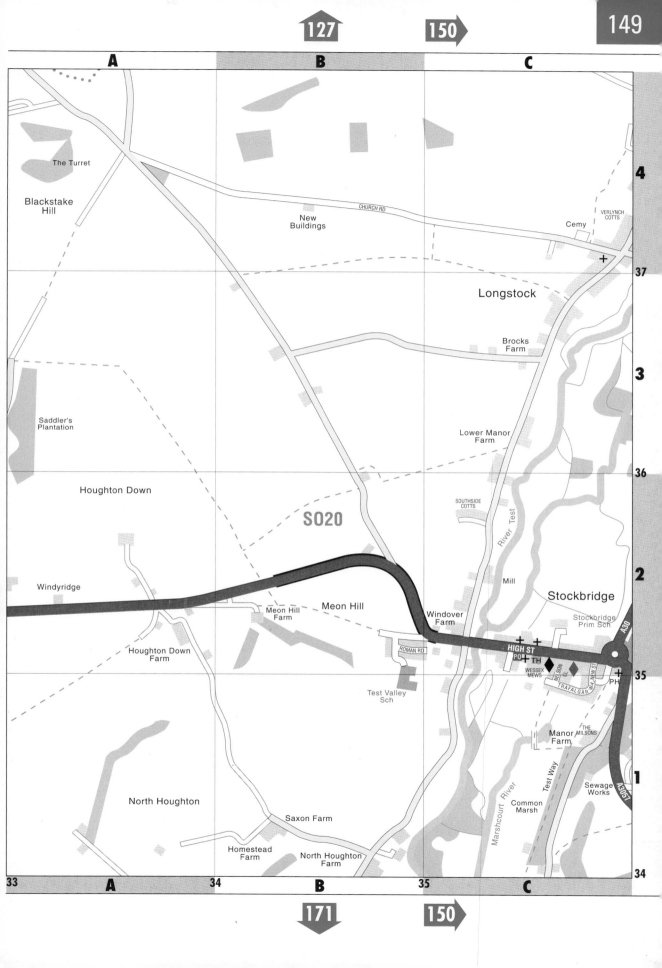

A   B   C

The Turret

Blackstake
Hill

New
Buildings

CHURCH RD

VERLYNCH
COTTS

Cemy

Longstock

Brocks
Farm

4

37

Saddler's
Plantation

Lower Manor
Farm

3

Houghton Down

SO20

SOUTHSIDE
COTTS

River Test

36

Windyridge

Meon Hill

Meon Hill
Farm

Windover
Farm

Mill

Stockbridge

Stockbridge
Prim Sch

A30

2

Houghton Down
Farm

ROMAN RD

HIGH ST
PO   TH
WESSEX
MEWS

NELSON CL

W NEW ST

TRAFALGAR

PH

35

Test Valley
Sch

Manor
Farm

THE
MILSONS

Test Way

North Houghton

Saxon Farm

Marshcourt River

Common
Marsh

Sewage
Works

A3057

1

Homestead
Farm

North Houghton
Farm

34

33   A   34   B   35   C   34

149
128

A   B   C

Abbotts
Manor
Farm

A3057

Leckford

Little Common

PO
LECKFORD

Leckford
Dairy

Leckford
Plantation

River Test

Great
Common

4

Leckford Abbas

Charity Farm
House

PH

Baker's
Farm

Aqueduct

37

Lone Barn

Leckford
Plantation

LECKFORD LA

CH

Riches
Plantation

3

Atners
Hill

Chilcombe
Copse

Atners
Towers

Test Way

SO20

Leckford
Camp

36

London Hill
Farm

LONDON RD

A30

Wynrush

Fair View
Farm

Sandydown
Farm

2

A3057

Little Dean
Farm

Woolbury Ring

A30

OLD LONDON RD

LITTLE
DEAN HO

LITTLE DEAN
CT

Sch

WINTON HILL

35

B3049

Cemetery

Stockbridge Down

Home
Farm

Lamberts

P

The
Plantation

P

1

PENNY LA

SOMBORNE PARK RD

Ridge's Grove

B3049

A3057

Teg
Down

Windovers

34

36   A   37   B   38   C

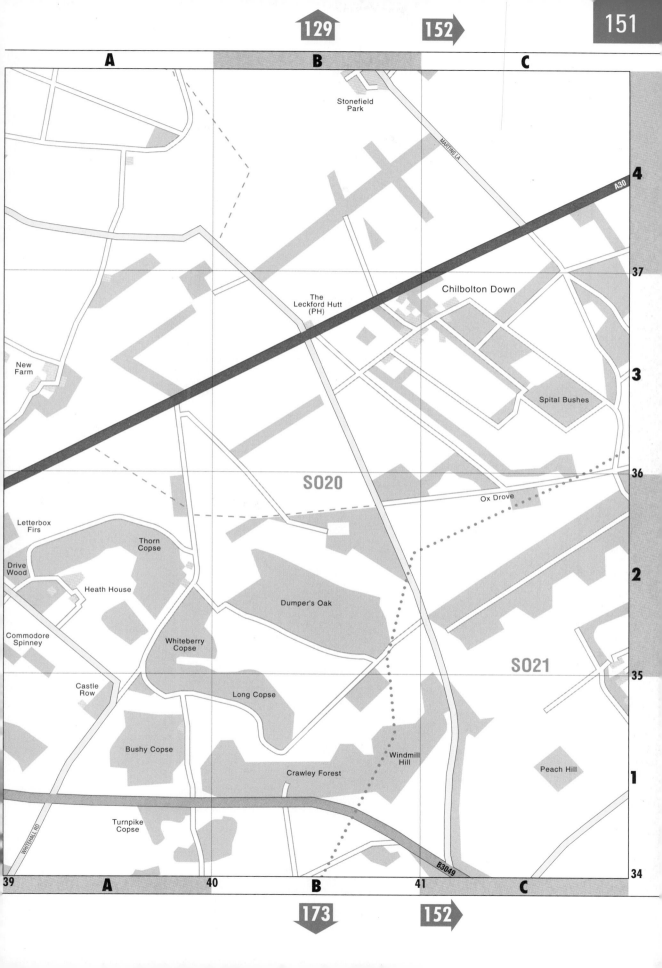

129
152
173
152

Stonefield Park

MARTINS LA

A30

Chilbolton Down

The Leckford Hutt (PH)

New Farm

Spital Bushes

SO20

Ox Drove

Letterbox Firs

Thorn Copse

Drive Wood

Heath House

Dumper's Oak

SO21

Commodore Spinney

Whiteberry Copse

Castle Row

Long Copse

Bushy Copse

Windmill Hill

Peach Hill

Crawley Forest

WHITEHALL RD

Turnpike Copse

B3049

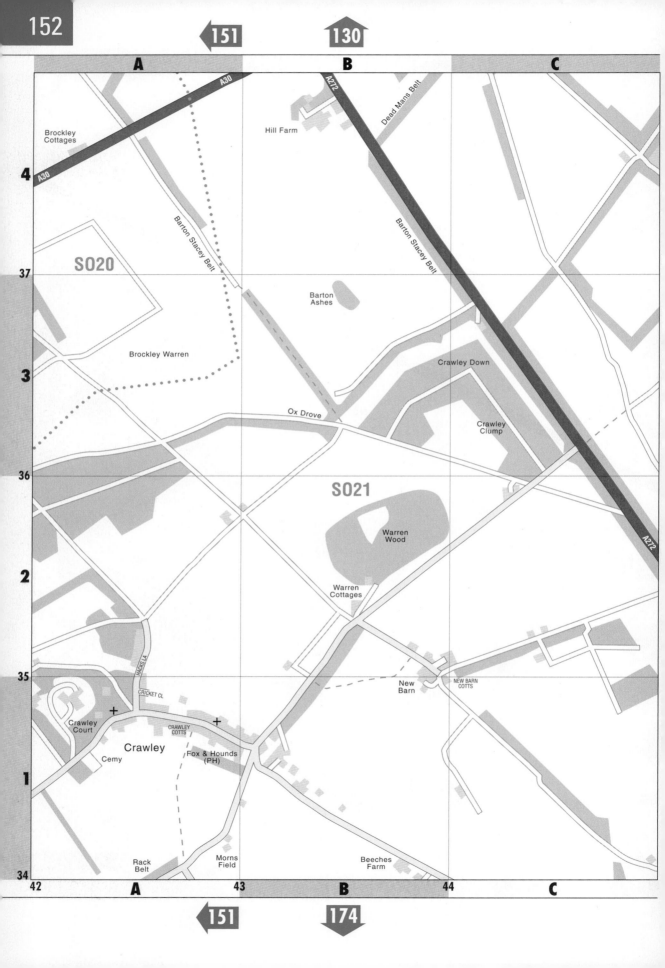

151
130

A · B · C

A30

Brockley
Cottages

A30

4

Hill Farm

A272

Dead Mans Belt

Barton Stacey Belt

Barton Stacey Belt

SO20

37

Barton
Ashes

Brockley Warren

Crawley Down

3

Ox Drove

Crawley
Clump

36

SO21

Warren
Wood

A272

2

Warren
Cottages

HACKS LA

35

New Barn

NEW BARN
COTTS

CRICKET CL

Crawley
Court

CRAWLEY
COTTS

+

+

Crawley

Cemy

Fox & Hounds
(PH)

1

Rack
Belt

Morns
Field

Beeches
Farm

34

42 · A · 43 · B · 44 · C

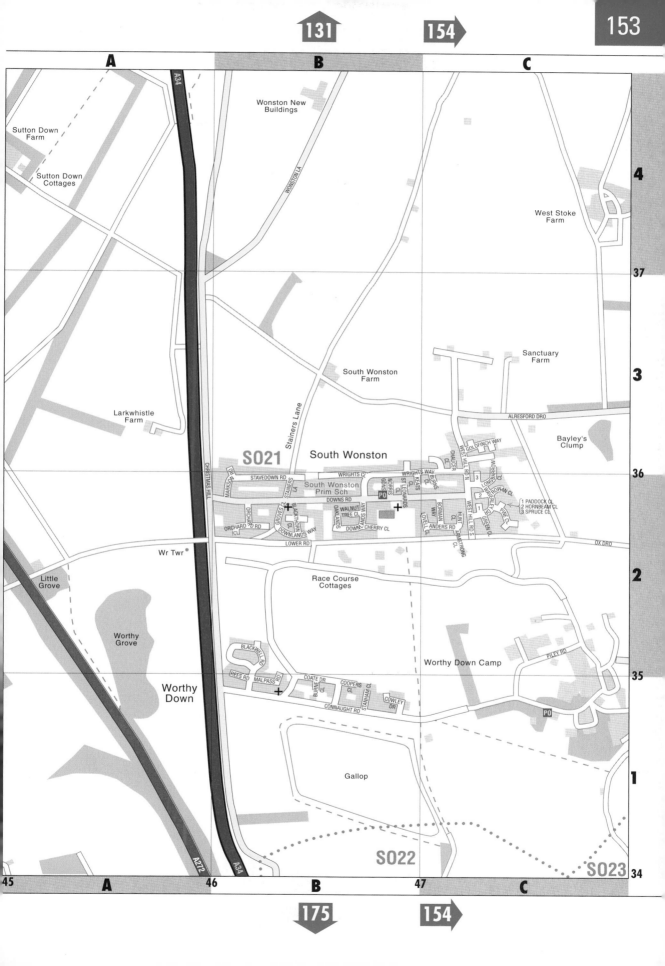

A   B   C

Sutton Down
Farm

Sutton Down
Cottages

A34

Wonston New
Buildings

WONSTON LA

West Stoke
Farm

4

37

Larkwhistle
Farm

Stainers Lane

CHRISTMAS HILL

South Wonston
Farm

Sanctuary
Farm

3

ALRESFORD DRO

SO21   South Wonston

Bayley's
Clump

GOLDFINCH WAY

WEST HILL RD N

CHAUCER CL

MORPHELY

MARKSON RD

STAVEDOWN RD

WRIGHTS CL

WRIGHTS WAY

KEATS CL

BURNS CL

ST LEONARDS CL

NORRIS GDNS

South Wonston
Prim Sch

PO

ROWAN CL

3

2

1

1 PADDOCK CL
2 HORNBEAM CL
3 SPRUCE CL

36

PINE CL

WAVERLEY RD

GREEN CL

WEST HILL RD S

DOWNS RD

WALNUT
TREE CL

OAKLANDS

DOWN...

BORMAN WAY

HUNT CL

ORCHARD RD

ORCHARD CL

GROVES

STAINERS LA

BLACKTHORN CL

DOWNLAND'S WAY

CHERRY CL

LOVELL CL

ANDERS RD

ARMSTRONG CL

DX DRO

LOWER RD

Wr Twr

Little
Grove

Race Course
Cottages

2

Worthy
Grove

Worthy Down Camp

PILEY RD

35

Worthy
Down

BLACKWELL RD

REES RD

MALPASS RD

COATE DR

BURNE CL

COOPERS CL

STANHAM CL

COWLEY DR

PO

CONNAUGHT RD

A34

Gallop

1

A272

SO22

SO23   34

45   A   46   B   47   C

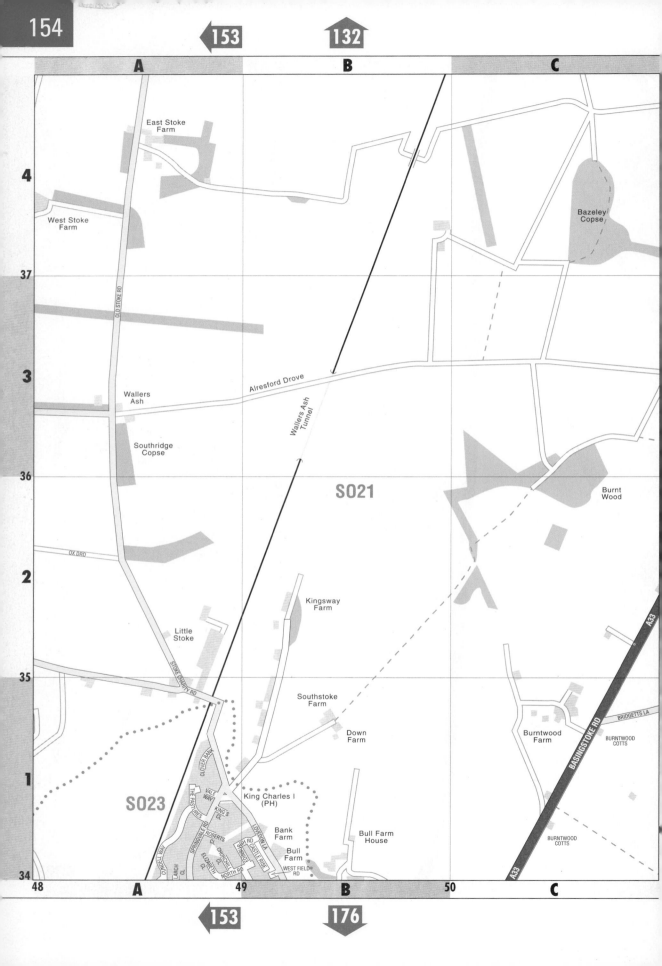

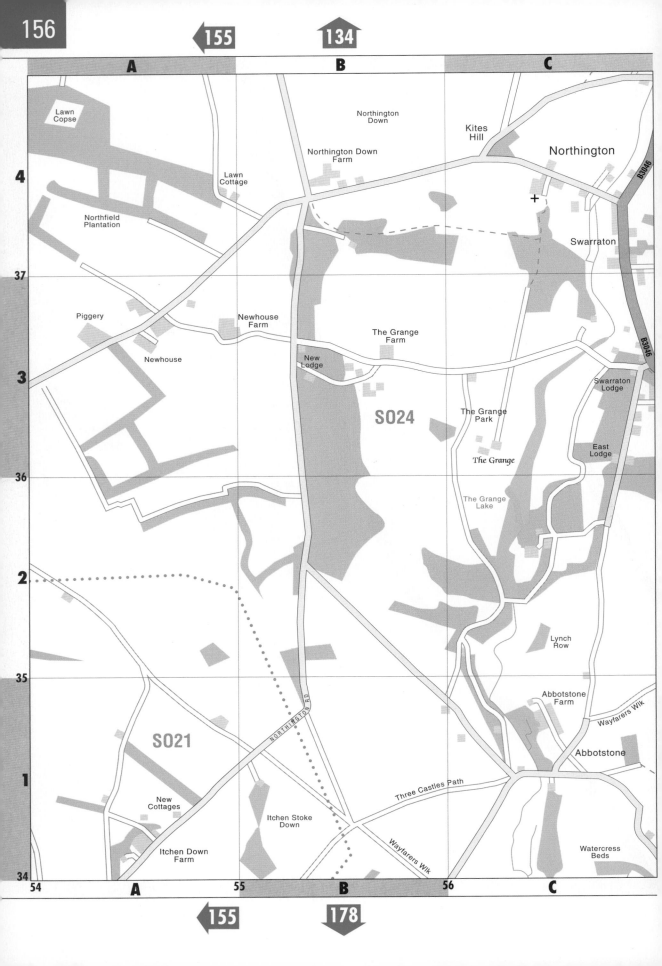

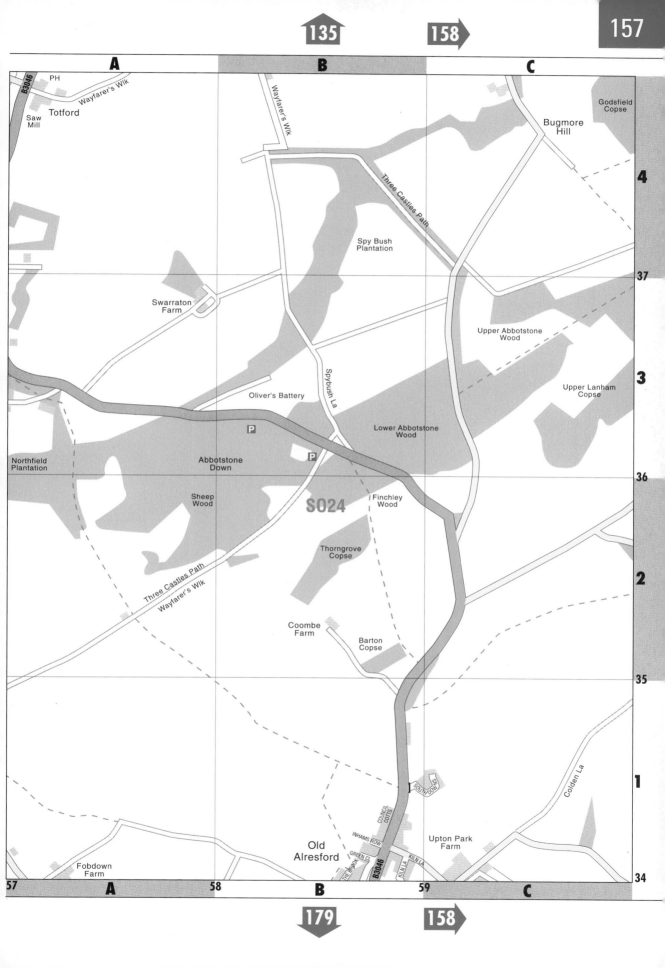

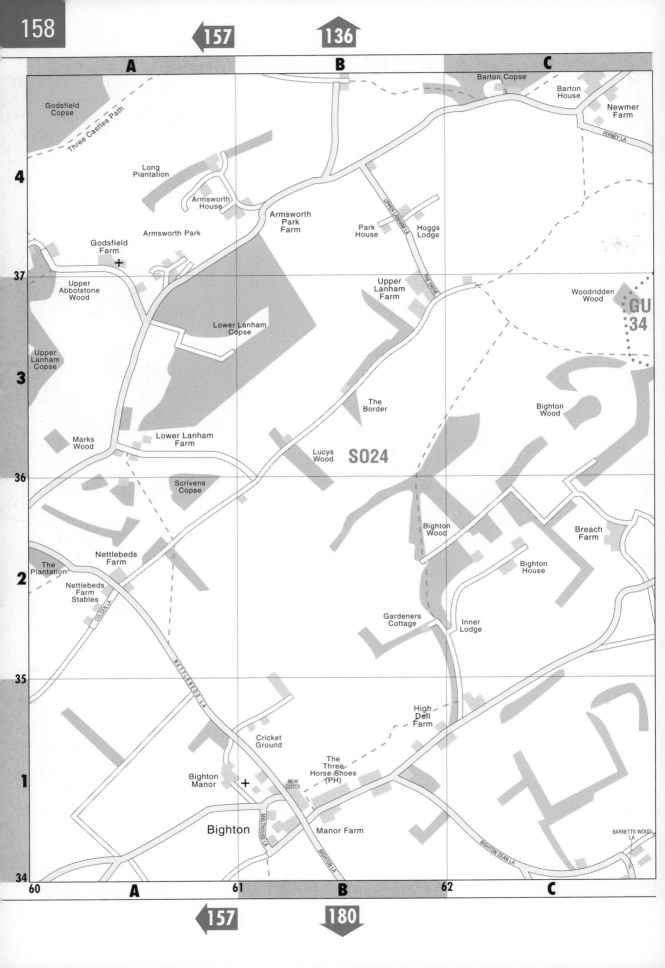

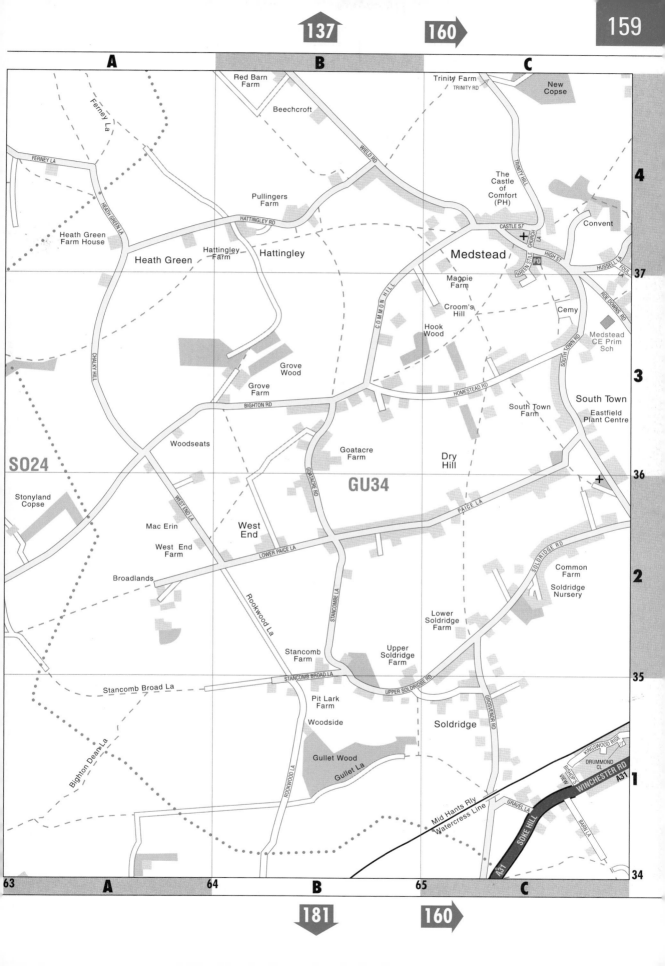

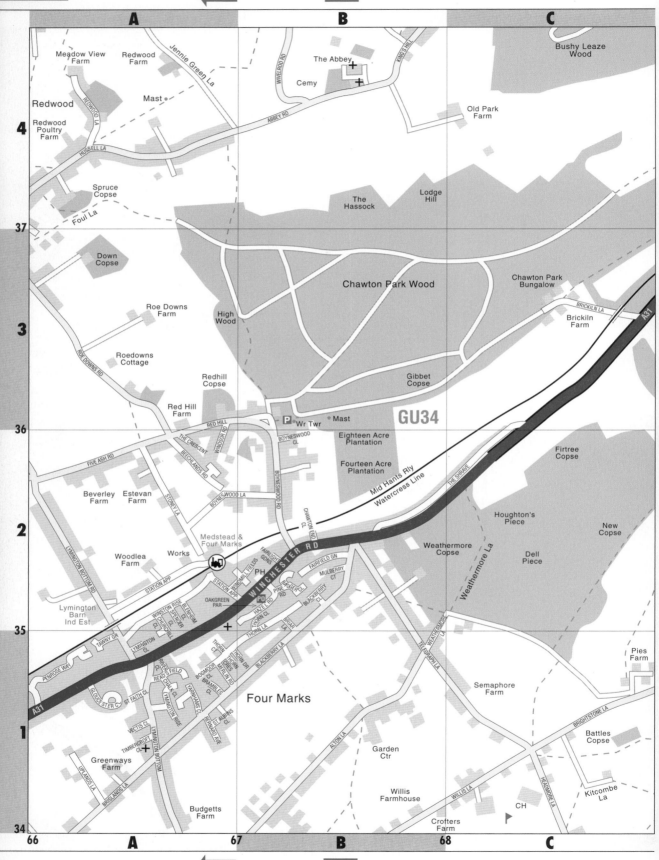

A B C

Bushy Leaze Wood

Meadow View Farm

Redwood Farm

Jennie Green La

The Abbey

Cemy

King's Hill

Redwood

Mast

Old Park Farm

Abbey Rd

Redwood Poultry Farm

Redwood La

Russell La

Spruce Copse

Foul La

The Hassock

Lodge Hill

Down Copse

Chawton Park Wood

Chawton Park Bungalow

Brickiln La

A31

Roe Downs Farm

Roe Downs Rd

Roedowns Cottage

High Wood

Brickiln Farm

Redhill Copse

Red Hill Farm

Gibbet Copse

The Crescent

Windsor Rd

Boyneswood Cl

Wr Twr

Mast

GU34

Five Ash Rd

Beechlands Rd

Eighteen Acre Plantation

Firtree Copse

Beverley Farm

Estevan Farm

Stoney La

Boyneswood La

Boyneswood Rd

Fourteen Acre Plantation

Mid Hants Rly

Watercress Line

The Shrave

Houghton's Piece

New Copse

Lymington Bottom Rd

Woodlea Farm

Works

Medstead & Four Marks

Chawton End Cl

Weathermore Copse

Weathermore La

Dell Piece

Station App

Station App

Fairlight Gdns

Winchester Rd

PH

Windmill Fields

PO

Fairfield Gn

Mulberry Ct

Lymington Barn Ind Est

Winston Rise

Blenheim

Spencer Cl

Churchill

Oakgreen Par

Hazel Rd

Pine Rd

Roger Cl

Blackberry Cl

Penrose Way

Tanny Gr

Lymington Cl

Thorn Cl

Thorn La

Brice Cl

Blackberry La

Telegraph La

Weathermore La

Pies Farm

A31

Gloucester Cl

St Faith Cl

Rivers Field

Read Cl

Chalk Cl

Lymington Bottom

Bogmoor Rd

Jones Cl

Merlin Rd

Brambles

Duncan Dr

Four Marks

Semaphore Farm

Battles Copse

Brightstone La

Uplands La

Victis Cl

Timbercroft Cl

Yarnhams Cl

Bernard Ave

St Aubins Cl

Alton La

Garden Ctr

Headmore La

Kitcombe La

Greenways Farm

Brislands La

Budgetts Farm

Willis Farmhouse

Willis La

Crofters Farm

CH

66 A 67 B 68 C

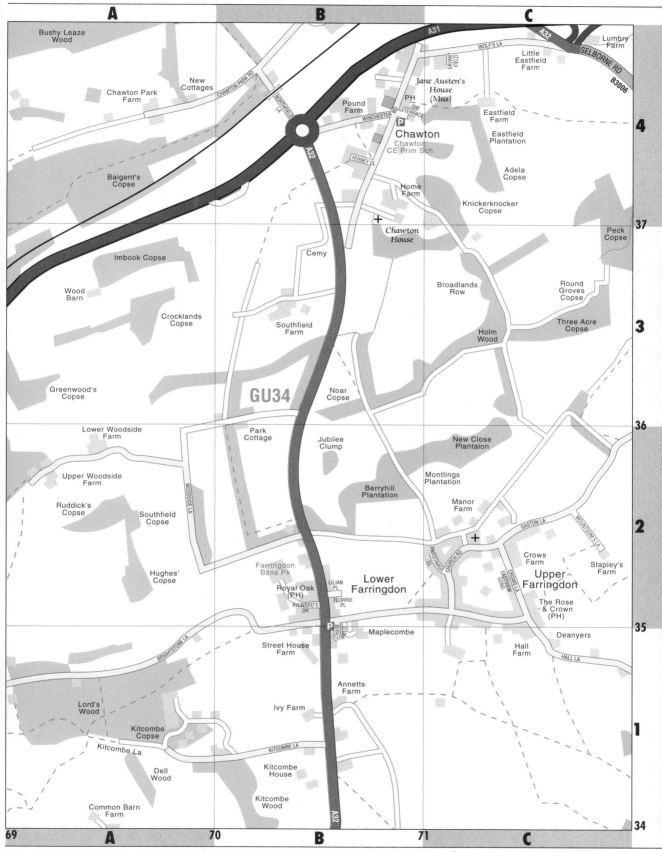

Bushy Leaze Wood

New Cottages

Chawton Park Farm

CHAWTON PARK RD

NORTHFIELD LA

WINCHESTER RD

A31

A32

WOLF'S LA

SELBORNE RD

B3006

Lumbry Farm

Little Eastfield Farm

LAVANT FIELD

Pound Farm

PH
THE TERRACE

Jane Austen's House (Mus)

Eastfield Farm

Eastfield Plantation

4

Baigent's Copse

FERNEY CL

P

Chawton

Chawton CE Prim Sch

Adela Copse

Home Farm

Knickerknocker Copse

Imbook Copse

Cemy

Chawton House

Broadlands Row

Peck Copse

37

Wood Barn

Round Groves Copse

Crocklands Copse

Southfield Farm

Holm Wood

Three Acre Copse

3

Greenwood's Copse

GU34

Noar Copse

Lower Woodside Farm

Park Cottage

Jubilee Clump

New Close Plantaion

36

Upper Woodside Farm

WOODSIDE LA

Berryhill Plantation

Montlings Plantation

Manor Farm

Ruddick's Copse

Southfield Copse

GASTON LA

MOUNTSM'S LA

Crows Farm

Stapley's Farm

2

Hughes' Copse

Farringdon Bsns Pk

Royal Oak (PH)

LILIAN PL

FLORRIE PL

AYLWARD'S DR

Lower Farringdon

PARSSNAGE CL

CHURCH RD

EASTVIEW GDNS

CROWS LA

Upper Farringdon

The Rose & Crown (PH)

P

CHASE PIECE

Maplecombe

Hall Farm

Deanyers

HALL LA

35

BRIGHTSTONE LA

Street House Farm

Annetts Farm

Lord's Wood

Ivy Farm

1

Kitcombe Copse

Kitcombe La

KITCOMBE LA

Kitcombe House

Dell Wood

Kitcombe Wood

Common Barn Farm

A32

34

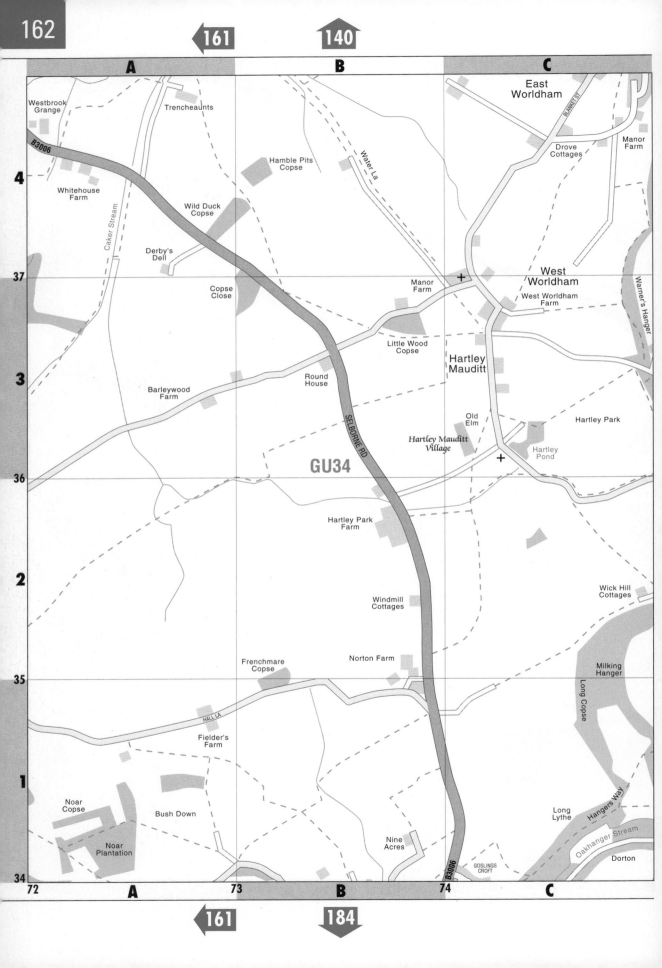

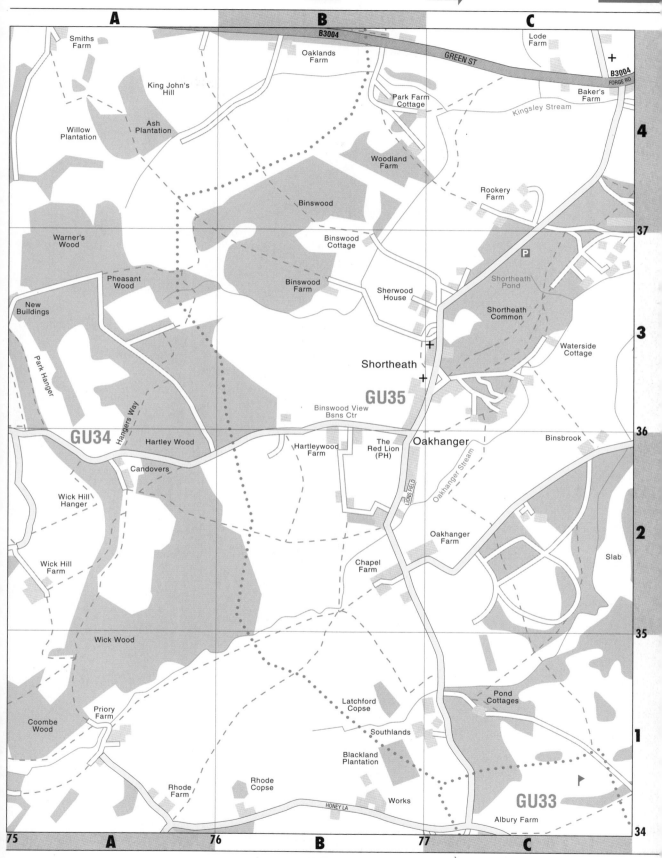

← 163
↑ 142

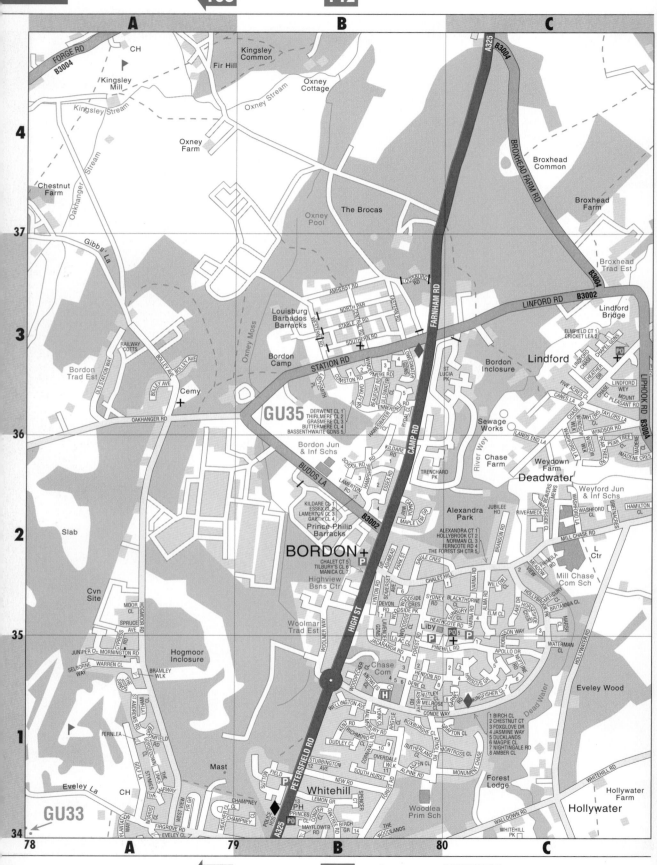

← 163
↓ 186

B1
1 WISTERIA DR
2 OAK LODGE
3 SHAFTESBURY CT
4 ASHLEY HO
5 COOPER HO
6 JOHN POUNDS HO
7 CONNAUGHT CL
8 BLUE TIMBERS CL
9 BEDFORD CL
10 NORTHUMBERLAND RD
11 OVERDALE PL
12 TWOWAYS CT
13 WITTCOMBE TERR
14 PELHAM CL

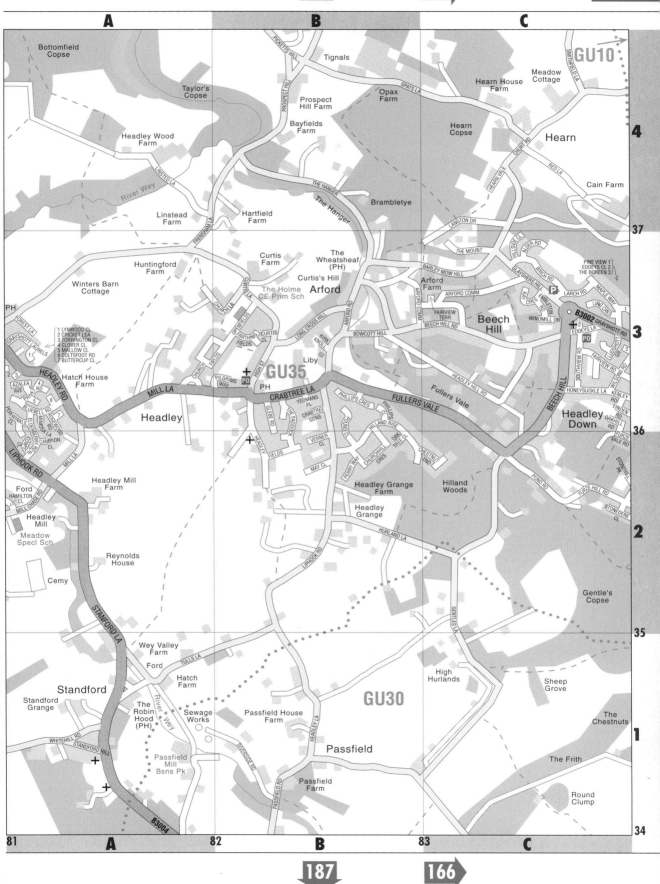

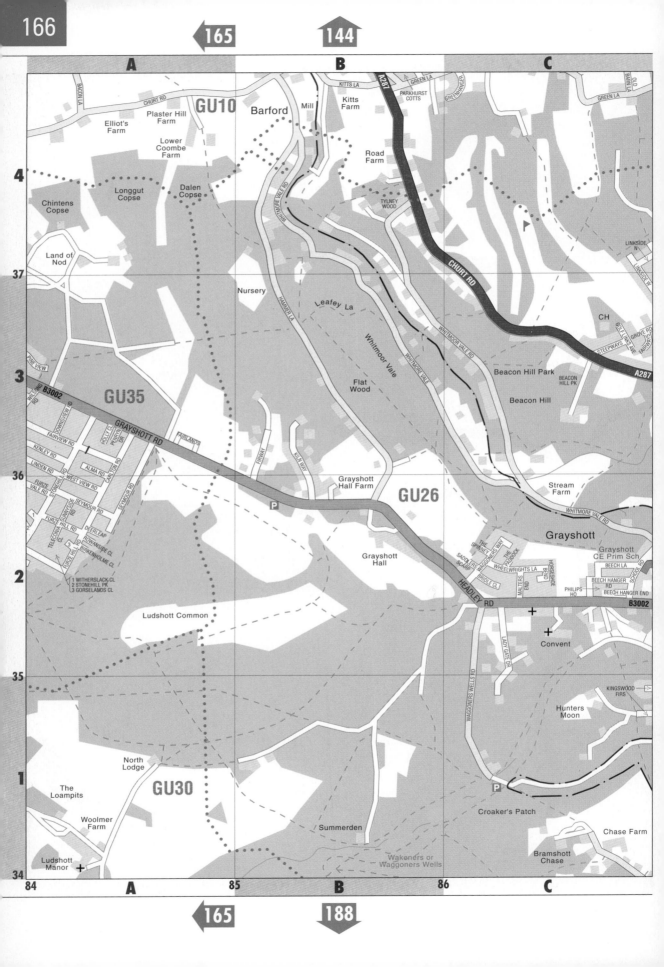

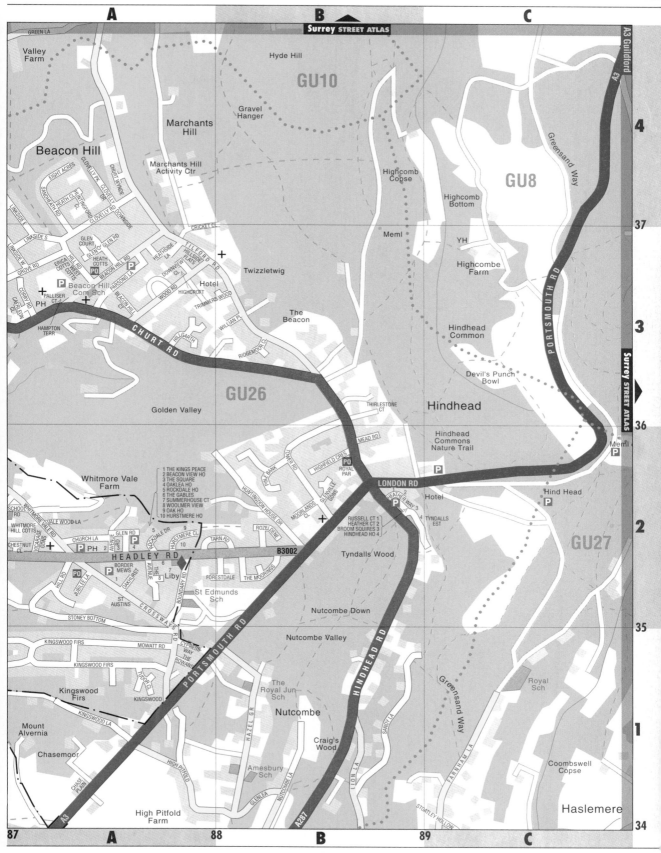

GU10

Valley Farm

Hyde Hill

Gravel Hanger

Marchants Hill

Beacon Hill

Marchants Hill Activity Ctr

Highcomb Copse

GU8

Greensand Way

A3 Guildford

A3

Highcomb Bottom

4

37

Meml

YH

Highcombe Farm

EIGHT ACRES

CLOVELLY PK

HEATH CLARENDON RD

CLOVELLY CL

DOWNSIDE

Twizzletwig

CRICKET CL

GLEN COURT

GLEN CV

GLEN RD

HEATH COTTS

HEATHSIDE LA

HILLSIDE FLATS

DOWNVIEW CL

Hindhead Common

Highcombe Farm

TILFORD RD

P

P

Beacon Hill Com Sch

PALLISER CT

PH

WOOD RD

HIGHCROFT

Hotel

High

TRIMMERS WOOD

The Beacon

PORTSMOUTH RD

3

Devil's Punch Bowl

CHURT RD

HAMPTON TERR

BEACON HILL CT

HILGARTH

WILLIAN PL

RIDGEMOOR CL

THIRLESTONE CT

Hindhead

GU26

Golden Valley

MEAD RD

Hindhead Commons Nature Trail

36

Meml

P

Whitmore Vale Farm

1 THE KINGS PEACE
2 BEACON VIEW HO
3 THE SQUARE
4 OAKLEA HO
5 ROCKDALE HO
6 THE GABLES
7 SUMMERHOUSE CT
8 WOOLMER VIEW
9 OAK HO
10 HURSTMERE HO

PINE BANK

TOWER RD

HIGHFIELD CRES

PO

ROYAL PAR

P

LONDON RD

Hind Head

P

SCHOOL RD

WHITMORE VALE WOOD LA

AVENUE GDNS

GLEN RD

P

MOORLANDS CL

GLENVILLE GDNS

ROYAL PAR

P

Hotel

HEATHER WAY 3

TYNDALLS EST

GU27

Whitmore Hill Cotts

CHURCH LA

VICARAGE GDNS

Chestnut Rd

PH

ROCKDALE DR

HURSTMERE CL

TARN RD

ROZELDENE

RUSSELL CT 1
HEATHER CT 2
BROOM SQUIRES 3
HINDHEAD HO 4

2

P

HEADLEY RD

B3002

Tyndalls Wood

HILL RD

PO

ABLETT LA

BORDER MEWS

P

OAKHURST

THE AVENUE

Liby

BOUNDARY RD

FORESTDALE

THE MOORINGS

St Edmunds Sch

Nutcombe Down

ST AUSTINS

CROSSWAYS

STONEY BOTTOM

35

KINGSWOOD FIRS

MOWATT RD

ROAD

CYPRESS WAY

THE ROWANS

St Edmunds Sch

Nutcombe Valley

Greensand Way

Royal Sch

KINGSWOOD FIRS

TUDOR CL

KINGSWOOD

PORTSMOUTH RD

The Royal Jun Sch

HINDHEAD RD

HAZEL GR

Kingswood Firs

Mount Alvernia

KINGSWOOD LA

Nutcombe

1

Chasemoor

Craig's Wood

LION LA

SANDY LA

Coombswell Copse

CHASE PLAIN

A3

High Pitfold

Amesbury Sch

GLENLEA

NUTCOMBE LA

A287

STOATLEY HOLLOW

FARNHAM LA

Haslemere

High Pitfold Farm

34

A   B   C

East
Winterslow

Red La

Howe
Copse

Burretts
Grove

Earthpits
Wood

Ramshill Dro

4

Hill
Farm

Ramshill
House

Warren
Farm

MILL LA

Cooper's
Farm

Noad's
Copse

Middle
Winterslow

33

THE CAUSEWAY

Birchen
Copse

STONE CL

THE FLASHETT

GLEBEFIELD CL

GUNVILLE HILL

Easton Common Hill

The Monarch's Way

WEAVERS
CL

PADDOCK

KINGS

SAXON LEAS

MIDDLETON RD

PO

PH

THE COMMON

GUNVILLE RD

Robin Hill
Farm

Clarendon Way

Little Buckholt
Farm

COMMON
VALE

Upper Noad's
Copse

3

WESTON LA

The
Common

WITT RD

TYTHERLEY RD

Lower Noad's Copse

Yarmley
Farm

BENTLEY
WAY

SP5

Witt's
End

Elevage
Breton

32

Hedgemoor
Copse

Tanglewood

Richwellsted
Copse

Wiltshire STREET ATLAS

2

Picked
Copse

Smokeway
Copse

Gravel Shoot
Copse

Home
Farm

Chickard
Wood

Three Sisters
Copse

Northaw
Sch

31

Hooping Oak
Copse

LIVERY RD

1

Bentley
Wood

Prior's
Copse

Park La

Coalpits
Copse

Beechways
Copse

Redman's
Gore

Park
Copse

30

24   A   25   B   26   C

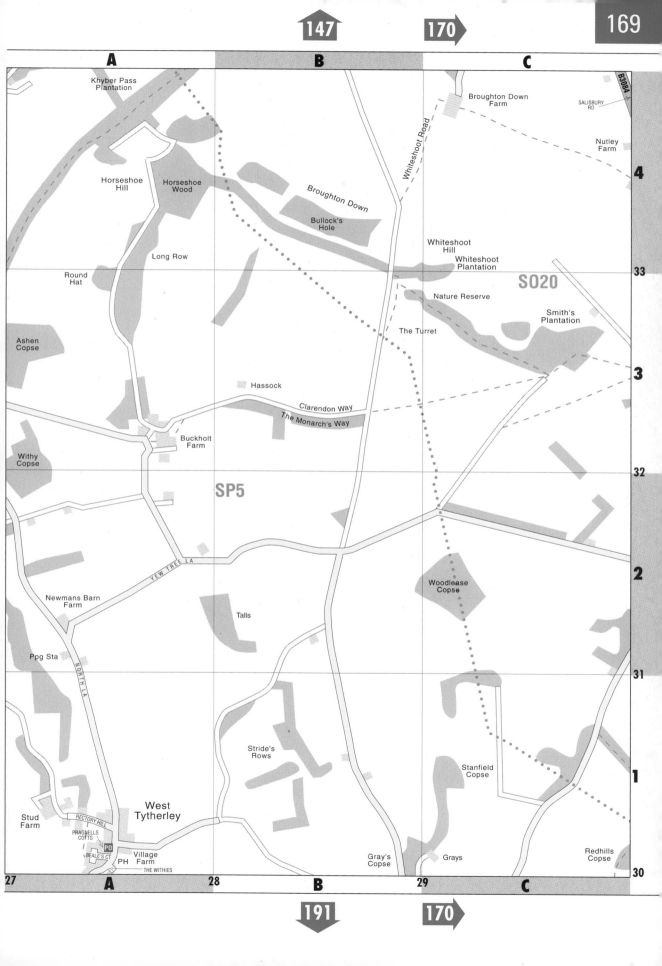

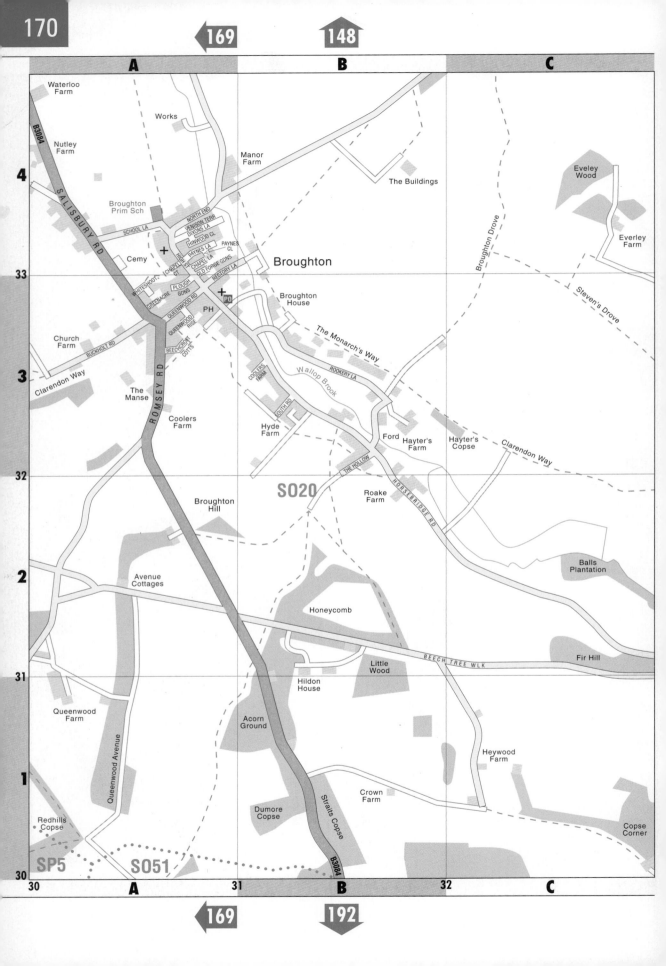

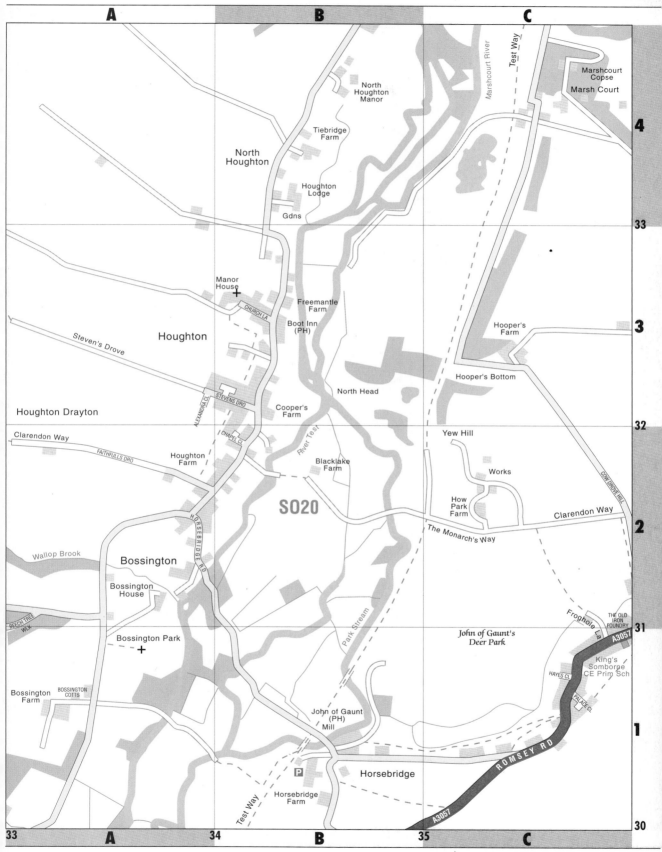

A B C

4

33

3

32

2

31

1

30

Marshcourt River
Test Way
Marshcourt Copse
Marsh Court

North Houghton Manor

Tiebridge Farm

North Houghton

Houghton Lodge

Gdns

Manor House

Freemantle Farm

CHURCH LA

Boot Inn (PH)

Houghton

Hooper's Farm

Steven's Drove

North Head

Hooper's Bottom

Houghton Drayton

STEVENS DRO

ALEXANDRA CL

Cooper's Farm

Yew Hill

Clarendon Way

FAITHFULLS DRO

CHAPEL CL

Houghton Farm

Blacklake Farm

River Test

Works

How Park Farm

Clarendon Way

COW DROVE HILL

SO20

HORSEBRIDGE RD

The Monarch's Way

Wallop Brook

Bossington

Bossington House

Park Stream

John of Gaunt's Deer Park

Froghole La

THE OLD IRON FOUNDRY

A3057

BEECH TREE WLK

Bossington Park

King's Somborne CE Prim Sch

HAYES CL

Bossington Farm

BOSSINGTON COTTS

John of Gaunt (PH)
Mill

PALACE CL

ROMSEY RD

A3057

Horsebridge

P

Test Way

Horsebridge Farm

A3057

33 34 B 35 C 30

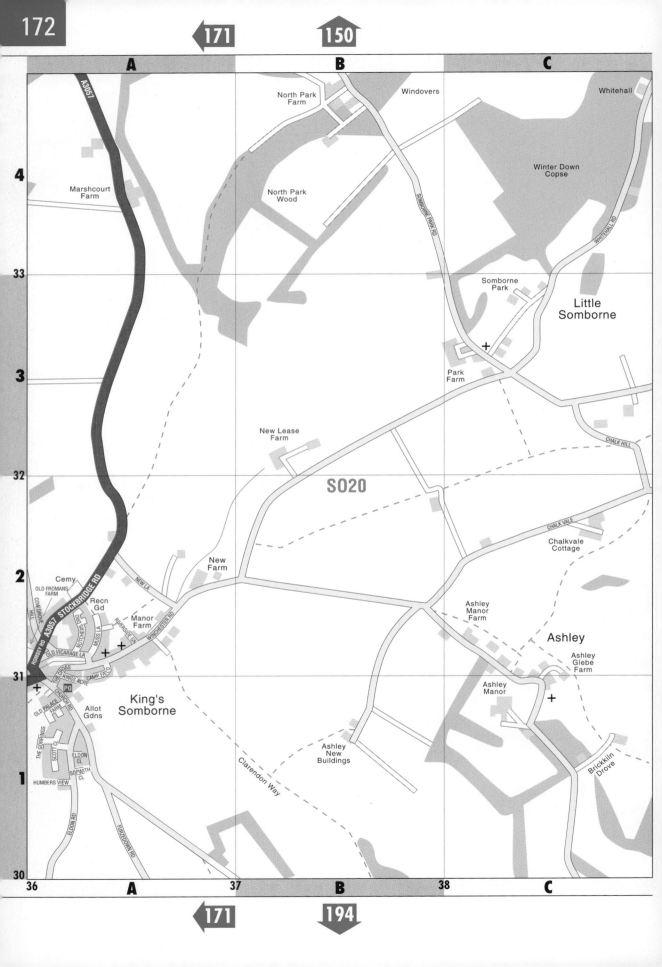

171
150

A   **B**   **C**

North Park Farm

Windovers

Whitehall

A3057

North Park Wood

Winter Down Copse

SOMBORNE PARK RD

WHITEHALL RD

Marshcourt Farm

4

Somborne Park

33

Little Somborne

Park Farm

3

CHALK HILL

New Lease Farm

32

SO20

CHALK VALE

Chalkvale Cottage

New Farm

New LA

Cemy

OLD FROMANS FARM

STOCKBRIDGE RD

A3057

COW DROVE

RIVERSIDE GN

WINCHESTER RD

Recn Gd

Manor Farm

MUSS LA

OLD NUTCHERS RD

ROMSEY RD

OLD VICARAGE LA

2

Ashley Manor Farm

Ashley

Ashley Glebe Farm

THE CROSS

KINGS ACRE

CAMP FIELD

HILL

PO

Ashley Manor

31

King's Somborne

Allot Gdns

OLD PALACE FARM

CHURCH RD

Ashley New Buildings

Brickkiln Drove

THE GORRINGS

SCOTT CL

ELDON CL

SOPWITH CL

HUMBERS VIEW

Clarendon Way

1

ELDON RD

FURZEDOWN RD

30

36   **A**   **37**   **B**   **38**   **C**

171
194

WHITEHALL RD

Fox Heath Copse

Folly Farm

B3049

4

Rookley Farm

33

Rookley Manor

COURT LA

Up
Somborne

3

Lovell's
Farm

COUNCIL
HOS

Ower Wood

SO20

Forest
Extra

No Man's
Land

SO21

32

CHALK VALE

Little
Up Somborne
Wood

No Man's Land

2

Great
Up Somborne
Wood

Sparsholt
Corner

Ashley
Wood

Corner
Plantation

31

Forest Round
Wood

Lawn
Copse

Well
Copse

1

Forest
Great
Wood

The
Oven

West Wood

30

39

40

41

A

B

C

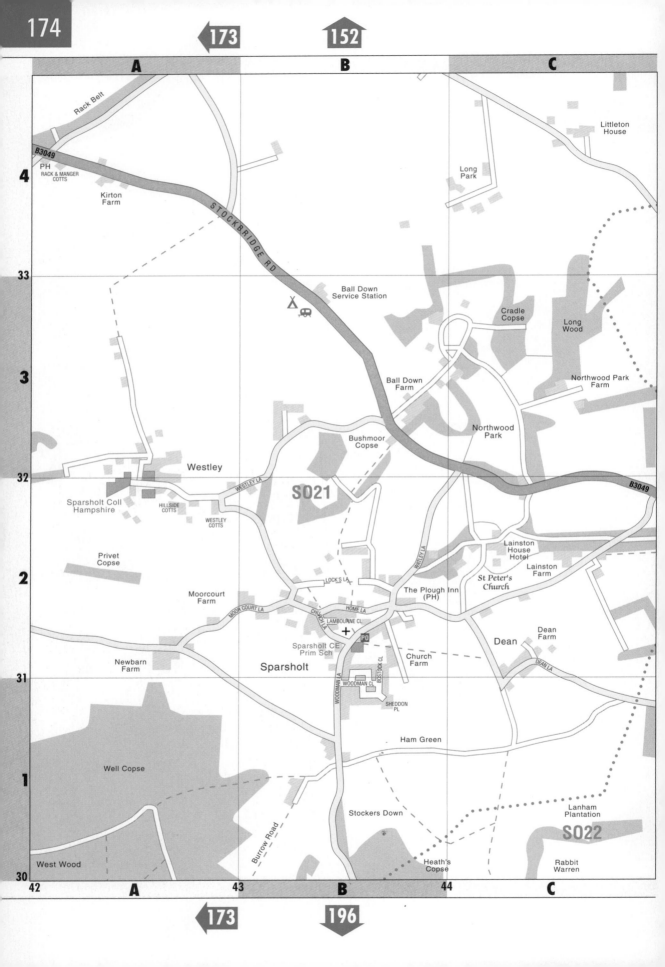

A   **B**   **C**

Rack Belt

B3049

4

PH
RACK & MANGER
COTTS

Kirton
Farm

Littleton
House

Long
Park

STOCKBRIDGE RD

33

Ball Down
Service Station

Cradle
Copse

Long
Wood

3

Ball Down
Farm

Northwood Park
Farm

Bushmoor
Copse

Northwood
Park

Westley

32

WESTLEY LA

SO21

B3049

Sparsholt Coll
Hampshire

HILLSIDE
COTTS

WESTLEY
COTTS

Lainston
House
Hotel

Lainston
Farm

Privet
Copse

Moorcourt
Farm

LOCK'S LA

St Peter's
Church

2

MOOR COURT LA

CHURCH LA

HOME LA

WATLEY LA

The Plough Inn
(PH)

Dean
Farm

LAMBOURNE CL

Dean

Newbarn
Farm

+

PO

Sparsholt CE
Prim Sch

Church
Farm

DEAN LA

31

Sparsholt

WOODMAN LA

BOSTOCK CL

WOODMAN CL

SHEDDON
PL

Ham Green

1

Well Copse

Stockers Down

Lanham
Plantation

SO22

Burrow Road

Heath's
Copse

Rabbit
Warren

West Wood

30

42   **A**   43   **B**   44   **C**

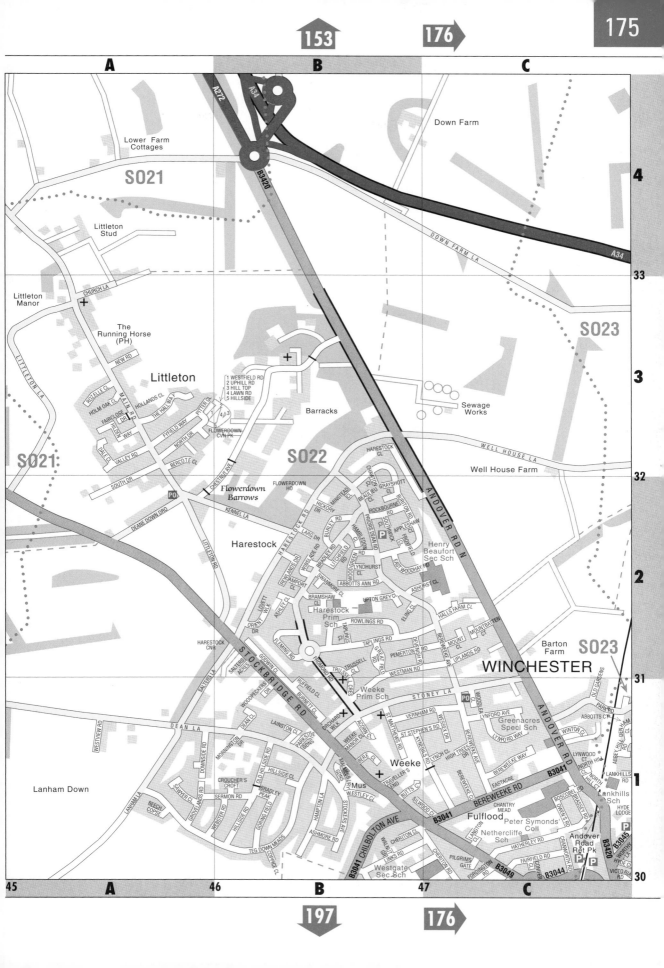

A1		
1 PARK CT	10 MERIDEN CT	20 THE TOLLGATE
2 HUSSEY CL	11 WARNER CT	21 HYDE LODGE
3 CORAM CL	12 ALTON CT	22 HYDE HOUSE GDNS
4 CONEY GN	13 WARWICK CL	23 DANES RD
5 SIMONDS CT	14 WARWICK CT	24 HYDE CHURCH PATH
6 COLBOURNE CT	15 TWYFORD CT	25 BARTHOLOMEW CL
7 COVENTRY CT	16 FARINGDON CT	26 ST BEDE'S CT
8 KENILWORTH CT	17 REGENT CT	27 ALSWITHA TERR
9 STRATFORD CT	18 WOODLANDS CT	28 ROSEWARNE CT
	19 DONNINGTON CT	29 KING ALFRED TERR

A1
30 ARLINGTON PL
31 DALZELL
32 YORK HO

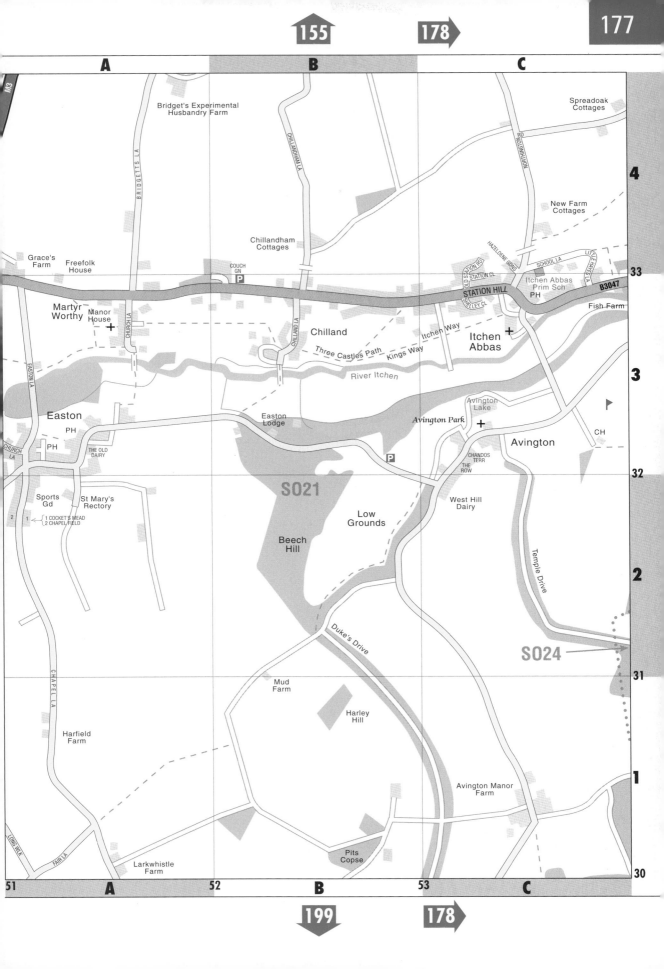

A B C

4

Bridget's Experimental
Husbandry Farm

Spreadoak
Cottages

New Farm
Cottages

Grace's
Farm

Freefolk
House

Chillandham
Cottages

COUCH
GN
P

Itchen Abbas
Prim Sch
PH

33

B3047

Martyr
Worthy

Manor
House

STATION HILL

Fish Farm

Chilland

Three Castles Path

Kings Way

Itchen Way

Itchen
Abbas

River Itchen

3

Avington
Lake

Easton

PH

Easton
Lodge

Avington Park

Avington

CH

PH

THE OLD
DAIRY

P

CHANDOS
TERR
THE
ROW

32

CHURCH LA

Sports
Gd

St Mary's
Rectory

SO21

West Hill
Dairy

2   1

1 COCKET'S MEAD
2 CHAPEL FIELD

Low
Grounds

Beech
Hill

Temple Drive

2

SO24

Duke's Drive

31

Mud
Farm

Harley
Hill

CHAPEL LA

Harfield
Farm

1

Avington Manor
Farm

LONG WALK

FAIR LA

Larkwhistle
Farm

Pits
Copse

30

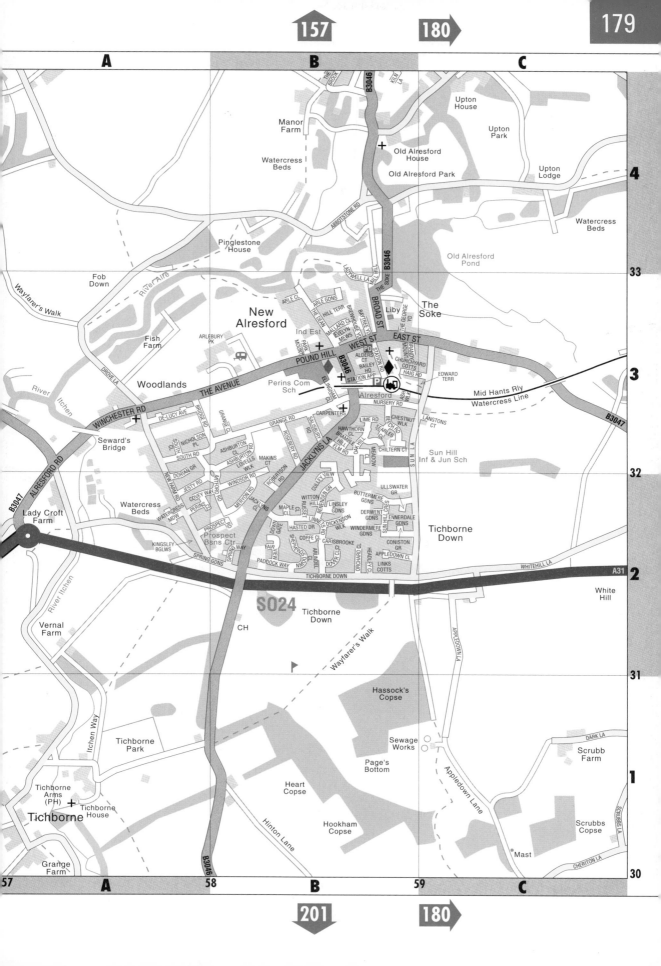

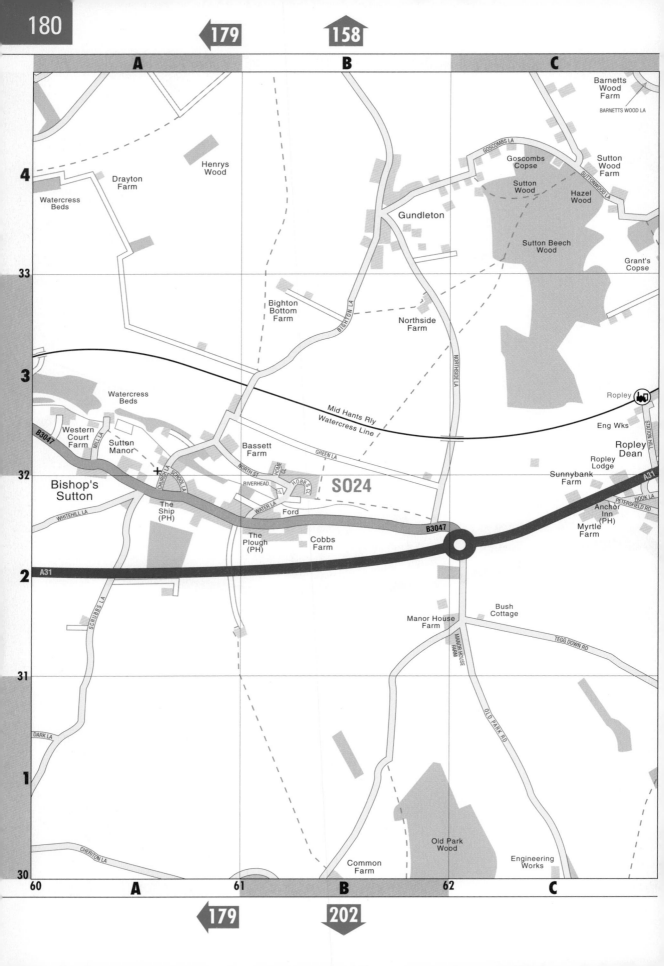

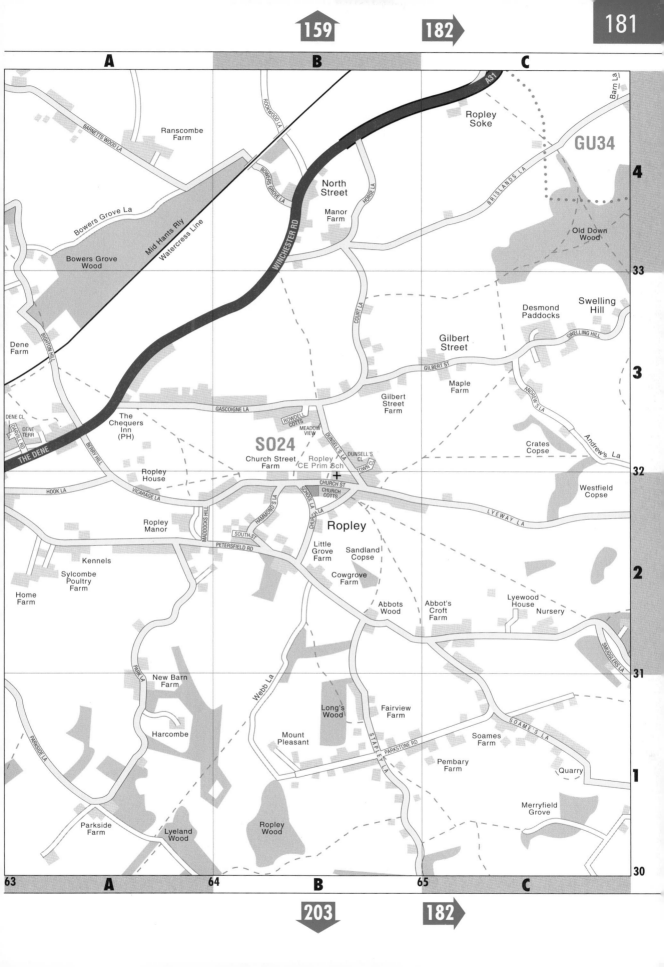

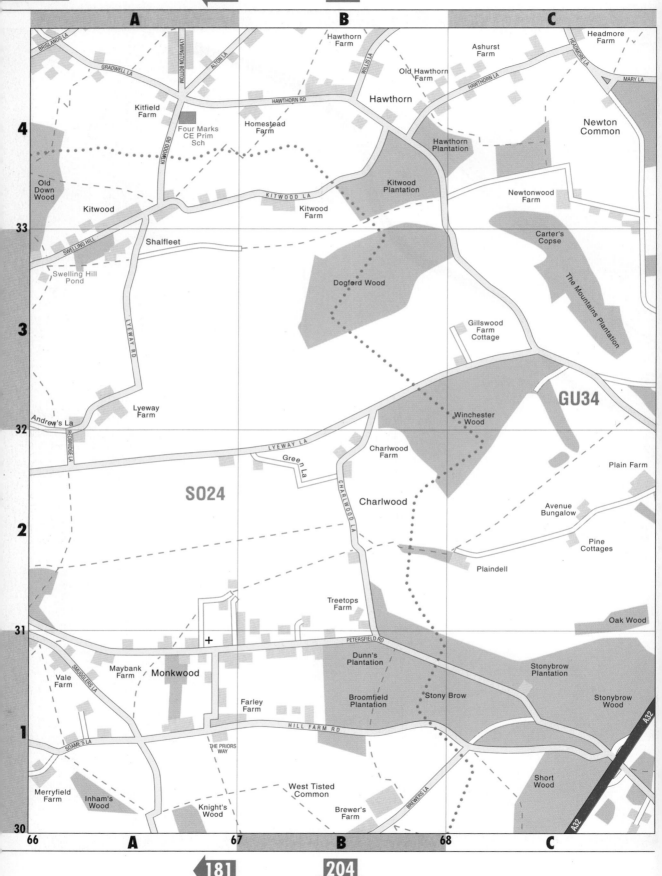

A   B   C

BRISLANDS LA
GRADWELL LA
LYMINGTON BOTTOM
ALTON LA
WILLIS LA
HEADMORE LA
MARY LA

Hawthorn Farm
Old Hawthorn Farm
Ashurst Farm
Headmore Farm

HAWTHORN RD
HAWTHORN LA

Kitfield Farm
Four Marks CE Prim Sch
Homestead Farm
Hawthorn
Newton Common

4

KITWOOD RD

Hawthorn Plantation

Old Down Wood
Kitwood
KITWOOD LA
Kitwood Farm
Kitwood Plantation
Newtonwood Farm

33

SWELLING HILL
Shalfleet
Carter's Copse

Swelling Hill Pond
Dogford Wood
The Mountains Plantation

LYEWAY RD

Gillswood Farm Cottage

3

Andrew's La
Lyeway Farm
Winchester Wood
GU34

REDBRIDGE LA

32
LYEWAY LA
Charlwood Farm
Plain Farm

Green La
Avenue Bungalow

SO24
CHARLWOOD LA
Charlwood
Pine Cottages

2
Plaindell

Treetops Farm
Oak Wood

31
PETERSFIELD RD

Dunn's Plantation
Stonybrow Plantation

Vale Farm
Maybank Farm
Monkwood
Stony Brow
Stonybrow Wood

SMUGGLERS LA
Farley Farm
Broomfield Plantation
A32

1
HILL FARM RD

SOAME'S LA
THE PRIORS WAY
Short Wood

Merryfield Farm
Inham's Wood
Knight's Wood
West Tisted Common
Brewer's Farm
BREWERS LA
A32

30

66   **A**   67   **B**   68   **C**

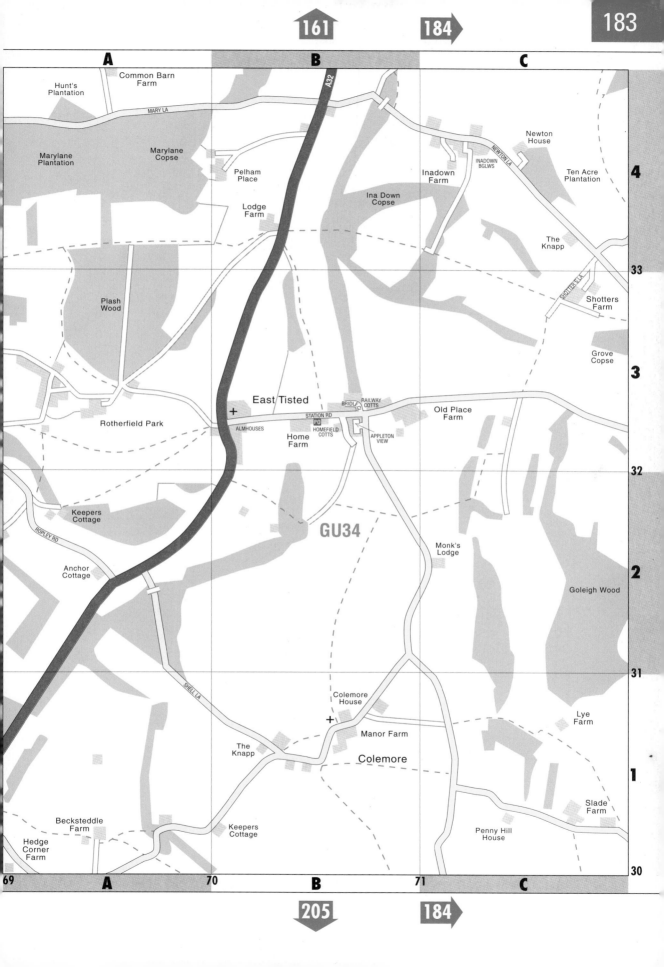

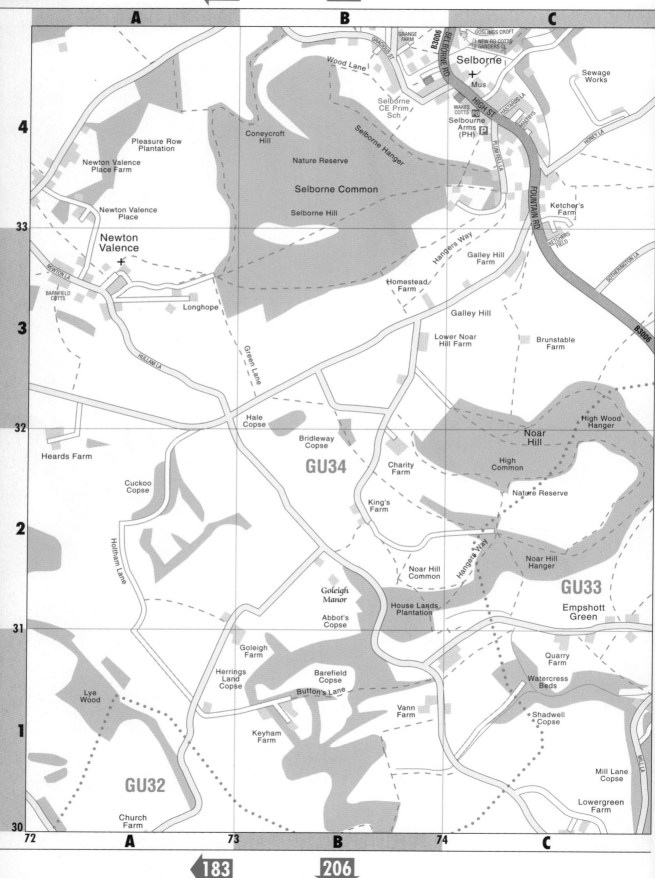

A B C

4

33

3

32

2

31

1

30

72 A 73 B 74 C

Selborne

Sewage Works

Goslings Croft
1 New Rd Cotts
2 Ganders Cl

Grange Farm

Gracious St

Wood Lane

Selborne CE Prim Sch

Selborne Hanger

Nature Reserve

Selborne Common

Selborne Hill

Pleasure Row Plantation

Newton Valence Place Farm

Coneycroft Hill

Wakes Cotts

Selbourne Arms (PH)

Mus

High St

Hastards La

Maltbys

Honey La

Ketcher's Farm

Ketchers Field

Fountain Rd

Plum Fell La

Newton Valence Place

Newton Valence

Hangers Way

Galley Hill Farm

Sotherington La

B3006

Newton La

Barnfield Cotts

Longhope

Huilam La

Green Lane

Homestead Farm

Galley Hill

Lower Noar Hill Farm

Brunstable Farm

Heards Farm

Hale Copse

Bridleway Copse

GU34

Charity Farm

High Wood Hanger

Noar Hill

High Common

Nature Reserve

Cuckoo Copse

King's Farm

Holtham Lane

Goleigh Manor

Abbot's Copse

Noar Hill Common

Hangers Way

House Lands Plantation

Noar Hill Hanger

GU33

Empshott Green

Lye Wood

Goleigh Farm

Herrings Land Copse

Barefield Copse

Button's Lane

Vann Farm

Quarry Farm

Watercress Beds

Shadwell Copse

Keyham Farm

GU32

Church Farm

Mill La

Mill Lane Copse

Lowergreen Farm

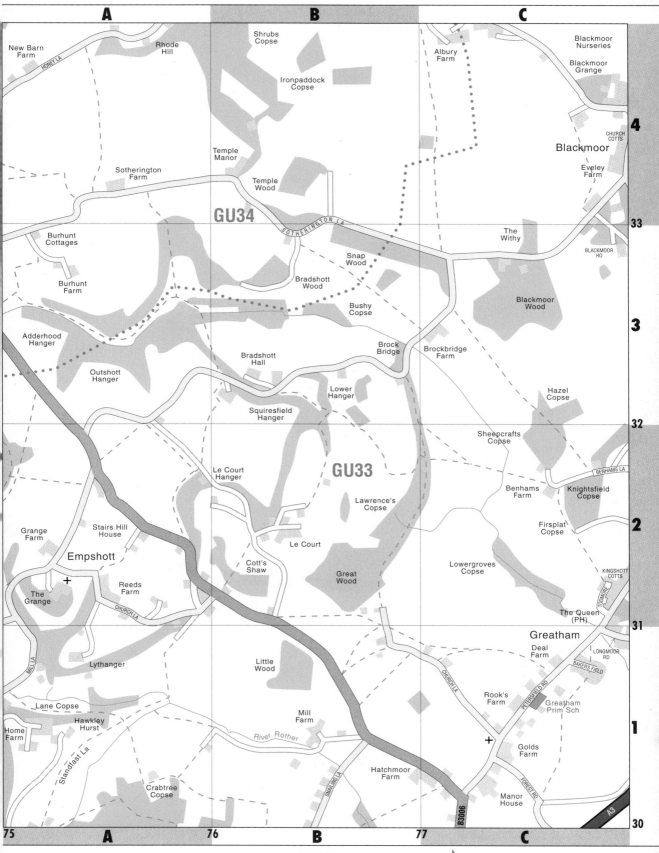

A   B   C

New Barn
Farm

HONEY LA

Rhode
Hill

Shrubs
Copse

Albury
Farm

Blackmoor
Nurseries

Blackmoor
Grange

4

CHURCH
COTTS

Blackmoor

Ironpaddock
Copse

Sotherington
Farm

Temple
Manor

Eveley
Farm

GU34

Temple
Wood

SOTHERINGTON LA

33

BLACKMOOR
HO

Burhunt
Cottages

The
Withy

Snap
Wood

Bradshott
Wood

Burhunt
Farm

Bushy
Copse

Blackmoor
Wood

Adderhood
Hanger

Bradshott
Hall

Brock
Bridge

Brockbridge
Farm

3

Outshott
Hanger

Lower
Hanger

Hazel
Copse

Squiresfield
Hanger

Sheepcrafts
Copse

32

BENHAMS LA

GU33

Le Court
Hanger

Lawrence's
Copse

Benhams
Farm

Knightsfield
Copse

Grange
Farm

Stairs Hill
House

Le Court

Firsplat
Copse

2

Empshott

Cott's
Shaw

Great
Wood

Lowergroves
Copse

KINGSHOTT
COTTS

Reeds
Farm

The
Grange

CHURCH LA

The Queen
(PH)

Greatham

31

Deal
Farm

LONGMOOR
RD

MILL LA

Lythanger

Little
Wood

CHURCH LA

BAKERS FIELD

Rook's
Farm

PETERSFIELD RD

Greatham
Prim Sch

Lane Copse

Hawkley
Hurst

Mill
Farm

River Rother

1

Home
Farm

Standfast La

Crabtree
Copse

SNAILING LA

Hatchmoor
Farm

B3006

Golds
Farm

FOREST RD

Manor
House

A3

30

75   A   76   B   77   C

185
164

A B C

St Matthew's CE Prim Sch

FVEY CL
PLANTATION WAY
BRACKEN LA

MAYFLOWER RD

A325

OAK TREE RD
THE MOUNT
SPRING RD
WALLDOWN RD

LIPHOOK RD

WHITEHILL PK
HOLLYWATER RD

PH

Hollywater Green

4

DRIFT RD

The Vicarage

Round Hill

Hollywater Clump

DANGER AREA

Rifle Range

GU35

Fern Hill

Park Hill

33

BLACKMOOR RD

PETERSFIELD RD

DANGER AREA

Cranmer Bottom

Horsebush Hill

Linchborough Park

3

Woolmer Cottages

Woolmer Forest

DANGER AREA

Queen's Bank

Long Down

Brimstone Inclosure

Keepers Cottage

Woolmer Pond Cottage

Woolmer Pond

GU33

Woolmer Down

Heifers Down

32

BENHAMS LA
WOOLMER TERR

PO

DIGBY WAY

GU30

Forest Side Farm

Inn

PETERSFIELD RD

Rifle Range

A3

2

WOOLMER RD
A325

DANGER AREA

King's Holt

HOPESWOOD

LONGMOOR RD

QUORN TERR

METHUEN RD
PLUMER RD
FRENCH RD
KITCHENER RD
RAILWAY RD

ROBERTS RD
WARREN RD
OLD HUNTERS RD
HAMI

31

WOLFMERE LA

Forest Side

WHITE AVE
KIMBERLEY RD
BADEN POWELL RD
PRETORIA
PATTERSON RD
IAN SMUTS CL
KNOLL RISE

Broad Hill

Longmoor Camp

1

A3

Greatham Moor

Palmer's Ball

Longmoor Inclosure

Weavers Down

30

78 A 79 B 80 C

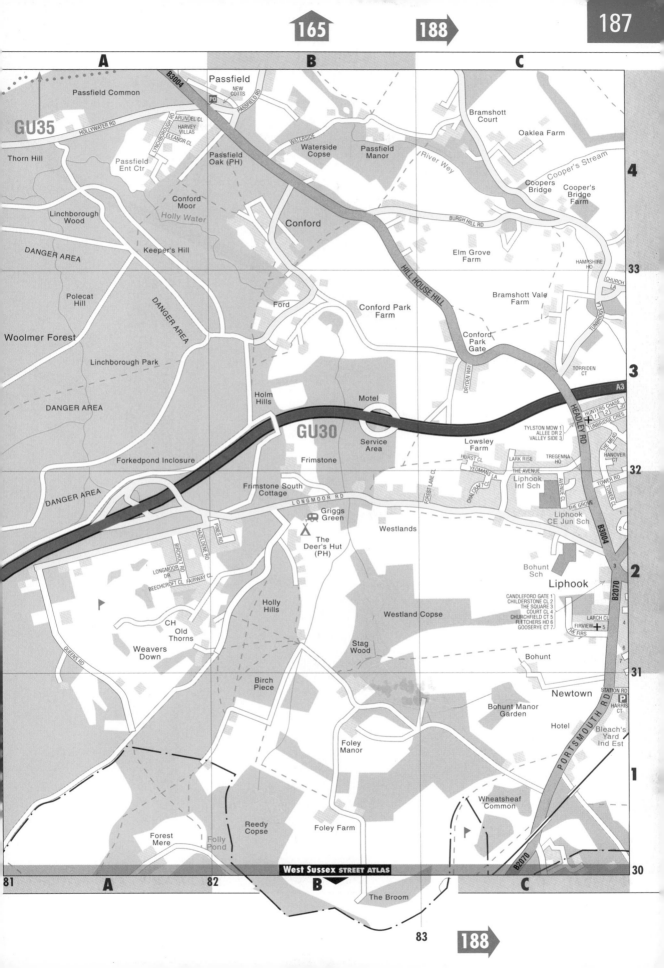

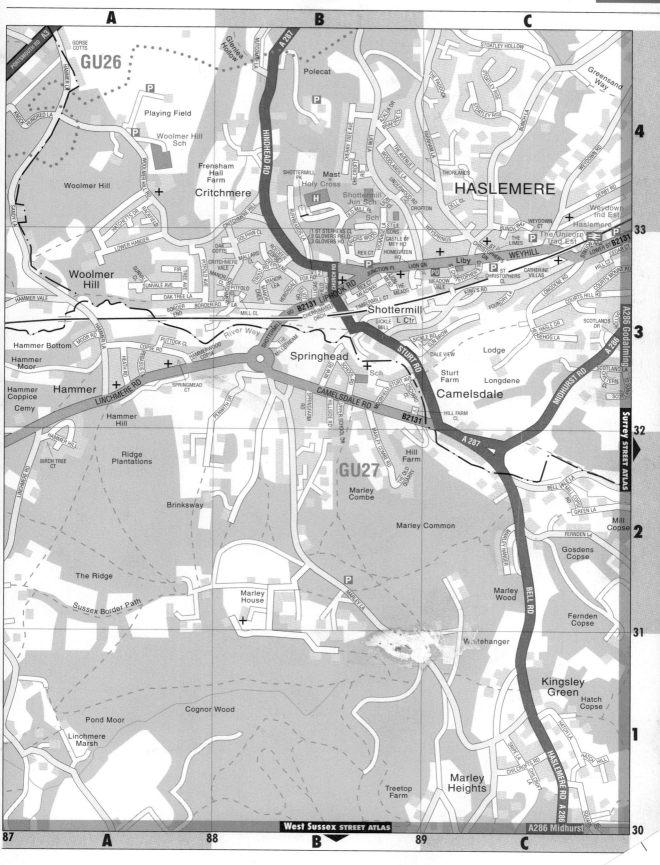

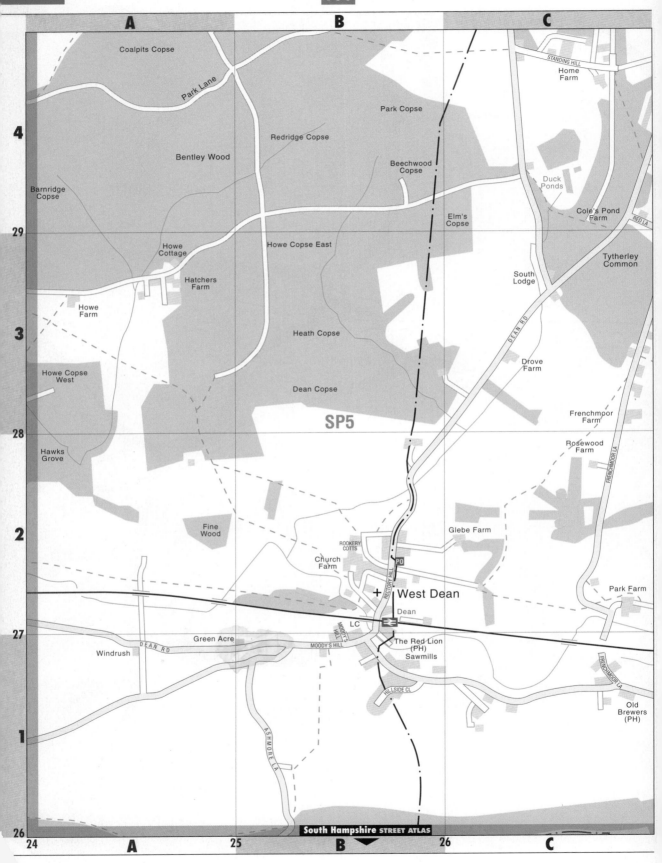

A
B
C

West Tytherley CE Prim Sch
Church Farm
Stony Batter
Stride's Farm
Manor Farm
East Tytherley

DEAN RD
Poplar Farm
Lye Farm
THE COACH RD
Sopp's Farm
MANOR RD

RED LA
The Green
White House
4

PUG'S HOLE
BONNER COTTS
Oaklands Farm
29

RED LA
BULL'S DROVE
Drove

FRENCHMOOR LA
Frenchmoor
SP5
Lockerley Hall Park

Upper Frenchmoor Copse
Lower Frenchmoor Copse
Bulls Drove
Lain Copse
3

Lockerley Hall

Pug's Hole
HOME FARM BSNS CTR
28

Holbury Wood
The Star Inn (PH)

Holbury Farm
MARK WAY
SO51
2

HOLBURY LA
PARK VIEW

Holbury Mill
Lockerley Water Farm

Mill Farm
27

Manor Farm
LC
River Dun
East Dean

GLEBE MDW
EAST DEAN RD
PO
1

Lockerley

Dean Hill Barn Farm
Deangate Farm
Top Green
PENOLE GREEN

Dean Hill
Curlew's Farm
Critchell's Green
Butt's Green

COOKS LA
BUTTS CL
26

27
A
28
B
29
C
26

192

A   B   C

Hackpits
Copse

Redhills
Copse

Deborah
Copse

Pittleworth
Manor

Pittleworth
Farm

4

Little Bentley
Farm

Great Bentley
Farm

Holm Moor
Copse

SP5

Bentley
Firs

SO20

29

Blackpits Wood

The
Bungalow

3

Lain Copse

Great
Copse

Clapgate
Copse

Snook's
Copse

Spearywell Wood

SO51

Newlyns
Farm

BACK LA

28

Blackmoor Firs

Culver
Leaze

Bushy
Copse

Woodland
Walk   P

Cadbury
Farm

Spearywell

2

Dummer
Copse

Test Way

Mottisfont Abbey
(National Trust)

Gardens   Priory

27

KEEPERS LA

BENGER'S LA

OAKLEY RD

Abbey
Farm

P

Mottisfont

Drove Copse

HATT LA

PO

Glebe
Farm

Monarch's Way

CHURCH LA

River Test

Hatt Farm
Hatt Hill

1

River Dun

Lockerley Endowed
CE Prim Sch

Dunbridge

LOCKERLEY RD

The School
Farm

LC   LC

OVAL RD

AVON

Butt's
Green

Test Way

River Dun

Dunbridge

26

RUSSELL DR 1
MILL RISE 2

DOCKERLEY RD

PH

DUNBRIDGE LA

B3084

30   A   31   B   32   C

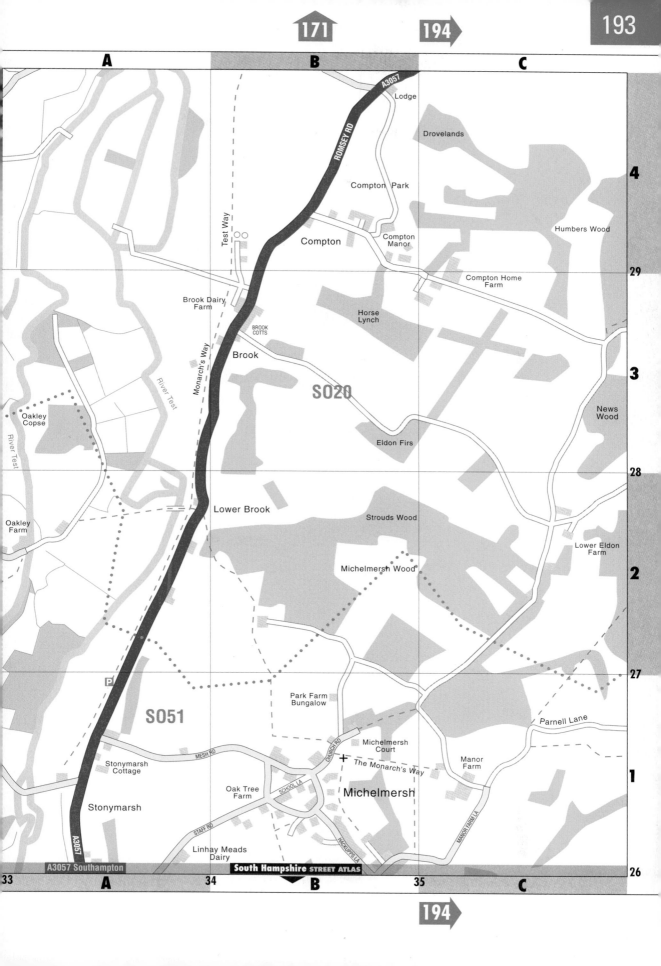

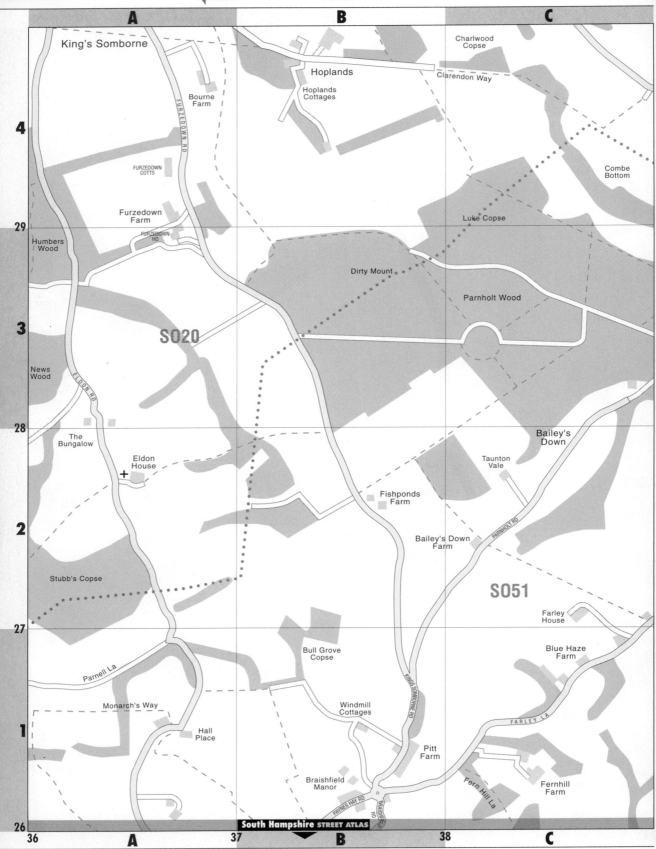

King's Somborne

Bourne Farm

FURZEDOWN RD

FURZEDOWN COTTS

Furzedown Farm

FURZEDOWN HO

Humbers Wood

News Wood

ELDON RD

The Bungalow

Eldon House

SO20

Hoplands

Hoplands Cottages

Charlwood Copse

Clarendon Way

Combe Bottom

Luke Copse

Dirty Mount

Parnholt Wood

Bailey's Down

Taunton Vale

Fishponds Farm

Bailey's Down Farm

PARNHOLT RD

SO51

Stubb's Copse

Farley House

Parnell La

Monarch's Way

Hall Place

Bull Grove Copse

Windmill Cottages

KINGS SOMBORNE RD

Blue Haze Farm

FARLEY LA

Pitt Farm

Fern Hill La

Fernhill Farm

Braishfield Manor

PAYNES HAY RD

BRAISHFIELD RD

4
29
3
28
2
27
1
26

36   A   37   B   38   C

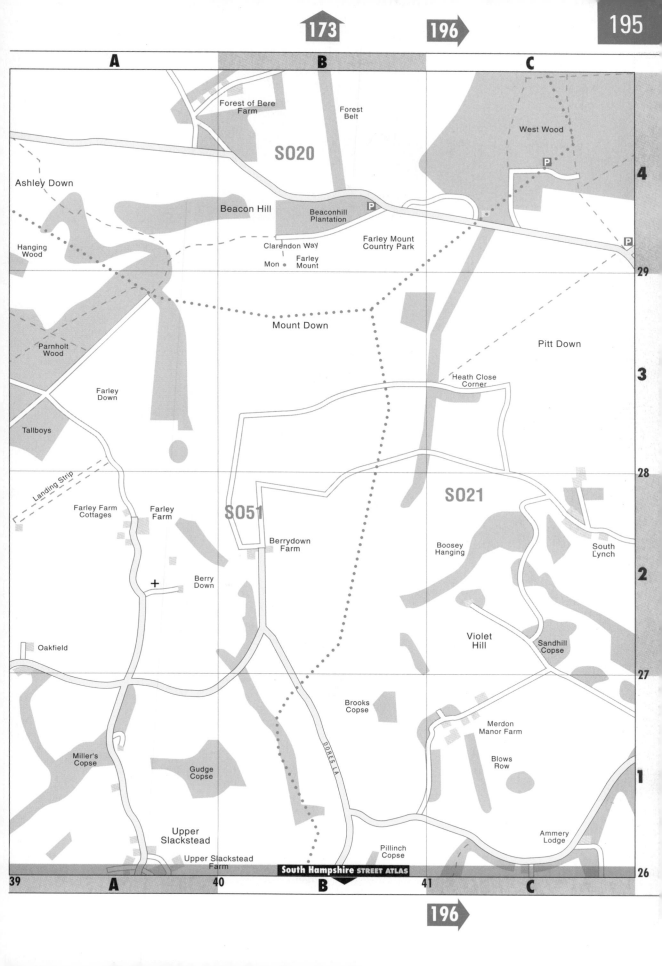

A B C

4

29

3

28

2

27

1

26

Forest of Bere Farm

Forest Belt

West Wood

SO20

Ashley Down

Beacon Hill

Beaconhill Plantation

Farley Mount Country Park

Clarendon Way

Mon

Farley Mount

Hanging Wood

Parnholt Wood

Mount Down

Pitt Down

Heath Close Corner

Farley Down

Tallboys

Landing Strip

Farley Farm Cottages

Farley Farm

SO51

SO021

Berrydown Farm

Boosey Hanging

South Lynch

Berry Down

Violet Hill

Sandhill Copse

Oakfield

DORES LA

Brooks Copse

Merdon Manor Farm

Blows Row

Miller's Copse

Gudge Copse

Upper Slackstead

Upper Slackstead Farm

Pillinch Copse

Ammery Lodge

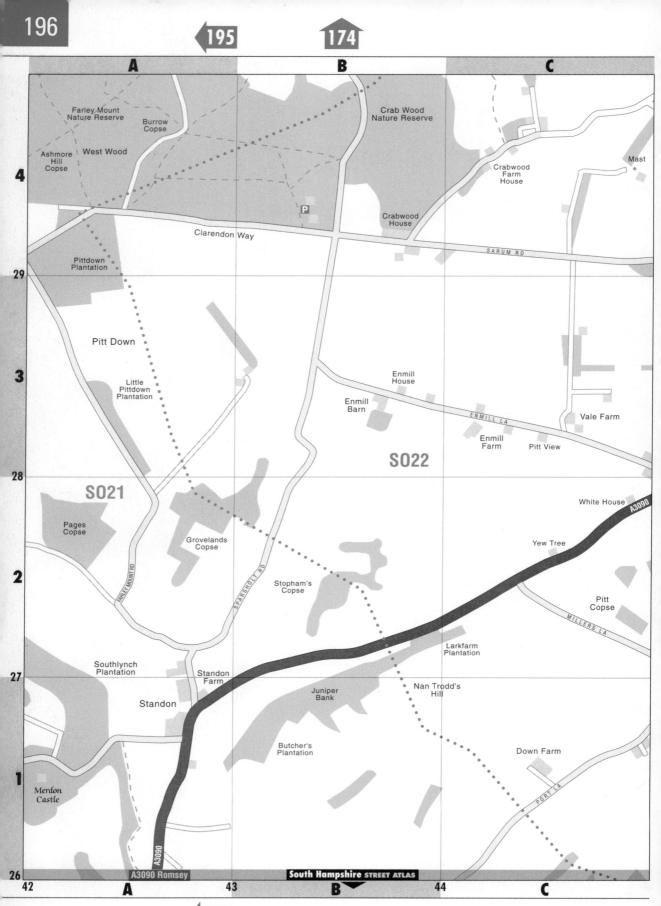

Farley Mount
Nature Reserve

Burrow
Copse

Crab Wood
Nature Reserve

Ashmore
Hill
Copse

West Wood

Crabwood
Farm
House

Mast

P

Crabwood
House

Clarendon Way

SARUM RD

Pittdown
Plantation

Pitt Down

Little
Pittdown
Plantation

Enmill
House

Enmill
Barn

ENMILL LA

Vale Farm

Enmill
Farm

Pitt View

SO22

SO21

Pages
Copse

Grovelands
Copse

FARLEY MOUNT RD

SPARSHOLT RD

Stopham's
Copse

White House

A3090

Yew Tree

Pitt
Copse

MILLERS LA

Larkfarm
Plantation

Southlynch
Plantation

Standon
Farm

Standon

Juniper
Bank

Nan Trodd's
Hill

Down Farm

Butcher's
Plantation

PORT LA

Merdon
Castle

A3090

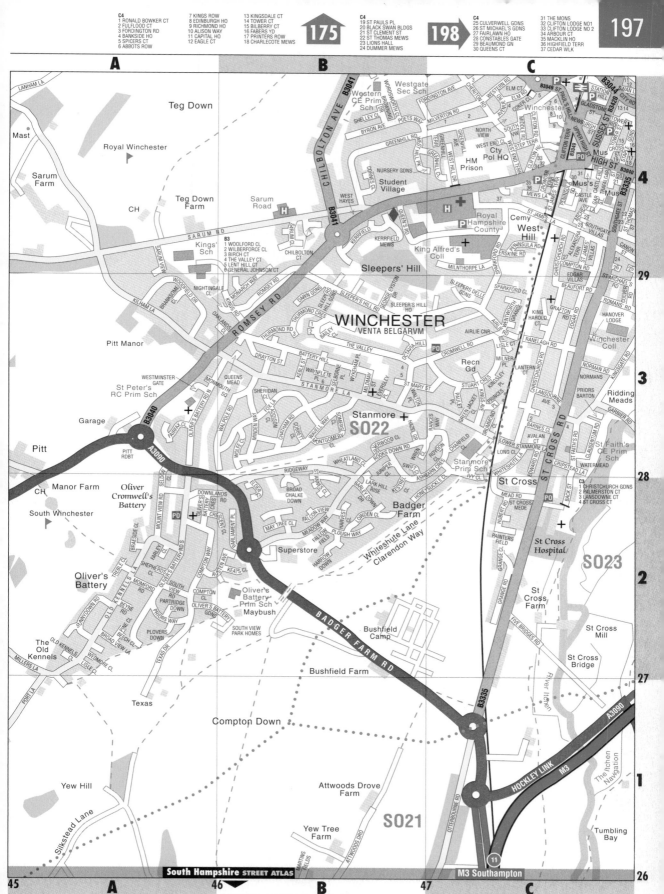

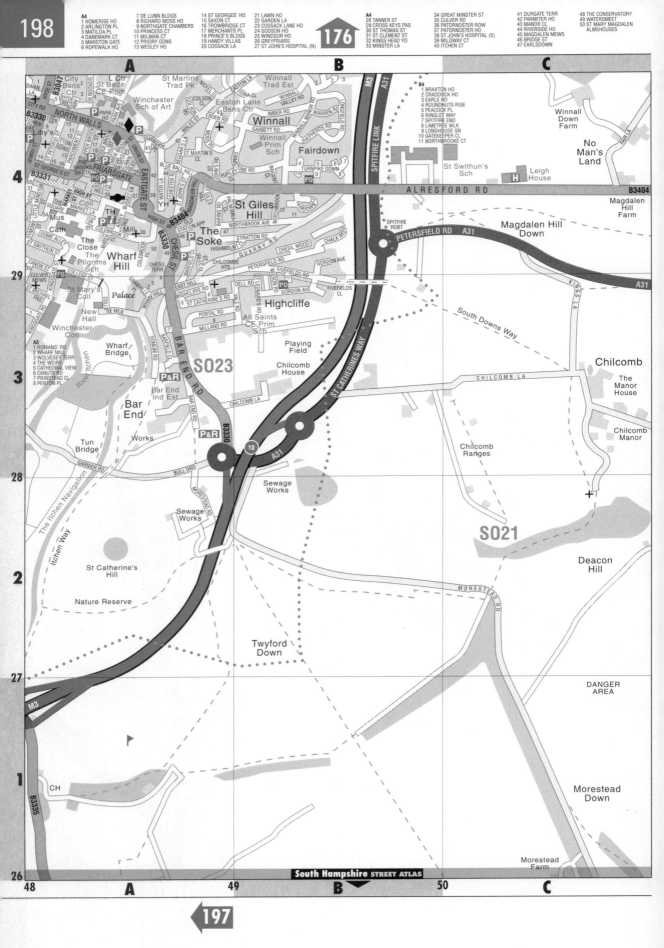

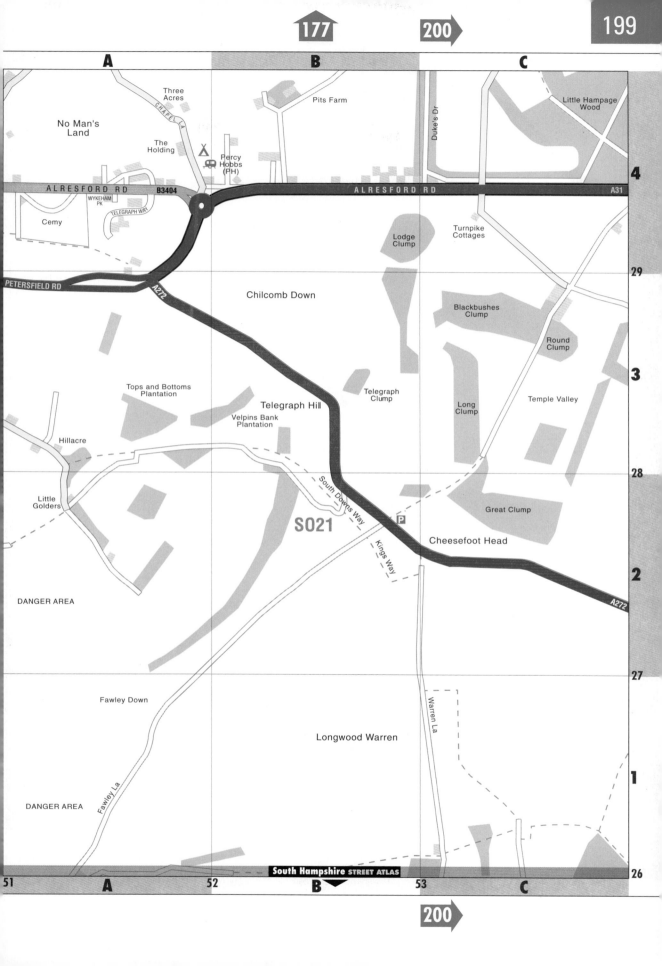

A
B
C

Three Acres

Pits Farm

Little Hampage Wood

No Man's Land

CHAPEL LA

The Holding

Duke's Dr

Percy Hobbs (PH)

4

ALRESFORD RD   B3404   ALRESFORD RD   A31

WYKEHAM PK

Cemy

TELEGRAPH WAY

Turnpike Cottages

Lodge Clump

29

PETERSFIELD RD   A272

Chilcomb Down

Blackbushes Clump

Round Clump

3

Tops and Bottoms Plantation

Telegraph Clump

Temple Valley

Telegraph Hill

Long Clump

Velpins Bank Plantation

Hillacre

28

South Downs Way

Little Golders

SO21

P

Great Clump

Cheesefoot Head

2

Kings Way

DANGER AREA

A272

27

Fawley Down

Warren La

Longwood Warren

1

Fawley La

DANGER AREA

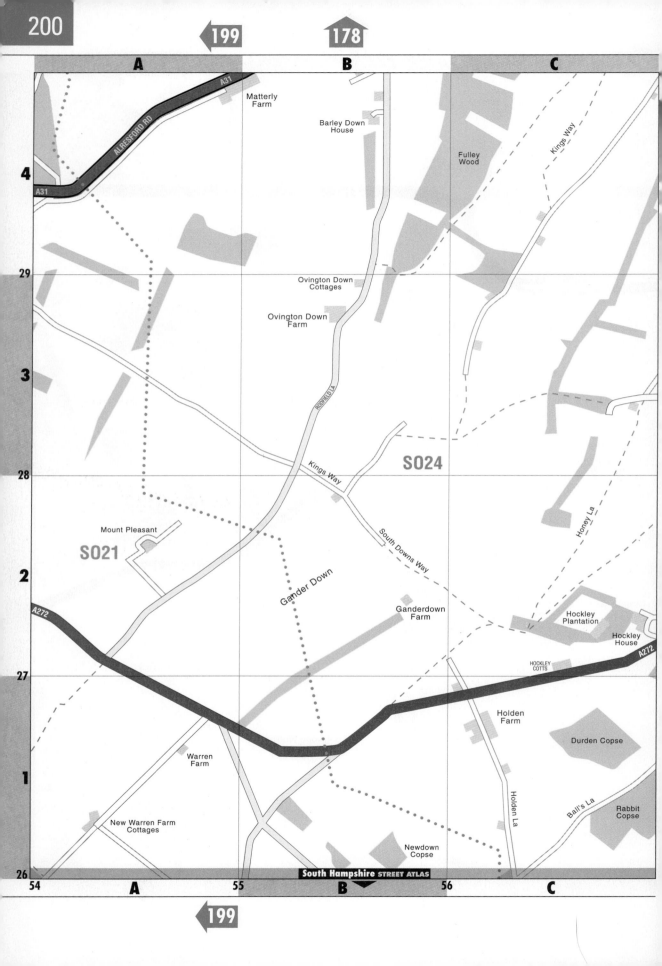

A · B · C

4

29

3

28

2

27

1

26

A31

ALRESFORD RD

A31

Matterly
Farm

Barley Down
House

Fulley
Wood

Kings Way

Ovington Down
Cottages

Ovington Down
Farm

ROPFIELD LA

Kings Way

SO24

Mount Pleasant

SO21

Gander Down

South Downs Way

Ganderdown
Farm

Honey La

Hockley
Plantation

Hockley
House

A272

A272

HOCKLEY
COTTS

Holden
Farm

Durden Copse

Warren
Farm

Holden La

Ball's La

Rabbit
Copse

New Warren Farm
Cottages

Newdown
Copse

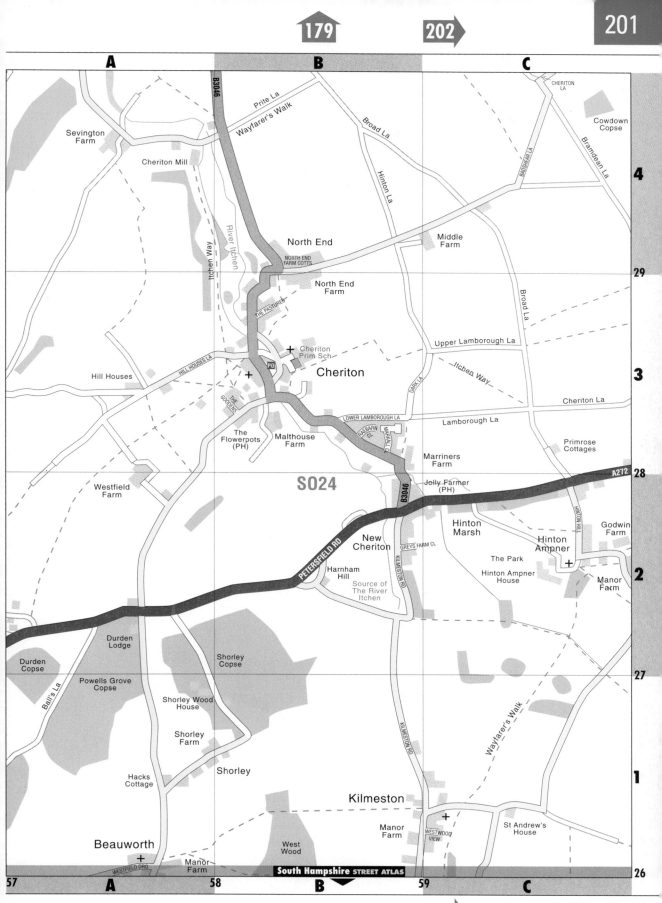

A B C

4

29

3

28

2

27

1

26

Sevington Farm

Cheriton Mill

B3046

Prite La

Wayfarer's Walk

Broad La

Hinton La

River Itchen

Itchen Way

North End

NORTH END FARM COTTS

North End Farm

THE PASTURES

Hill Houses

HILL HOUSES LA

Cheriton Prim Sch

PO

Cheriton

THE GODENS

The Flowerpots (PH)

Malthouse Farm

LOWER LAMBOROUGH LA

RAEBARN CL

MARKAL CL

Upper Lamborough La

Itchen Way

DARK LA

Lamborough La

Cheriton La

Primrose Cottages

Marriners Farm

SO24

Westfield Farm

Jolly Farmer (PH)

A272

Middle Farm

Broad La

BADSHEAR LA

BRAMDEAN LA

CHERITON LA

Cowdown Copse

PETERSFIELD RD

New Cheriton

Harnham Hill

Source of The River Itchen

KILMESTON RD

GREYS FARM CL

Hinton Marsh

The Park

Hinton Ampner House

Hinton Ampner

HINTON HILL

Godwin Farm

Manor Farm

Durden Copse

Durden Lodge

Powells Grove Copse

Ball's La

Shorley Copse

Shorley Wood House

Shorley Farm

Hacks Cottage

Shorley

KILMESTON RD

Wayfarer's Walk

Kilmeston

Manor Farm

WESTWOOD VIEW

St Andrew's House

Beauworth

WESTFIELD DRO

Manor Farm

West Wood

57 A 58 B 59 C

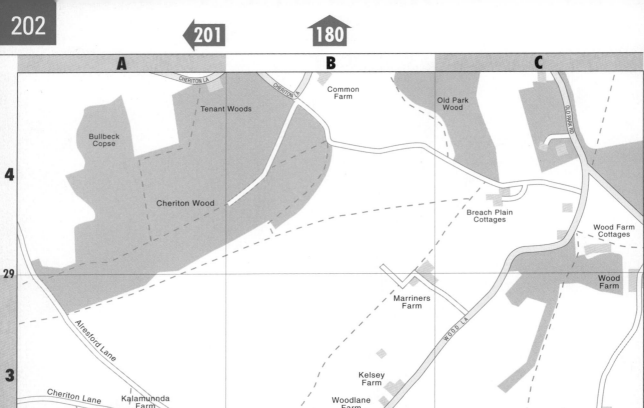
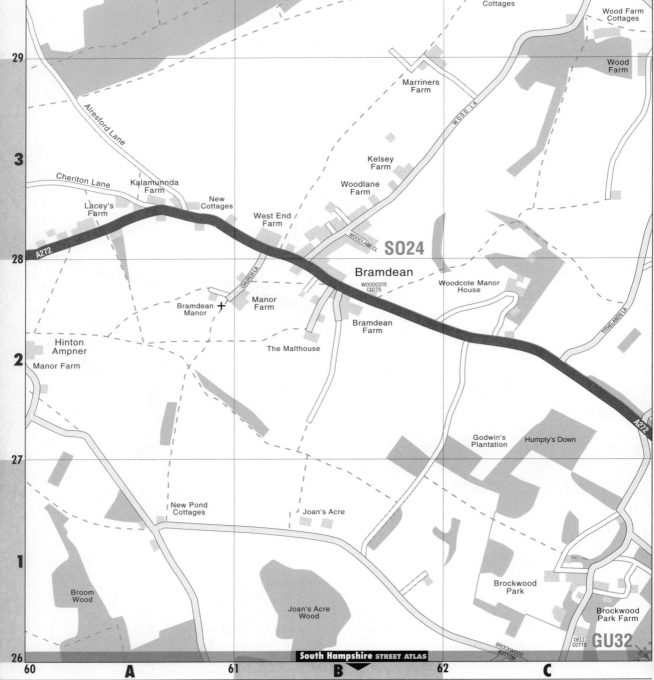

A B C

CHERITON LA
CHERITON ST

Common Farm

Old Park Wood

OLD PARK RD

Tenant Woods

Bullbeck Copse

Cheriton Wood

4

Breach Plain Cottages

Wood Farm Cottages

29

Marriners Farm

WOOD LA

Wood Farm

Alresford Lane

3

Kelsey Farm

Cheriton Lane

Kalamunnda Farm

Woodlane Farm

New Cottages

Lacey's Farm

West End Farm

WOODLANE CL

SO24

A272

28

Bramdean

WOODCOTE COTTS

Woodcote Manor House

CHURCH LA

Bramdean Manor

Manor Farm

Bramdean Farm

TITHELANDS LA

Hinton Ampner

The Malthouse

2

Manor Farm

Godwin's Plantation

Humpty's Down

27

A272

New Pond Cottages

Joan's Acre

1

Broom Wood

Brockwood Park

Brockwood Park Farm

Joan's Acre Wood

DELL COTTS

GU32

BROCKWOOD BOTTOM

26

60 A 61 B 62 C

A
B
C

Wr Twr

Daylesford

Bonniesfield
Farm

West Tisted

Bramdean Common

The
Plantation

Manor
Farm

BRICK KILN LA

4

Clinkley Road

St
Christopher

Green Lane

PO

Home Farm

Saw
Mill

Long
House

29

Manor Farm
Stud

Court
Farm

Woodland
Gate

3

Wolfhanger
Farm

Frenchleys

PUNSHOLT LA

SO24

Parsonage
Farm

Slys Farm

28

Tithelands Lane

Punsholt
Farm

Purser's

Punsholt
Cottages

A32

2

Hinton Woodlands
Farm

Woodlands
Farm

Purser's La

Old
Wheatsheaf

FILMOREHILL LA

GU34

Three Horse Shoes
Farm

THREE HORSE SHOES LA

27

The
Grove

West Meon
Woodlands

KITT'S LA

The Dean

P

Woodlands
Farm

1

Inwood
Copse

Shutt's
Copse

The West Meon Hut
(PH)

GU32

Pest Houses

Garage

A32

A272

Martin's Wood

26

A
B
C

63
64
65

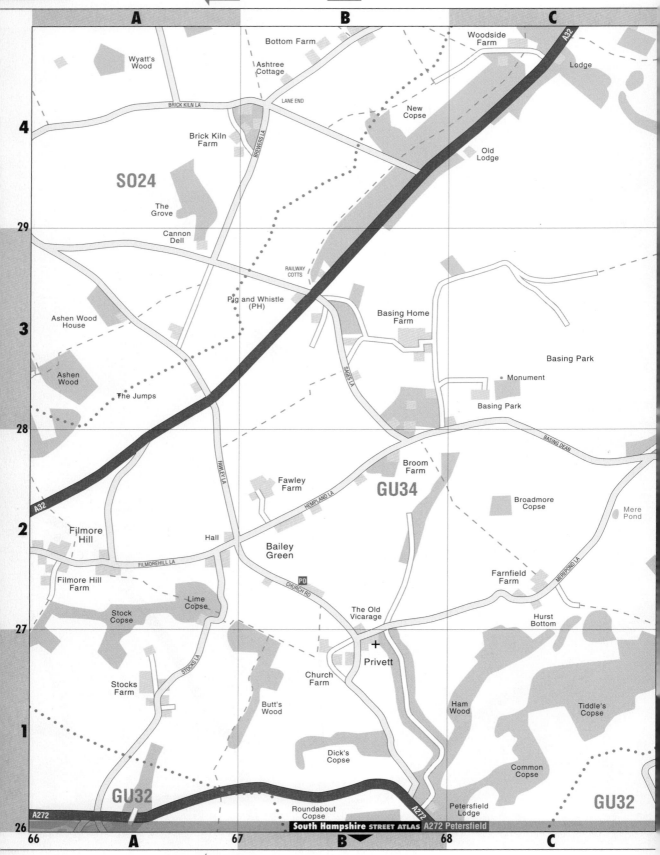

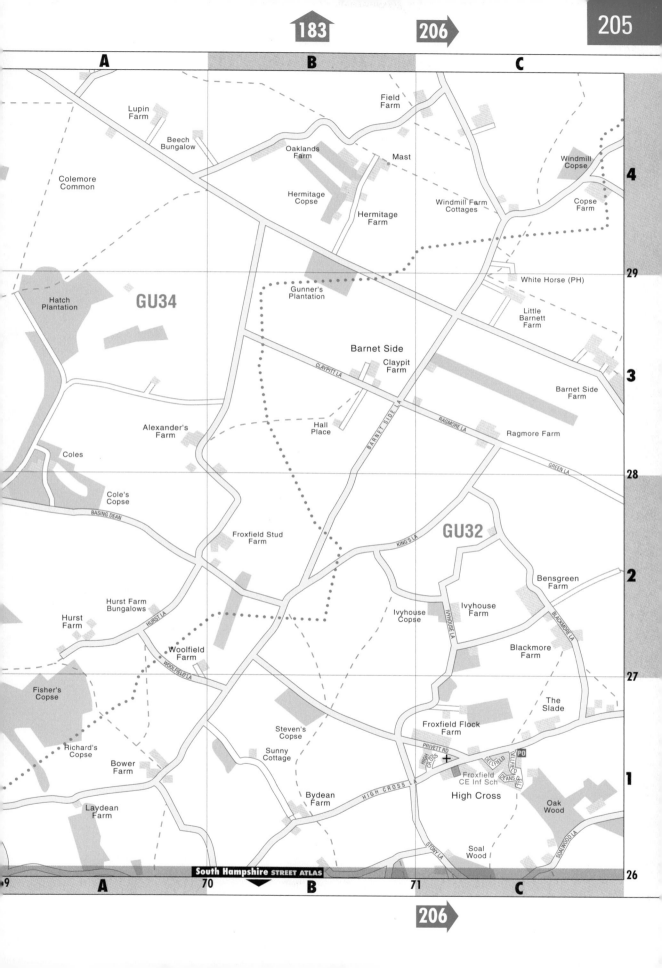

A B C

Field Farm

Lupin Farm

Beech Bungalow

Oaklands Farm

Mast

Windmill Copse

4

Colemore Common

Hermitage Copse

Windmill Farm Cottages

Copse Farm

Hermitage Farm

White Horse (PH)

29

GU34

Hatch Plantation

Gunner's Plantation

Little Barnett Farm

Barnet Side

Claypit Farm

Barnet Side Farm

3

CLAYPIT LA

Alexander's Farm

Hall Place

RAGMORE LA

Ragmore Farm

Coles

BARNET SIDE LA

GREEN LA

28

Cole's Copse

BASING DEAN

Froxfield Stud Farm

KING'S LA

GU32

Bensgreen Farm

2

Hurst Farm Bungalows

HURST LA

Ivyhouse Copse

IVYHOUSE LA

Ivyhouse Farm

BLACKMORE LA

Hurst Farm

Woolfield Farm

Blackmore Farm

WOOLFIELD LA

27

Fisher's Copse

The Slade

Richard's Copse

Steven's Copse

Froxfield Flock Farm

PRIVETT RD

PO

Bower Farm

Sunny Cottage

HIGH CROSS

DELLFIELD

DEANS CL

CHITTY LA

1

Froxfield CE Inf Sch

Laydean Farm

Bydean Farm

HIGH CROSS LA

High Cross

Oak Wood

STONY LA

Soal Wood

SOALWOOD LA

26

A   **B**   **C**

Church
Farm

Manor
House

GU34

Lowergreen
Farm

Lower Green

4

Hawkley
Hanger

Champlers
Farm

Five Ash
Farm

Hawkley

PH

Upper Gn   Pococks La

29

Warren
Farm

Tubb's
Farm

Cheesecombe
Farm

3

The
Warren

Reston
Hanger

Oakshott
Farm

Oakshott Stream

Moore's
Copse

GU33

Warren
Corner

Shaw
Wood

Roundhills
Hanger

Windmill
Cottage

WARREN LA

28

Parsons

Happersnapper
Hanger

GU32

Oakshott

GREEN LA

Hill
Farm

Lower Oakshott
Farmhouse

TROOPER
BOTTOM

HONEYCRITCH LA

Hanger's Way

2

Ringsgreen
Copse

PH

Oakshott
Hanger

COTTAGE LA

Wheatham
Hill

Rings
Green

Ringsgreen Lane

WOODFIELD
COTTS

Woodfield
Copse

OLD LITTEN LA

Old Litten Lane

27

Shoulder of Mutton
Hill

HIGH CROSS LA

Ashford
Hill

COCKSHOTT LA

Southdean
Farm

Week
Green
Farm

Ashford
Farm

1

ASHFORD
CHACE

SOALWOOD LA

Wyke
Green Farm

Lutcombe
Bottom

MILL LA

Bushy
Hill

STONER HILL RD

Pipers
Farm

Wyke Green
Cottage

Little
Langleys

26

72   **A**   73   **B**   74   **C**

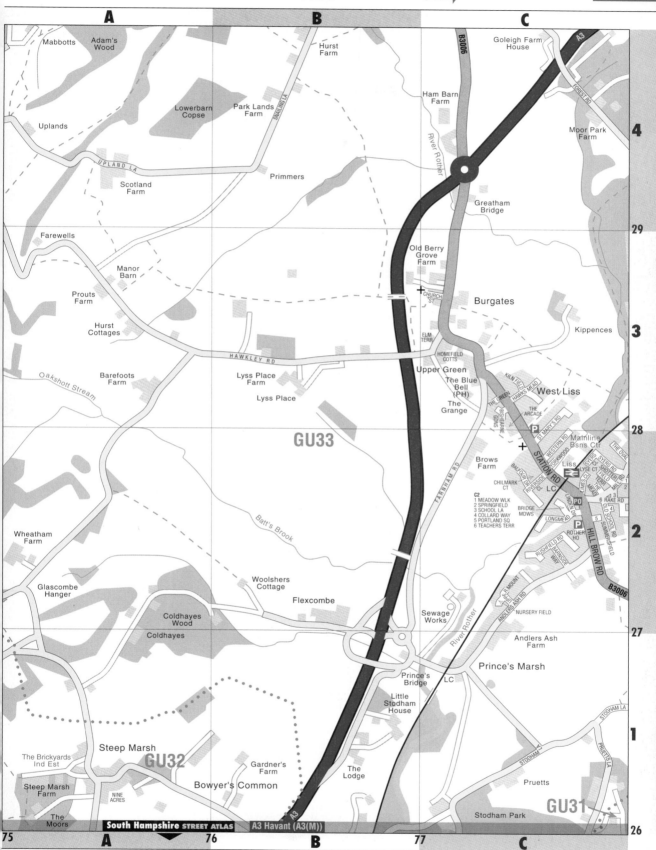

A
B
C

Mabbotts
Adam's Wood
Hurst Farm
Goleigh Farm House
A3
B3006
FOREST RD

Uplands
Lowerbarn Copse
Park Lands Farm
SHARLING LA
Ham Barn Farm
Moor Park Farm

4

UPLAND LA

Scotland Farm
Primmers
River Rother
Greatham Bridge

Farewells

29

Manor Barn
Old Berry Grove Farm
CHURCH ST
Burgates

Prouts Farm
Kippences

Hurst Cottages
HAWKLEY RD
ELM TERR.
HOMEFIELD COTTS

3

Oakshott Stream
Barefoots Farm
Lyss Place Farm
Upper Green
The Blue Bell (PH)
West Liss

Lyss Place
The Grange
KILN FIELD
HANKS MEAD
THE GREEN
THE ARCADE
ST MARY'S RD
THE OVAL

GU33
BUSHBARNE GDNS
WESTERN RD
CORKWOOD
Mainline Bsns Ctr
SYSTERS
SYERS RD
SHOTTER
MILL
THE MEAD

28

Brows Farm
BALFOUR DR
Liss
LYSE CT
KIMES CL

CHILMARK CT
RIVERSIDE CL
STATION RD
LC
KIMES CL

C2
1 MEADOW WLK
2 SPRINGFIELD
3 SCHOOL LA
4 COLLARD WAY
5 PORTLAND SQ
6 TEACHERS TERR
BRIDGE MDWS
LONGMEAD
ROTHER HO
6 RAKE RD
5
OLD SCHOOL RD

Wheatham Farm
Batt's Brook
RUSHFIELD RD
BARNSIDE WAY
SUMMERSFIELD
HILL BROW RD

2

B3006

Glascombe Hanger
Woolshers Cottage
Flexcombe
F. MOUNT
ANDLERS ASH RD
NURSERY FIELD

Coldhayes Wood
Sewage Works
Andlers Ash Farm

Coldhayes

27

River Rother
Prince's Marsh

Prince's Bridge
LC

STODHAM LA
PRUETTS LA

1

Steep Marsh
Little Stodham House

The Brickyards Ind Est
GU32
Gardner's Farm
STODHAM

Steep Marsh Farm
NINE ACRES
Bowyer's Common
The Lodge
Pruetts
Pruetts

GU31

The Moors
A3
Stodham Park

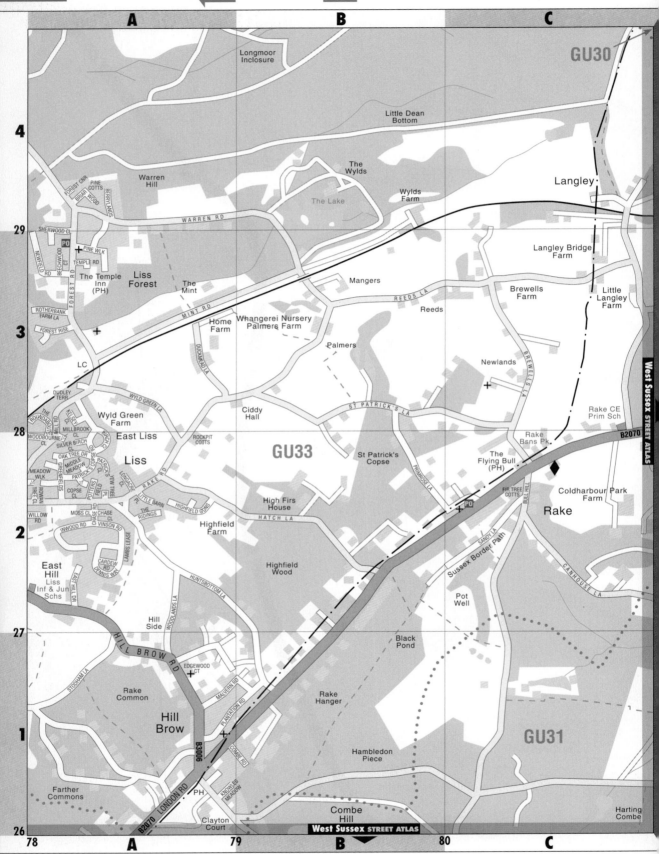

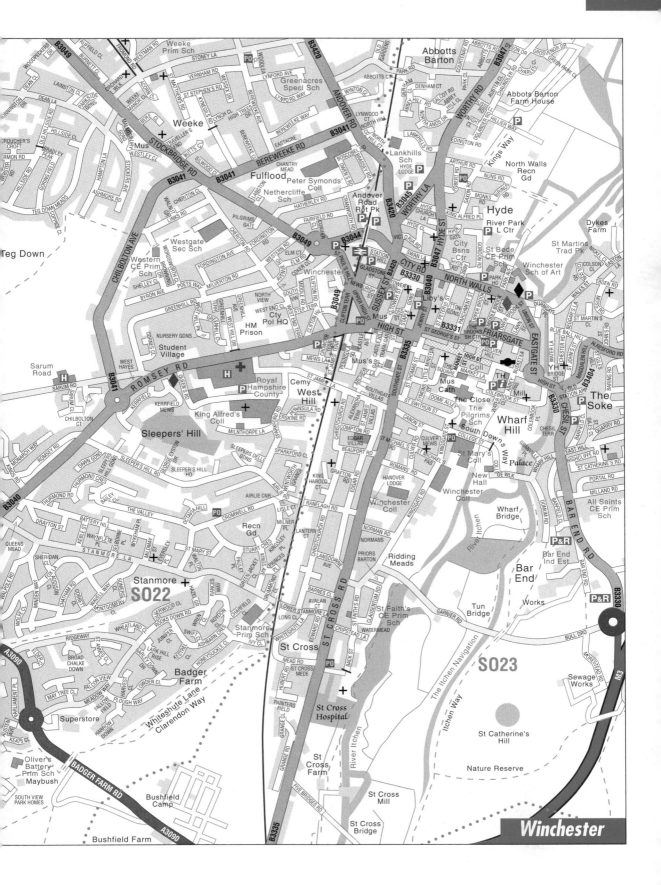

Winchester

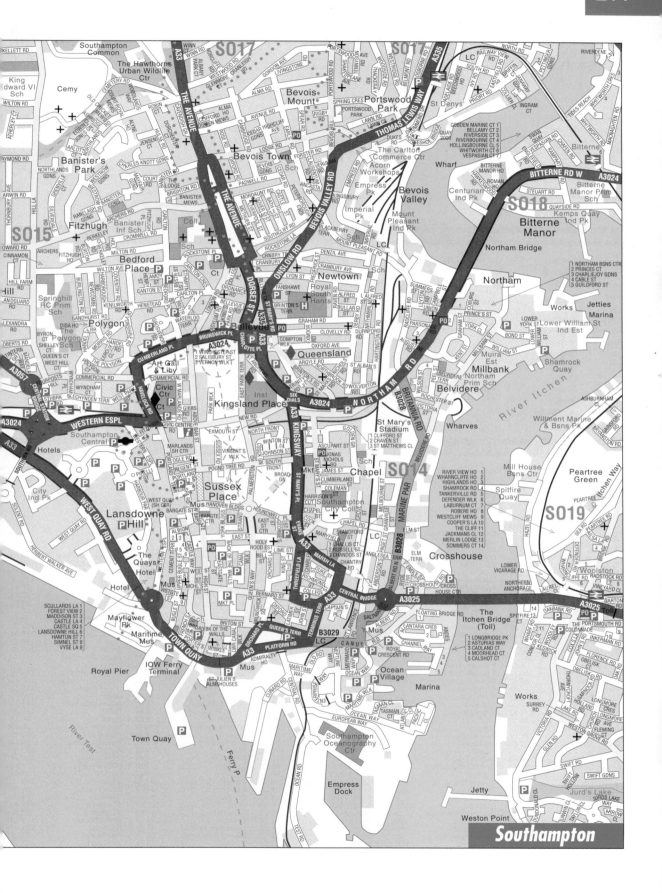

Southampton

Index

Church Rd **6** Beckenham BR2..........**53** C6

Place name	**Location number**	**Locality, town or village**	**Postcode district**	**Page and grid square**
May be abbreviated on the map	Present when a number indicates the place's position in a crowded area of mapping	Shown when more than one place has the same name	District for the indexed place	Page number and grid reference for the standard mapping

Public and commercial buildings are highlighted in magenta   **Places of interest** are highlighted in blue with a star★

Abbreviations used in the index

Acad	**Academy**	Comm	**Common**	Gd	**Ground**	L	**Leisure**	Prom	**Prom**
App	**Approach**	Cott	**Cottage**	Gdn	**Garden**	La	**Lane**	Rd	**Road**
Arc	**Arcade**	Cres	**Crescent**	Gn	**Green**	Liby	**Library**	Recn	**Recreation**
Ave	**Avenue**	Cswy	**Causeway**	Gr	**Grove**	Mdw	**Meadow**	Ret	**Retail**
Bglw	**Bungalow**	Ct	**Court**	H	**Hall**	Meml	**Memorial**	Sh	**Shopping**
Bldg	**Building**	Ctr	**Centre**	Ho	**House**	Mkt	**Market**	Sq	**Square**
Bsns, Bus	**Business**	Ctry	**Country**	Hospl	**Hospital**	Mus	**Museum**	St	**Street**
Bvd	**Boulevard**	Cty	**County**	HQ	**Headquarters**	Orch	**Orchard**	Sta	**Station**
Cath	**Cathedral**	Dr	**Drive**	Hts	**Heights**	Pal	**Palace**	Terr	**Terrace**
Cir	**Circus**	Dro	**Drove**	Ind	**Industrial**	Par	**Parade**	TH	**Town Hall**
Cl	**Close**	Ed	**Education**	Inst	**Institute**	Pas	**Passage**	Univ	**University**
Cnr	**Corner**	Emb	**Embankment**	Int	**International**	Pk	**Park**	Wk, Wlk	**Walk**
Coll	**College**	Est	**Estate**	Intc	**Interchange**	Pl	**Place**	Wr	**Water**
Com	**Community**	Ex	**Exhibition**	Junc	**Junction**	Prec	**Precinct**	Yd	**Yard**

Index of localities, towns and villages

A

Abb – Avo 213

Abbatt Cl SP11 57 A1
Abberbury Cl (Almshouses)
RG14 1 B3
Abbetts La GU15 35 C2
Abbey Bsns Pk GU9 122 B4
Abbey Cl RG14 5 C4
Abbey Ct
4 Andover SP10 105 C4
Basingstoke RG24 48 A1
Camberley GU15 36 A3
4 Farnham GU9 99 A1
Abbey Hill Cl SO23 176 A1
Abbey Hill Rd SO23 175 C1
Abbey Pas SO23 198 A4
Abbey Rd Alton GU34 160 B4
Basingstoke RG24 69 A4
Medstead GU34 160 B4
Abbey Sch The GU9 99 A1
Abbey St GU9 99 A1
Abbey Way GU14 56 A2
Abbot's Ride GU9 99 B1
Abbots Cl Fleet GU51 54 A1
North Tidworth SP9 78 C4
Abbots Ct GU47 34 B4
Abbots Rd Newbury RG14 1 C1
North Tidworth SP9 78 C4
Abbots Row 6 SO22 197 C4
Abbots Wood Forest Wlk*
GU10 143 A3
Abbotstone Rd SO24 179 B4
Abbotswood Cl RG26 26 C4
Abbott Cl RG22 68 B1
Abbott's Ann CE Prim Sch
SP11 104 C2
Abbott's Ann Rd SP11 104 B3
Abbotts Ann SP11 105 A2
Abbotts Ann Rd SO22 175 B2
Abbotts Cl
Abbotts Ann SP11 105 A2
Winchester SO23 176 A1
Abbotts Cotts GU10 143 B3
Abbotts Ct SO22 175 C1
Abbotts Hill SP11 105 A2
Abbotts Rd SO23 176 A1
Abex Rd RG14 2 A2
Abingdon Rd GU47 35 A4
Above Town SP11 105 C2
Acadamey Gate GU15 35 C3
Academy Cl GU15 36 B4
Accentors Cl GU34 139 C3
Acheulian Cl GU9 122 A4
Achilles Cl RG24 48 C2
Ackender Rd GU34 139 C2
Acorn Cl RG21 69 C3
Acorn Keep GU9 99 A4
Acorn Mews GU14 55 C4
Acorn Rd GU17 34 C3
Acre Almshouses 7
SP10 106 A4
Acre Ct SP10 106 A4
Acre Path SP10 106 A4
Acton Ho RG22 68 C2
Adam Cl RG26 9 B1
Adampur Rd SP9 78 B2
Adams Cl
North Tidworth SP11 79 B3
North Warnborough RG29 72 A2
Adams Dr GU51 54 B1
Adams Ho GU34 140 A2
Adams Park Rd GU9 99 A2
Adams Way GU34 140 A2
Addison Cl SO22 197 B3
Addison Gdns RG29 72 C2
Addison Rd GU16 56 B4
Adelaide Rd SP10 106 A4
Adlington Pl GU14 56 B1
Admers Cres GU30 188 A1
Admirals Way SP10 83 B1
Admiralty Way GU15 35 B2
Adrian Cl RG27 52 B3
Aerospace Bvd GU11 76 C4
Aghemund Cl RG24 48 C2
Agra Rd SP9 78 B2
Agricola Wlk SP10 83 A2
Ainger Cl GU12 77 A2
Aintree Cl RG14 2 A1
Airborne Forces Mus*
GU11 76 C3
Aircraft Espl GU14 56 A1
Aird Cl RG20 21 B4
Airlie Cnr SO22 197 C3
Airlie Rd SO22 197 C3
Ajax Cl RG24 48 C2
Alamein Rd
Aldershot GU11 76 C1
Enham Alamein SP11 83 A4
Alanbrooke Cl RG27 52 B3
Alanbrooke Rd GU11 77 A3
Albany Cl GU51 75 A4
Albany Ct Camberley GU16 36 A1
Fleet GU51 54 A1
Albany Mews SP10 105 C4
Albany Park Ind Est
GU16 36 A1
Albany Pk GU16 36 A1
Albany Rd Andover SP10 105 C4
Fleet GU51 75 A4
Albert Rd Aldershot GU11 76 C1
Alton GU34 139 C1
Camberley GU15 36 A3
Farnborough GU14 56 A1
Newbury RG14 1 C2
Albert St GU51 54 A1
Albert Yd 8 RG21 69 A2
Albion Pl RG27 52 B3
Albion Rd GU47 34 C4
Alder Cl Alton GU34 139 C3
Ash GU12 77 C4
Newbury RG14 2 A2
Alder Gr GU46 34 A3
Alder Rd GU35 165 C3
Aldermaston CE Prim Sch
RG7 9 B4
Aldermaston Rd
Basingstoke RG24 68 C4
Pamber End RG26 27 A2
Sherborne St John RG24,
RG26 47 B3
Aldermaston Rd S RG21 68 C4
Alderney Ave RG22 91 A4
Alders Ct SO24 179 B3
Alders The GU9 99 C3
Aldershot Military Mus*
GU11 77 A3
Aldershot Rd Ash GU12 77 B1
Fleet GU51 75 A4
Fleet, Church Crookham
GU52 75 B3
Aldershot Sta GU11 76 C1
Alderwood RG24 48 C2
Alderwood Dr RG27 51 A1
Aldrin Cl SP10 82 C2
Aldrin Pl GU14 55 A2
Aldwick Cl GU14 55 C3
Aldworth Cres RG22 68 C2
Aldwych Cotts RG14 1 B3
Alencon Link RG21 69 A3
Alexander Cl SO20 171 A3
Alexander Ho 6 SP9 78 C4
Alexander Rd RG25 88 A4
Alexander Terr RG29 72 B2
Alexandra Ave GU15 35 C3
Alexandra Ct
Bordon GU35 164 C2
9 Farnborough GU14 56 A1
Alexandra Rd
Aldershot GU11 76 B1
Alton GU34 139 C3
Andover SP10 105 C4
Ash GU12 77 B1
Basingstoke RG21 68 C3
Farnborough GU14 56 A1
Alexandra Terr
1 Aldershot GU11 76 C1
Winchester SO23 197 C4
Alexandria Rd SO21 131 B3
Alfonso Cl GU12 100 A4
Alfred Rd GU9 99 A1
Alfred St GU11 76 C1
Alice Holt Cotts GU10 120 C1
Alice Holt Forest Visitor Ctr*
GU10 143 A4
Alice Rd GU11, GU12 76 C1
Alison Cl GU14 55 B2
Alison Dr GU15 36 B3
Alison Way
Aldershot GU11 76 B1
10 Winchester SO22 197 C4
Alison's Rd GU11 76 C2
All Hallows RC Sch GU9 99 B4
All Saints CE Jun Sch
GU51 74 B4
All Saints CE Prim Sch
SO23 198 A3
All Saints Cres GU14 35 B1
Allden Ave GU12 100 A4
Allden Gdns GU12 100 A4
Allee Dr GU30 187 C3
Allen Cl Alton GU34 140 A3
Basingstoke RG21 68 C2
Allen Gallery & Curtis Mus*
GU34 139 C2
Allenby Rd GU15 35 C3
Alliston Way
Basingstoke RG22 68 A2
Whitchurch RG28 86 B2
Allnutt Ave RG21 69 B3
Alma Cl GU12 77 A1
Alma La GU9 99 A4
Alma Rd Bordon GU35 164 C2
Headley GU35 166 A3
Alma Sq GU14 77 A4
Alma Way GU9 99 A4
Almhouses SO24 183 B3
Almond Ave RG14 1 C3
Almond Cl
2 Farnborough GU14 55 C4
Old Basing RG24 70 A3
Almond Ct GU52 75 A3
Almondale Ct GU14 55 C3
Almshouses 2 RG21 69 A2
Almswood Rd RG26 9 C1
Aloes The GU51 75 A4
Alpha Rd GU12 77 A1
Alphington Ave GU16 36 B1
Alphington Gn GU16 36 B1
Alpine Cl GU14 55 A2
Alpine Ct RG22 68 A2
Alpine Rd GU35 164 B1
Alresford Dro SO21 153 C3
Alresford Rd
Chilcomb SO21, SO23 199 B4
Ovington SO24 178 C1
Winchester SO21, SO23 198 B4
Alresford Sta* SO24 179 B3
Alsace Wlk GU15 35 C1
Alswitha Terr 27 SO23 176 A1
Alton Bsns Ctr GU34 140 A2
Alton Coll GU34 139 C3
Alton Com Hospl GU34 139 B1
Alton Convent Sch
GU34 140 A3
Alton Ct 12 SO23 176 A1
Alton Inf Sch GU34 140 A2
Alton La GU34 160 B1
Alton Rd Farnham GU10 121 A4
Fleet GU51 75 B4
Odiham RG29 95 A3
Alton Ride GU47 35 A4
Alton Road Cotts RG29 94 C2
Alton Sta GU34 140 A2
Altona Gdns SP10 82 C2
Alverstoke Gdns GU11 76 B1
Alwin Pl GU9 99 A4
Amazon Cl RG21 68 C2
Amber Cl GU35 164 C1
Amber Ct 2 GU12 77 A1
Amber Gdns SP10 105 B4
Amber Hill GU15 36 C2
Amberley Cl RG14 1 B2
Amberley Grange GU11 99 B4
Amberwood Dr GU15 36 B4
Ambleside Cl
Farnborough GU14 55 B2
Mytchett GU16 56 C1
Ambleside Cres GU9 98 C3
Ambrose Rd RG26 26 C4
Amery Hill GU34 139 C2
Amery Hill Sch GU34 139 C2
Amery St GU34 139 C2
Amesbury Ho 3 SP9 79 A3
Amesbury Rd
Cholderton SP4 101 A1
Newton Toney SP4 123 A3
Penton Grafton SP11 81 A1
Amesbury Sch GU26 167 B1
Amherst Rd GU35 164 B3
Ampere Rd RG14 1 C2
Amport CE Prim Sch
SP11 104 A3
Amport Cl
Old Basing RG24 70 A4
Winchester SO22 175 B2
Amport Firs SP11 104 A3
Amport Park Mews
SP11 103 C3
Ancells Ct GU51 54 B3
Ancells Rd GU51 54 B2
Anchor Mdw GU14 55 B2
Anchor Rd RG20 24 B1
Anchor Yd 1 RG21 69 A2
Andeferas Rd SP10 82 C2
Anders Rd SO21 153 C2
Anderson Ho GU9 99 A1
Andlers Ash Rd GU33 207 C2
Andover CE Prim Sch
SP10 106 A4
Andover Com Hospl
SP10 82 C1
Andover Dr 1 GU51 53 B2
Andover Dro RG20 4 C2
Andover La SP11 80 A4
Andover Rd
Blackwater GU17 35 A3
Fyfield SP11 80 C3
Micheldever SO21 111 A1
Monxton SP11 104 B3
Newbury RG14 5 A3
Oakley RG23,RG25 66 B1
Winchester SO21, SO22,
SO23 175 C1
Andover Rd N SO22 175 C2
Andover Road Ret Pk
SO23 175 C1
Andover Sta SP10 105 C4
Andover Way GU11 99 C4
Andrew Cl RG29 72 A2
Andrew Ct GU14 55 B4
Andrew's La
Long Sutton RG29 95 C2
Ropley SO24 181 C3
Andrewartha Rd GU14 56 B1
Andrews Cl GU52 75 A3
Andrews Endowed CE Prim
Sch GU34 140 B3
Andrews Rd GU14 55 B3
Andwell La
Mapledurwell RG24 71 A3
Newnham RG27 71 A3
Angel Ct RG14 1 C2
Angel Mdws RG29 72 C2
Angelsey Rd GU12 77 A1
Anglesey Ave GU14 55 B4
Anglesey Cl
Andover SP10 106 A3
Basingstoke RG24 48 B1
Angora Way GU51 54 A2
Annandale Dr GU10 122 A3
Anne Armstrong Cl GU11 77 A3
Annes Way GU52 75 A3
Annettes Croft 4 GU52 74 C2
Ansell Rd GU16 36 B1
Anson Cl GU11 76 B2
Anstey Cl RG21 69 A1
Anstey Jun Sch GU34 139 C2
Anstey La GU34 139 C4
Anstey Mill Cl GU34 140 A3
Anstey Mill La GU34 140 A3
Anstey Rd GU34 140 A3
Antar Cl RG21 68 C2
Anton Cl RG23 67 A1
Anton Inf Sch SP10 106 A3
Anton Jun Sch SP10 106 A3
Anton La SP11 83 A3
Anton Mill Rd SP10 106 A4
Anton Rd SP10 106 A3
Anton Trad Est SP10 106 A4
Antrim Cl RG22 68 A2
Anvil Way RG26 28 C2
Anzio Cl GU11 76 C1
Apex Dr GU16 36 A1
Apollo Dr GU35 164 C1
Apollo Ho RG7 9 B1
Apollo Rise GU14 55 A2
Apple Tree Cl RG14 5 B4
Apple Tree Gr SP10 82 B1
Apple Way RG24 70 A3
Appledore Mews GU14 55 C4
Appledown Cl SO24 179 B2
Appledown La SO24 179 C2
Applegarth Cl RG21 69 B2
Applelands Cl GU10 121 C2
Appleshaw CE Inf & Jun Sch
SP11 81 A4
Appleshaw Cl
12 Tadley RG26 26 C4
Winchester SO22 175 B2
Appleshaw Dene SP11 81 A3
Appleshaw Way SP11 79 B3
Appleton Cl SO20 125 B1
Appleton Mews SP10 106 A3
Appleton View SO24 183 B3
Appletree Mead RG27 51 B1
Appley Ct GU15 35 C3
Appley Dr GU15 35 C3
Approach Rd GU9 99 A1
April Cl GU15 36 A1
Apsley Cl SP10 105 C3
Arboretum The RG25 94 A3
Arbour Ct 34 SO22 197 C4
Arcade The
11 Aldershot GU11 76 C1
Liss GU33 207 C3
12 Newbury RG14 1 C2
Archaeological Trail*
SO24 155 C3
Archery Fields RG29 72 C2
Archery La SO22 197 C4
Archery Rise GU34 139 C1
Arcot Rd SP9 78 C2
Ardglen Rd RG28 86 B3
Ardrossan Ave GU15 36 C3
Arena L Ctr GU15 36 A3
Arena La GU11 76 B3
Arford Comm GU35 165 B3
Arford Rd GU35 165 B3
Argent Terr GU47 35 B4
Argente Cl GU51 54 A2
Argyle Cl GU35 164 B1
Argyle Rd RG14 1 B1
Arkle Ave RG19 2 B2
Arkwright Cl RG20 21 B3
Arkwright Gate SP10 82 A1
Arle Cl SO24 179 B3
Arle Gdns SO24 179 B3
Arlebury Pk SO24 179 B3
Arlington Pl 2 SO23 198 A4
Arlington Terr GU11 76 B1
Arlott Dr RG21 69 A4
Armitage Dr GU16 36 B1
Armstrong Cl SO21 153 C2
Armstrong Mall GU14 55 A2
Armstrong Rd RG24 69 C4
Armstrong Rise SP10 82 C2
Arne Cl RG22 91 B4
Arnett Ave RG40 16 B4
Arnewood Ave RG26 10 A1
Arnhem Cl GU11 76 C1
Arnhem Rd RG14 1 C2
Arran Cl RG23 67 A1
Arrow Ind Est GU14 55 B1
Arrow La RG27 52 A4
Arrow Rd GU14 55 B1
Arthur Cl GU9 98 C1
Arthur Ct 22 RG21 69 A3
Arthur Rd Farnham GU9 99 A1
Newbury RG14 1 B1
Winchester SO23 176 A1
Arthur St GU11 76 C1
Arthur's La SP11 20 A1
Artillery Rd
Aldershot GU11 76 C1
Farnborough GU11 77 A4
Artists Way SP10 83 A1
Arun Ct RG21 69 B3
Arundel Cl Fleet GU51 75 A4
Liphook GU30 187 A4
New Alresford SO24 179 B2
Arundel Gdns RG23 68 B4
Arundell Pl 8 GU9 98 C1
Ascension Cl RG24 48 B1
Ascot Cl Alton GU34 140 A1
Newbury RG14 6 A4
Ascot Ct GU11 76 C1
Ash Church Rd GU12 77 C1
Ash Cl Ash GU12 77 C2
Blackwater GU17 35 A3
North Tidworth SP9 79 A4
Ash Ct 6 RG14 1 C2
Ash Gr Kingsclere RG20 24 B1
Liphook GU30 188 A2
Old Basing RG24 70 B3
Ash Grange Cty Prim Sch
GU12 77 C1
Ash Green La W GU10 100 B4
Ash Hill Rd GU12 77 C2
Ash La Baughurst RG26 9 B1
Latchmere Green RG26 28 A3
Ash Lodge Cl GU12 77 C1
Ash Lodge Dr GU12 77 C1
Ash Manor Sch GU12 100 B4
Ash Park Cotts RG25 89 A4
Ash Path SO20 126 A2
Ash Rd Aldershot GU12 100 A4
Bishop's Green RG20 6 B2
Ash St GU12 77 C1
Ash Sta GU12 77 C1
Ash Terr RG18 2 C4
Ash Tree Cl GU14 55 A2
Ash Tree Gr RG20 3 C4
Ash Tree Rd SP10 105 B4
Ash Vale Sta GU12 77 C4
Ash Wlk SO24 179 B3
Ashbarn Cres SO22 197 C3
Ashbourne Way RG19 2 C2
Ashburton Cl SO24 179 B3
Ashburton Rd SO24 179 B3
Ashbury Dr GU17 35 C1
Ashbury Rd GU35 164 B1
Ashdell Rd GU34 140 A2
Ashdene Cres GU12 77 C2
Ashdene Rd GU12 77 C1
Ashdown Ave GU14 56 B1
Ashdown Terr SP9 78 C3
Ashfield RG24 48 C2
Ashfield Gn GU17 34 B3
Ashfield Rd SP10 105 B4
Ashfields SO21 130 B3
Ashford Chace GU32 206 C1
Ashford Hill Prim Sch
RG19 8 B1
Ashford Hill Rd RG19 7 B1
Ashlawn Gdns SP10 106 A3
Ashlea RG27 51 A1
Ashley Cl Camberley GU16 56 C3
Crondall GU10 97 B4
Winchester SO22 175 B2
Ashley Ct GU34 140 A2
Ashley Dr GU17 35 A2
Ashley Dro SN8 17 C3
Ashley Ho 4 GU35 164 B1
Ashley Lodge 16 RG21 69 A2
Ashley Rd
Bentworth GU34 138 A3
Farnborough GU14 56 A2
Ashmead GU35 164 B2
Ashmoor La RG24 70 C4
Ashmore Green Rd RG18 2 C4
Ashmore La SP5 190 B1
Ashmore Rd SO22 175 B1
Ashridge GU14 55 B4
Ashridge Ct 2 RG14 1 C1
Ashton Rd RG14 1 C1
Ashtree Cnr RG20 4 A4
Ashtrees The GU12 77 C1
Ashurst Cl Tadley RG26 26 C4
Winchester SO22 175 B2
Ashurst Rd GU12 77 B2
Ashwell Ave GU15 36 B3
Ashwood Dr RG14 2 A2
Ashwood Way RG23 68 B4
Ashwood Way Rdbt RG23 68 B4
Aspen Cl GU35 164 B1
Aspen Gdns RG27 51 A1
Aspen Ho GU11 100 A4
Aspin Way GU17 34 C3
Aster Ct SP10 105 B3
Aster Rd RG22 91 A4
Atbara Rd GU52 75 A2
Athlone Cl SP11 83 A4
Atholl Ct SP10 83 A2
Atholl Rd GU35 164 B1
Attenborough Cl GU51 54 A2
Attfield Cl GU12 77 B1
Attlee Gdns GU52 74 C2
Attwood Cl RG21 68 C2
Attwoods Dro SO21 197 B1
Auchinleck Ho 3 SP9 78 C4
Auchinleck Way GU11 76 B1
Audley Cl RG14 2 A3
Audley Ho GU9 122 A4
Augustine Cl SP10 82 B2
Augustus Dr RG23 68 B4
Augustus Wlk SP10 83 A2
Aukland Cl SP9 79 A3
Auklet Cl RG22 90 C4
Austen Ave SO22 197 B2
Austen Cl SO23 176 A1
Austen Gdns RG14 5 C4
Austen Gr RG22 68 C1
Austen Rd GU14 55 C3
Austin's Cotts GU9 98 C1
Avalan Ct SO23 197 C3
Aveley La GU9 122 A4
Avenue Cl Andover SP10 105 C4
Liphook GU30 187 C2
Avenue Rd
Farnborough GU14 56 A2
Fleet GU51 53 C1
Grayshott GU26 167 A2
Lasham GU34 116 B2
Winchester SO22 197 C4
Avenue Sucy GU15 35 C2
Avenue The
Aldershot GU12 100 A4
Andover SP10 105 C4
Barton Stacey SO21,SP11 108 B2
Camberley GU15 35 C3
Farleigh Wallop RG22 91 B1
Farnham GU10 121 B2
Fleet GU51 53 C1
Grayshott GU26 167 A2
Haslemere GU27 189 B4
Hatherden SP11 59 C1
Liphook GU30 187 C2
Mortimer RG7 11 C3
New Alresford SO24 179 B3
South Tidworth SP9 78 C2
Avery Cl RG40 16 B3
Avery Ct 18 GU11 76 C1
Aviary Ct RG24 69 C4
Aviemore Dr RG23 67 A1
Avington Pk* SO21 177 C3
Avocet Cres GU47 35 B4

Lincoln Cl
Basingstoke RG22 91 A4
Camberley GU15 36 C2
Farnborough GU12 77 B3
Lincoln Ct
2 Liphook GU30 188 A2
Newbury RG14 1 B1
Lincoln Gn GU34 139 C1
Linden Ave Odiham RG29 72 C2
Old Basing RG24 70 A3
Linden Cl Ludgershall SP11 57 A1
Newbury RG14 1 B2
Linden Ct Camberley GU15 36 B4
Old Basing RG24 70 A3
Linden Dr GU33 207 C2
Linden Rd
Bishop's Green RG20 6 B2
Headley GU35 166 A3
Lindens The GU9 99 A1
Lindenwood RG24 48 C2
Lindford Chase GU35 164 C3
Lindford Rd GU35 164 C3
Lindford Wey GU35 164 C3
Lindum Cl 8 GU11 76 C1
Lindum Dene GU11 76 C1
Lines Rd GU11 77 A4
Lines The RG20 24 B2
Linford Rd GU35 164 C3
Ling Cres GU35 165 C3
Lingen Cl SP10 82 C2
Lingfield Cl Alton GU34 139 C1
Old Basing RG24 70 B3
Lingfield Rd RG14 6 A4
Lingmala Gro GU52 75 A3
Link Ho 4 RG14 1 C1
Link Rd Alton GU34 140 A3
Kingsclere RG20 24 C1
Newbury RG14 1 C1
Link The Andover SP10 105 B4
Yateley GU46 34 A4
Link View RG14 1 B4
Link Way Oakley RG23 67 A1
Thatcham RG18 2 C2
Linklater's Cotts GU17 54 C3
Links Cotts SO24 179 B2
Links Rd SO22 175 B1
Links The GU35 164 A1
Links Way GU14 55 A2
Linkside E GU26 167 A4
Linkside N GU26 166 C4
Linkside S GU26 167 A3
Linkway Camberley GU15 36 A2
Fleet GU52 75 A3
Linkway Par GU52 74 C3
Linnet Cl RG22 68 A1
Linnet La RG20 6 B2
Linnets Rd SO24 179 B2
Linnets Way GU34 139 C3
Linsford Bsns Pk GU16 56 B2
Linsford La GU16 56 B2
Linsley Gdns SO24 179 B2
Linstead Rd GU14 55 B4
Linsted La GU35 165 A4
Linton Cl RG26 27 A4
Linton Dr SP10 83 A1
Lion & Lamb Way 5
GU9 98 C1
Lion & Lamb Yd 13 GU9 98 C1
Lion Cl Haslemere GU27 189 B4
Overton RG25 88 A4
Lion Ct RG24 69 C3
Lion Gn GU27 189 B3
Lion La GU27 189 B4
Lion Mead GU27 189 B3
Lion Way GU52 75 A3
Lions Field GU35 163 B2
Lions Hall 23 SO22 197 C4
Liphook CE Jun Sch
GU30 187 C2
Liphook Inf Sch GU30 187 C2
Liphook Rd Bordon GU35 186 B4
Haslemere GU27 189 B3
Headley GU30,GU35 165 B2
Linchmere GU27 188 C2
Lindford GU35 164 C3
Liphook Sta GU30 188 A1
Lipscombe Cl RG14 1 B1
Lipscombe Rise GU34 139 C3
Lisa Ct 9 RG21 69 A2
Liskeard Dr GU14 55 C3
Lisle Cl Newbury RG14 1 B3
Winchester SO22 197 A2
Lisle Ct SO22 197 C3
Lismoyne Cl GU51 53 C1
Liss Dr 9 GU51 53 B2
Liss Inf & Jun Schs
GU33 208 A2
Liss Sta GU33 207 C2
Lister Rd RG22 68 C1
Litchfield Cl SP10 82 B2
Litchfield Dr GU51 53 B2
Litchfield Ho 2 RG26 26 C4
Litchfield Rd SO22 175 B2
Litten The RG20 24 B1
Little Aldershot La RG26 8 C1
Little Austins Rd GU9 122 A4
Little Barn Pl GU33 208 A2
Little Basing RG24 69 C4
Little Copse
Andover SP10 105 C3
Fleet GU52 74 C4
Yateley GU46 34 A4
Little Copse Chase RG24 48 C1
Little Croft GU46 34 A3
Little Dean Ct SO20 150 A2
Little Dean Ho SO20 150 A2
Little Dean La
South Warnborough RG25 94 C3
Little Dean La *continued*
Upton Grey RG25 94 C3
Little Drove Rd SO20 129 A2
Little Fallow RG24 70 A4
Little Green La GU9 121 C3
Little Hatherden SP11 59 C1
Little Hayes La SO21 177 C4
Little Hoddington Cl
RG25 94 B3
Little Knowl Hill RG20 24 C2
Little London Rd RG7 27 C4
Little Minster St SO23 198 A4
Little Paddock GU15 36 C4
Little Thurbans Cl GU9 121 C3
Little Vigo GU46 33 C2
Little Wellington St
GU11 76 C1
Little-Ann Bridge Farm
SP11 105 B3
Littlefield Cl GU12 77 C1
Littlefield Gdns GU12 77 C1
Littlefield Rd GU34 140 A2
Littlefield Sch GU30 188 A1
Littleton Cotts SP11 80 B2
Littleton La SO21 175 A3
Littleton Rd SO22 175 A2
Littleworth Rd GU10 100 B1
Litton Gdns RG23 67 A1
Livery Rd SP5 168 A1
Livingstone Rd
Andover SP10 83 C1
Newbury RG14 1 C1
Lock Rd GU11 77 A3
Lock Sq SP10 83 B1
Lock's La SO21 174 B2
Locke Cl SP11 124 C4
Locke Rd GU30 188 A2
Locke's Dro SP11 60 A4
Lockerley Endowed CE Prim
Sch SO51 192 A1
Lockerley Rd
Lockerley SO51 192 A1
Mottisfont SO51 192 B1
Lockram La RG7 12 A4
Locksmead 9 RG21 69 B3
Lockwood Cl GU14 55 B4
Loddon Bsns Ctr The
RG24 69 C4
Loddon Cl GU15 36 C3
Loddon Ct RG21 69 B1
Loddon Ctr RG24 69 C4
Loddon Dr RG21 69 B3
Loddon Mall 15 RG21 69 A3
Loddon Rd GU14 55 A3
Loddon Sch The RG27 49 B3
Loddon Way GU12 77 C1
Lodge Cl Aldershot GU11 100 A4
Andover SP10 105 C4
Lodge Dr SP11 81 B1
Lodge Gr GU46 34 B3
Lodge Hill Cl GU10 122 A3
Lodge Hill Rd GU10 122 B3
Lodge La SP11 58 A2
Lodge The Farnham GU9 99 B2
Newbury RG14 1 C2
Lodsworth GU14 55 A2
Loggon Rd RG21 69 A1
Loman Rd GU16 56 C2
Lomond Cl RG23 67 A1
Londlandes GU52 74 C2
London Ct RG14 2 A2
London Rd Alton GU34 140 B3
Andover SP10 106 B4
Andover SP10,SP11 106 C4
Basingstoke RG21 69 B2
Blackwater GU15 35 B3
Camberley GU15 36 B4
Camberley GU15 36 A3
Hartley Wintney RG27 52 B3
Hill Brow GU33 208 A1
Hook RG27 51 B1
Kings Worthy SO23 176 A3
Laverstoke RG28 87 A3
Liphook GU30 188 A3
Newbury RG14 2 A2
Odiham RG29 72 C2
Odiham RG29 72 C3
Old Basing RG24,RG27 70 B3
Overton RG25 88 A4
Stockbridge SO20 150 B2
Whitchurch RG28 86 C3
London St Andover SP10 106 A4
Basingstoke RG21 69 A2
Whitchurch RG28 86 B3
Long Beech Dr GU14 55 A2
Long Bridge GU9 99 A1
Long Cl SO23 197 C3
Long Copse Chase RG24 48 C2
Long Cross Hill GU35 165 B3
Long Cross La RG22 91 A3
Long Garden Mews 11
GU9 98 C1
Long Gdn Way GU9 98 C1
Long Gdn Wlk GU9 98 C1
Long Gdn Wlk E GU9 98 C1
Long Gdn Wlk W GU9 98 C1
Long Gr RG26 9 A1
Long Hill GU10 100 B1
Long La Chineham RG24 49 A1
Long Sutton RG29 96 A3
Newbury RG14 2 A4
Long Leaze SP11 61 B2
Long Rd The GU10 121 C2
Long Sutton CE Prim Sch
RG29 95 C2
Long Sutton Dr 11 GU51 53 B2
Long Wlk SO21 176 C2
Longacre Ash GU12 77 C1
Longacre *continued*
Newbury RG14 5 A4
Longacre Cl GU33 208 A2
Longacre Rise RG24 48 C1
Longbarrow Cl SO21 153 C2
Longbridge Cl RG27 29 C1
Longbridge Rd RG26 28 C2
Longcroft GU10 120 A3
Longcroft Cl 11 RG21 69 A2
Longcroft Rd RG20 24 B2
Longdene Rd GU27 189 C3
Longdown GU52 74 C3
Longdown Cl GU10 122 A3
Longdown Lodge GU47 34 C4
Longdown Rd GU10 122 A3
Longfellow Par RG24 69 B4
Longfield RG23 67 A2
Longfield Cl
Farnborough GU14 55 C4
North Waltham RG25 89 C1
Longfield Rd Ash GU12 77 C1
Winchester SO23 198 B4
Longford Cl GU15 36 A2
Longhope Dr GU10 121 C3
Longhouse Gn 9 SO23 198 B4
Longleat Sq GU14 56 A2
Longley Rd GU9 99 A1
Longmead Fleet GU52 75 A3
Liss GU33 207 C2
Woolton Hill RG20 4 B1
Longmeadow GU16 36 B2
Longmoor Cl RG40 16 B3
Longmoor Ct 10 GU51 53 B2
Longmoor Dr GU30 187 A2
Longmoor La RG7 11 C4
Longmoor Rd
Basingstoke RG21 69 A2
Greatham GU33 186 A2
Liphook GU30 187 B2
Longparish CE Prim Sch
SP11 108 A2
Longparish Ct 11 SP10 106 A4
Longparish Rd
Hurstbourne Priors RG28 85 B1
Longparish SP11 107 C1
Longs Ct RG28 86 B3
Longstock Cl
Andover SP10 105 C4
Chineham RG24 49 A2
Longstock Ct 13 SP10 106 A4
Longstock Rd SP11 128 A4
Longwater La
Eversley GU46 33 B4
Finchampstead RG40 16 B1
Longwater Rd RG40 16 B1
Lopcombe Cnr SP5 146 A2
Lord Wandsworth Coll
RG29 95 C1
Lordsfield Rd RG25 88 A4
Lordswood RG7 27 C4
Lorraine Rd GU15 36 B4
Lorraine Sch GU15 36 B4
Louisburg Rd GU35 164 B3
Louise Margaret Rd
GU11 76 C2
Loundyes Cl RG18 2 C2
Love La Andover SP10 106 A4
Kingsclere RG20 24 B1
Newbury RG14 1 C3
Odiham RG29 72 B1
Lovedon La SO23 176 B4
Lovegroves RG24 49 A2
Lovell Cl
South Wonston SO21 153 C2
Thruxton SP11 103 B4
Lovells Wlk SO24 179 B3
Loveridge Cl
Andover SP10 83 A2
Basingstoke RG21 69 A1
Lovers La GU10 144 A4
Loves Wood RG7 11 B3
Lovett Ho 2 GU9 98 C1
Lovett Wlk SO22 175 B2
Lovington La SO24,SO21 178 B2
Low La GU9 99 C3
Lowa Rd SP9 78 C3
Lowden Cl SO22 197 B2
Lowe Cl GU11 76 B2
Lower Brook St
Basingstoke RG21 68 C3
Winchester SO23 198 A4
Lower Canes GU46 33 C3
Lower Charles St GU15 36 A3
Lower Chestnut Dr RG21 68 C2
Lower Church La 16 GU9 98 C1
Lower Church Rd GU47 34 B4
Lower Comm RG27 15 B1
Lower Evingar Rd RG28 86 B3
Lower Farm Ct RG14 2 B1
Lower Farnham Rd
GU11,GU12 100 A4
Lower Hanger GU27 189 A3
Lower Lamborough La
SO24 201 B3
Lower Moor GU46 34 A3
Lower Mount St 19 GU51 53 B2
Lower Neatham Mill La
Alton GU34 140 B3
Alton, Neatham GU34 140 C3
Lower Nelson St GU11 76 C1
Lower Newport Rd GU12 77 A1
Lower Paice La GU34 159 B2
Lower Pool Rd RG27 32 A2
Lower Raymond Almshouses
12 RG14 1 B1
Lower Rd SO21 153 B2
Lower Sandhurst Rd
RG40 16 C1
Lower South View GU9 99 A2
Lower St GU27 189 C3
Lower Stanmore La
SO23 197 C3
Lower Turk St GU34 139 C2
Lower Way RG19 2 C2
Lower Weybourne La
GU9 99 C3
Lower Wote St RG21 69 A3
Loweswater Gdns GU35 164 B3
Lowicks Rd GU10 144 C3
Lowlands Rd
Basingstoke RG22 68 A2
Blackwater GU17 35 A2
Lowndes Bldgs GU9 98 C2
Lowry Cl GU47 35 A3
Lowry Ct SP10 82 C1
Loxwood Ave GU51 74 C4
Loyalty La RG24 70 A3
Lubeck Dr SP10 82 C2
Lucas Cl GU46 34 A3
Lucas Field GU27 189 B3
Ludgershall Castle Prim Sch
SP11 57 A1
Ludgershall Rd SP9 78 C4
Ludlow Cl
Basingstoke RG23 68 B3
Camberley GU16 56 C4
Newbury RG14 2 B2
Ludlow Gdns RG23 68 B3
Ludshott Gr GU35 165 C3
Luke Rd GU11 99 B4
Luke Rd E GU11 99 B4
Lulworth Cl GU14 55 C4
Lundy Cl RG24 48 B1
Lune Cl 4 RG21 69 B3
Lune Ct 43 SP10 83 B1
Lupin Cl RG22 91 A4
Lutyens Cl
Basingstoke RG24 69 C4
Chineham RG24 48 C1
Lyall Pl GU9 98 C4
Lych Gate Cl GU47 34 B4
Lyde Cl RG23 67 A1
Lydford Cl
Camberley GU16 56 C4
Farnborough GU14 55 C4
Lye Copse Ave GU14 55 C4
Lyeway La GU34,SO24 182 B2
Lyeway Rd SO24 182 A3
Lyford Rd RG21 69 A3
Lymington Ave GU46 34 A3
Lymington Barn Ind Est
GU34 160 A2
Lymington Bottom
GU34 160 A1
Lymington Bottom Rd
Four Marks GU34 160 A2
Medstead GU34 160 A2
Lymington Cl
Basingstoke RG22 91 A4
Four Marks GU34 160 A1
Lymington Rise GU34 160 A1
Lyn Ct 5 RG21 69 B3
Lynams GU52 74 C2
Lynch Cl SO22 175 C1
Lynch Hill RG28 86 B3
Lynch Hill Pk RG28 86 B3
Lynch Rd GU9 99 B1
Lynch The Overton RG25 87 C4
Whitchurch RG28 86 B3
Lynchborough Rd GU30 187 A4
Lynchford Rd
Farnborough GU14 77 A4
Farnborough GU14 77 B4
Lyndale Dr GU51 54 B1
Lyndford Terr GU52 74 C4
Lyndhurst Ave
Aldershot GU11 100 A3
Blackwater GU17 35 A3
Lyndhurst Cl SO22 175 B2
Lyndhurst Dr RG22 91 B3
Lyndhurst Sch GU15 35 C3
Lyndsey Cl GU14 54 C2
Lynford Ave SO22 175 C1
Lynford Way SO22 175 C1
Lynn Way GU14 55 B4
Lynton Cl GU9 121 C4
Lynton Ct RG14 1 C2
Lynton Mdw SO20 129 A2
Lynton Rd GU35 164 B2
Lynwood Cl GU35 165 A3
Lynwood Ct SO22 175 C1
Lynwood Dr
Andover SP10 105 C4
Mytchett GU16 56 C2
Lynwood Gdns RG27 51 A1
Lyon Way GU16 36 A1
Lyon Way Ind Est GU16 36 A1
Lyse Ct GU33 207 C2
Lysons Ave GU12 77 B4
Lysons Rd GU11 76 C1
Lysons Way GU12 77 C4
Lytham Cl GU35 164 A1
Lytton Rd RG21 69 B3

M

Mabbs La RG27 52 B2
Mac Callum Rd SP11 83 A4
Macadam Way SP10 82 A1
Macdonald Rd GU9 98 C4
MacDonald's Almshouses 21
GU9 98 C1
Macklin Ho 35 SO22 197 C4
Macnaghten Woods
GU15 36 B3
Macrae Rd GU46 34 A3
Maddocks Hill SO24 181 A2
Madeira Cl RG24 48 B1
Madeira Pl 5 RG14 1 C1
Madeley Rd GU52 75 A3
Madox Brown End GU47 35 B3
Madrid Rd SP10 83 B1
Magdalen Hill SO23 198 A4
Magdalen Mews 45
SO23 198 A4
Magellan Cl SP10 83 C1
Magnolia Cl SP10 105 C4
Magnolia Ho RG24 48 A1
Magnolia Way GU52 75 A4
Magnus Dr RG22 91 A4
Magpie Cl
Basingstoke RG22 90 C4
Bordon GU35 164 C1
Ewshot GU10 98 A4
Thatcham RG19 2 C2
Mahler Cl RG22 91 C4
Maida Rd GU11 76 C2
Maidenthorn La RG25 90 A1
Main Rd Littleton SO22 175 A3
Tadley RG26 27 A3
Main St RG19 6 C3
Mainline Bsns Ctr GU33 207 C2
Maitland Rd GU14 76 C4
Maitlands Cl GU10 100 B3
Majendie Cl RG14 1 A3
Majestic Rd RG22 91 A3
Majorca Ave SP10 83 B1
Makins Ct SO24 179 B3
Maldive Rd RG24 48 B1
Malham Gdns RG22 91 A3
Mall The Andover SP10 106 A4
South Tidworth SP9 78 B2
Mallard Cl Andover SP10 83 A1
Ash GU12 77 A1
Basingstoke RG22 90 C4
Haslemere GU27 189 B3
New Alresford SO24 179 B3
Mallard Ct RG14 1 B2
Mallard Way 4 GU46 33 C3
Mallards GU34 139 C3
Mallards The GU16 36 B1
Mallow Cl GU35 165 A3
Malmesbury Gdns SO22 175 B1
Malmesbury Ho 2 SP9 79 A3
Malmsbury Rd GU35 164 B1
Malpass Rd SO21 153 B1
Malshanger La RG23 67 A2
Malta Cl RG24 48 A1
Maltbys GU34 184 C4
Malters End GU26 166 C2
Malthouse Bridge Cotts
GU51 74 B3
Malthouse Cl Fleet GU52 74 C3
Itchen Abbas SO21 176 C2
Malthouse Cotts RG29 72 B2
Malthouse Ct GU30 188 A2
Malthouse La
Bighton SO24 158 B1
Smannell SP11 83 B4
Tadley RG26 27 A3
Upper Chute SP11 58 A4
Malthouse Mdws GU30 188 A2
Malthouse Mews GU34 140 B3
Maltings Cl GU34 139 C2
Maltings The
Bramley RG26 28 C1
Liphook GU30 188 A2
Malvern Cl RG22 68 A2
Malvern Ct RG14 1 B1
Malvern Rd
Farnborough GU14 55 A4
Hawley GU47 34 B1
Hill Brow GU33 208 A1
Mandarin Ct Farnham GU9 99 A3
Newbury RG14 2 A1
Mandora Rd GU11 76 C2
Manfield Rd GU12 77 C1
Manica Cl GU35 164 B2
Manley Bridge Rd GU10 121 B3
Manley James Cl RG29 72 C2
Mann Cl RG28 86 B2
Manningford Cl SO23 176 A2
Manor Bridge Ct SP9 78 C4
Manor Cl
Abbotts Ann SP11 105 A2
Alton GU34 140 A3
Basingstoke RG22 91 A3
Haslemere GU27 189 B3
Shipton Bellinger SP9 101 C4
Tongham GU10 100 B4
43 Winchester SO23 198 A4
Manor Copse SP10 83 A3
Manor Cotts RG28 87 A3
Manor Cres GU27 189 B3
Manor Ct GU52 75 A2
Manor Farm Bsns Ctr
GU10 100 B3
Manor Farm Cl GU12 77 A1
Manor Farm Cotts SO21 131 A1
Manor Farm La SO51 193 C1
Manor Field Inf Sch
RG22 91 C4
Manor Field Jun Sch
RG22 91 C4
Manor Fields
Liphook GU30 188 A2
Seale GU10 100 C2
Manor Gdns GU10 122 A3
Manor Ho The
Camberley GU15 36 A3

Moorlands Cl *continued*
Hindhead GU26 ....167 B2
Moorlands Pl GU15 .....35 C2
Moorlands Rd GU15 .....35 C2
Moors Ct RG40 ....16 B4
Moors The GU10 ....100 B4
Moorside Cl GU14 ......35 C1
Moorside Rd SO23 ......176 B1
Moot Cl SP10 ....83 A2
Moray Ave GU47 ....35 A4
More House Sch GU10 .122 A1
Moreland Cl GU34 .....140 A1
Morestead Rd
Winchester SO21 ....198 C2
Winchester SO23 ....198 A2
Moreton Cl Churt GU10 ..144 B1
Fleet GU52 ....74 C2
Morgaston Rd RG24,RG26 47 C4
Morland Rd GU11 ......100 A3
Morley Cl GU46 ....33 C3
Morley Rd
Basingstoke RG21 ....69 A1
Farnham GU9 ....99 A1
Mornington Ave RG40 ...16 B4
Mornington Cl
Andover SP10 ....106 A3
Baughurst RG26 ....9 B1
Mornington Dr SO22 ...175 B1
Mornington Rd GU35 ...164 A1
Morris Rd GU14 ....77 A4
Morris St RG27 ....71 C4
Morse Rd RG22 ....68 C2
Mortimer Cl
Hartley Wintney RG27 .....52 A2
Kings Worthy SO23 ......176 A3
Mortimer Gdns RG26 ....27 A4
Mortimer Hall RG7 ......12 A3
Mortimer La
20 Basingstoke RG21 .....69 A3
Stratfield Mortimer RG7 ...12 A4
West End Green RG7 .....29 A4
Mortimer St John's CE Sch
RG7 ....11 C3
Mortimer Sta RG7 ....12 B3
Morton Cl GU16 ....56 B4
Morval Cl GU14 ....55 B2
Morval Rd GU46 ....34 B1
Moselle Cl GU14 ....55 A3
Moss Cl GU33 ....208 A2
Moss Rd SO23 ....198 A4
Mothes Ho RG26 ....27 A4
Mottisfont Abbey (NT)★
SO51 ....192 C1
Mottisfont Abbey Gdns★
SO51 ....192 C2
Moulsham Copse La
GU46 ....33 C4
Moulsham La GU46 ......33 C4
Mount Carmel Rd SP11 .124 C3
Mount Cl Highclere RG20 ..21 B3
Newbury RG14 ....1 C1
Winchester SO22 ....175 C2
Mount Hermon Rd
SP11 ....124 C3
Mount Hts SP5 ....146 B2
Mount Pleasant
Amport SP11 ....104 A3
Farnham GU9 ....98 C1
Hartley Wintney RG27 .....52 B3
Kings Worthy SO23 ......176 B3
Laverstoke RG28 ....87 A3
Tadley RG26 ....26 C4
Mount Pleasant Dr RG26 26 C4
Mount Pleasant Rd
Aldershot GU12 ....77 A1
Alton GU34 ....139 C1
Lindford GU35 ....164 C3
Mount Rd RG20 ....21 B4
Mount The Fleet GU51 ....54 A1
Headley GU35 ....165 C3
Mount View GU11 ....76 C1
Mount View Rd SO22 ...197 A2
Mountbatten Cl RG14 .....2 A3
Mountbatten Ct
14 Aldershot GU11 ....76 C1
Andover SP10 ....83 B1
Winchester SO22 ....175 C2
Mountbatten Pl SO23 ...176 B4
Mounter's La GU34 .....139 B1
Mounters La GU34 ......139 B1
Mounts Way GU51 ....53 B2
Mountsom's La GU34 ...161 C2
Mourne Cl RG22 ....68 A2
Mowatt Rd GU26 ....167 A1
Mozart Cl RG22 ....91 C4
Mud La RG27 ....15 B1
Mulberries The GU9 .....99 B2
Mulberry Cl Ash GU12 ...77 C2
Sandhurst GU47 ....35 A4
Mulberry Ct GU34 ......160 B2
Mulberry Ho 3 SP10 ...106 A4
Mulberry Mead RG28 ....86 B3
Mulberry Way RG24 ......48 C2
Mulfords Hill 3 RG26 ...26 C4
Mulgrave Rd GU16 ....36 B1
Mull Cl RG23 ....67 A1
Mullins Cl RG21 ....69 A4
Mulroy Dr GU15 ....36 C3
Munnings Cl RG21 ....69 B2
Munnings Ct SP10 ....82 C1
Munnings Dr GU47 ......35 B3
Munro Way GU11 ....77 A4
Murray Cl SP10 ....105 C3
Murray Rd GU14 ....55 B2
Murray's Rd GU11 ....77 A3
Murrell Green Bsns Pk
RG27 ....51 C1
Murrell Rd GU12 ....77 C2
Murrells La GU15 ....35 C2
Mus of Army Flying
Explorers' World★
SO20 ....126 A2
Muscott Cl SP9 ....101 B4
Museum of the Iron Age★
SP10 ....106 A4
Musgrave Cl RG22 ....91 B4
Musgrove Gdns GU34 ..139 C2
Musket Copse RG24 .....70 A3
Muss La SO20 ....172 A2
Myland Cl RG21 ....69 B4
Mylen Bsns Ctr SP10 ...105 C4
Mylen Rd SP10 ....82 C1
Myrtle Dr GU17 ....35 A3
Mytchett Heath GU16 ....56 C2
Mytchett Lake Rd GU16 ..56 C1
Mytchett Place Rd GU16 .56 C1
Mytchett Prim Sch GU16 .56 B2
Mytchett Rd GU16 ....56 B2

N

Naafi Rdbt GU11 ....76 C1
Nadder Rd SP9 ....78 C3
Nairn Cl GU16 ....36 B1
Napier Cl Ash GU11 ......77 B4
North Tidworth SP9 ....79 A3
Napier La GU12 ....77 C2
Napier Wlk SP10 ....83 B1
Napoleon Ave GU14 ......55 C3
Napoleon Dr RG23 ....68 B4
Naseby Rise RG14 ....2 A3
Nash Cl Basingstoke RG21 .69 B4
Farnborough GU14 ....55 B2
Nash Grove La RG40 .....16 B4
Nash Mdws RG29 ....95 A2
Nateley Rd RG29 ....71 C1
Nations Hill SO23 ......176 B3
Naylors The RG7 ....14 A3
Neath Rd RG21 ....69 B3
Neelem Ct 5 GU14 ....56 A1
Nelson Cl Aldershot GU12 .77 A1
Farnham GU9 ....99 A4
Stockbridge SO20 ....149 C1
Nelson Rd Farnham GU9 ..99 A4
Winchester SO23 ....198 B3
Nelson St GU11 ....76 C1
Nelson Way GU15 ....35 B2
Nelson Wlk SP10 ....83 B1
Nene Ct 47 SP10 ....83 B1
Nepaul Rd SP9 ....78 C4
Neptune Rd GU35 ......164 C1
Nestor Cl SP10 ....82 C1
Nether St 15 GU34 .....139 C2
Nether Vell-Mead GU52 .74 C2
Nethercliffe Sch SO22 ..175 C1
Netherfield Cl GU34 ....139 C2
Netherhouse Ct GU51 ....74 B3
Netherhouse Moor GU51 74 B3
Netley St GU14 ....77 A4
Nettlebeds La SO24 ....158 A1
Neuvic Way RG28 ....86 B2
Nevada Cl GU14 ....55 A2
Neville Cl Andover SP10 .106 A3
Basingstoke RG21 ....69 A1
Neville Duke Rd GU14 ...55 B4
New Barn Cl GU51 ....74 B4
New Barn Cotts SO21 ...152 C1
New Barn La Alton GU34 139 C1
Wherwell SP11 ....128 C4
New Bldgs SP11 ....58 B4
New Bridge La 10 RG21 ..69 B3
New Cotts Bighton SO24 .158 B1
South Warnborough RG29 ..95 A2
Sutton Scotney SO21 ....131 B2
New Ct SO21 ....131 B2
New Dawn Cl GU14 ......55 A2
New Farm Cotts RG29 ...95 B1
New Farm Rd
East Stratton SO21 ......134 A2
New Alresford SO24 .....179 A2
New Hall SO23 ....198 A3
New House La SP11 .....81 A4
New La SO20 ....172 A2
New Mill La RG27 ....15 B1
New Mill Rd RG40 ....15 B2
New North Dr RG27 ......49 C4
New Odiham Rd GU34 ..139 B3
New Paddock Cl GU34 .140 B3
New Rd Basingstoke RG21 .69 A2
Blackwater GU17 ....35 B2
Bordon GU35 ....164 B1
Eversley GU46 ....33 B4
Fleet GU52 ....75 A3
Hartley Wintney RG27 .....52 B3
Hook RG27 ....72 A4
Linchmere GU27 ....189 B3
Littleton SO22 ....175 A3
Micheldever SO21 ....111 A1
Newbury RG14,RG19 ....6 A4
North Warnborough RG29 ..72 B2
Over Wallop SO20 ....147 B4
Pamber End RG26 ....27 B2
Sandhurst GU47 ....34 C4
Stratfield Mortimer RG7 ...12 A4
Tadley RG26 ....26 C4
Tongham GU10 ....100 B3
New Rd Cotts GU34 ....184 C4
New St Andover SP10 .....83 A1
Basingstoke RG21 ....69 A2
Stockbridge SO20 ....149 C2
Stratfield Saye RG7 ......29 C4
New The GU12 ....77 C1
New Villas RG20 ....3 C2
Newall Rd SP11 ....105 A4
Newark Rd GU47 ....34 B1
Newbold Rd RG14 ....1 A3
Newburgh St SO23 .....197 C4
Newbury Coll RG14 ....1 B2
Newbury Com Hospl RG14 1 B1
Newbury Rd
Andover SP10,SP11 ....83 A3
Enham Alamein SP10,SP11 .83 A3
Kingsclere RG20 ....24 A2
Whitchurch RG28 ....86 B4
Newbury Ret Pk RG14 .....5 C4
Newbury St RG28 ....86 B3
Newbury St Nicolas CE Jun
Sch RG14 ....1 C1
Newbury Sta RG14 ....1 C1
Newchurch Rd RG26 ......9 C1
Newcomb Cl SP10 ....106 A3
Newcome Pl GU12 ......100 A4
Newcome Rd GU9 ....99 B3
Newfield Ave GU14 ......55 B3
Newfield Rd Ash GU12 ...77 C3
Liss GU33 ....208 A3
Newlands Cl GU46 ....34 A3
Newlands Dr GU12 ....77 C2
Newlands Prim Sch
GU46 ....34 A3
Newlands Rd GU15 ....35 C1
Newman La GU34 ....140 A3
Newmans Ct GU9 ....98 C4
Newnham La RG24 ....70 C4
Newnham Pk RG27 ....71 C4
Newnham Rd RG27 ....71 C4
Newport Cl RG14 ....1 C2
Newport Jun Sch GU12 ..77 A1
Newport Rd
Aldershot GU12 ....77 A1
Newbury RG14 ....1 C2
Newton La GU34 ....183 C4
Newton Pk SP10 ....82 A1
Newton Rd GU14 ....56 A3
Newton Toney CE Prim Sch
SP4 ....123 A3
Newton Villas SP11 ......57 A1
Newton Way GU10 ......100 B4
Newtown Tadley RG26 ....26 C4
Tadley RG26 ....9 C1
Newtown Cl SP10 ....105 C4
Newtown Rd
Liphook GU30 ....188 A2
Newbury RG14,RG19,RG20 ..5 C4
Sandhurst GU47 ....34 C4
Nexus Pk GU12 ....77 B4
Nicholson Pl SO24 ......179 A3
Nickel Cl SO23 ....198 A4
Nicola Ct GU12 ....77 A1
Nicotiana Ct 7 GU52 ....74 C2
Night Owls RG19 ....6 A4
Nightingale Cl
Farnborough GU14 ....55 A3
Winchester SO22 ....197 B3
Nightingale Dr GU16 ....56 C2
Nightingale Gdns
Hook RG27 ....51 A1
Sandhurst GU47 ....34 C4
Sherborne St John RG24 ...68 B4
Nightingale La RG7 ......12 A3
Nightingale Rd GU35 ...164 C1
Nightingale Rise RG25 ...88 A4
Nightingales The RG14 ...5 C4
Nightjar Cl GU10 ....98 A4
Nine Acres GU32 ....207 A1
Nine Mile Ride RG40 .....16 B3
Nine Mile Ride Ind RG40 16 A3
Nine Mile Ride Prim Sch
RG40 ....16 B3
Norden Cl RG21 ....69 A3
Norman Cl GU35 ....164 C2
Norman Court La SP11 .105 C2
Norman Ct GU9 ....99 A1
Norman Gate Sch SP10 ..83 B1
Norman Rd SO23 ....197 C3
Normandy Mews 10
GU34 ....139 C2
Normandy St GU34 .....140 A2
Normans SO23 ....197 C3
Normanton Rd RG21 ....69 A4
Normay Rise RG14 ....5 A3
Norn Hill RG21 ....69 B4
Norn Hill Cl RG21 ....69 B3
Norris Cl GU35 ....164 A1
Norris Gdns SO21 ......153 B2
Norris Hill Rd GU51 .....75 B4
Norris Ho RG25 ....88 A4
North Acre SP11 ....108 B3
North Ave GU9 ....99 A4
North Camp Sta GU12 ...77 B4
North Cl Aldershot GU12 ..77 B1
Farnborough GU14 ....55 C4
North Dr SO22 ....175 A3
North End SO20 ....170 A4
North End Farm Cotts
SO24 ....201 B4
North Farm Rd GU14 .....55 B4
North Farnborough Inf Sch
GU14 ....56 A3
North Field RG25 ....65 A1
North Foreland Lodge Sch
RG27 ....49 C3
North Fryerne GU46 .....34 A4
North Gate Rd GU14 ....56 A1
North Hampshire Hospl The
RG24 ....68 C4
North Hill Cl SO22 ......175 C1
North Hill Ct SO22 ......175 C1
North La Aldershot GU12 ..77 A1
West Tytherley SP5 .....169 A1
North Lodge Ind Pk
GU30 ....188 A1
North Mall 13 GU51 .....53 C1
North Par GU35 ....164 B3
North Rd Ash GU12 ....77 B2
Farnborough GU11 ....77 A4
Kings Worthy SO23 ......154 A1
North Row RG26 ....28 C2
North Side GU10 ....100 B4
North St
Bishop's Sutton SO24 ....180 B3
Kingsclere RG20 ....24 B1
North View SO22 ....197 C4
North View Gdns 14 RG14 .1 C2
North View Rd RG26 .....27 A4
North Walls SO23 ....198 A4
North Waltham Prim Sch
RG25 ....89 C1
North Warnborough St
RG29 ....72 A2
North Way SP10 ....83 C1
Northanger Cl GU34 ....139 C2
Northaw Sch SP5 ....168 C1
Northbrook SO21 ....132 C2
Northbrook Ave SO23 ...198 B4
Northbrook Cl SO23 ....198 B4
Northbrook Pl RG14 ......1 C2
Northbrook Rd GU11 .....99 C4
Northbrooke Ct 11
SO23 ....198 B4
Northcote Rd Ash GU12 ..77 C4
Farnborough GU14 ....55 B3
Northcroft Ct RG29 .....95 A2
Northcroft La RG14 ....1 B2
Northcroft Terr RG14 .....1 B2
Northern Ave
Andover SP10 ....83 A1
Newbury RG14 ....1 C3
Northfield Cl
Aldershot GU12 ....77 A1
Fleet GU52 ....75 B3
Northfield Rd Fleet GU52 .75 B3
Sherfield on Loddon RG27 ..29 B1
Thatcham RG18 ....2 C2
Northfields La GU34 ....161 B4
Northgate Chambers 9
SO23 ....198 A4
Northgate La RG25 ......92 A1
Northgate Way RG22 .....91 A3
Northington Cnr SO21 ..134 A2
Northington Rd SO21 ...177 C4
Northlands Dr SO23 ....176 A1
Northmead GU14 ....55 C2
Northside La SO24 .....180 C3
Northtown Trad Est
GU12 ....77 B1
Northumberland Rd 10
GU35 ....164 B1
Northway RG14 ....1 C1
Northwick GU46 ....33 B4
Northwood Dr RG14 ......2 A2
Norton Cl RG14 ....5 A3
Norton Cotts SO21 ......131 B4
Norton Rd RG7 ....14 A2
Norton Ride RG24 ....69 C4
Norwich Ave GU15 ....36 B2
Norwich Cl RG22 ....91 A4
Novello Cl RG22 ....91 B4
Nuffield Rd RG2 ....15 B4
Nuns Rd SO23 ....176 A1
Nursery Cl
Camberley GU16 ....56 B4
Chineham RG24 ....49 A2
Fleet GU51 ....75 B4
Hook RG27 ....51 A1
Nursery Field GU33 .....207 C2
Nursery Gdns SO22 .....197 B4
Nursery Rd Alton GU34 ..140 A2
New Alresford SO24 .....179 B3
Nursery Terr RG29 ....72 B2
Nutbane Cl SP10 ....105 C4
Nutbane La SP11 ....81 C4
Nutbeam La RG7 ....14 B3
Nutbourne GU9 ....99 B4
Nutchers Dro SO20 .....172 A2
Nutcombe La GU27 .....189 B4
Nutfield Ct GU15 ....36 A4
Nuthatch Cl GU10 ....98 A4
Nutley Cl Bordon GU35 ..164 B1
Yateley GU46 ....34 A3
Nutley Dr 16 GU51 ......53 B2
Nutmeg Ct GU14 ....55 A3
Nutshell La GU9 ....99 A3
Nutter's La RG2 ....14 C4

O

O'Bee Gdns RG26 ....9 B1
O'Connor Rd GU11 ......77 B4
O'Gorman Rd GU14 ......55 C1
Oak Bank SP10 ....106 A3
Oak Cl Basingstoke RG21 ..69 B3
Baughurst RG26 ....26 A4
Kingsclere RG20 ....24 C1
Middle Wallop SO20 .....126 A2
North Tidworth SP9 ......79 A4
Oakley RG23 ....67 A1
Overton RG25 ....88 A4
Oak Cotts GU27 ....189 B3
Oak Ct Farnborough GU14 .56 B1
Farnham GU9 ....98 C1
Oak Dr RG14 ....1 B1
Oak Farm Cl GU17 ....35 A3
Oak Farm Com Sch GU14 55 B3
Oak Grove Cres GU15 ....35 B3
Oak Hanger Cl RG27 .....51 A1
Oak Hill SO24 ....179 B3
Oak Ho 3 GU14 ....55 C4
Oak Lodge 2 GU35 .....164 B1
Oak Rd GU14 ....56 A2
Oak Ridge Cl RG14 ....5 B4
Oak Tree Cl
Aldershot GU12 ....100 B4
Ash GU12 ....56 B1
Chilbolton SO20 ....129 A2
Headley GU35 ....165 B2
6 Tadley RG26 ....9 C1
Oak Tree Cotts RG25 ....70 C3
Oak Tree Dr GU33 ......208 A2
Oak Tree La GU27 ....189 A3
Oak Tree View GU9 ......99 B3
Oak Tree Way RG27 ......51 A1
Oakdene GU34 ....139 C3
Oaken Copse GU52 ......75 A2
Oaken Copse Cres GU14 .55 C4
Oaken Gr RG14 ....5 A4
Oakfield Rd
Blackwater GU17 ....35 B2
Pamber Heath RG26 ......10 B1
Oakfields GU15 ....35 C3
Oakfields Cl RG20 ....23 B2
Oakgreen Par GU34 .....160 B2
Oakhanger Rd GU35 ....164 A3
Oakhill Rd GU35 ....165 C3
Oakhurst GU26 ....167 A2
Oakland Ave GU9 ....99 B4
Oakland Rd RG28 ....86 B3
Oakland Terr RG27 ....52 B3
Oaklands
Hartley Wintney RG27 .....52 B3
South Wonston SO21 ....153 B2
Yateley GU46 ....34 A3
Oaklands Cl SO22 ......197 B3
Oaklands Way RG23 .....68 B4
Oaklea GU12 ....77 C3
Oaklea Dr RG27 ....15 B1
Oaklea Gdns RG26 ....29 A1
Oaklea Ho GU26 ....167 A2
Oakley CE Jun Sch RG23 67 A1
Oakley Dr GU51 ....75 A4
Oakley Inf Sch RG23 .....67 A1
Oakley La RG23 ....67 A1
Oakley Pl 15 Fleet GU51 ...53 C1
Hartley Wintney RG27 .....52 B3
Oakley Rd Bordon GU35 .164 B3
Camberley GU15 ....35 C2
Hannington RG26 ....44 C1
Mottisfont SO51 ....192 C2
Newbury RG14 ....2 A2
Oakmead RG26 ....28 C2
Oakridge Ctr RG21 ......69 B4
Oakridge Jun & Inf Schs
RG21 ....69 A4
Oakridge Rd RG21 ....69 A4
Oakridge Twrs 1 RG21 ..69 B4
Oaks The Andover SP10 ..105 C4
Blackwater GU17 ....35 B2
Farnborough GU14 ....55 A2
Fleet GU51 ....53 B1
Tadley RG26 ....26 C4
Yateley GU46 ....34 A3
Oaktree Rd GU35 ....164 B1
Oaktrees Ash GU12 ....77 B1
Farnham GU9 ....98 C3
Oakway Aldershot GU12 .100 B4
Bentley GU10 ....120 A3
Oakway Dr GU16 ....36 B1
Oakwood Chineham RG24 .48 C2
Fleet GU52 ....75 A2
Oakwood Dr GU34 ......139 C1
Oakwood Inf Sch RG27 ...52 B3
Oast House Cres GU9 ....99 A3
Oast House La GU9 ......99 A3
Oast La GU11 ....99 C4
Oasthouse Dr GU51 ......54 B2
Oasts The RG29 ....95 B2
Oates Mus, Gilbert White's
Ho★ GU34 ....184 C4
Oban Cl RG23 ....67 A1
Obelisk Way GU15 ....36 A3
Oberursel Way GU11 .....76 B1
Ochil Cl RG22 ....68 A2
Ockham Hall GU35 .....142 A1
Octavia Hill SO22 ......197 B3
Octavian Cl RG22 ....91 A4
Oddfellows Rd RG14 ......1 B1
Odette Gdns RG26 ....10 A1
Odiham Cottage Hospl
RG29 ....72 C1
Odiham Rd Ewshot GU10 ..98 B4
Heckfield RG7 ....14 A1
Odiham RG29 ....73 A4
Officers Row RG26 ......29 A1
Oglander Rd SO23 ......176 A1
Olaf Cl SP10 ....83 A2
Old Acre Rd GU34 ......139 C1
Old Barn Cl RG25 ....89 C1
Old Barn La GU10 ......144 C1
Old Basing Inf Sch RG24 .70 A3
Old Basing Mall 14 RG21 .69 A3
Old Bath Rd RG14 ....1 B2
Old Beggarwood La
RG22 ....91 A3
Old Bisley Rd GU16 ......36 C2
Old Brick Kiln Trad Est The
RG26 ....46 C4
Old Brickfield Rd GU11 ..99 C4
Old Canal Pl RG21 ....69 B3
Old Chapel La GU12 .....77 C1
Old Church La GU9 .....122 A4
Old Common Rd RG21 ...69 B2
Old Common Way SP11 ..57 A1
Old Compton La GU9 ....99 B1
Old Cove Rd GU51 ....54 A2
Old Ct RG29 ....72 C1

Old Dairy The SO21 177 A3
Old Dean Rd GU15 36 A4
Old Down Cl RG22 68 A1
Old Down Rd SP10 82 C1
Old English Dr SP10 82 C2
Old Farm Pl GU12 77 B2
Old Farnham La
Bentley GU10 97 C1
Farnham GU9 122 A4
Old Forge End GU47 34 C4
Old Forge Gdns SO20 170 A4
Old Frensham Rd GU10 122 B2
Old Fromans Farm SO20 172 A2
Old Gdns SO22 175 C1
Old Green La GU15 36 A4
Old Guildford Rd GU16 56 C3
Old Heath Way GU9 99 A4
Old Hill The SP11 128 C4
Old Hillside Rd SO22 175 B1
Old Iron Foundry The SO20 171 C2
Old Kempshott La RG22 68 A2
Old Kennels Cl SO22 197 A2
Old Kennels La SO22 197 A2
Old Kiln GU9 98 C1
Old Kiln Cl GU10 144 B1
Old Kiln Ctyd 12 GU9 98 C1
Old Kiln La GU10 144 B1
Old La Aldershot GU11 99 C4
Ashford Hill RG19 8 B1
Frensham GU10 143 B2
Kintbury RG20 3 B4
Old Litten La GU32 206 B2
Old London Rd SO20 150 A2
Old Micheldever Rd SP11 107 A3
Old Mill Pl GU27 189 B4
Old Newtown Rd RG14 1 B1
Old Odiham Rd GU34 139 C3
Old Orchard The GU9 121 C4
Old Palace Farm SO20 172 A1
Old Park Cl GU9 98 C3
Old Park Farm GU35 142 B1
Old Park La GU9 98 C2
Old Park Rd SO24 180 C1
Old Pasture Rd GU16 36 B2
Old Pond Cl GU15 36 A1
Old Portsmouth Rd GU15 36 C3
Old Potbridge Rd RG27 52 A1
Old Pump House Cl GU51 54 A1
Old Quarry The GU27 189 B2
Old Reading Rd RG21 69 B3
Old Rectory Dr GU12 77 C1
Old Rectory Gdns
Farnborough GU14 56 A2
Kings Worthy SO21 176 B3
Old Salisbury Rd SP11 105 A2
Old School Cl Ash GU12 77 C2
Fleet GU51 54 A1
Hartley Wintney RG27 52 B3
Old School La GU46 34 A3
Old School Rd Hook RG27 71 C4
Liss GU33 207 C2
Old School Terr 12 GU51 54 A1
Old Station App SO23 198 A4
Old Station Rd SO21 177 C3
Old Station Way GU35 164 A3
Old Stockbridge Rd
Middle Wallop SO20 125 B3
Over Wallop SO20 125 B3
Old Stoke Rd
South Wonston SO21 154 A4
Wonston SO21 154 A4
Old Town Mews 19 GU9 98 C1
Old Vicarage La SO20 172 A2
Old Vyne La RG26 26 B1
Old Welmore GU46 34 B3
Old Winton Rd SP10 106 A3
Old Worting Rd RG22 68 B2
Oldberg Gdns RG22 91 C4
Oldbury Cl GU16 56 B4
Oldcorne Hollow GU46 33 C3
Olde Farm Dr GU17 34 C3
Oldenburg Cl SP10 82 C2
Oldfield View RG27 52 B3
Oldwood Chase GU14 55 A2
Oliver Rise GU34 139 C2
Oliver's Battery Cres SO22 197 A2
Oliver's Battery Gdns SO22 197 A2
Oliver's Battery Prim Sch SO22 197 B2
Oliver's Battery Rd N SO22 197 A3
Oliver's Battery Rd S SO22 197 A2
Oliver's La RG26 29 A2
Oliver's Wlk RG24 69 C4
Olivers Cl RG26 29 A1
Omega Pk GU34 140 A2
Omni Bsns Ctr GU34 140 A2
Onslow Cl RG24 48 C1
Ontario Way GU30 188 A2
Openfields GU35 165 B3
Orange Gr SP11 124 C3
Orange La SO20 125 B1
Orbit Cl RG40 16 B3
Orchard Cl Ash GU12 77 C3
Farnborough GU17 35 B1
Farnham GU9 99 C3
Linchmere GU27 189 B3
New Alresford SO24 179 B2
Orchard Cl *continued*
Newbury RG14 2 A3
South Wonston SO21 153 B2
Orchard Cotts SP11 58 A2
Orchard Ct GU10 97 B3
Orchard End GU10 121 B2
Orchard Fields GU51 53 C1
Orchard Gate GU47 34 C4
Orchard Gdns GU12 100 A4
Orchard Ho Alton GU34 140 A2
Tongham GU10 100 B4
Orchard La GU34 140 A2
Orchard Rd Andover SP10 82 C1
Basingstoke RG22 68 B2
Farnborough, Cove Green GU14 55 C2
Farnham GU9 99 C3
Mortimer RG7 11 C3
South Wonston SO21 153 B2
Orchard Terr GU34 140 A2
Orchard The
Kingsclere RG20 24 B1
Overton RG25 88 A4
Tadley RG26 27 A4
Orchard Way GU12 100 A4
Orchard Wlk SO22 175 B1
Orchardene RG14 1 C2
Orchid Ct SP10 105 B3
Ordnance Rd
Aldershot GU11 77 A2
North Tidworth SP9 78 C3
Ordnance Rdbt GU11 76 C1
Oregon Wlk RG40 16 B4
Oriel Hill GU15 36 A2
Orient Dr SO22 175 B2
Orkney Cl RG24 48 B1
Orpheus Ho 2 RG7 9 B1
Orts Rd RG14 1 C1
Orwell Cl GU14 55 B3
Osborn Rd GU9 99 A2
Osborn Way RG27 72 A4
Osborne Cl Alton GU34 139 B2
Camberley GU16 56 B4
Osborne Ct GU14 77 A4
Osborne Dr GU52 75 A4
Osborne Rd
Andover SP10 106 A4
Farnborough GU14 77 A4
Osbourne Cl RG21 69 A4
Osgood Ct GU10 100 B4
Osier Ho 9 RG26 26 C4
Osler Cl RG26 28 C2
Osnaburgh Hill GU15 35 C3
Osprey Gdns GU11 99 C4
Osprey Rd RG22 67 C1
Otterbourne Cres RG26 26 C3
Ottrebourne Rd SO21 197 C1
Ouse Ct 49 SP10 83 B1
Oval Rd SO51 192 A1
Oval The Andover SP10 83 B2
Liss GU33 207 C2
Overbridge Sq RG14 2 B2
Overdale Pl 11 GU35 164 B1
Overdale Rise GU15 36 B2
Overdale Wlk GU35 164 B1
Overlord Cl GU15 36 A4
Overton CE Prim Sch RG25 65 A1
Overton Cl GU11 100 A3
Overton Ho RG25 88 A4
Overton Mews RG25 88 A4
Overton Rd SO21 111 B2
Overton Sta RG25 65 A1
Ovington Dr 15 GU51 53 B2
Owen Rd RG14 1 C3
Owen's Rd SO22 175 C1
Owlsmoor Rd GU47 35 A4
Ox Dro
Picket Piece SP10,SP11 84 A1
South Wonston SO21 153 C2
Ox Drove Rise SP11 84 A2
Oxenden Ct GU10 100 B4
Oxenden Rd GU10 100 B4
Oxford Rd
Farnborough GU14 56 A1
Newbury RG14 1 B3
Sutton Scotney SO21 131 B2
Oxford St RG14 1 B2
Oyster Cl RG22 91 A4

P

Pack La Basingstoke RG23 67 B1
Oakley RG23 67 B1
Pack Way GU9,GU10 122 B4
Packenham Rd RG21 68 C2
Paddington Ho 7 RG21 69 A3
Paddock Cl
Camberley GU15 36 C3
South Wonston SO21 153 C2
Paddock Ct RG27 52 B3
Paddock Field SO20 129 A3
Paddock Rd
Basingstoke RG22 68 B2
Newbury RG14 5 B4
Paddock The
Farnham GU10 121 B2
Grayshott GU26 166 C2
Hartley Wintney RG27 52 B4
Haslemere GU27 189 C4
Headley GU35 165 B3
Kings Worthy SO23 176 B3
Kingsclere RG20 24 B1
Newbury RG14 2 A1
Paddock Way
Liphook GU30 188 A3
New Alresford SO24 179 B2
Paddockfields RG24 70 A4
Padwick Cl RG21 69 A2
Padworth Rd RG7 11 A4
Pages Yd RG28 86 B2
Paget Cl Camberley GU15 36 C4
North Tidworth SP9 78 B4
Paice La GU34 159 C2
Paices Hill RG7 9 C2
Painters Field SO23 197 C2
Painters Pightle RG27 50 C1
Pakenham Dr GU11 76 B2
Palace Cl SO20 171 C1
Palace Gate RG29 72 B2
Palace Gate Farm RG29 72 B2
Pale La Fleet RG27 53 A1
Hartley Wintney RG27 53 B2
Palestine Rd SP11 124 B3
Palliser Ct
Beacon Hill GU26 167 A3
Grayshott GU26 167 A2
Palm Hall Cl SO23 198 B4
Palmer Cl RG21 69 B4
Palmer Dr SP10 106 B4
Palmerston Cl GU14 55 A2
Palmerston Ct 2 SO22, SO23 197 C3
Palmerston Pl SP10 106 C4
Pamber Dr 17 GU51 53 B2
Pamber Heath Rd RG26 10 B1
Pamber Rd
Charter Alley RG26 46 C4
Silchester RG7 10 C1
Pammers Mead GU52 74 C2
Pan's Gdns GU15 36 B2
Pankridge St GU10 97 B4
Pannells GU10 122 A3
Pantile Dr RG27 51 B1
Pantings La RG20 21 B4
Paper Mill La GU34 140 A2
Papermakers RG25 88 A4
Parade The Ash GU12 77 C2
Basingstoke RG21 69 B3
8 Tadley RG26 9 C1
Parchment St SO23 198 A4
Pardown RG23 90 A4
Parfitts Cl GU9 98 C1
Parish Cl Ash GU12 77 C1
Farnham GU9 98 C3
Parish Rd GU14 77 A4
Park Ave Camberley GU15 36 A2
Old Basing RG24 70 A3
Winchester SO23 198 A4
Park Cl Binsted GU10 120 C1
Kingsley GU35 142 B1
Oakley RG23 67 A1
Winchester SO23 176 A1
Park Close Rd GU34 140 A3
Park Corner Rd RG27 52 B4
Park Ct Farnham GU9 99 A2
1 Winchester SO23 176 A1
Park Dro SO20 125 C2
Park End RG14 1 C2
Park Farm GU9 99 C3
Park Farm Ind Est GU16 36 A1
Park Gdns RG21 69 B2
Park Hill GU52 74 C3
Park Ho SO23 198 A4
Park House Mews SP4 101 C2
Park House Sch RG14 5 B3
Park La Arborfield RG40 15 C3
Camberley GU15 36 A3
Hamstead Marshall RG20 3 C4
Kings Worthy SO21 176 B3
Lower Froyle GU34 119 B3
Newbury RG14 1 C2
Old Basing RG24 70 A3
Quarley SP11 103 A2
Ropley SO24 181 A2
Silchester RG7 12 A1
Park Mount SO24 179 B3
Park Pl GU52 74 C3
Park Prim Sch GU11 100 A4
Park Rd Aldershot GU11 100 A4
Camberley GU15 36 A2
Farnborough GU14 77 B4
Farnham GU9 99 A2
Sandhurst GU47 35 A4
South Tidworth SP9 78 C3
Winchester SO22,SO23 175 C1
Park Row GU9 98 C2
Park St Bordon GU35 164 B2
Camberley GU15 36 A3
Newbury RG14 1 C2
Park Terr RG14 1 C2
Park View Beech Hill RG7 13 A3
Lockerley SO21 191 C2
Park View Inf & Jun Sch RG22 68 B1
Park Way RG14 1 C2
Parkfields GU46 34 A3
Parkhill Cl GU17 35 A2
Parkhill Rd GU17 35 A2
Parkhouse Cnr SP4 101 C2
Parkhouse Cross SP4 101 B2
Parkhouse Rd SP9 101 B4
Parkhurst Cotts GU10 166 B4
Parkhurst Fields GU10 144 B1
Parkland Gr GU9 99 B4
Parkside GU9 99 A3
Parkside Gdns SO22 175 B1
Parkside La SO24 181 A1
Parkside Rd RG21 69 B2
Parkstone Dr GU15 36 A2
Parkstone Rd SO24 181 B1
Parkview Cl SP10 82 C1
Parkway GU15 36 A2
Parkwood Cl RG24 48 C2
Parliament Pl SO22 197 B2
Parmiter Ho 42 SO23 198 A4
Parnell Ct SP10 82 B1
Parnholt Rd SO51 194 C2
Parsonage Cl GU34 161 C2
Parsonage Farm Inf Sch GU14 55 A3
Parsonage Way GU16 36 B1
Parsons Cl Arborfield RG2 15 C4
Fleet GU52 74 C3
Newbury RG14 1 B1
Parsons Down Inf & Jun Schs RG19 2 C2
Parsons Field GU47 34 C4
Parsons La GU26 167 A3
Part La RG7 14 B2
Partridge Ave GU46 33 C3
Partridge Cl
Barton Stacey SO21 130 B4
Basingstoke RG22 90 C4
Camberley GU16 36 B1
Ewshot GU10 98 A4
Partridge Down SO22 197 A2
Partridge Gn GU34 139 C3
Paschal Rd GU15 36 B4
Passet Mead GU52 74 C2
Passfield Ent Ctr GU30 187 A4
Passfield Mill Bsns Pk GU30 165 A1
Passfield Rd GU30 165 B1
Pastures The
Cheriton SO24 201 B3
Kings Worthy SO23 154 A1
Paternoster Ho 37 SO23 198 A4
Paternoster Row 36 SO23 198 A4
Paterson Cl RG22 91 B4
Paterson Rd GU33 186 B1
Pathfinders The GU14 55 A2
Patrick's Cl GU33 208 A2
Patrick's Copse Rd GU33 208 A2
Patten Ave GU46 34 A3
Pattinson Cres SP11 105 A4
Paul Cl GU11 99 B4
Paul's Field GU46 33 A4
Paulet Pl Old Basing RG24 70 A3
Winchester SO22 197 C3
Pavilion Rd GU11 76 B1
Pavilions End The GU15 36 A2
Paviors GU9 99 A2
Pawley Cl GU10 100 B4
Pax Hill GU34 119 C2
Paxton Cl RG22 91 A4
Payne's Mdw RG24 70 A4
Paynes Cl
Broughton SO20 170 A4
Headley, Nr Greenham RG19 24 B4
Paynes Hay Rd SO51 194 B1
Paynes La SO20 170 A4
Paynesdown Rd RG19 2 C2
Peabody Rd GU14 77 A4
Peach Gr SP11 124 C3
Peach Tree Cl GU14 55 C4
Peacock Pl 5 SO23 198 B4
Peake Cl RG24 69 C4
Peakfield GU10 144 A4
Pear Tree Ave 4 GU51 53 C1
Pear Tree Cl GU35 164 C2
Pear Tree Ct GU15 36 C4
Pear Tree La
Farnham GU10 121 B2
Newbury RG14 2 A3
Pear Tree Rd GU35 164 C2
Pearces Pl RG20 24 B1
Pearl Ho SP11 57 A1
Pearman Dr SP10 106 B4
Peatmoor Cl GU51 53 C1
Peckmoor Dr RG19 6 A4
Peddlars Gr GU46 34 B3
Peel Ave GU16 56 C4
Peel Ct Farnborough GU14 77 A4
Hartley Wintney RG27 52 B3
Peel Gdns RG20 24 B2
Pegasus Ave GU12 77 B1
Pegasus Cl
Linchmere GU27 189 A3
Thatcham RG19 2 C2
Pegasus Ct
Farnborough GU14 56 B1
Fleet GU51 53 C1
Whitchurch RG28 86 B3
Pegasus Rd GU14 55 B4
Pelham Cl
14 Bordon GU35 164 B1
Old Basing RG24 70 A3
Pelham Pl GU10 121 C2
Pelican La RG14 1 C2
Pelican Rd RG26 10 B1
Pelton Rd RG22 68 C3
Pembroke Bwy GU15 36 A3
Pembroke Ct SP10 106 A4
Pembroke Rd
Basingstoke RG23 68 A3
Newbury RG14 1 B2
Pembury Pl GU12 77 A1
Pemerton Rd
Basingstoke RG21 69 B4
Winchester SO22 175 B2
Pen Cl SP10 106 B4
Pendennis Cl RG23 68 A3
Pendle Gn SO51 191 C1
Penfold Croft GU9 99 B2
Pengilly Rd GU9 98 C1
Peninsula Rd SO22 197 C4
Peninsula Sq SO23 197 C4
Peninsular Cl GU15 36 C4
Penn Rd RG14 1 A3
Pennefather's Rd GU11 76 B2
Pennine Cl RG22 68 A2
Pennine Way
Basingstoke RG22 68 A2
Farnborough GU14 55 B4
Pennings Rd SP9 78 C4
Penns Wood GU14 56 A1
Penny La SO20 150 A1
Penny's Hatch RG20 24 C1
Penrhyn Cl GU12 76 C1
Penrith Rd RG21 69 A2
Penrose Cl RG14 1 B3
Penrose Way GU34 160 A1
Penryn Dr GU35 166 A3
Penshurst Rise GU16 56 B4
Pentangle The RG14 1 C2
Pentland Cl RG22 68 A2
Pentland Pl GU14 55 B4
Penton La SP11 81 C3
Penton Pl 8 SO23 198 A3
Penwith Dr GU27 189 B3
Penwood Hts RG20 21 C4
Penwood Rd RG20 5 A2
Perham Cres SP11 57 A1
Perins Cl SO24 179 A2
Perins Com Sch SO24 179 B3
Periwinkle Cl GU35 165 A3
Perowne St GU11 76 B1
Perring Ave GU14 55 B4
Perry Dr GU51 53 B1
Perry Way Farnham GU9 98 C4
Headley GU35 165 B2
Pershore Rd RG24 48 A1
Perth Cl SP11 79 B4
Peshawar Cl SP9 78 B4
Peter Symonds' Coll SO22 175 C1
Petersfield RG23 90 A4
Petersfield Cl RG24 49 A2
Petersfield Gn SP9 78 C3
Petersfield Rd
Cheriton SO24 201 B2
East Tisted GU34,SO24 182 B1
Greatham GU33 186 A3
Greatham GU33 185 C1
Ropley SO24 181 B2
Winchester SO21, SO23 198 B4
Petrel Croft RG22 90 C4
Petty's Brook Rd RG24 49 A2
Petunia Cl RG22 91 A4
Petworth Cl
Basingstoke RG22 91 A3
Camberley GU16 56 B4
Petworth Ct GU15 36 B2
Pevensey Way GU16 56 C4
Peveral Way RG22 68 B2
Peveral Wlk RG22 68 B2
Pewsey Ho 4 SP9 78 C3
Pheaben's Field RG26 28 C2
Pheasant Cl
Barton Stacey SO21 130 C4
Basingstoke RG22 90 C4
North Tidworth SP9 79 A3
Pheasant Copse GU51 53 C1
Pheasant La RG20 6 B2
Pheasantry Dr RG27 32 A2
Pheby Rd RG22 68 B1
Pheonix Ct RG27 52 A2
Pheonix Terr RG27 52 A2
Philips Ho GU26 166 C2
Phillips Cl Headley GU35 165 B3
Tongham GU10 100 B4
Phillips Cres GU35 165 B3
Phoenix Ct
15 Aldershot GU11 76 C1
Kingsclere RG20 24 B1
Phoenix Park Terr RG21 69 A3
Phoenix Wlk RG14 5 A3
Pickaxe La RG29 118 A3
Picket Twenty SP11 106 C4
Picketts Hill GU35 143 A1
Pickford St GU11 76 C1
Pickwick Gdns GU15 36 C2
Picton Rd SP10 106 A3
Pierrefondes Ave GU14 55 C3
Pigeon Cl RG26 29 A1
Pigeonhouse Cotts SO21 131 B2
Pigeonhouse Field SO21 131 B2
Pigeons Farm Rd RG19 6 A4
Pike St RG14 1 C2
Pilcot Rd GU51,RG27 74 B3
Piley Rd SO21 153 C2
Pilgrims Cl GU9 121 C4
Pilgrims Gate SO22 175 C1
Pilgrims Sch The SO23 198 A4
Pilgrims Way
Andover SP10 83 B1
Headley GU35 165 B3
Pilgrims' Way Sch The GU9 121 C4
Pimpernel Way RG24 69 C4
Pinchington La RG14,RG19 5 C4
Pindar Pl RG14 2 B3
Pine Ave GU15 36 A2
Pine Bank GU26 167 B2
Pine Cl Ash GU12 77 C3
Middle Wallop SO20 126 A2
Sandhurst GU15 35 B4
South Wonston SO21 153 C2
Winchester SO22 197 A2
Pine Cotts GU33 208 A4
Pine Dr Blackwater GU17 35 B2
Finchampstead RG40 16 C4
Mortimer RG7 11 B3
Pine Gr Farnham GU10 122 B3
Fleet GU52 75 A3

Reynards Cl RG26 ... 26 C4
Reynolds Cl RG21 ... 69 C2
Reynolds Ct SP10 ... 82 C1
Reynolds Gn GU47 ... 35 A3
Reynolds Ho RG22 ... 68 B1
Reyntiens View RG29 ... 72 C1
Rhine Banks GU14 ... 55 A3
Rhodes Sq SP10 ... 83 B2
Rhododendron Cnr RG40 16 C2
Rhododendron Rd GU16 . 56 C4
Ribble Ct 51 SP10 ... 83 B1
Ribble Pl GU14 ... 55 B4
Ribble Way 17 RG21 ... 69 B3
Richard Aldworth Com Sch The RG22 ... 68 B1
Richard Cl GU51 ... 74 C4
Richard Moss Ho 8 SO23 ... 198 A4
Richards Cl GU12 ... 77 C3
Richborough Dr SP10 ... 82 B2
Richmond Ave RG19 ... 2 C2
Richmond Cl
Bordon GU35 ... 164 B1
Camberley GU16 ... 36 B1
Farnborough GU14 ... 55 A2
Fleet GU52 ... 74 C3
Richmond Ho
Sandhurst GU47 ... 35 B4
9 Winchester SO22 ... 197 C4
Richmond Rd
Basingstoke RG21 ... 69 A3
Sandhurst GU47 ... 35 B4
Riddings La RG19 ... 8 A1
Rideway Cl GU15 ... 35 C2
Ridge Cl RG22 ... 91 B3
Ridge La Hook RG27 ... 50 C1
Newnham RG27 ... 50 C1
Ridgemoor Cl GU26 ... 167 B3
Ridges Cl SP11 ... 83 B4
Ridges View SP11 ... 83 B4
Ridgeway SO22 ... 197 B3
Ridgeway Com Sch The GU9 ... 122 A4
Ridgeway Par GU52 ... 75 A3
Ridgeway The GU34 ... 139 C1
Ridgway Hill Rd GU9 ... 122 A4
Ridgway Rd GU9 ... 122 A4
Ridings The
Camberley GU16 ... 36 C2
Liss GU33 ... 208 A2
Ridley Cl GU52 ... 74 C4
Ridleys Piece RG29 ... 95 A2
Rifle Way GU14 ... 55 A2
Riley La RG24 ... 70 A4
Rimbault Cl GU11 ... 77 A4
Rimes's La RG26 ... 26 B3
Ringlet Way 6 SO23 ... 198 B4
Ringshall Gdns RG26 ... 28 C2
Ringway Ctr The RG21 ... 68 C4
Ringway E RG21 ... 69 C3
Ringway N RG21 ... 69 A4
Ringway S RG21 ... 69 B2
Ringway W RG22 ... 68 C3
Ringwood Rd
Blackwater GU17 ... 35 A3
Farnborough GU14 ... 56 A4
Ripon Rd GU46 ... 34 B1
Ripplesmore Cl GU47 ... 34 C4
Rise The RG40 ... 15 C1
River Cl GU34 ... 160 A1
River Ho 59 SP10 ... 83 B1
River La GU9,GU10 ... 121 B4
River Park L Ctr SO23 ... 176 A1
River Pk RG14 ... 1 C2
River Rd GU46 ... 33 C4
River Row Cotts GU9 ... 121 B4
River View Cl SP11 ... 128 C2
River View Cotts GU34 ... 140 A2
River Way SP10 ... 83 B1
River Wlk RG14 ... 2 A2
Riverdale GU10 ... 121 B4
Riverhead SO24 ... 180 B2
Rivermead Ho GU47 ... 34 B4
Rivermead Rd GU15 ... 35 C1
Rivermede GU35 ... 164 C2
Rivers Cl GU14 ... 56 B1
Riverside Bsns Pk GU9 ... 99 A2
Riverside Cl
Farnborough GU14 ... 55 B3
Liss GU33 ... 207 C2
Old Basing RG24 ... 70 A4
Overton RG25 ... 88 A4
Riverside Cotts RG28 ... 86 A1
Riverside Ct GU9 ... 99 A2
Riverside Gn SO20 ... 172 A2
Riverside Ho 44 SO23 ... 198 A4
Riverside Ind Pk GU9 ... 99 A2
Riverside Rd GU30 ... 165 B1
Riverside Way GU15 ... 35 C2
Riverwey Ind Est GU34 ... 140 A2
Robert May's Sch RG29 ... 72 B2
Robert Mays Rd RG29 ... 72 B1
Robert Sandilands Prim Sch RG14 ... 1 B2
Robert Way GU16 ... 56 B2
Roberts Cl SO23 ... 154 A1
Roberts Rd
Aldershot GU12 ... 77 A1
Barton Stacey SO21 ... 130 C4
Bordon GU33 ... 186 B1
Camberley GU15 ... 35 C3
Sandhurst GU15 ... 35 C3
Robertsfield RG19 ... 2 B2
Robertson Cl RG14 ... 5 C4
Robertson Rd SO24 ... 179 B2
Robertson Way GU12 ... 77 B1
Robin Cl Alton GU34 ... 140 A3
Ash GU12 ... 77 C3
Basingstoke RG22 ... 91 A4
Robin Hill Dr GU15 ... 36 C2
Robin Hood Cl GU14 ... 55 C4
Robin La
Bishop's Green RG20 ... 6 B2
Sandhurst GU47 ... 34 C4
Robin Way SP10 ... 83 A1
Robin's Bow GU15 ... 35 C2
Robins Cl RG14 ... 5 B4
Robins Grove Cres GU46 . 33 C3
Robinson Way GU35 ... 164 C1
Rochester Cl RG22 ... 91 A4
Rochester Gr GU51 ... 75 A4
Rochford Rd RG21 ... 69 A3
Rock Gdns GU11 ... 76 B1
Rock La GU10 ... 121 C3
Rockbourne Rd SO22 ... 175 B2
Rockdale Dr GU26 ... 167 A2
Rockdale Ho GU26 ... 167 A2
Rockery The GU14 ... 55 B2
Rockfield Way GU47 ... 35 A4
Rockingham Rd RG14 ... 1 B1
Rockmoor La SP11 ... 18 B1
Rockpit Cotts GU33 ... 208 A2
Rodfield La SO24 ... 200 B3
Roding Cl RG21 ... 69 B3
Rodmel Ct GU14 ... 56 B1
Rodney Ct SP10 ... 83 B1
Roe Downs Rd GU34 ... 160 A3
Roebuts Cl RG14 ... 5 B4
Roedeer Copse GU27 ... 189 B3
Roentgen Rd RG24 ... 69 C4
Rogers Ct 16 GU34 ... 139 C2
Roke La RG29 ... 96 A4
Rokeby Cl RG14 ... 5 C4
Rokes Pl GU46 ... 33 C3
Roman Rd
Basingstoke RG23 ... 68 A3
Stockbridge SO20 ... 149 B2
Roman Way Andover SP10 83 A2
Barton Stacey SO21 ... 130 C4
Basingstoke RG23 ... 68 A3
Farnham GU9 ... 99 B2
Thatcham RG18 ... 2 C2
Roman Way Prim Sch SP10 ... 83 A2
Romano Ct RG14 ... 1 C1
Romans Bsns Pk GU9 ... 99 A2
Romans Field RG7 ... 10 C1
Romans Gate RG26 ... 10 B1
Romans Ind Pk GU9 ... 99 A2
Romans' Rd 1 SO23 ... 198 A3
Romayne Cl GU14 ... 55 C3
Romley Ct GU9 ... 99 A1
Romsey Cl
Aldershot GU11 ... 100 A3
Basingstoke RG24 ... 48 A1
Blackwater GU17 ... 35 A3
Romsey Rd
Broughton SO20 ... 170 A3
King's Somborne SO20 ... 171 C1
Nether Wallop SO20 ... 147 C3
Wherwell SP11 ... 128 B3
Winchester SO22, SO23 ... 197 B3
Ronald Bowker Ct 1 SO22 ... 197 C4
Rook La SO21 ... 133 A2
Rookery Cotts SP5 ... 190 B2
Rookery Ct RG40 ... 15 C3
Rookery La SO20 ... 170 B3
Rookery The RG28 ... 86 B3
Rooks Down Rd SO22 ... 197 B3
Rooksbury Rd SP10 ... 105 C3
Rooksdown Ave RG24 ... 68 B4
Rooksdown La RG24 ... 47 B1
Rooksfield RG20 ... 6 C1
Rookswood GU34 ... 139 C3
Rookswood Cl RG27 ... 51 A1
Rookwood La GU34 ... 159 B1
Rookwood Sch SP10 ... 105 C4
Room Cotts SO20 ... 129 A3
Ropewalk Ho 6 SO23 ... 198 A4
Ropley CE Prim Sch SO24 ... 181 B2
Ropley Cl RG26 ... 26 C4
Ropley Rd SO24 ... 183 A2
Ropley Sta* SO24 ... 180 C3
Rorkes Drift GU16 ... 56 C2
Rosary Gdns GU46 ... 34 A3
Rose Cl RG22 ... 91 A4
Rose Cotts GU12 ... 77 C1
Rose Est The RG27 ... 72 A4
Rose Gdns GU14 ... 55 B2
Rose Hodson Pl RG23 ... 68 B4
Rose Wlk GU51 ... 53 C1
Rosebank Cl 5 RG26 ... 26 C4
Rosebay Gdns RG27 ... 51 B1
Roseberry Cl RG22 ... 91 A3
Rosebery Rd SO24 ... 179 B3
Rosedale GU12 ... 77 A1
Rosedene Gdns GU51 ... 53 C1
Rosedene La GU47 ... 35 A4
Rosehip Way RG24 ... 69 C4
Rosemary Ave GU12 ... 77 C4
Rosemary Cl GU14 ... 55 A2
Rosemary Dr RG26 ... 26 C3
Rosemary Gdns GU17 ... 35 A3
Rosemary La
Blackwater GU17 ... 35 A3
Farnham GU10 ... 121 B2
Rosemary Terr RG14 ... 1 B1
Rosetree Cotts GU34 ... 140 A2
Rosewarne Ct 23 SO23 ... 176 A1
Rosewood Chineham RG24 48 C2
Mytchett GU16 ... 56 C2
Rosewood Ct 4 SP9 ... 79 A4
Rosewood Rd GU35 ... 165 A3
Ross Cl RG21 ... 69 A1
Ross Terr 16 RG14 ... 1 B1
Rossini Cl RG22 ... 91 C4
Rossmore Gdns GU11 ... 76 B1
Rothay Ct 18 RG21 ... 69 B3
Rother Cl GU47 ... 35 A4
Rother Ho GU33 ... 207 C2
Rother Rd GU14 ... 55 B4
Rotherbank Farm La GU33 ... 208 A3
Rotherwick Ct GU14 ... 77 A4
Rotherwick Ho GU51 ... 53 B2
Rotherwick La RG27 ... 50 B4
Rotherwick Rd RG26 ... 27 A4
Rotten Green Rd RG27 ... 53 C3
Rotten Hill RG25,RG28 ... 87 C3
Rotunda Est The 19 GU11 ... 76 C1
Round End RG14 ... 5 A3
Roundabouts The GU33 . 208 A3
Roundaway La SP11 ... 58 C2
Roundhuts Rise 4 SO23 ... 198 B4
Roundmead Rd RG21 ... 69 A2
Roundway Ct SP10 ... 105 C4
Rounton Rd GU52 ... 75 A3
Row The SO21 ... 177 C3
Rowan Chase GU10 ... 121 C3
Rowan Cl Camberley GU15 36 B4
Fleet GU51 ... 54 B1
South Wonston SO21 ... 153 C2
Tadley RG26 ... 27 A4
Rowan Ct 8 SP9 ... 78 C4
Rowan Dale GU52 ... 74 C3
Rowan Dr RG14 ... 1 C3
Rowan Rd RG26 ... 27 A4
Rowan Tree Cl GU33 ... 208 A2
Rowans The Andover SP10 82 C1
Grayshott GU26 ... 167 A1
Rowanside Cl GU35 ... 166 A2
Rowanwood RG40 ... 15 C3
Rowcroft Cl GU12 ... 77 C3
Rowcroft Rd RG2 ... 15 B4
Rowdell Cotts SO24 ... 181 B3
Rowhill Ave GU11 ... 99 B4
Rowhill Cres GU11 ... 99 B4
Rowhill Nature Trail* GU11 ... 99 A4
Rowhills GU9 ... 99 A4
Rowhills Cl GU9 ... 99 B4
Rowland's Cl RG7 ... 11 A3
Rowledge CE Prim Sch GU10 ... 121 B2
Rowlings Rd SO22 ... 175 B2
Roxburghe Cl GU35 ... 164 B1
Royal Cl RG22 ... 91 A3
Royal Greenjackets Mus* SO23 ... 197 C4
Royal Hampshire Cty Hospl SO22 ... 197 C4
Royal Hampshire Regiment Mus* SO23 ... 197 C4
Royal Jun Sch The GU26 ... 167 B1
Royal Military Academy Hospl GU15 ... 35 C4
Royal Oak Cl GU46 ... 34 B3
Royal Par GU26 ... 167 B2
Royal Sch GU27 ... 167 C1
Royale Cl GU11 ... 100 A4
Royce Cl SP10 ... 82 A1
Roycroft La RG40 ... 16 B4
Roydon Cl SO22 ... 197 C3
Royston Ctr GU12 ... 77 B4
Rozeldene GU26 ... 167 B2
Rozelle Cl SO22 ... 175 A3
Rubens Cl RG21 ... 69 B1
Rucstall Prim Sch RG21 . 69 B2
Rudd Hall Rise GU15 ... 36 A2
Ruffield Cl SO22 ... 175 B1
Rufford Cl GU52 ... 75 A3
Rune Dr SP10 ... 82 C2
Runfold-St George GU10 99 C3
Runnymede Ct 1 GU14 ... 55 C4
Runwick La GU10 ... 98 A1
Rupert Rd RG14 ... 5 B4
Rural Life Ctr Mus* GU10 ... 122 B2
Rushden Way GU9 ... 99 A4
Rushes The 12 RG21 ... 69 B3
Rushmoor Cl GU52 ... 75 A4
Rushmoor Ct GU14 ... 77 A4
Rushmoor Ind Sch GU14 . 56 A1
Rushmoor Rd GU11 ... 76 A2
Ruskin Cl RG21 ... 69 C2
Russel Rd RG21 ... 69 A2
Russell Ct
Blackwater GU17 ... 35 A3
Hindhead GU26 ... 167 B2
Russell Dr SO51 ... 192 B1
Russell Rd Newbury RG14 ... 1 B1
Winchester SO23 ... 176 A1
Russet Cl
New Alresford SO24 ... 179 B2
Tongham GU10 ... 100 B4
Russet Gdns GU15 ... 36 A2
Russet Glade GU11 ... 99 B4
Russett Rd GU34 ... 140 A2
Russetts Dr GU51 ... 75 A4
Rustic Glen GU52 ... 74 C3
Ruth Cl GU14 ... 55 A3
Rutherford Rd RG24 ... 69 B4
Rutland Cl GU11 ... 76 C2
Ryan Mount GU47 ... 34 C4
Rydal Cl Basingstoke RG22 68 A1
Bordon GU35 ... 164 B3
Rydal Cl *continued*
Farnborough GU14 ... 55 A2
Rydal Dr Fleet GU52 ... 74 C3
Thatcham RG19 ... 2 C2
Ryde Ct 7 GU11 ... 77 A1
Ryde Gdns GU46 ... 33 C3
Rye Cl Farnborough GU14 ... 55 B4
Fleet GU51 ... 54 B3
Rye Croft 8 GU52 ... 74 C2
Ryebeck Rd GU52 ... 75 A3
Ryecroft Gdns GU17 ... 35 B2
Ryeland Cl GU51 ... 54 B3
Ryelaw Rd GU52 ... 75 A3
Ryle Rd GU9 ... 121 C4
Ryon Cl SP10 ... 83 A2
Ryves Ave GU46 ... 33 C3

S

Sabre Ct 3 GU11 ... 76 B1
Saddleback Rd GU15 ... 36 B4
Saddleback Way GU51 ... 54 A2
Saddler Cnr GU47 ... 34 C4
Saddlers Cl SO21 ... 131 B2
Saddlers Ct RG14 ... 1 B2
Saddlers Scarp GU26 ... 166 C2
Saddlewood GU15 ... 36 A2
Saffron Cl Chineham RG24 49 A2
Newbury RG14 ... 1 B2
Saffron Ct GU14 ... 55 A2
Sages La GU34 ... 204 B3
Sainfoin La RG23 ... 90 A4
Sainsbury Cl SP10 ... 105 C3
St Albans Rdbt GU14 ... 77 A4
St Andrew's Ct 5 GU9 ... 99 A1
St Andrew's Inf Sch GU9 98 C1
St Andrew's Rd RG22 ... 68 B2
St Andrew's Way GU16 ... 56 B4
St Andrews Rd
Bordon GU35 ... 164 A1
North Tidworth SP9 ... 78 C3
St Ann's Cl SP10 ... 105 C4
St Anne's RC Prim Sch RG22 ... 68 B2
St Annes Cl SO22 ... 197 B2
St Aubins Cl GU34 ... 160 A1
St Augustine's Cl GU12 ... 77 A1
St Augustine's RC Prim Sch GU16 ... 36 B1
St Austins GU26 ... 167 A2
St Barbara's Cl RG26 ... 29 A1
St Bartholomew Sch RG14 1 B1
St Bede CE Prim Sch SO23 ... 198 A4
St Bede's Ct 26 SO23 ... 176 A1
St Bede's RC Prim Sch RG24 ... 48 A1
St Benedict's Convent Sch SP11 ... 82 A2
St Benedicts Cl GU11 ... 76 C1
St Bernadette RC Prim Sch GU14 ... 55 C3
St Catherine's Hill RG7 ... 11 B3
St Catherine's Rd SO23 198 A3
St Catherine's Sch GU15 . 36 A2
St Catherines Rd GU16 ... 56 C4
St Catherines Way SO23,SO21 ... 198 B3
St Christopher's Gn GU27 ... 189 C3
St Christopher's Rd GU27 ... 189 C3
St Christophers Cl
Aldershot GU12 ... 77 A1
Basingstoke RG22 ... 68 B2
Haslemere GU27 ... 189 C3
St Christophers Pl GU14 . 55 B2
St Christophers Rd GU14 55 C2
St Clement St
21 Winchester SO22 ... 197 C4
31 Winchester SO23 ... 198 A4
St Clements Ct GU14 ... 55 C4
St Cross Ct 4 SO23 ... 197 C3
St Cross Hospl* SO23 ... 197 C2
St Cross Mede SO23 ... 197 C2
St Cross Rd
Camberley GU16 ... 56 C4
Crondall GU10 ... 97 B3
Farnham GU9 ... 99 A2
Winchester SO22 ... 197 C3
St David's Cl
Farnborough GU14 ... 55 B4
Farnham GU9 ... 99 B4
St David's Ct GU11 ... 76 C1
St David's Rd
Basingstoke RG22 ... 68 C2
Newbury RG14 ... 1 B1
St Davids Cl RG29 ... 72 B1
St Donats Pl RG14 ... 1 C1
St Edmunds Sch GU26 ... 167 A2
St Faith Cl GU34 ... 160 A1
St Faith's CE Prim Sch SO22 ... 197 C3
St Faith's Rd SO22 ... 197 C3
St Gabriel's Sch RG20 ... 5 C3
St George's Cl GU9 ... 99 C3
St George's Cl SP9 ... 78 C3
St George's Ho 14 SO23 198 A4
St George's Rd
Aldershot GU12 ... 76 C1
Farnham GU9 ... 99 A1
St George's Rd E GU12 ... 76 C1
St George's St SO23 ... 198 A4
St Georges Ave RG14 ... 1 B1
St Georges Ind Est GU15 35 C2
St Georges Mews GU9 ... 99 A2
St Georges Rd
Farnham GU9,GU10 ... 99 C3
North Tidworth SP9 ... 78 C3
St Georges Yd GU9 ... 99 A1
St Giles Cl SO23 ... 198 A4
St Giles Hill SO23 ... 198 A4
St Helens Cres GU47 ... 34 C4
St Hubert Rd SP10 ... 105 C4
St James Cl RG26 ... 29 A1
St James Ct Farnham GU9 99 A2
Fleet GU51 ... 74 C4
St James Rd
Finchampstead RG40 ... 16 B4
Fleet GU51 ... 74 C4
St James' Ave GU9 ... 99 A2
St James' La SO22,SO23 197 C4
St James' Terr
Farnham GU9 ... 99 A2
Winchester SO23 ... 197 C4
St James' Villas SO23 ... 197 C4
St John Cl RG26 ... 29 A1
St John the Baptist RC Prim Sch SP10 ... 105 B4
St John the Evangelist Inf Sch RG14 ... 1 B1
St John's CE Prim Sch RG21 ... 69 A2
St John's Cotts RG27 ... 71 C4
St John's Cross SP11 ... 105 A1
St John's Ct
Farnborough GU14 ... 55 A3
14 Fleet GU51 ... 54 A1
St John's Gdns 15 RG14 ... 1 B1
St John's Hospital (Almshouses)(N) 27 SO23 ... 198 A4
St John's Hospital (Almshouses)(S) 38 SO23 ... 198 A4
St John's Piece RG23 ... 90 A4
St John's Rd
Andover SP10 ... 106 A4
Farnborough GU14 ... 55 B3
Farnham GU9 ... 121 C4
Mortimer RG7 ... 11 C3
Newbury RG14 ... 1 C1
Oakley RG23 ... 67 B1
Sandhurst GU47 ... 34 C4
Winchester SO23 ... 198 A4
St John's St SO23 ... 198 A4
St John's Wlk 13 RG21 ... 69 A3
St Johns CE Inf Sch GU10 ... 144 B1
St Johns Cl RG27 ... 51 A1
St Johns Gr GU9 ... 121 C4
St Johns Rd RG27 ... 52 B3
St Joseph's Cres RG24 ... 48 C1
St Joseph's RC Prim Sch RG14 ... 1 C2
St Joseph's Rd GU12 ... 76 C1
St Josephs Ct RG14 ... 1 C2
St Josephs RC Prim Sch GU11 ... 99 C4
St Just Cl SP4 ... 123 A3
St Lawrence CE Prim Sch GU34 ... 139 C2
St Lawrence Rd GU34 ... 139 C2
St Leger Ct RG14 ... 1 B2
St Leonard's Ave RG24 ... 49 A2
St Leonard's Rd SO23 ... 198 B3
St Leonards Cl SO21 ... 153 B2
St Lucia Pk GU35 ... 164 C3
St Lukes Cl RG22 ... 68 B2
St Margarets SP11 ... 81 C4
St Mark's CE Prim Sch
Basingstoke RG22 ... 91 A3
Farnborough GU14 ... 77 A4
St Marks Cl Bramley RG26 29 A1
Farnborough GU14 ... 56 A1
St Marks Pl GU9 ... 98 C4
St Martin Cl SO23 ... 198 A4
St Martin's CE Prim Sch RG20 ... 20 C4
St Martins Trad Pk SO23 ... 198 A4
St Mary Bourne Prim Sch SP11 ... 61 C1
St Mary Magdalen Almshouses 50 SO23 ... 198 A4
St Mary St SO22 ... 197 B3
St Mary's Almshouses 14 RG14 ... 1 B1
St Mary's Ave RG26 ... 29 A1
St Mary's CE Inf Sch GU10 ... 144 A4
St Mary's CE Jun Sch RG24 ... 70 A3
St Mary's Cl
Kings Worthy SO21 ... 176 B3
Old Basing RG24 ... 70 A3
St Mary's Coll SO23 ... 198 A3
St Mary's Cotts GU10 ... 144 A4
St Mary's Ct
Basingstoke RG21 ... 69 B3
Bramley RG26 ... 29 A1
4 Newbury RG14 ... 1 C2
St Mary's Mdw SP11 ... 105 A2
St Mary's Pl Farnham GU9 99 A2
Newbury RG14 ... 1 C2
St Mary's Rd Ash GU12 ... 77 C3
Camberley GU15 ... 36 A3
Hartley Wintney RG27 ... 52 B3
Kingsclere RG20 ... 24 B1
Liss GU33 ... 207 C2
Mortimer RG7 ... 11 C3
Newbury RG14 ... 1 C2
St Marys Bentworth CE Prim Sch GU34 ... 138 A3

St Marys CE Jun Sch
RG7 .....12 A3
St Marys Cl Alton GU34 .139 C2
Sandhurst GU47 .....35 A4
St Matthew's CE Prim Sch
GU33 .....186 A4
St Matthews Rd SO22 ..175 B1
St Michael's CE Inf Sch
GU11 .....99 C4
St Michael's CE Jun Sch
GU11 .....100 A4
St Michael's CE Prim Sch
GU47 .....34 B4
St Michael's Cl RG25 ...89 C1
St Michael's Gdns 26
SO22 .....197 C4
St Michael's Hall GU11 ..99 C4
St Michael's Pas SO23 .198 A3
St Michael's Rd
Aldershot GU12 .....76 C1
Basingstoke RG22 .....68 B2
Farnborough GU14 .....55 C3
Newbury RG14 .....1 B1
Sandhurst GU47 .....34 B4
Winchester SO22 .....197 C3
St Michaels Ave SP9 ...78 C3
St Michaels Cl GU51 ...75 A4
St Michaels Rd GU15 ...35 C3
St Michaels Sch RG20 ...21 B3
St Neot's Rd RG27 .....32 B4
St Neot's Sch RG27 .....32 B4
St Nicholas Cl Fleet GU51 53 C1
Ludgershall SP11 .....57 A1
St Nicholas Ct RG22 ...68 B2
St Nicholas Rd RG14 .....1 B1
St Nicholas Rise SO23 ..176 A3
St Nicholas Sch GU52 ..74 C1
St Patrick's La GU33 ...208 B3
St Patrick's RC Prim Sch
GU14 .....56 A2
St Patrick's Rd RG22 ....68 C2
St Patricks Ave SP9 .....78 C3
St Paul's Hill SO22 .....197 C4
St Paul's Rd RG22 .....68 C2
St Pauls Cl GU10 .....100 B4
St Pauls Pl 19 SO22 ....197 C4
St Peter St SO23 .....198 A4
St Peter's CE Jun Sch
Farnborough GU14 .....56 A2
Yateley GU46 .....34 B3
St Peter's CE Prim Sch
GU10 .....121 C3
St Peter's Cl SP11 .....106 A1
St Peter's Cl RG26 .....26 C4
St Peter's Gdns
Farnham GU10 .....121 B3
Yateley GU46 .....34 A3
St Peter's RC Prim Sch
SO22 .....197 A3
St Peter's Rd RG22 .....68 B2
St Peter's Way GU16 ....56 B4
St Peters Cl
Headley, Nr Greenham RG19 .7 A1
Shipton Bellinger SP9 ....101 C4
St Peters Mead GU12 ....77 C1
St Peters Pk GU11 .....99 B4
St Philips Ct 4 GU51 ....54 A1
St Polycarp's RC Prim Sch
GU9 .....99 A1
St Richards Rd RG14 .....1 C3
St Stephen's Rd SO22 ..175 B1
St Stephens Cl GU27 ...189 B3
St Swithun St SO23 ....198 A4
St Swithun's Sch SO21 .198 B4
St Thomas Cl SP10 .....82 C2
St Thomas Mews 22
SO23 .....197 C4
St Thomas St SO22 .....197 C4
St Thomas' Cl RG21 .....69 A4
St Thomas' Inf Sch
RG20 .....21 A4
Salcombe Rd RG14 .....1 B1
Salcot Rd SO23 .....176 A1
Salerno Cl GU11 .....76 C1
Sales Ct 5 GU11 .....76 C1
Salesian Coll GU14 .....56 A1
Salesian View GU14 .....77 B4
Salisbury Cl Alton GU34 .140 A1
Odiham RG29 .....72 B1
Salisbury Gdns RG22 ....68 B2
Salisbury Gr GU16 .....56 C2
Salisbury Ho 12 SP9 .....78 C4
Salisbury La SO20 .....147 B4
Salisbury Rd
Abbotts Ann SP11 .....105 A2
Andover SP10 .....105 C3
Ash GU12 .....77 C1
Blackwater GU17 .....35 A3
Broughton SO20 .....169 C4
Farnborough GU14 .....56 A2
New Alresford SO24 .....179 B3
Over Wallop SP11 .....124 C3
Shipton Bellinger SP9 ....101 C3
Upper Clatford SP11 .....105 C3
Salisbury Terr GU16 .....56 C2
Salmon Rd GU11 .....77 A3
Salmond Rd SP11 .....105 A4
Salmons Rd RG29 .....72 B1
Salters Acres SO22 .....175 B2
Salters Heath Rd RG26 ...47 A4
Salters La SO22 .....175 A1
Saltram Rd GU14 .....56 B1
Sam Whites Hill SP11 ..105 C2
Samarkand Cl GU15 .....36 C2
Sampson Bsns Pk GU15 ..35 C2
Sampson's Almshouses 22
GU9 .....98 C1
Samuel Cody Ho GU12 ...77 C4
Samuel Cody Sch The
GU14 .....76 C4
San Carlos App GU11 ...77 A1
Sand Hill GU14 .....55 C4
Sand Hill Ct GU14 .....55 C4
Sandbanks Dr RG22 .....91 A4
Sandford Cl RG20 .....24 C1
Sandford Ct GU11 .....76 B1
Sandford Ho RG20 .....24 C2
Sandford Rd
Aldershot GU11 .....76 B1
Farnham GU9 .....98 C4
Tadley RG26 .....26 C3
Sandham Meml Chapel*
Bishop's Green RG20 .....6 A1
* Burghclere RG20 .....22 B3
Sandheath Rd GU26 ....167 A4
Sandhurst La GU17 .....34 C3
Sandhurst Rd
Finchampstead RG40 .....16 C4
Yateley GU46 .....34 B4
Sandhurst Royal Military
Acad GU15 .....35 C4
Sandhurst Sch GU47 .....35 A4
Sandhurst Sta GU47 .....34 C4
Sandleford Hospl RG14 ....5 C4
Sandleford Rise RG14 .....5 C4
Sandown Cl Alton GU34 .140 A1
Blackwater GU17 .....35 A3
Sandown Cres GU11 .....99 C4
Sandown Dr GU16 .....36 A1
Sandown Way RG14 .....2 A1
Sandpiper Way RG22 .....90 C4
Sandpit Cotts GU10 .....75 A1
Sandpit Hill RG20 .....5 A2
Sandpit La RG7 .....14 C3
Sandringham Cl
Alton GU34 .....139 B2
Farnborough GU14 .....76 C4
Sandringham Ct RG22 ....68 B2
Sandringham Ho 5
SP10 .....83 A2
Sandringham Inf Sch
GU16 .....56 B4
Sandringham Way GU16 .56 B4
Sandrock Hill Rd GU10 .121 C3
Sands Cl GU10 .....100 B1
Sands Rd GU10 .....100 A1
Sands The GU35 .....164 A1
Sandy Cross GU10 .....100 B2
Sandy Hill Rd GU9 .....98 C4
Sandy La
Bramshott GU27 .....189 A4
Camberley GU15 .....36 B3
Farnborough GU14 .....55 A4
Fleet GU52 .....75 A2
Frensham GU10 .....144 C3
Frensham GU10 .....122 A1
Hartley Wintney RG27 .....52 B3
Haslemere GU26 .....167 B1
Rake GU33 .....208 C2
Tadley RG26 .....27 A4
Sandys Cl RG22 .....68 C2
Sandys Rd RG22 .....68 C2
Sandys Road Rdbt RG22 .68 C2
Sankey La GU51 .....54 B2
Santina Cl GU9 .....99 A4
Saor Mews 3 SP10 .....105 C4
Sapley La RG25 .....88 A4
Sarah Way GU14 .....55 C2
Sarisbury Cl RG26 .....26 C4
Sarson Cl SP11 .....104 A3
Sarson La SP11 .....104 A4
Sarum Cl
Over Wallop SO20 .....147 B4
Shipton Bellinger SP9 ....101 B4
Winchester SO22 .....197 B4
Sarum Hill RG21 .....69 A2
Sarum Rd Tadley RG26 .....9 C1
Winchester SO22 .....197 A4
Sarum Road Hospl
SO22 .....197 B4
Sarum View SO22 .....197 A4
Saturn Ho 9 RG7 .....9 B1
Saunders Gdn 6 RG26 ...26 C4
Saunton Gdns GU14 .....55 C3
Savernake Ho 2 SP9 .....78 C3
Savile Cres GU35 .....164 B2
Saville Gdns GU15 .....36 C3
Savoy Cl SP10 .....106 A4
Savoy Ct GU15 .....36 A3
Savoy Gr GU17 .....35 A2
Sawyer Cl SO22 .....175 A1
Sawyers Ley RG7 .....12 A4
Saxon Croft GU9 .....99 A1
Saxon Ct 1 Andover SP10 83 A2
Thatcham RG19 .....2 C2
Saxon Leas SP5 .....168 A3
Saxon Mews 9 GU34 ....139 C2
Saxon Rd SO23 .....176 A1
Saxon Way Charlton SP10 .82 C2
Old Basing RG24 .....69 C4
Saxon Wood Sch RG24 ....68 A4
Saxton Ct 15 SO23 .....198 A4
Sayers Cl Camberley GU16 .56 B4
Newbury RG14 .....5 C4
Scamblers Mead SP11 ....81 C2
Scarlatti Rd RG22 .....91 C4
Scarlet Oaks GU15 .....36 B2
Scarlett's Rd GU11 .....76 C2
School Cl SP11 .....38 B3
School Fields GU35 .....142 A1
School Hill
Farnham GU10 .....121 B3
Seale GU10 .....100 C2
School La Bentley GU10 .120 A3
Bishop's Sutton SO24 ....180 A2
Broughton SO20 .....170 A4
School La *continued*
Ewshot GU10 .....98 A4
Farnham GU10 .....122 A3
Itchen Abbas SO21 .....177 C4
Kings Worthy SO23 .....176 A3
3 Liss GU33 .....207 C2
Michelmersh SO51 .....193 B1
Middle Wallop SO20 .....147 C4
Riseley RG7 .....14 B2
Ropley SO24 .....181 B2
Silchester RG7 .....10 C1
Yateley GU46 .....33 C3
School Lane Cotts SO20 147 C4
School Rd Bordon GU35 .164 B2
Farnham GU10 .....121 B2
Grayshott GU26 .....166 C2
Linchmere GU27 .....189 B3
Riseley RG7 .....14 B2
Schroeder Cl RG21 .....69 A1
Schubert Rd RG22 .....91 C4
Scotland Cl GU12 .....77 C3
Scotland Farm Rd GU12 ..77 C3
Scotland Hill GU47 .....34 C4
Scotland La GU27 .....189 C3
Scotlands Cl GU27 .....189 C3
Scotlands Dr GU27 .....189 C3
Scotney Rd RG21 .....69 A4
Scott Cl Andover SP10 ....83 C1
King's Somborne SO20 ...172 A1
Scott's Ct GU14 .....55 C4
Scrubbs La SO24 .....180 A3
Scures Rd RG27 .....50 C1
Seagull Cl RG22 .....90 C4
Seal Rd
15 Basingstoke RG21 .....69 A2
Basingstoke RG21 .....69 A3
Searing Way RG26 .....9 C1
Searle Rd GU9 .....122 A4
Searle's La Hook RG27 ....51 A2
Hook RG27 .....51 B1
Searles Cl SO24 .....179 B3
Seaton Rd GU15 .....35 C3
Sebastopol Rd GU11 .....76 C1
Second Ave RG7 .....10 A1
Second St E RG19 .....6 C3
Second St W RG19 .....6 B2
Sedgefield Rd RG14 .....6 A4
Sedgemoor GU14 .....55 C4
Seebys Oak GU17 .....35 A3
Sefton Ho 12 GU11 .....76 C1
Sek Kong Cl SO20 .....126 A2
Selborne Ave GU11 .....100 A3
Selborne CE Prim Sch
GU34 .....184 B4
Selborne Cl
Blackwater GU17 .....35 A3
Hook RG27 .....51 A1
Selborne Pl SO22 .....197 B3
Selborne Rd Alton GU34 .162 B3
East Worldham GU34 .....162 B3
Selborne GU34 .....162 B3
Selborne Way GU35 .....164 A1
Selborne Wlk RG26 .....26 C4
Selbourne Gdns GU9 ...121 C4
Selbourne Rd GU34 .....139 C1
Selby Wlk RG24 .....48 A1
Seldon Cl SO22 .....197 A2
Selwyn Dr GU46 .....33 C3
Sepen Meade GU52 .....74 C2
Seremban Cl SO20 .....126 A3
Sermon Rd SO22 .....175 A1
Seton Dr RG27 .....71 C4
Sett The GU46 .....33 C3
Seventh St RG19 .....6 B3
Severals The RG24 .....47 C2
Severn Cl Sandhurst GU47 .35 A4
Thatcham RG18 .....2 C3
Severn Ct 52 SP10 .....83 B1
Severn Gdns RG23 .....67 A1
Severn Rd GU14 .....55 B3
Severn Way 29 RG21 .....69 B3
Seville Cres SP10 .....83 B1
Seymour Ct GU51 .....54 A1
Seymour Dr GU15 .....36 C4
Seymour Pl RG29 .....72 C2
Seymour Rd
Basingstoke RG22 .....68 B1
Headley GU35 .....166 A2
Shackleton Cl GU12 .....77 B3
Shackleton Sq SP10 .....83 B1
Shady Nook GU9 .....98 C3
Shafer Ct RG14 .....1 C1
Shaftesbury Ct
3 Bordon GU35 .....164 B1
Farnborough GU14 .....77 A4
Shaftesbury Mount GU17 35 A2
Shakespeare Ave SP10 ..82 B1
Shakespeare Gdns GU14 .55 A3
Shakespeare Rd RG24 ...69 B4
Shalbourne Rise GU15 ..36 A3
Shalden La GU34 .....138 C4
Shalden Rd GU12 .....100 A4
Shamrock Cl GU16 .....56 A4
Shanklin Ct GU12 .....77 A1
Shannon Ct 53 SP10 .....83 B1
Shapley Heath RG27 .....52 A1
Shapley Hill RG27 .....52 B1
Shaw Cl SP10 .....105 B4
Shaw cum Donnington
Parochial Sch RG14 .....1 B3
Shaw Farm Rd RG14 .....1 C3
Shaw Hill RG14 .....1 C3
Shaw Ho SP11 .....81 A3
Shaw La RG26 .....26 B4
Shaw Mill RG14 .....1 C3
Shaw Pightle RG27 .....50 C1
Shaw Rd RG14 .....1 C2
Shawfield La GU12 .....77 B1
Shawfield Prim Sch
GU12 .....77 C2
Shawfield Rd GU12 .....77 C1
Sheddon Pl SO21 .....174 B1
Sheep Dro SO20 .....147 B2
Sheep Fair SP10 .....106 B4
Sheep Fair Cl SP10 .....106 B4
Sheephatch La GU10 ....122 C3
Sheephouse GU9 .....122 A4
Sheepwash La
Burghclere RG20 .....5 C1
Ramsdell RG26 .....46 B4
Sheerlands Rd RG2,RG40 .15 B3
Sheffield Cl GU14 .....55 B2
Shefford Lodge 7 RG14 ..1 C1
Sheldon's La RG27 .....51 A1
Sheldon's Rd RG27 .....51 A1
Shell La SO24 .....183 A1
Shelley Cl
Basingstoke RG24 .....69 B4
Fleet GU51 .....75 A4
Itchen Abbas SO21 .....177 C3
Winchester SO22 .....197 B4
Shelley Ct GU15 .....36 A3
Shelley Rise GU14 .....55 B3
Shelleys La GU34 .....140 C1
Shenstone Cl RG40 .....16 C4
Shepherd & Flock Rdbt
GU9 .....99 B2
Shepherds Cl SO22 .....197 A2
Shepherds Ct GU9 .....122 A4
Shepherds Down SO24 .179 B2
Shepherds Rd SO23 .....198 B4
Shepherds Rise SP11 .....38 B3
Shepherds Row SP10 ...106 B4
Shepherds Spring La
SP10 .....83 A1
Shepherds Spring Schs
SP10 .....83 A2
Shepherds Way GU30 ..188 A2
Shepherds Wlk GU14 ....55 B4
Sheppard Almshouses
SP11 .....104 A3
Sheppard Cl RG28 .....86 B2
Sheppard Rd RG21 .....69 A1
Sheppard Sq SP10 .....83 B1
Sheraton Ave RG22 .....91 A4
Sheraton Cl GU17 .....35 B2
Sherborne Rd
Basingstoke RG21 .....69 A4
Farnborough GU14 .....77 A4
Sherborne St John RG24 ...47 C1
Sherborne St John CE Prim
Sch RG24 .....47 C2
Sherbrooke Cl SO23 ....176 B4
Sherfield Rd RG26 .....29 A1
Sheridan Cl
Aldershot GU11 .....99 C4
Winchester SO22 .....197 B3
Sheridan Cres RG26 .....9 B1
Sheridan Ct
Camberley GU16 .....56 A4
Newbury RG14 .....2 A2
Sheridan Rd GU16 .....56 A4
Sherlock Lea GU17, GU46 .33 B4
Sherrard Mead RG14 .....1 C3
Sherrington Way RG22 ..68 C1
Sherwin Cres GU14 .....56 A4
Sherwood Cl
Basingstoke RG22 .....91 B3
Liss GU33 .....208 A4
Sherwood Terr GU34 ...140 A2
Shetland Rd RG24 .....48 B1
Shetland Way GU51 .....54 A2
Ship Alley GU14 .....56 A4
Ship La GU14 .....56 A3
Shipley Cl GU34 .....140 A3
Shipley Ct 3 GU30 .....188 A2
Shipton Bellinger Prim Sch
SP9 .....101 B4
Shipton Way RG22 .....68 B1
Shire Ave GU51 .....54 B2
Shire Ct 2 GU11 .....76 B1
Shires Way GU46 .....34 A4
Shoddesden La
Kimpton SP11 .....80 B3
Ludgershall SP11 .....57 A1
Shoe La GU11,GU14 .....76 C3
Shooters Way RG21 .....69 B3
Shop La RG14 .....1 B3
Short Dale Rd GU11 ....100 A3
Short La SP11 .....82 A1
Short St Aldershot GU11 ..76 C1
Ludgershall SP11 .....57 A1
Shortfield Rd GU10 .....122 A1
Shortheath Crest GU10 .121 B3
Shortheath Rd GU9 ....121 C3
Shotter's La GU34 .....183 C3
Shotterfield Terr GU33 .207 C2
Shottermill Fst Sch
GU27 .....189 B4
Shottermill Jun Sch
GU27 .....189 B4
Shottermill Pk GU27 ...189 B4
Shottermill Rd GU27 ...189 B3
Shrave The GU34 .....160 C2
Shrewsbury Terr RG14 ....1 B1
Shrivenham Cl GU47 .....35 A4
Shrubbery The GU14 ....55 A2
Shrubbs La GU10 .....121 B2
Shyshack La RG26 .....9 B1
Sian Cl GU52 .....75 A3
Sibelius Cl RG22 .....91 C4
Sickle Mill GU27 .....189 B3
Sickle Rd GU27 .....189 C3
Sickles Rd GU35 .....142 A1
Sidbury Circular Rd SP9 .78 B4
Sidbury Hill Ave SP9 ....78 C4
Sidestrand Rd RG14 .....5 B4
Sidings The GU11 .....77 A2
Sidlaw Cl RG22 .....68 A2
Sidlaws Rd GU14 .....55 A3
Sidmouth Rd SP10 .....106 B4
Silchester CE Prim Sch
RG7 .....10 C1
Silchester Cl SP10 .....82 C1
Silchester Dr GU51 .....53 B2
Silchester Rd
Bramley RG26 .....28 B2
Pamber End RG7,RG26 .....27 C2
Pamber Heath RG7,RG26 ...10 B1
Silk Mill La RG25 .....87 C4
Silkweavers Rd SP10 ...106 A4
Silver Birch Cl Fleet GU52 74 C3
Liss GU33 .....208 A2
Silver Birch Rd SP10 ....82 C1
Silver Hill Sandhurst GU47 35 B4
Winchester SO23 .....198 A4
Silver La RG7 .....10 C4
Silver Park Cl GU52 .....75 A3
Silverdale GU52 .....75 A3
Silverdale Rd RG26 .....9 C1
Silverglades GU46 .....34 A2
Silverwood Cl SO22 .....197 B3
Silverwood Dr GU15 .....36 C4
Silvester Cl RG21 .....69 B4
Silvester Way GU52 .....74 C3
Silwood Cl SO22 .....175 B1
Simmondstone La GU10 144 A1
Simmons Wlk 27 RG21 ....69 B3
Simms Farm La RG7 .....11 B2
Simonds Ct 5 SO23 .....176 A1
Simons Cl RG24 .....48 C1
Simons Rd RG24 .....48 C1
Sims Cl RG26 .....29 A1
Sine Cl GU14 .....55 C4
Sinhurst Rd GU15 .....35 C2
Sixth Form Coll The
GU14 .....55 C3
Sixth St RG19 .....6 B3
Skates La RG26 .....27 A3
Skew Rd SP11 .....103 A2
Skinners Green La RG14 ..4 C4
Skippetts La E RG21 .....69 B1
Skippetts La W RG21 .....69 A1
Skippons Cl RG14 .....5 A3
Skylark Rise RG28 .....86 A3
Skylings RG14 .....2 A2
Slade Hill Gdns RG20 .....4 B1
Sleeper's Hill Ho SO22 .197 B3
Sleeper's Hill Rd SO22 .197 B3
Sleepers Delle Gdns
SO22 .....197 C3
Sleepers Hill Gdns
SO22 .....197 B3
Sleepy Hollow (Cvn Pk)
RG26 .....27 A4
Slessor Cl SP11 .....105 A4
Slim Cl GU11 .....77 B4
Slim Rd GU15 .....35 C4
Smallfield Dr RG27 .....51 B1
Smallridge RG20 .....5 A2
Smannell & Enham CE Prim
Sch SP11 .....83 C4
Smannell Rd
Andover SP10,SP11 .....83 B2
Smannell SP10,SP11 .....83 B2
Smay Down La SN8 .....17 A2
Smeaton Rd SP10 .....82 A1
Smithfield La GU10,
GU35 .....143 C1
Smiths Mead RG25 .....89 C1
Smithy Cl GU34 .....140 B4
Smithy La GU10 .....143 B1
Smithy The RG26 .....28 C2
Smugglers La SO24 .....182 A1
Smugglers' Way GU10 ..100 B1
Snailing La GU33 .....207 B4
Snailslynch GU9 .....99 A1
Snipe La
Bishop's Green RG20 .....6 B1
Linchmere GU27 .....189 C1
Snoddington Rd SP11 ...80 A1
Snode Hill GU34 .....139 A2
Snowdon Rd GU14 .....55 B4
Snowdrop Cl RG22 .....91 A4
Snowdrop Wlk 2 GU51 ...53 C1
Soalwood La GU32 .....205 C1
Soame's La SO24 .....181 C1
Sobers Sq SP10 .....83 B1
Society of St Pius X St
Michael's Sch RG20 ....22 B3
Soke Hill SO24 .....159 C1
Soke Rd RG7 .....10 B2
Soke The SO24 .....179 B3
Solarton Rd GU14 .....55 C2
Solby's Rd 21 RG21 .....69 A3
Soldridge Rd GU34 .....159 C2
Solent Dr RG22 .....91 A4
Somborne Park Rd
SO20 .....172 B4
Somers Cl SO22 .....197 B3
Somerset Ave GU35 .....164 B2
Somerset Ct 11 GU14 ....56 A1
Somerset Rd GU14 .....56 A1
Somerville Cres GU47 ....34 B3
Somerville Ct SP10 .....83 B1
Somerville Rd SO23 ....176 B4
Somme Rd SP11 .....79 B4
Sonnige Cl GU47 .....35 A4
Sonning Cl RG22 .....90 C4
Soper Gr RG21 .....69 A3
Sopwith Cl SO20 .....172 A1

Whins Dr GU15 35 C2
Whistler Cl RG21 69 B2
Whistler Gr GU47 35 A3
Whistlers La RG26 10 C1
Whitakers Cl RG18 2 C2
Whitby Cl GU14 56 B1
Whitchurch CE Prim Sch RG28 86 B2
Whitchurch Cl GU11 100 A3
Whitchurch Rd GU51 53 C2
Whitchurch Silk Mill★ RG28 86 B2
Whitchurch Sta RG28 86 B3
White Acres Rd GU16 56 B2
White Ave GU33 186 B1
White Cottage Cl GU9 99 A3
White Farm La SN8 18 A3
White Hart Ho GU17 35 B2
White Hart Ind Est GU17 35 B3
White Hart La
Basingstoke RG21 69 B2
Charter Alley RG26 46 C4
White Hart Par GU17 35 B2
White Hill
Burghclere RG20 22 A1
Ecchinswell RG20 23 B2
Kingsclere RG20 44 A3
Long Sutton RG29 96 A1
White Ho The SP9 78 C3
White Horse La RG40 16 A3
White House Cl RG22 68 C1
White House Gdns GU46 34 A4
White House Wlk GU9 99 A4
White La Greywell RG29 71 B1
Hannington RG26 66 B3
White Lion Way GU46 34 A4
White Oak Way SP11 105 B2
White Post La GU10 121 C2
White Rd GU15 35 B3
White Rose La GU10 121 C4
White Swan Ct SO21 131 B2
Whitebeam Gdns GU14 55 A2
Whitebines GU9 99 A1
Whitedown GU34 139 C1
Whitedown Cotts 1 GU34 139 C2
Whitedown La GU34 139 B1
Whitedown Rd RG26 26 B4
Whitedown Sch GU34 139 C1
Whitehall Dr RG2 15 B4
Whitehall Rd SO20 172 C4
Whitehead Cl RG24 69 C4
Whitehill Cl GU15 36 A4
Whitehill La SO24 179 C2
Whitehill Pk GU35 186 C4
Whitehill Rd GU35 164 C1
Whitehouse Cl GU14 55 C3
Whites Cl RG27 50 C1
Whites Rd GU14 56 B1
Whiteshoot SO20 170 A3
Whiteshute La SO23 197 C3
Whitestones RG22 91 B3
Whitethorn Cl GU12 77 C1
Whitewater CE Prim Sch RG27 50 C3
Whitewater Rd RG29 72 B2
Whitewater Rise RG27 51 B1
Whiteways End GU10 100 A2
Whitewood RG24 48 C2
Whitlet Cl GU9 98 C1
Whitley Rd GU46 34 A2
Whitmoor Vale Rd GU26 166 C3
Whitmore Cl GU47 35 A4
Whitmore Gn GU9 99 B2
Whitmore Vale GU26 166 B3
Whitmore Vale Rd
Grayshott GU26 166 C2
Headley GU26 166 B4
Whitney Rd RG24 69 C4
Whittle Cl
Farnborough GU12 77 B3
Finchampstead RG40 16 B4
Whittle Cres GU14 55 B4
Whittle Rd SP10 82 A1
Whittle Rdbt GU14 55 A1
Whitworth Rd RG40 15 C4
Whynot La SP10 105 C4
Whyte Ave GU12 100 A4
Wick Hill La RG40 16 C3
Wicket Hill GU10 121 C3
Wickham Cl Alton GU34 139 B1
Fleet GU52 74 C3
Tadley RG26 26 C4
Wickham Ct GU52 74 C3
Wickham Pl GU52 74 C3
Wickham Rd
Camberley GU15 36 B4
Fleet GU52 74 C3
Wicklow Cl RG22 68 A2
Widgeons GU34 139 C3
Widmore Rd RG22 68 B1
Wield Grange SO24 136 C1
Wield Industries SO24 137 A2
Wield Rd GU34 159 B4
Wights Wlk RG22 91 A4
Wigmore Rd RG26 9 B1
Wilberforce Cl 2 SO22 197 B3
Wild Briar RG40 16 B4
Wild Herons RG27 51 B1
Wilderness Rd GU16 36 B1
Wilders Cl GU15 36 A2
Wildhern SP11 59 C1
Wildmoor La
Church End RG27 49 B3
Sherfield on Loddon RG27 49 C4
Wildwood Dr RG26 9 A1
Wildwood Gdns GU46 34 A2
Will Hall Cl GU34 139 B2
Willems Ave GU11 76 B1
Willems Rdbt GU11 76 B1
William Cobbett Jun Sch GU9 99 B3
William Ct GU14 55 C2
William Farthing Cl GU11 76 C1
William Hitchcock Ho 5 GU14 55 C4
William Ho SP11 83 A4
William Way GU34 140 A3
Williams Way GU51 54 B1
Willian Pl GU26 167 B3
Willington Cl GU15 35 C3
Willis La GU34 160 C1
Willis Mus The★ RG21 69 A2
Willis Waye SO23 176 B3
Willoughby Cl GU34 139 C2
Willoughby Way RG23 68 B3
Willow Cl Bordon GU35 164 C2
Liphook GU30 188 A2
Mytchett GU16 56 B2
Newbury RG14 1 B1
Willow Cres GU14 55 C4
Willow Ct Alton GU34 139 C2
Ash GU12 77 C4
Camberley GU16 36 A1
Willow Gdns GU30 188 A2
Willow Gr SP10 105 C4
Willow Ho RG24 49 A2
Willow La GU17 35 A2
Willow Mews 3 SP9 79 A4
Willow Pk GU12 77 B1
Willow Rd
Bishop's Green RG20 6 B1
Liss GU33 208 A2
Tadley RG26 26 C4
Willow Way
Aldershot GU12 100 B4
Basingstoke RG23 68 B4
Farnham GU9 99 A3
Middle Wallop SO20 126 A2
Sherfield on Loddon RG27 29 B1
Willowdale RG40 16 B4
Willowford GU46 34 A3
Willowmead Cl RG14 5 A3
Willows End GU47 34 C4
Willows The
Andover SP10 105 C3
Farnham GU10 100 A2
North Warnborough RG29 72 B2
Wilmot Way
Basingstoke RG23 68 B3
Camberley GU15 36 B2
Wilmot Wlk RG14 5 A3
Wilsom Rd GU34 140 A2
Wilson Cl Alton GU34 140 A2
Middle Wallop SO20 126 A2
Wilson Ho 14 SP9 78 C4
Wilson Rd Aldershot GU12 77 A1
Farnborough GU14 55 B2
Wilson Valkenburg Ct RG14 1 B2
Wilsons Rd GU35 165 C3
Wilton Ct GU14 56 A2
Wilton Pl RG21 68 C2
Wilton Rd GU15 35 C2
Wilton Terr SP9 101 C4
Wimborne Ho GU14 56 A1
Wimbushes RG40 16 A3
Wincanton Cl GU34 140 A1
Winchcombe Cl GU51 75 A4
Winchcombe Jun & Inf Schs RG14 1 C2
Winchcombe Rd
Basingstoke RG21 69 A2
Newbury RG14 1 C1
Winchester Cath★ SO23 198 A4
Winchester Coll
Winchester SO22 197 C3
Winchester SO23 198 A3
Winchester Cty Mill★ SO23 198 A4
Winchester Cty Mus★ SO23 198 A4
Winchester Gdns SP10 106 A3
Winchester Hill SO21 131 B2
Winchester Rd
Andover SP10 106 A2
Ash GU12 77 C2
Basingstoke RG22 91 A4
Chawton GU34 161 B4
Four Marks GU34 160 B2
Frensham GU10 144 C4
Goodworth Clatford SP11 106 A2
King's Somborne SO20 172 A2
Kingsclere RG20 44 B4
Micheldever SO21 133 A1
New Alresford SO24 179 A3
Ropley SO24 181 B4
Upper Clatford SP10, SP11 106 A2
Whitchurch RG28 86 B2
Winchester Road Rdbt RG21 68 C2
Winchester Sch of Art SO23 198 A4
Winchester St
16 Andover SP10 106 A4
7 Basingstoke RG21 69 A2
Chilbolton SO20 129 A3
Farnborough GU14 77 A4
Overton RG25 88 A4
Whitchurch RG28 86 B2
Winchester Sta SO22 197 C4
Winchester Way GU17 35 A3
Winchfield Cl GU51 53 C2
Winchfield Ct RG27 53 A1
Winchfield Gdns RG26 27 A4
Winchfield Hurst RG27 52 C1
Winchfield Sta RG27 52 B1
Windermere Ave RG22 68 A1
Windermere Cl GU14 55 B2
Windermere Ct GU12 77 B2
Windermere Gdns SO24 179 B2
Windermere Rd GU35 164 B3
Windermere Way
Farnham GU9 98 C3
Thatcham RG19 2 C2
Winding Wood Dr GU15 36 C2
Windmill Cnr RG7 11 C3
Windmill Ct
4 Aldershot GU12 77 A1
Alton GU34 139 C1
Mortimer RG7 11 C3
Windmill Dr GU35 165 C3
Windmill Fields
East Worldham GU34 141 A1
Four Marks GU34 160 B2
Windmill Hill GU34 140 A1
Windmill La Alton GU34 140 A1
Hurstbourne Tarrant SP11 60 B4
Windmill Rd
Aldershot GU12 77 A1
Mortimer RG7 11 C3
Windmills The GU34 139 C2
Windrush Cl 28 RG21 69 B3
Windrush Hts GU47 34 C4
Windsor Cl GU34 139 B2
Windsor Cres GU9 98 C3
Windsor Ct
Camberley GU15 36 A2
9 Fleet GU51 54 A1
Newbury RG14 1 C1
Windsor Gdns Ash GU12 77 A1
Basingstoke RG22 91 A3
Windsor Ho 25 SO23 198 A4
Windsor Pk GU34 139 C1
Windsor Rd
Andover SP10 105 C4
Farnborough GU14 56 A1
Lindford GU35 164 C3
Medstead GU34 160 A2
New Alresford SO24 179 B2
Windsor Ride
Finchampstead RG40 16 C4
Sandhurst GU15 35 C4
Windsor Rise RG14 6 A4
Windsor Way
Aldershot GU11 76 C1
Camberley GU16 56 B4
Windsor Wlk GU35 164 C3
Wingate Ct GU11 76 B1
Wingate La RG29 95 B2
Wings Cl GU9 98 C3
Wings Rd GU9 98 C3
Winklebury Ctr RG23 68 B3
Winklebury Inf & Jun Sch RG23 68 B3
Winklebury Way RG23 68 B3
Winkworth La RG7,RG26 10 A1
Winkworth Pl GU9 99 A2
Winnall Cl SO23 176 B1
Winnall Manor Rd SO23 198 B4
Winnall Prim Sch SO23 198 B4
Winnall Trad Est SO23 198 B4
Winnall Valley Rd SO23 198 B4
Winnipeg Cl GU30 188 A2
Winslade La RG25 115 B4
Winslade Rd SO22 175 B2
Winston Ave RG26 27 A3
Winston Cl GU16 56 B3
Winston Rise GU34 160 A2
Winston Way RG19 2 B2
Winston Wlk GU10 122 A3
Winterbourne Ho RG22 68 B1
Winterbourne Wlk GU16 56 B4
Winterdyne Mews SP10 105 C4
Winterthur Way RG21 69 A3
Winterton Dr RG14 1 A3
Winton Chase SP10 106 B4
Winton Cl
South Tidworth SP9 78 C2
Winchester SO22 175 C1
Winton Cres GU46 34 A3
Winton Hill SO20 150 A2
Winton Rd
26 Aldershot GU11 76 C1
Farnham GU9 99 A2
Winton Sch SP10 106 B4
Winton Sq RG21 69 A2
Wiremead La SP11 103 C4
Wishanger La GU10 143 C1
Wishmoor Cl GU15 36 B4
Wishmoor Rd GU15 36 B4
Wisley Gdns GU14 55 A1
Wisley Rd SP10 105 C4
Wistaria Ct SP10 105 B4
Wistaria La GU46 34 A3
Wisteria Ct GU9 99 A2
Wisteria Dr 1 GU35 164 B1
Wisteria Mews GU34 140 B3
Witan Cl SP10 83 A2
Witan Ct RG28 86 A3
Wither Rise RG23 67 A1
Witherslack Cl GU35 166 A2
Withes The GU10 97 B3
Withies The
Longparish SP11 108 A3
West Tytherley SP5 169 A1
Witt Rd SP5 168 A3
Wittcomb Terr 13 GU35 164 B1
Wittmead Rd GU16 56 B2
Witton Hill SO24 179 B2
Wivelrod Rd GU32 138 B1
Woburn Ave GU14 56 A2
Woburn Cl GU16 36 C1
Woburn Gdns RG22 68 B2
Wokefield Row RG7 12 A4
Wolds The RG22 68 A2
Wolf's La GU34 161 C4
Wolfe Cl SO22 197 B3
Wolfe Rd GU12 77 A1
Wolfmere La GU33 186 A1
Wolseley Rd GU11 76 C1
Wolverdene Specl Sch SP10 106 A4
Wolversdene Cl SP10 106 B4
Wolversdene Gdns SP10 106 B4
Wolversdene Rd SP10 106 B4
Wolverton La RG26 25 B1
Wolverton Rd
Ashford Hill RG26 25 C3
Baughurst RG26 25 C3
Wolverton Towns End RG26 25 C1
Wolvesey Castle (Old Bishop's Palace)★ SO23 198 A3
Wolvesey Terr 3 SO23 198 A3
Wonston Cl SO21 131 B2
Wonston La SO21 131 B1
Wood Cl RG21, RG22 91 A3
Wood End RG24 48 C1
Wood Hill La RG29 95 B2
Wood La Beech Hill RG7 13 B3
Bramdean SO24 202 C3
Farnborough GU14 55 C2
Fleet GU51 54 B1
Hook RG27 71 B3
Seale GU10 100 C3
Wood Moor RG40 16 B1
Wood Rd
Beacon Hill GU26 167 A3
Camberley GU15 35 C1
Farnham GU9 99 A4
Wood Ridge RG14 5 B4
Wood St GU12 77 C3
Woodbarn The GU9 99 A1
Woodbine Cl GU47 35 A4
Woodbine La RG20 5 B1
Woodbourne GU9 99 B4
Woodbourne Cl
Liss GU33 208 A2
Yateley GU46 34 A3
Woodbridge Dr GU15 36 A4
Woodbridge Rd GU17 34 C3
Woodbury Rd RG22 91 A3
Woodcock Cl SP9 78 C3
Woodcot Gdns GU14 55 A2
Woodcote Cotts SO24 202 B2
Woodcote Gn GU51 74 B4
Woodcote Rd SN8 18 A4
Woodcott Ho 1 RG26 26 C4
Woodcott Terr GU12 100 A4
Woodcut Rd GU10 121 B3
Woodend Camberley GU15 36 C4
Farnborough GU14 56 A2
Woodfield GU35 142 A1
Woodfield Cotts GU32 206 A2
Woodfield Dr SO22 197 A3
Woodgarston Dr RG22 91 A3
Woodgate GU51 54 B2
Woodgreen Rd SO22 175 B2
Woodhouse La RG7,RG19 8 B1
Woodland Cres GU14 56 A3
Woodland Dr
Bramley RG26 29 A1
Farnham GU10 121 C3
Woodland Rise GU52 74 C3
Woodland Wlk★ SO51 192 B2
Woodlands
Andover SP10 106 B4
Chineham RG24 49 A2
Farnham GU10 100 A2
Fleet GU51 53 C1
Highclere RG20 21 C4
Overton RG25 88 A4
Yateley GU46 34 A2
Woodlands Ave GU9 99 B4
Woodlands Bsns Village RG21 69 B3
Woodlands Cl Ash GU12 77 C3
Farnborough GU17 35 B1
Woodlands Ct
Alton GU34 139 B1
18 Winchester SO23 176 A1
Woodlands La
Haslemere GU27 189 B4
Liss GU33 208 A2
Woodlands Rd
Baughurst RG26 9 A1
Camberley GU15 35 C3
Farnborough GU14 55 A3
Woodlands The
Bordon GU35 186 B4
Kings Worthy SO23 176 B3
Woodlands Way SP10 106 B4
Woodlands Wlk GU17 35 B1
Woodlane Cl SO24 202 B3
Woodlea Cl SO22 175 C1
Woodlea Prim Sch GU35 164 B1
Woodleigh GU51 75 A4
Woodleys RG20 23 B2
Woodman Cl SO21 174 B1
Woodman La SO21 174 B1
Woodmanfield RG25 94 B3
Woodmere Croft RG22 90 C4
Woodpecker Cl
Basingstoke RG22 90 C4
Woodpecker Cl *continued*
Bordon GU35 164 B1
Ewshot GU10 98 A4
Woodpeckers 1 SP10 106 A4
Woodpeckers Dr SO22 175 B1
Woodridge Manor GU15 36 A4
Woodroffe Dr RG22 68 B1
Woods La RG25 91 C4
Woodside
Blackwater GU17 35 A2
Farnborough GU14 55 C4
Newbury RG14 5 A4
Sandhurst GU15 35 B4
Woodside Cl
Bordon GU35 164 B2
Finchampstead RG40 16 B4
Mortimer RG7 11 C3
Woodside Cres GU35 164 B2
Woodside Gdns
Chineham RG24 49 A2
Fleet GU51 54 B1
Woodside La GU34 161 A2
Woodside Pk GU35 164 B2
Woodside Rd
Farnborough GU11 76 B4
Farnham GU9 99 B4
Woodstock Mead RG22 91 A3
Woodstocks GU14 56 A3
Woodville Cl
Blackwater GU17 34 C3
Chineham RG24 48 C1
Woodville Rise RG24 48 C1
Woodway GU15 35 C3
Wool Gr SP10 106 B4
Wooland Ct 3 GU52 74 C2
Wooldings Farm Vineyard★ RG28 63 C1
Wooldridge Cres RG29 95 B4
Woolfield La GU32,GU34 205 A2
Woolford Cl 1 SO22 197 B3
Woolford Way RG23 68 B3
Woollards Rd GU12 77 C2
Woolley Sq SP10 83 B2
Woolmead Ct GU9 99 A2
Woolmead Rd GU9 99 A2
Woolmead The GU9 99 A2
Woolmead Wlk GU9 99 A2
Woolmer Hill Rd GU27 189 A4
Woolmer Hill Sch GU27 189 A4
Woolmer La GU30 188 A4
Woolmer Rd GU33 186 A2
Woolmer Terr GU33 186 A2
Woolmer Trad Est GU35 164 B2
Woolmer View GU26 167 A2
Woolton Hill Jun Sch RG20 21 B4
Woolton Lodge Gdns RG20 4 B1
Wootey Inf & Jun Schs GU34 139 C3
Wooteys Way GU34 139 C3
Worcester Ave RG25 91 A4
Worcester Cl GU14 55 C4
Wordsworth Ave GU46 33 C2
Wordsworth Cl
Basingstoke RG24 69 B4
Winchester SO22 197 B4
Worldham Hill GU34 141 A1
Wormersley Rd RG19 6 A4
Worrell Sq SP10 83 B2
Worsley Rd GU16 56 B4
Worthy La SO23 175 C1
Worthy Rd SO23 176 A1
Worting Inf & Jun Schs RG22 68 A2
Worting Rd
Basingstoke RG21,RG22 68 C2
Basingstoke RG22,RG23 68 A2
Worting Road Rdbt RG22 68 B2
Wote St RG21 69 A2
Wouldham Cl SP11 79 B4
Wrecclesham Hill GU10 121 B3
Wrecclesham Rd GU9 121 B4
Wrekin Cl RG22 68 A2
Wrekin The GU14 56 B1
Wren Cl Alton GU34 140 A3
Winchester SO22 197 B3
Yateley GU46 33 C3
Wren Ct GU12 77 C2
Wren Way GU14 55 B4
Wrights Cl SO21 153 B2
Wrights Way SO21 153 B2
Wuthering Hts SO22 197 C3
Wychwood Cl GU12 77 B1
Wychwood Pl GU15 36 C4
Wyck La Binsted GU34 141 C3
Binsted, Wyck GU34 141 A2
Wye Ct 55 SP10 83 B1
Wykeham Ct RG29 95 B4
Wykeham Dr RG23 68 A2
Wykeham Ho GU14 77 A4
Wykeham Ind Est The SO23 176 B2
Wykeham Pk SO21 199 A4
Wykeham Pl SO22 197 B3
Wykeham Rd GU9 99 A2
Wykwood GU30 188 A2
Wyld Green La GU33 208 A3
Wylye Rd SP9 78 C4
Wymering Ct GU14 56 A2
Wyndham Cl GU46 34 A4
Wyndham Rd
Andover SP10 105 C3
Newbury RG14 2 A3
Wyndham St GU12 77 A1

Using the Ordnance Survey National Grid

Any feature in this atlas can be given a unique reference to help you find the same feature on other Ordnance Survey maps of the area, or to help someone else locate you if they do not have a Street Atlas.

The grid squares in this atlas match the Ordnance Survey National Grid and are at 1 kilometre intervals. The small figures at the bottom and sides of every other grid line are the National Grid kilometre values (**00** to **99** km) and are repeated across the country every 100 km (see left).

To give a unique National Grid reference you need to locate where in the country you are. The country is divided into 100 km squares with each square given a unique two-letter reference. Use the administrative map to determine in which 100 km square a particular page of this atlas falls.

The bold letters and numbers between each grid line (**A** to **C**, **1** to **4**) are for use within a specific Street Atlas only, and when used with the page number, are a convenient way of referencing these grid squares.

The map on the left shows the two-letter National Grid references: NG, NH, NJ, NK, NM, NN, NO, NP, NR, NS, NT, NU, NX, NY, NZ, SC, SD, SE, TA, SH, SJ, SK, TF, TG, SM, SN, SO, SP, TL, TM, SR, SS, ST, SU, TQ, TR, SW, SX, SY, SZ, TV.

Example *The railway bridge over DARLEY GREEN RD in grid square A1*

Step 1: Identify the two-letter reference, in this example the page is in **SP**

Step 2: Identify the 1 km square in which the railway bridge falls. Use the figures in the southwest corner of this square: Eastings **17**, Northings **74**. This gives a unique reference: **SP 17 74**, accurate to 1 km.

Step 3: To give a more precise reference accurate to 100 m you need to estimate how many tenths along and how many tenths up this 1 km square the feature is. This makes the bridge about **8** tenths along and about **1** tenth up from the southwest corner.

This gives a unique reference: **SP 178 741**, accurate to 100 m.

Eastings (read from left to right along the bottom) come before Northings (read from bottom to top). If you have trouble remembering say to yourself "Along the hall, THEN up the stairs"!

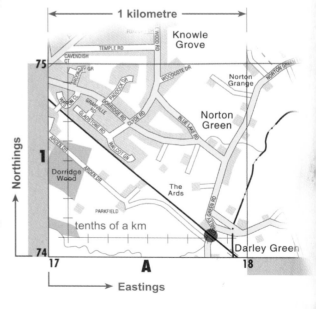

Name and Address	Telephone	Page	Grid reference

Street Atlases from Philip's

Philip's publish an extensive range of regional and local street atlases which are ideal for motoring, business and leisure use. They are widely used by the emergency services and local authorities throughout Britain.

Key features include:

◆ Superb county-wide mapping at an extra-large scale of 3½ inches to 1 mile, or 2½ inches to 1 mile in pocket editions

◆ Complete urban and rural coverage, detailing every named street in town and country

◆ Each atlas available in two handy sizes – standard spiral and pocket paperback

'The mapping is very clear... great in scope and value'

★★★★ BEST BUY   AUTO EXPRESS

PHILIP'S STREET ATLAS Cambridgeshire — With complete coverage of Peterborough — BEST BUY — Unique comprehensive coverage — Plus Cambri... Town maps ...

PHILIP'S STREET ATLAS Glasgow and West Central Scotland — with tim...

PHILIP'S STREET ATLAS Cardiff, Swansea and the Valleys — Unique comprehensive coverage

PHILIP'S STREET ATLAS London — The definitive London atlas — from Britain's national maps...

PHILIP'S STREET ATLAS East Sussex — With complete coverage of Brighton and Hove — BEST BUY — The definitive East Sussex atlas

PHILIP'S STREET ATLAS North Yorkshire — Unique comprehensive coverage — BEST BUY — Auto Express

PHILIP'S STREET ATLAS Wiltshire and Swindon — Unique compreh...

PHILIP'S STREET ATLAS Devon — Unique comprehensive coverage — BEST BUY — Auto Express — with time-saving through-routes — Includes Lyme Regis, Saltash and Wellington, plus Exeter and Plymouth city centres at extra-large scale — Plus town maps of Ar...

1 Bedfordshire
2 Berkshire
3 Birmingham and West Midlands
4 Bristol and Bath
5 Buckinghamshire
6 Cambridgeshire
7 Cardiff, Swansea and The Valleys
8 Cheshire
9 Cornwall
10 Derbyshire
11 Devon
12 Dorset
13 County Durham and Teesside
14 Edinburgh and East Central Scotland
15 North Essex
16 South Essex
17 Glasgow and West Central Scotland
18 Gloucestershire
19 North Hampshire
20 South Hampshire
21 Hertfordshire
22 East Kent
23 West Kent
24 Lancashire
25 Leicestershire and Rutland
26 London
27 Greater Manchester
28 Merseyside
29 Norfolk
30 Northamptonshire
31 Nottinghamshire
32 Oxfordshire
33 Somerset
34 Staffordshire
35 Suffolk
36 Surrey
37 East Sussex
38 West Sussex
39 Tyne and Wear and Northumberland
40 Warwickshire
41 Worcestershire
42 Wiltshire and Swindon
43 East Yorkshire and Northern Lincolnshire
44 North Yorkshire
45 South Yorkshire
46 West Yorkshire

How to order

The Philip's range of street atlases is available from good retailers or directly from the publisher by phoning 01903 828503